59 455
D0897576

How to Write *and Sell*
Magazine Articles

Also by Richard Gehman:

NOVELS—

A Party at the Buchanan Club

Driven

The Slander of Witches

NON-FICTION—

A Murder in Paradise

Sardi's (with Vincent Sardi, Sr.)

ANTHOLOGY—

Eddie Condon's Treasury of Jazz (with Eddie Condon)

How to Write *and Sell* Magazine Articles

by RICHARD GEHMAN

HARPER & BROTHERS, PUBLISHERS, NEW YORK

HOW TO WRITE AND SELL MAGAZINE ARTICLES

Printed in the United States of America

M-H

Grateful acknowledgment is made to the following for permission to use stories and articles included in this book:

Cosmopolitan Magazine for "How I Stole a Fortune" by Richard Crowe, from the November, 1950, issue; "She Plumb Give It All Away" from the September, 1956, issue; and "The Writer" ("The Business of Being a Writer") from the August, 1957, issue. Reprinted by permission.

The Crowell-Collier Publishing Company for "Old Buddy, Stay 'Way from My Door" from the April 2, 1949, issue of *Collier's;* "Confucius in Louisville" from the May 21, 1949, issue of *Collier's;* and "Ralph Bunche" ("Ralph Bunche, American Peacemaker"), from the June 11, 1949, issue of *Collier's.*

The Curtis Publishing Company for "The Doodads Women Wear" ("Sam Kramer Jewelry? Gee! Wow!"), originally published in *The Saturday Evening Post,* © 1955 by The Curtis Publishing Company; "He Digs Hollywood Gold" ("Swifty"), originally published in *The Saturday Evening Post,* © 1957 by The Curtis Publishing Company; "The Noblest Sandwich of Them All," originally published in *The Saturday Evening Post,* © 1955 by The Curtis Publishing Company.

Esquire, Inc., for "Red Means Go." Reprinted from *Esquire,* November, 1954. © 1954 by Esquire, Inc.

The New York Herald Tribune for "The Hospital Bit" from the February 8, 1953, issue of *This Week Magazine.*

Playboy for "Birth of a Broadway Show" ("The Making of a Broadway Show"), which first appeared in its issue of April 16, 1958.

Popular Publications, Inc., for "Where'd You Foul Up?" from the January, 1953, issue of *Argosy.*

True, The Man's Magazine, for "The Rat Catchers" ("The Rat Catchers of London"). Used with their permission.

Library of Congress catalog card number: 58-10133

This book is dedicated to the memory of
LOUIS RUPPEL,
a great editor, my good friend

Contents

Note

This book began as a collection of magazine articles, each introduced by a short piece of personal reminiscence. The editor suggested that perhaps I could incorporate some advice into the prefaces, and at first I demurred; I did not believe I had much that was valuable to communicate about my craft. Originally I had planned to call the book *How to Write Magazine Articles*—an ironic title suggested by Ring Lardner's collection *How to Write Short Stories,* which I had read with great admiration as a boy. The editors suggested adding the "*and Sell*" and I agreed, somewhat against my better judgment. I still don't know any sure way to sell magazine articles—or how to present any iron-clad rules. But in order to justify those two words, I have put into the book as many personal experiences and tips as I can remember after nearly twenty years in the magazine-writing business. I also have put in a good deal about my writing background, primarily because I have found that aspiring writers like to hear or read such material, and secondarily because I always have felt a deep obligation to those kind people who helped me along. It occurs to me that there are many, many editors who have given me important bits of advice and/or assistance who are not mentioned in the book, and I would like to acknowledge them here: Douglas Kennedy, Charles Barnard and Don McKinney of *True,* as well as the editorial director of Fawcett, Inc., Ralph Daigh; Bart Sheridan, of *Good Housekeeping;* Arnold Gingrich, editor of *Esquire,* and a former editor, Bruce Colen; Ray Russell of *Playboy;* Harry Steeger, publisher of *Argosy,* and Ken Purdy, former editor there; Brooks Roberts of *This Week;* Ernest V. Heyn and Charles Robins of *The American Weekly;* Lew Gillenson, Jim Skardon and Bernie Glaser of *Coronet;* Eileen Tighe and Emily Paley of *Woman's Day;* and Donald Congdon, once an editor, now an agent. My debt to my own agents, Kenneth Littauer and Maxwell Wilkinson, is incalculable. Special thanks are due to Stephanie Molnar, who typed parts of the manuscript. Finally, there are my co-workers at *Cosmopolitan:* the editor, John J. O'Connell, Tom Fleming, Harriet LaBarre, Jack Scott and Robert Atherton, without whose encouragement and indulgence, etc. etc. etc. I thank them all.

RICHARD GEHMAN

How to Write *and Sell* Magazine Articles

1 · *My Beginnings—and Yours*

It is hard for me to remember when I first decided to write. I never wanted to be anything but a writer, preferably a well-to-do one, for during the depression of the thirties our family was hit hard, as indeed was nearly every other family in Lancaster, Pennsylvania, where I was born. When I was four, my mother taught me to read. She was not especially fond of reading herself, as I remember —her taste ran mainly to *True Story* and other confession magazines —but I believe she thought that teaching me to read might give me some sort of accomplishment that would take people's minds off the fact that I was skinny, puny, and nervous. My first-grade teacher, Mrs. Elizabeth Kenneson, encouraged me to make up stories and write them down, and permanently scarred me when I had been in second grade only a few days by skipping me to third and thereby causing me to miss the multiplication tables, which all second-graders were required to commit to memory. My fourth-grade teacher, Miss Lillian E. Howell, a beauty with brown hair and slender legs, further encouraged me; if she had urged me to learn undertaking I would be in that business today, for I fell in love with her—I was eight—and fiercely resented the young man who called for her every Friday afternoon when school was out. In the fifth grade, my teacher was a Mrs. Annie Brand, who also apparently thought I had some talent and bade me pursue it. There are days today when I am in the middle of a tough story, stuck and inspirationless, when I would gladly line up all four of these ladies and shoot them dead, but on the whole I am grateful to them. They more or less foreordained my life. I have never been anything but a writer, although I have delivered newspapers, worked as a water boy on a construction project, set up pins in a bowling alley, attempted to promote a beauty contest while acting as a public relations man for an amusement park, pretended to be a soldier, worked for a high-minded and largely ineffectual group called Americans United for World Government, and taught in a university. I also have been a student for varying periods of time; although I never went to college, I was admitted to the Kenyon School of English, which offered courses on a graduate level. All these were minor interests, dictated principally by necessity. Writing has always been my preoccupation.

My first writing to appear in print was done for *The Quill*, the student newspaper of the West End Junior High School in Lancaster. I became editor in the ninth grade, and thought I had arrived. I had every intention of becoming editor of the Boys' High magazine, which was called *The Vidette*, and sure enough, after earning my Varsity "L" (in those days they gave school letters to the writers as well as the athletes), I was appointed editor in my senior year. This position enabled me to get myself expelled from high school four days before my graduation. As editor, I was given one free period of an hour per day in order to work on the newspaper. I used to clear up all my newspaper work for the monthly magazine in three or four days. That left twenty-odd days per month in which I had nothing to do in my free magazine period. My schedule was arranged so that each day I had plane trigonometry for the first hour, gymnasium for the second, a study hall for the third, and my free period. There was no way of getting out of trig, which was too bad, for without the multiplication table it and all other math were mysteries I could not fathom. But because I had neatly forged my mother's name to a permanent excuse which removed the necessity of my going to gymnasium class (I put down that I had incipient tuberculosis, and the instructor, a fool, did not bother to check, as I had known he would not), I therefore had, with the study hall and the free period, three uninterrupted hours with nothing to do. I used to leave school with a purposeful look on my face, acting as though I were heading for the printer's office with a sheaf of proofs clutched in my hand. Mounting my bicycle, I would ride out to a suburban section of Lancaster where an aunt of mine, Mary Marshall, lived. Mary was extraordinarily broad-minded, which distressed my mother. She permitted me to read as much as I wanted to (my mother evidently had come to regret her original instruction, feeling that reading was bad for the eyes), she let me smoke cigarettes, she did not mind my atrocious and profane vocabulary (swearing made me feel older), she did not make me take my hat off in the house (I wore a hat constantly, because I had seen newspapermen in the movies), and above all, she was genuinely interested in my budding, but hardly noticeable, ability.

My parents had not the slightest interest in my becoming a newspaperman or a writer. They thought it all foolishness. My father, manager of the record department in a music shop, believed it was something I would get over, like chicken pox or my fondness for jazz records. My mother was genuinely alarmed. She knew, from the accounts she read in *True Story*, that writers were degenerate, worthless rascals, and that newspapermen were even worse. Somehow I had acquired a typewriter—much as I got my bicycle, by paying for it at the rate of a dollar a week—but I had to do my writing so that the family could not hear me. I used to take the typewriter into the clothes closet in my room, padding the walls with old blankets I tacked up. The only possible advantage this had was that I also could smoke in the closet—until the smoke got so thick I began to choke. (I also had been forbidden to smoke. Drinking was unheard of in our house; my maternal grandfather had been a breeder of trotters and a gay blade, and his spendthrift ways had bred in my mother a terror of booze.)

Anyhow, I used to go and visit Mary Marshall at every opportunity. She would give me lunch and we would sit around and discuss what we were reading and argue. I was fifteen; I was treated as though I were much, much older. Her husband, my half-uncle Ray Marshall (he was my father's half-brother) was the most intelligent, wittiest man I ever had known. He had been my idol from boyhood; he was eight years older than I and was attending Franklin and Marshall College. He felt that I too should go to college. My excuse was that my parents couldn't afford it. Actually, I had no intention of going—I wanted only to be a newspaperman, first in Philadelphia and then in New York and then in London, and I felt that college would only slow me down.

One morning, five days before graduation, I got on my bicycle at the beginning of my free three hours, as usual, and started out the school driveway for the street that led to Mary's house. On the sidewalk, coming toward me, was Donald B. Witmer, the assistant principal. As I rode by, I waved in a familiar, friendly manner. He waved back but frowned. That afternoon, when I returned to school, he pulled me out of class and asked where I had been. I told him I had been out visiting my aunt. He told me he had checked and found that I had been out of school for three hours nearly every day of the semester, and he said he had no choice but to expel me. Shaking with fear, I went downtown and stammered the news to my father. I was certain he would whip me. At that time I thought of him as a distant, forbidding man, with as little understanding of my life as Witmer had. To my amazement he said, "Well, I'll see what I can do to get you back in—but not a word of this to your mother. She'll worry." He went out to the school and spoke to Witmer and to B. B. Herr, the principal. They finally agreed to let me graduate with my class, but refused to give me the Quill and Scroll Award—Quill and Scroll was a national honorary association of high school journalists—that I had earned as editor of *The Vidette.*

I graduated. My mother did not learn of my expulsion until about five years later, at which time she exhibited the same alarm she would have shown if she had known of it at the time.

I have gone into the incident at this length because it strengthened my determination to be a writer-newspaperman, no matter what. I already was one then, in fact. At fourteen I had begun reading O. O. McIntyre's column in the local afternoon paper, and for fun I had done some columns in imitation of his style. My aunt thought they were good enough to be printed. The afternoon paper —*The New Era*—was too lofty a goal for me, but at that time there was a throwaway sheet, *The Lancaster Independent,* published by a printer at the edge of the city, and I resolved to offer my columns there. It took me a long time to make up my mind to see the editor, and when after weeks I finally screwed up the courage to go out to his office, I became tongue-tied when the telephone operator at the front desk asked what I wanted. Presently I managed to make clear that I wanted to see Mr. William Young (I had learned his name from the masthead).

In one sense this book should be dedicated to William Young as well as to Louis Ruppel, for although it is doubtful that Young could see that I had talent, he was the first professional man who was kind enough to give me the feeling that I might amount to something in the work to which I was drawn. He was compact and rather handsome, with strong cheekbones and warm, smiling eyes. He took the columns I timidly extended and glanced at them—and then, to my dismay, he began to read one, frowning. At length he said, "These aren't bad, young man. They're unashamed imitations of Odd McIntyre, of course—but I think we could publish one each week. However, you must understand that we operate on a limited budget around here, and we can't pay you much."

The idea of being paid was so overwhelming, I could not speak. I had not even dared hope that he might print them.

Somehow, I managed to tell him that he could have the columns for whatever he wished to pay.

He said, "How will a dollar a week be to start?"

I tore out to Mary's house as fast as my legs could pump the pedals of my Schwinn. Babbling out the news, I accepted her congratulations in a paroxysm of triumph and raced home, where my mother was cooking supper. To my astonishment, she reacted strangely. The news seemed to make her apprehensive. Nor did my achievement particularly impress my father.

My column began appearing in the *Independent* each week. It caused no comment whatever from my schoolmates, none of whom ever read the paper. Nor did any of my relatives ever mention it. About the only persons who ever said anything about it were Mary and Ray. But my delight—my pride, actually—in seeing my by-line in print, and reading the words I had written the week before, more than compensated for the fact that I had no audience.

One thing struck me. For some reason, apart from the tremendous boost the mere fact of being in print had given my ego, my words seemed curiously flat on the page. They were not nearly as exciting as they had been when I was in the process of setting them down. Something was lacking; worse, I continually saw places where I should have made changes before handing in the manuscript. Although I was not aware of it, I was already developing what every writer must somehow acquire if he is to survive—an ability to criticize himself, a dissatisfaction with his own output. The complacent writer is a worthless one. The standards must go up and up and up, continually and unendingly if the writer is to live with himself. (See the comments by other writers in Article: "The Business of Being a Writer," P. 20) F. Scott Fitzgerald once told a friend that nothing he had written really satisfied him. He always wanted to change a word here, to put in a comma there. I have never seen a piece of mine in print (including this one, I'll warrant) that did not make me feel later that it was not quite my best work. I have had pieces that seemed satisfactory as I handed them in—but later on I have wished to make changes. It is this habit of writers that has led most of the mass magazines, during the past few years, to abandon the practice of sending out proofs. "They just can't stop fooling with their work," Herbert Mayes, editor of *Good Housekeeping,* once said to me, "and we just can't afford to give them that privilege." Among the mass-circulation magazines, only *The Saturday Evening Post, Ladies' Home Journal,* and *Holiday* adhere to the ancient custom of giving authors their proofs. This is too bad, for there are so many inexperienced and inept editors in the magazine business these days that what starts out as a competent piece often appears as a horror, and the writer is blamed by the unfortunate reader for the editor's bad grammar, lack of taste, and stupidity.

William Young taught me that, after a piece is finished, it ought to be put away to "season" for a couple of days—for a week or two, if possible. I had begun showing him short stories I was trying to write, asking for his frank criticism. He said, "You write too fast and you're too easily satisfied with what you do. The very act of putting down words is so exciting to you, you are inclined to forget the writer's responsibilities—thoughtfulness, factual reporting, and clarity of expression.

"Every time you finish a piece," he went on, "you ought to put it aside and start something else. Then, after a while, get the first one out and read it over critically. This will help you get some perspective on it. You'll see things you weren't able to see before in the heat of creation."

I worked for Bill Young—although "worked" is hardly the word, since I regarded writing as pure pleasure—all through my junior year in high school. When the senior year began he asked me to do a weekly sports column as well as my regular column, which was made up of gossip about friends (even though none ever read it) and personal observations which I believed to be perceptive and penetrating (they were neither; I was, after all, fourteen turning fifteen). I began covering the high school basketball and football games, and was suffered entry to the press box by the older reporters from the dailies. One night in Reading, Pennsylvania, as I was settling down to cover a basketball game between Reading and Lancaster high schools, a reporter arrived drunk. He was an old Reading newspaperman who was a stringer for the Lancaster morning sheet, the *Intelligencer-Journal*. He fell asleep several times during the game. I was horrified and outraged. First, I was full of school spirit, and it angered me to think that dear old Lancaster High, enjoying one of its rare wins in any sport, was being covered badly; second, my idealistic sense of a newspaperman's duty was being trampled by this sot. (I did not realize then that most writers, with the possible exception of James A. Michener and Frances Parkinson Keyes, drink like fish.)

The story printed in the next day's newspaper, which the drunk had telephoned in after the game, stirred me even more. It was badly written and inaccurate in several spots. I could have done much, much better. I resolved to go and see F. Melvin Martin, the sports editor of the *Intelligencer Journal*. I called him up and asked for an appointment, my voice shaking. To my amazement, he asked me to go in and see him that afternoon. "And bring some of your work," he added.

I have been trying to recall that initial meeting. Nothing comes back. I was so eager, yet so terrified, all details have vanished. He asked me about my school and about my interest in sports (it is hard for me to believe today that I was then an avid sports fan; my passion vanished the year after I got out of high school, when I covered 163 basketball games in one season and grew to loathe all sports except football). He asked to see my columns, and when I showed them to him, he raised his eyebrows. I do recall that he said, "I've seen this column in the *Independent*—and I thought it was written by someone much older." That set me up, of course;

but what was absolutely stunning was his offer of a job as one of his assistants on the Saturday night sports desk of the *Sunday News.* I was to begin immediately and was to receive five dollars a week. This time I must have staggered a little as I made my way out of the office.

Again, my parents were not especially pleased. My mother was downright distressed. The hours of my job were to be from four P.M. until at least two A.M., with an hour off for dinner. Getting home at three or three-thirty, I told my mother, would mean that I would be unable to get up to go to Sunday School the next day. She was by then already convinced that I was going straight to hell, and now that I had the job on the immoral newspaper, she resigned herself to the fact that it would be only a matter of time before my horns and forked tail appeared.

Frank Melvin Martin—he signed himself "F. Melvin," but everybody called him "Jack" for some reason—taught me more than any other individual except Louis Ruppel. He was a small, stout man, with regular Pennsylvania Dutch features that once must have been fine-boned but which his overweight condition blurred slightly—a straight nose, keen blue eyes, and a square jaw. His voice was customarily soft, even when he was openly angry, which was seldom. A stickler for good manners, he was invariably polite to everyone, even people he hated; his regular habits were typified by the way he carefully removed his hat each evening as he came to work and placed it in the self-same straight position on the office coat rack. His formality could not conceal a certain constitutional bitterness; he suffered from a persecution complex, and although he pretended that many of his sarcastic remarks were meant in jest, there was a sincere undercurrent that always got through to his listeners. What was working inside Jack, I had no way of knowing then and cannot tell to this day; I worked with him, desk to desk, for three years, but whatever knowledge I have of human motives had not yet begun to form. I accepted him for what he was—and what he was to me, in those days, was the greatest newspaperman, and the hardest and most impatient taskmaster, who ever lived.

Jack was not a good writer, technically speaking. He was rather like the Westbrook Pegler of the past few years. He wrote conversationally, rambling along with various side excusions and digressions, ungrammatically and idiomatically, his hatred and bitterness undisguised (he especially hated the Lancaster School Board and the Superintendent of Schools, a harmless old fellow, because he felt they were stifling scholastic sports). At the same time, he recognized good writing when he saw it, and he insisted upon seeing it on his page. Time and again, during my first few months of Saturdays with him, he would hurl a story back on my desk, shaking his head in disgust, saying, "Do you think you'll ever amount to anything?" or "I go to hell if that isn't the worst piece of copy I ever saw in my life." He once made me rewrite an account of a baseball game eleven times. In the end he printed my first version, saying cruelly, "I just wanted to see how many different ways you could do it, kid."

I hated him, at first. Time and again, I wanted to quit—but there was always the desperate desire to learn to write, and the welcome relief from going to that accursed Sunday School of my mother's. So I stuck. And one Saturday night, after I had been working for Jack for about three months, he asked me to go along to dinner with him. We went to The Red Rose, a greasy spoon a few blocks from the newspaper office. It was only about the third or fourth time in my life I had eaten in a restaurant, and I was thrilled. During dinner, Jack became a different person. He asked me questions about school, about my work as editor of the magazine, about my ambitions. He told me he thought I showed promise—which so excited me I could scarcely finish my baked beans. When we returned to the office he changed back into his office personality, but now I knew that at bottom he could be a kindly, generous man, and that he was my friend and advocate. And I worked even harder. After a few weeks I became bold enough to banter with him. When he said, "Do you honestly think you'll ever amount to anything?" I would answer, "Well, at least I won't be a broken-down sports editor on a two-bit paper, like you." And he would say, "Jesus, if you keep on writing copy like this, I'm going to have to send you back to the *Independent*." I loved those dialogues; they seemed to me to be real newspaperman talk. It was during my association with Jack that I bought my first hat and wore it everywhere, especially indoors. The trouble was, I couldn't type with a cigarette dangling from my mouth; the smoke curled up into my eyes. I learned to type with two fingers, because Jack did—which meant that I had to unlearn the touch-typing I had learned in a course in school.

Martin worked on me until his principles of newspaper reporting and writing became second nature to me. He insisted upon absolute accuracy, clear writing, and brevity. He also demanded speed—the two of us, plus one more man who worked only three hours, had a four-page sports section to fill every Saturday night. Over and over he would say, "You must never put an opinion in a story unless you are signing it—and even then you ought to think it over carefully before you set it down. We're not paying you to think; we're paying you to report." Even after he gave me a column of my own, with my name at the head of it, he insisted that I stick to straight reporting. It is only today, now that I have been writing for nearly twenty-five years, that I can express an opinion in print without the uneasy feeling that Jack's ghost—he died a few years ago of a heart attack—is looking over my shoulder.

I finally graduated from high school in 1938. I worked for Jack through that summer vacation, resisted my mother's entreaties to go out to Armstrong Linoleum and try for a respectable job, and earned ten dollars a week as publicity man for Maple Grove, a Lancaster amusement park. I wrote a daily story about some incident or event at the park and took it down and handed two versions of it to the city editors of the morning and afternoon newspapers. They printed the stories because the Park was an advertiser. The management of the Park thought I was doing a great job, and I did nothing to persuade them otherwise.

In the fall the question of college came up again. My parents were not urging me—no one in our family ever had been to college, except my half-uncle Ray—but Jack felt that I should go. I told him I wanted to be a newspaperman more than I wanted to go to college, and asked if there might not be an opening on the *Intelligencer Journal*. There was not, but he spoke to George Kirchner, the sports editor of *The New Era*, the afternoon paper, who hired me as scholastic sports correspondent. He paid me nine cents per column inch for everything I wrote that got into print. I began working for Kirchner in September, 1938, and it is unnecessary to say that every story I handed in was at least twice as long as it deserved to be. Kirchner ruthlessly cut my copy in half—but my disappointment at getting less money was somewhat offset by his custom of giving me a by-line each day. I learned a good deal from him, too. He was neither as stern nor as demanding as Martin, but he was a first-rate reporter. The trouble with the job, as I saw it, was that he expected me to do much more than write copy at space rates. I was his errand boy, copy boy and rewrite man, and he demanded that I arrive at the office at eight A.M. to cut the copy off the teletype machines. I never could get in at eight. One day I didn't get in until noon; he warned me that he did not want me to be late again. A few days later I was late again, and he said, patiently enough, that summer was coming on and he wouldn't be needing me for a while. That was that.

That summer I filled in on the *Intelligencer Journal* for various two-week spells while reporters were on holiday. The managing editor, the late Earl E. Keyser, an ulcerous matrinet when working and a jovial companion when not, took an interest in me and gave me a sampling of odd jobs to do. I covered the police beat, the court house, fires, minor crimes and, as usual, sports. Keyser said he would see if he could fit me in as a regular in the autumn, and I was in transports. Meanwhile I was still working on the Sunday sports desk with Jack, and augmenting my income by acting as a press agent for the Manheim Barons, a ball club managed by a friend of Jack's. The friend, whom I remember today only as Bob, was a jovial saloonkeeper in Manheim, a small town about twelve miles from Lancaster, noted principally for the fact that Baron Steuben, the famous glassmaker, had once had his headquarters there. The Barons were financed by the citizens of the town, by public subscription, to play in a league made up of teams from Lancaster, Berks and Lebanon counties. Bob paid me ten dollars a week to write stories about the team for the local newspapers and act as official scorer at all home games.

Everything was going along nicely until Bob suddenly was fired as manager of the club. He was replaced by a man named Hunter, whom I met only once, at which time he told me he wished me to continue acting as flack. Unfortunately, Hunter was a total mess as manager. He paid players who did not play in the games and he spent the citizens' money unwisely, I felt. Worse, he never paid me. A month went by and I still was not paid. Presently I wrote him a note asking him for my salary. He did not bother to answer. Then I wrote another. Again there was no reply. Finally, in a fury, I sat down and wrote a note resigning as press agent and telling Hunter that unless I was paid at once I was going to ask questions about his mismanagement of the ball club in my column in the *Sunday News*.

Hunter was not only a man who did not pay his employees, he was also a friend of the late Austin E. McCullough, the distinguished, nationally-respected editor of the *Intelligencer Journal*. My letter reeked of blackmail, although I was not aware of that. Hunter took it to McCullough, and the following Saturday, when I reported for work as usual, I was told that I was through—and, moreover, that I would never work for Lancaster Newspapers, Inc., again. It was the worst blow I ever had received, and I have seldom experienced anything since to equal it. Doing my best to hold back the tears, I ran home, so mortified and ashamed I could not look in the mirror as I washed my face. My life, it seemed, was over; the newspaper had been my universe. Nothing else had mattered to me but my apprenticeship. Fortunately, my mother was not in the house. I hastily threw some clothes in a bag, left a note, and hitch-hiked to New York. The city terrified me. I wandered around in a daze and grew so frightened that about six A.M. I walked back down to the Holland Tunnel, got a ride through to the other end, walked over the Pulaski Skyway, and presently was picked up by four Negroes barreling home to Philadelphia after an all-night dance in Jersey City. There I hitched another ride back to Lancaster. Thus my first assault on the big city ended in utter disgrace.

Going back to the *Independent* was impossible. As for Lancaster Newspapers, Inc., both Jack Martin and Earl Keyser had interceded for me with McCullough, and he had agreed to give me a second chance. But I could not return to the newspaper and face my former colleagues, knowing they knew what I had done. For the rest of the summer I worked as a water boy on a construction gang, earning more money than I had dreamed of as a newspaperman—over thirty dollars a week. In September I went back to New York, stayed at the Y. M. C. A. known as William Sloane House, and made the rounds of the newspapers armed with references from Jack and Earl, hoping to get a job as a copy boy. The editors to whom I spoke were friendly but discouraging. They all told me I had not yet had enough experience. When I showed them front-page by-lined stories I had had in the Lancaster journals, including an exclusive interview with Paul Whiteman and several features in the magazine section, they told me that their waiting-lists were so long it would be years before they could even consider me. I returned to Lancaster with my savings gone and my hope all but. During the next few weeks I remained in my room, trying to write pulp-paper magazine fiction for *Astounding* and *Unknown,* and making occasional sorties to nearby Reading, York and Harrisburg, hoping to get a job on a newspaper in one of those cities. There were no openings. In Philadelphia, when I went there, I was told substantially what I had been told in New York. "Every newspaperman in eastern Pennsylvania wants to work on a Philly paper," one editor told me. "We've got the pick of the lot." Years later I was to use the depressing, apparently useless period of my life as background for *The Snob,* a novelette I published in *Ladies' Home Journal,* but of course at the time I had no notion that anything would come of it. (See Chapter II on wasting time.) All I knew was that I felt worthless and dispirited. The stories snapped back from the pulps with agonizing regularity, and even though I did get a personal note from an editor every once in a while, rather than a rejection slip, I was gradually beginning to believe that my mother's oft-expressed opinion—that I was wasting my time in trying to be a writer—was true.

Unexpectedly, I got a job writing publicity for the local Community Chest campaign. I heard of it through one of my friends on the newspaper, went to see the fund-raiser, and was hired on the spot. He was a jovial soul named H. A. Waldkoenig, who appeared completely disorganized but who was an expert at cajoling people into giving away money. I wrote a story each day for both the dailies, and distinguished myself during the first week by backing into a typewriter and knocking it off its stand, smashing it. Waldkoenig, who had a high, explosive laugh, went into hysterics but nevertheless charged me for the machine. I paid the fifty dollars—two weeks' salary—five dollars at a time. From then on I moved more deliberately.

While I was working away at that job, Margaret Smith, a reporter on the *Intelligencer Journal,* told me that the man with whom she was keeping company, Maurice Miller, was looking for someone to take a job in his organization. Miller, a local man who had spent some time as an editor in New York with D. Appleton-Century, had returned home and founded a kind of radio script syndicate. He leased half-hour and one-hour plays to radio stations all over the English-speaking world, paying royalties to their authors for the privilege. He had been instantaneously successful and was thinking of expanding. He had in mind a service which he would call Custom-Built Commercial Continuities—a weekly booklet of seventy-five spot announcements covering twenty-five different businesses, ranging from automobile dealers to women's wear shops. Each announcement would contain three blank spaces wherein the local radio stations could insert the name of the companies to which its salesmen peddled the service. Miller was looking for someone to write these commercials, and after we had had a talk he opined that the job was mine, on a trial basis, if I wanted it.

Miller was a brilliant man. Tall and ruggedly built, he resembled an athlete but was more of an aesthete, albeit a shrewd one. I liked him at once. He had read widely, his conversation was full of literary allusions, and he had traveled in Europe. He had returned to Lancaster for two reasons—to care for his aging and ailing father, for one, and because he himself was going blind. He suffered from a condition that made it impossible for his eyes to focus as other people's do. If he switched his gaze from one object to another, seconds elapsed before he could make out the details of the second. He ultimately died of a coronary occlusion, the aftermath of an operation which had been designed to restore normal sight.

The work I did for Miller was harder than anything I previously had attempted. It often seemed to me that I would never get the hang of writing material to be read aloud. What was perfectly acceptable in type did not sound effective—or punchy, as Miller put it—when spoken. He was extraordinarily patient. He gave me an office, permitted me to keep my own hours—and, for the first six weeks, gave me back everything I wrote to be rewritten. Gradually I learned to write those accursed commercials, and before long I became accustomed to the dreadful prospect of coming up with seventy-five entirely new ideas each week. Looking at it one way, it was wonderful experience. I lost some of the self-consciousness about writing itself that handicaps so many young writers. Jack Martin and George Kirchner had helped me overcome my initial stiffness at the typewriter, and Miller destroyed what was left of it. Perhaps I would be better off today if I wrote more slowly, but I cannot seem to work at any pace but my customary one.

While slaving away at the commercials I also did scripts for a syndicated morning radio program designed to be broadcast by disc jockeys. In doing this I discovered that I had a certain knack for what passed as humor. This show, *Morning Mirth,* at one time was being broadcast by ninety-two different radio stations in the United States and Canada. It was terrible; I still have some of the scripts, and I can scarcely bear to read them. But for some inscrutable reason Miller thought that I was potentially a writer of humorous material, and suggested that I do some things and submit them to the Post Scripts page of *The Saturday Evening Post.* I wrote a few short things, none more than five paragraphs long, and sent them off. They came back as quickly as my stories had come back from the pulps . . . no, more quickly, for the *Post* has always been the fastest-reporting magazine in the business (a writer gets a "No" or a check within a week at the most).

Then, one day, they bought one. It must have been my fifteenth or sixteenth try; I can't remember how many I wrote previously. A letter from Marione Derrickson (now Marione Nickles) said, "We like this Post Script and would like to keep it and pay you thirty dollars for it." The Marshalls were then living in Elizabethtown, a village eighteen miles from Lancaster; I got Mary on the telephone and shouted the news. She was naturally as excited as I. I ran into Miller's office, waving the letter. He stood up and shook my hand. "An historic day, m'boy," he said in the English accent he sometimes affected to amuse his friends. Then I ran home and told my mother. "What does that mean?" she said, worriedly. "It means I've sold my first story to a big magazine!" I yelled. "Oh," she said.

Hindsight, as well as a certain amount of psychoanalysis, even at the hands of a relatively unstable man like the one whose patient I was for three years, gives us a certain amount of insight. At the time, I was furious. My mother's comment seemed to me to be the final straw. On the most triumphant day of my life, her antagonism to my lifework remained steadfast. I realize now that she was not being antagonistic; that she wanted the best for me, that she could not understand what I was up to and therefore feared it, and that she could not actually express her fears for fear of provoking me. I also know why I became enraged. Writing, to me, was then primarily a compensation for some inadequacy I felt, some way of asserting myself. I had asserted myself in a spectacular manner, and had failed to command her respect or even attention.

From that point on—I was twenty—I was published in the national magazines with a certain amount of regularity. I sold Post Scripts two or three more little pieces, including one or two after I was drafted into the Army in 1942. In 1943, while enduring a totally unnecessary course of instruction in the art of setting and dismantling booby traps at Fort Belvoir, Virginia, I sat down on two successive evenings at a coin-operated typewriter in a Service Club and wrote a short story which Whit Burnett accepted for *Story* and later included in one of those innumerable anthologies he is always editing. A few months later I sold a short story to *The New Yorker*. Then I sold *Esquire, Collier's*, and several smaller, less well-known magazines. When the Army sent me to Oak Ridge, Tennessee, to put out a weekly newspaper for the workers and residents of the atomic bomb project, I met Fleta Campbell Coe, a lady who had been a prolific writer during the twenties and thirties. She generously read my stories critically, and with her help I became more adept. After my discharge in 1946 I continued to write, and I have been at it ever since.

I have put all this personal material on paper because people, especially aspiring writers, frequently ask me how I got started or what special training I had. I had none, except my life. Another question frequently asked is, "What rules would you set down for the beginning writer?" It is a hard question to answer, if not an impossible one, for the simple reason that no two individuals are much alike (if they were, the writers would be as out of business here as they appear to be in the Soviet Union). I cannot say, "Work on your school papers, get a job on a daily under a hard-driving perfectionist, write in your spare time, get into the Army and meet an experienced writer." Nevertheless, there are a few things I can say without being too presumptuous. They are:

1. *Read.* In order to gain at least some familiarity with what has

been written, an aspiring writer ought to read no less than an hour a day. I don't mean, necessarily, that he ought to read critically or selectively; he should read whatever happens to strike him, and cast aside what does not. He ought to know what other writers in his field have attempted and whether they have succeeded or failed. He ought to attempt to absorb the methods and techniques of the ones he admires and blend them with his own ideas into some semblance of an original style. This is usually an unconscious process. Nearly all writers begin as imitators without realizing it; but nearly all deliberate imitators are unsuccessful—with a few exceptions, such as Max Schulman, who began by imitating S. J. Perelman and wound up a spectacular success.

2. *Get some sort of education.* A writer ought to know the fundamentals of his craft, whether he learns them by reading or by going to school. He also ought to know a little about everything from mathematics to history, and a good deal about one or two things, for the most expert magazine writers are specialists more often than not. Most important, however, is the business of learning the language he uses. Mere power is not enough. The time is long past when a Dreiser, who used the language with unbelievable clumsiness, can get by on strength and intensity. The majority of the bad notices for James Jones' second novel, *Some Came Running,* attacked his careless usage. The fact that his book sold well must have been a hollow triumph in the light of what the reviewers said. Our audience has grown up somewhat since Dreiser's day—not enough, considering the politicians we send to office—but enough to scorn the man who writes despite a lack of knowledge of technique. I sometimes regret my unwillingness to go to college. There is so much I wish I knew.

3. *Waste Time.* A writer ought to sit around with friends, hang out in bars, go on the bum if he feels like it, or sit by himself doing nothing but thinking. He ought to let himself go to pieces if he is so inclined. He ought to fall in and out of love with unsuitable girls if he is so moved, smoke marijuana if it appeals to him, even become a porch-climber if that is his bent. No time is wasted for a writer; all experience, especially painful experience, contributes to his ability to communicate.

4. *Practice.* I already have mentioned the stiffness and self-con-

sciousness that almost always attends a young writer's first attempts. From the very first day when he decides that he will write—if indeed he can recognize the day—he ought to do what he can to get rid of that awareness of self, that I-am-a-writer-and-I-am-going-to-write-like-a-writer attitude. He ought to write like himself. To do this, he must first *be* himself, and second he must write and write and write in order to develop some ease and fluency. The best performers in the world are those whose performances give the impression of being effortless—and they are the hardest workers in the world. Picasso did not become the greatest living painter by sitting around in his youth and thinking that some day he would paint a picture. He painted all the time—and still does. He is still developing; he will not stop developing, or practicing, until he dies. I do not mean here that a writer ought simply to sit down and write something, anything that comes into his head; I do mean that when the time arrives for him to write, he should not permit the writing process to get in his way.

There are any number of ways to practice. One can go to work on a newspaper, as I did, where one is required to turn out large amounts of copy in a short time. One can write long letters to friends. One can write articles, sketches, short stories, poetry or plays, with or without the hope of publishing them (there is always the hope, no matter what some individuals say). Or one can do exercises out of English texts, writing essays on "What I Did Today," "An Interesting Bird I Know," "My Grandfather," "My Neighbor's Toby Collection" (if one has enough skill, one can then sell these masterpieces to a digest magazine). Several writers I know practice by sitting at their machines or at their tablets and writing down their streams-of-consciousness, and working from those into the chores at hand. The method has never worked for me. Even the discipline and training of an advertising agency can aid in removing self-consciousness or in creating an ability to "turn on" when it is necessary, or one feels that it is necessary, to do so.

If this were a class, some overanxious pupil would raise his hand at this point and tell me how Sinclair Lewis, addressing a writing class, began by asking what the pupils were doing in it, and went on to say they all should have been home writing. I personally regard Lewis' reputation as fraudulent. I imagine our country's tender years had something to do with creating it, for he was a straight writer who wrote so badly he was thought to be comic, and he bolstered his comic reputation by continuing to write straight. But his advice was sound. Writers become writers by writing.

5. *Develop a point of view.* Nobody can tell a human being how to develop a point of view any more than anyone can tell a human being how to be himself. The best writers are those who are themselves, even if they write as carelessly as James Jones, or as pompously as, say James Gould Cozzens, or in an eccentric manner, as Clementine Paddleford, the food columnist of the *New York Herald Tribune,* does so effectively. Whatever may be said against Sinclair Lewis, he at least wrote like Sinclair Lewis and like nobody else. The aim of the young writer ought to be individual, distinctive expression; to write in a manner that is entirely his own. As I stated before, it is almost impossible to begin without imitating another writer or writers—but it is also imperative to keep some perspective on the work and to attempt to eliminate the imitation.

6. *Be disciplined.* Most writers, in the beginning, have trouble getting themselves to work on a regular schedule. Part of this is due to timidity, I think. Discipline is absolutely necessary if a writer is going to produce with some consistency. In his book *Park Row,* Allen Churchill quotes the novelist David Graham Phillips as follows:

> "I write every night from eleven to five or six in the morning," he once told an aspiring writer. "Sometimes it is seven or eight. I write every night seven nights a week. Let me urge you to work the same number of hours every day and never, never, never to let anything interfere between you and those working hours. I don't wait for mood or inspiration and I don't give up because I don't begin right or am writing rubbish. I think it is fatal to give way to moods."

In ten years, this appalling schedule enabled Phillips to produce twenty-three books and several hundred short stories and articles—"a literary output unprecedented for that length of time," Churchill says. I would hesitate to recommend such a schedule—but I do believe that the young writer should set aside certain periods of time when he will do nothing but write, and should stay on his schedule in spite of everything.

The above are long-range principles. I do not claim they will work for everyone—but they have worked for a good many writers

I know, even though they sometimes were applied without the writers' being aware that they were applying them. The truth is that there are no set methods of becoming a writer—no rules, no maxims. For every one that exists there is a workable contradiction. After nearly a quarter-century of doing what I know best how to do I am convinced that I know very little indeed.

For that reason, the reader should approach the first piece in this collection with the same attitude that an atomic scientist might use in approaching the theories of Velikovsky. It is a job I did for *Cosmopolitan* in the summer of 1957. Because it contains a good deal of information about the life of a working writer, I have decided not only to print it in full but to expand it.

ARTICLE: "THE BUSINESS OF BEING A WRITER"

(Expanded from the original in *Cosmopolitan*)

One of the first rules a young reporter learns is to keep himself out of his material, and another rule he learns when he gets older is that all rules must be broken. This is meant to be a realistic appraisal of the business of being a writer in the modern market; it is not meant to be overly encouraging, it is meant to be practical and factual. Unlike those spurious pieces which declare that anyone who can write a simple friendly letter has it in him to be a writer, this one begins with the premise that not everyone can write, not even some writers (any magazine editor will hastily affirm the truth of the last). But it also holds that people can learn. Because I have developed certain definite notions, all of them fragile but definite nonetheless, about writing as an art and a craft and a business, I have decided to put myself into this material, thereby breaking the first rule but keeping the second intact. So.

I am a writer who learned. Today I earn my family's living, plus that of a couple of other families I seem to be supporting, from my writing. I write magazine articles, mainly, and occasional newspaper pieces, and now and again a book. It is not especially a distinction to be a writer, and I do not proclaim my occupational classification with any great pride. Writing is something I can do better than I can do anything else, but in the apartment below me lives a man who can take out gall bladders better than he can do anything else. He wishes he were a writer, and there have been times when I have longed for a nice, simple gallbladderectomy to perform. At present there are between 130 and 140 members of the Society of Magazine Writers, all of whom are doing just about what I am doing, and at last count there were around 3500 members of the Authors League of America, most of whom, presumably, are getting paid for their writing. That makes around 3700 professional writers that I know of, but there are many, *many*, MANY more writers than that alive and scribbling in the United States.

Indeed, it often strikes me that there is not one single living human being in this vast nation who is not, or who does not believe that he could be (if only he could find the time), a writer. There are even some animal writers. Lassie wrote a book a few years ago, as told to her trainer, Rudd B. Weatherwax. I know, because Lassie and I have the same agent representing us. Some indication of how very many writers there are may be gleaned from what happened after I published a magazine story about Irving Paul Lazar in January, 1957. Lazar is the most successful lone-wolf literary agent prowling the Beverly Hills. He persuades film producers to pay fabulous prices to his writer-clients for their material. His life has not been the same since that story of mine. Everyone who read it was instantaneously gripped with inspiration and immediately decided that Lazar could be his guide to fame and fortune in the writing business. Manuscripts engulfed Lazar (which did not take long, since he is about the size of one of those iron jockeys outside "21"). They came from all over the country by the hundreds. They arrived express collect. Western Union boys attempted to deliver manuscripts that were telegraphed in—collect. Poor Lazar fled to Europe, where at last report he was contemplating an easier profession, such as bullfighting.

There are so many would-be writers because, to the non-writer, writing looks easy and, in the classic phrase of John Lardner, it appears to beat working. The non-writer believes that writing requires no physical equipment except pencil, paper and perhaps a typewriter, and very little time beyond that needed to set down a given number of words. He imagines that the profits are immense and that a writer's life consists mainly of the stuff of which Igor Cassini's columns are made. Well, little of this is true. In a poll I recently took among fifty first-grade magazine writers, few of them said that they believed they were performing any kind of public service. I am now going to perform one, by attempting to show what the life of a writer actually is and by trying to set afire some of the myths about writers which the public now accepts as gospel.

The first nonsensical notion is that writers look like writers. In cartoons, writers have black, bushy hair and wear thick-rimmed glasses and disheveled clothes. The only writers I can think of offhand who look like that are James T. Farrell and Jean-Paul Sartre. Herman Wouk, on the jacket of his latest book, in Chesterfield, hair slicked down, looks like a distant cousin of the House of Rothschild. Kathleen Winsor could be one of those women one sees shopping custom-corset row along New York's East 58th Street. T. S. Eliot resembles a bank clerk (which he was for many years; he worked in a bank to support his poetry-writing). Lionel White appears to be a country squire, Walt Grove an airline pilot, John D. McDonald the treasurer of a wholesale grocery house. Frances Parkinson Keyes is the chairlady of a Cake Committee for a church covered-dish social. William Faulkner, in overalls, could be a member of his own Snopes family.

Yet there is something about most writers that sets them apart and brands them, some vague unrest, some terrible intensity, even a little insanity, in some cases an air of genuine sophistication, and above all a curiosity. There never has been a valuable writer who was not powerfully curious, if only about himself; Thomas Wolfe, despite his interest in his own navel, was continually asking questions. To me, the writer who looked most like a writer was a dear lady named Fleta Campbell Coe, who published many articles and short stories during the twenties and the thirties. She died a couple of years ago. She was a small, compact woman with fuzzy blondish bangs and a leathery skin and a burned-down cigarette always sticking out of the corner of her mouth; she had a hoarse voice and a lovely coarse candor. When she was conversing she cocked her head to one side to listen, squinting her eyes against the smoke from the the cigarette, and she listened so closely the speaker was inclined to say more, perhaps, than he originally had intended. She had an extensive knowledge of law, religion, fine art, cookery and even—although she pretended not to—nuclear science; but she was not essentially interested in any of those subjects, she was interested in people. Along with that primary interest she had a sense of perspective, which is to say a sense of humor, and an acceptance of human fallibility and mortality—which is what characterizes the real writers, even the pontifical ones like Thomas Mann.

Even when she was not actually writing, Mrs. Coe was continually working at her trade—for she knew (and taught me) that the actual transmission of words to paper is in some ways the least important act in the writing process. She worked all the time. Nearly every writer I know does. It is hard for non-writers to grasp that, and it is particularly hard for writers' wives, as Stanley Frank and others have pointed out. Nor do children ever seem to understand the business of writing; the late Wolcott Gibbs, the drama critic, once wrote that his small son was convinced that he was a burglar because Gibbs sat around the house all day in his pajamas and went out only at night. Indeed, society's whole attitude toward the writer makes many of us feel that we *are* criminals; when Eli Waldron was living in his home town of Oconto Falls, Wisconsin, he always felt that his neighbors were staring at him suspiciously, clearly indicating that they thought he had just stolen a horse. Of course, some writers really are criminals. Many writers I know would be happy to earn a tenth of what Caryl Chessman did from his death cell writings.

Despite appearances, all successful writers probably work harder, proportionately speaking, than any other class of laborers. Hemingway rises at a shudderingly early hour and writes in longhand four straight hours before going out fishing, fighting, hunting or drinking or whatever else he wants to do. S. J. Perelman goes to his office at ten, knocks off about a half-hour for lunch, then returns and sits at his machine until about six. Jim Bishop puts in a twenty-five hour day, it often seems to his friends; actually, the author of *The Day Christ Died* only works a twelve-hour day and, most nights, a four-hour night. W. Somerset Maugham has written at least three hours each day every day of his life since he began over sixty years ago.

Then there are the writing factories—those ravingly prolific individuals whose output sometimes staggers even themselves. The late Edgar Rice Burroughs, author of the *Tarzan* books and once termed by the reporter Alva Johnston the richest writer in the world, could knock out four books a year as casually as some men eat three meals a day. Kathleen Norris used to be good for two book-length serials a year for *Collier's*; so, in fact did a whole gaggle of lady writers whose names used to turn up regularly in the magazines —Sophie Kerr, Ursula Parrott, Faith Baldwin, Fannie Hurst and Nelia Gardner White. The astonishing thing about these ladies was that most of then managed to keep house and raise children between spasms at the typewriter or writing-pad. Some managed to combine their two lives neatly; there was usually a dinner party, with the menu fully described, in Sophie Kerr's books (she once wrote a wonderful cookbook, by the way, called *The Best I Ever Ate*). The females' output seems small indeed, however, beside some of the males. Dashiell Hammett sometimes wrote whole issues of *Black Mask Detective Magazine*, month after month—a serial and eight or nine stories. Erle Stanley Gardner used to turn out four books a year, two under his own name and two under his pen-name of A. A. Fair, which his publishers lately have taken to identifying as Erle Stanley Gardner. This is a new trend in publishing circles, by the way. It used to be that a writer could write under a pseudonym and keep his identity a secret. No more. When "John Phillips" published his first novel, his publisher proudly pointed out on the jacket that their writer was none other than J. P. Marquand, Jr. I might as well make a clean breast of it; I am Martin Scott. (And I had six articles, under six different names, in the August, 1958, *Cosmopolitan*.)

These days, John D. McDonald is the wonder of us all. He has been known to write four paper-backed books, four 25,000-word novelettes, and two dozen short stories in a single year. It makes other writers tired just to think of him. Moreover, he *writes* the stories; he does not dictate, as Erle Stanley Gardner does, or even as John P. Marquand, Sr., does. Prolific as he is, McDonald still seems like a small boy compared to some of Philip Wylie's performances when he was actively writing for the magazines (before he became the author of angry books like *Generation of Vipers*). S. J. Perelman once told me that Wylie arrived at his country house for a week end, vanished in the morning into a converted corn crib Perelman used as a study, and emerged that evening with the manuscript of a 25,000-

word novelette (which he sold at a handsome price the following Monday in New York). The performance amazed Perelman, who writes slowly and carefully, always looking for the exact phrase and the indispensable word. Flaubert was such a writer; he sometimes spent days stewing over a sentence or the proper location of a semi-colon.

Even some of the more studious writers are unexpectedly prolific. Allan Nevins, the historian, not only lectures at Columbia University but has turned out an enormous body of work. The late Bernard DeVoto found time not only to teach, to get arrested in behalf of civil liberties, and to write lively histories of the opening of the West; he also wrote detective stories under the name of John August. It is not uncommon for the intellectual to divert himself—and fatten his wallet—by turning out thrillers on the side, usually under pen-names. Francis Steegmuller, the Flaubert authority and critic, writes whodunits under two different names.

All writers, even the most successful ones, work against such tremendous odds that it is a wonder that any of us bother. Not even the most incurable horseplayer would attempt to go against such chancy figures. The man in Tusitala, New Mexico, who right this minute is banging away at a short story in the hope of selling it to *Cosmopolitan* does not realize it, but the likelihood of its being bought figures at 6 in 1,000—for we receive around 1,000 short stories each month and buy only six (well, some months we buy seven or eight, but not frequently). The odds against being published in a weekly are even higher. It takes a long, long time to learn to write saleable material; Joseph Hergesheimer, one of the great American romantic novelists, wrote away for more than a dozen years before he began to sell his work. Steady, consistent sales do not guarantee more steady, consistent sales. Every writer knows—to his despair—that he is bound to turn out a dog once in a while, which he will ultimately consign to his trunk, where it will lie as mute and profitless testimony to days, even weeks and months, of uncompensated work. However, the most expert cabinet-maker can turn out a table with one short leg. There is a story about Hugh McNair Kahler that illustrates how even a pro can miss.

Kahler had written and sold ninety-nine consecutive short stories to the *Saturday Evening Post*. The fiction editors were looking forward to a small celebration when he turned in the hundredth. He turned it in, they read it and sent it along to George Horace Lorimer, the editor, for final approval. Lorimer bounced it. "Look here, Mr. Lorimer," said one, "do you realize this is Hugh's hundredth story?" Lorimer said he didn't care; he was publishing a magazine, not helping a writer set a record. He would not buy it. Kahler subsequently became an editor—although not, I hasten to add, because of that incident; he went on to write many more successful short stories.

The hard, seemingly endless hours that must be spent at the desk may account in part for the peculiar turns that some writers' personalities take. Eccentricity in one form or another is almost a prerequisite, and has been since the days of Samuel Johnson; the world appears to take for granted the fact that all writers are a trifle crazy. Curiously, writers' personalities often seem diametrically opposed to the selves they exhibit to the world in print. In general the humorists are a morose, even vicious, lot, and the grimly serious ones are the most unrestrained carousers. Sometimes as I sit by my window in the mornings I see one of America's foremost wits walking by, his brow furrowed, his head bent, his posture plainly limning his dejection and anger at the world. Conversely, some of the most hilariously disorderly nights I ever have spent have been with such sober and thoughtful novelists as James Jones, Merle Miller, Robert Paul Smith and Robert Presnell, Jr. Novelists named "Robert" are demonstrably unrestrained for some reason. Very late one night a few years ago, Presnell, Jr. bet me he could walk a city block in New York without touching his feet to the ground; he nearly did it, too, by hopping from roof to roof of parked automobiles—until he happened to hit a convertible with a rotten top. Another night, Smith, staying late at a party at Merle Miller's house, discovered he had missed the last commuter's train; he happily called an ambulance, explaining that he always had wanted to ride home in an ambulance, got in and lay down and slept happily all the way to Scarsdale. Smith denies this, vehemently; the truth is, he doesn't remember it.

As the hard work breeds peculiarity, it also spawns exceptional restlessness. Writers are always going somewhere—not necessarily to look for material, but in the hope that they will bump into it. Usually they travel lightly, and fairly casually, too. Tom O'Reilly, the sportswriter, once showed up at Idlewild airport in New York, all ready for a month-long tour of England, with nothing but a toothbrush in his pocket. Robert Ruark once told me of an argument he'd had with his wife which ended with her saying, "Go away! Go *far* away!" Ruark left the house, got on an airplane, and presently landed in Australia. There he sent his wife a cable: IS THIS FAR ENOUGH?

My all-time favorite example of rootlessness came to my attention a few years ago when I happened to overhear a conversation in the San Remo, a Greenwich Village home away from home for writers and would-bes. A novelist—Marc Brandel, I believe—had just come back to town and was having a drink with a friend. The latter asked where he was living.

"My books are at Ted's house," I recall Brandel saying, "my clothes are at Joe's, my records are at Jerry's, and I've been working at Barbara's and sleeping on Dick's couch."

The friend, also a writer (it need hardly be mentioned), nodded sympathetically. "Nice that you're settled," he said.

Still, there apparently is a desire in all writers to settle down and lead a fairly normal life; why else would they get married so many times? Hemingway has been married four times, which is about par for the average writer. Artie Shaw, who has always considered himself more writer than clarinet player (he wrote a book called *The Trouble with Cinderella*), is perhaps the all-time champion. He has been espoused nine times. There are two reasons why writers get married impulsively. It is rare that one meets a girl who appears to have the slightest understanding of the problems of being a writer, and when a writer does meet such a girl, he automatically proposes (he then finds, almost immediately, that she has no more understanding of what it means to be a writer than his mother did). In January, 1957, just before I left on an assignment in London, James Jones stood in my living room, raised his glass-laden hand aloft and proclaimed that he would be a bachelor all his life. Two weeks later he was married. The second reason for the writer's habit of plunging into matrimony is the abject loneliness of the life. Most other occupations are conducted in group circumstances, even newspaper writing or working on magazines. The writer must have solitude if he is to do his best work, and the solitude sometimes drives one near-crazy. Josephine Herbst, the novelist (*Rope of Gold*) told me once that as she works she talks to herself absent-mindedly just to hear sounds.

Nevertheless, despite a writer's normal desire for companionship, being married to a writer is a chore, as all writer's wives (including this one's) will attest. That is perhaps what makes for the high divorce rate among writers. Writing is often such a frustrating business that it creates enormous hostility, which is turned inward upon one's self and then outward upon the world. The process of writing does nothing to get rid of this anger, despite what the old-timers used to say. I can remember becoming so furious, one day, at my inability to write a certain paragraph so that it said exactly what I wished to say that I walked over and belted a plaster wall, breaking a finger (and the wall as well). I usually get up in a fine humor, even with a hangover, but by the time I have been at this accursed machine for two hours I am ready to throw it out the window. I become moody, perverse, crotchety, argumentative and altogether like the writer in James Thurber's *The Case of Dimity Ann*, badly in need of drink or Miltown. If my wife looks in upon me, I snarl at her; if she does not look in, I go and find her and snarl at her.

Wives of writers cannot grasp the fact that there is nothing personal in the writer's occupational anger. "You're so nice when you're not working, Eric," the wife of a writer friend of mine once said to him, whereupon he resolved that he would be nice all the time. The next morning, as he was brooding over a situation in a short story that he could not seem to solve, she put her head in the door and asked if she could have some money for the egg man. He threw a paper-weight at her.

When a writer does settle down in something resembling a normal marriage, hypochondria sets in almost immediately. It seems to me I have never known a writer who was not sick at least part of the time. One summer I was fortunate enough to get to know Allen Tate, the distinguished poet and critic; our acquaintance arose, I believe, because neither of us ever felt quite right. Tate was always certain that he was on the verge of a heart attack, and I relieved his mind somewhat by telling him about the time I had a brain tumor which a surgeon later correctly diagnosed as an ingrown hair. He later autographed one of his books to me, "FROM ANGINA (A.T.) TO BRAIN TUMOR (R.G.)" James Boswell's *Journals* are full of imagined ailments, most of them venereal. Mrs. Charlotte Zolotow, herself a writer, once said of her husband, Maurice, "He doesn't feel himself unless he's a little sick." "Neither does Richard," said the asp in my bosom.

The hypochondria is, of course, a manifestation of a deep insecurity. The average writer's life is one of feast or famine, mostly the latter, as Robert M. Heilbroner has pointed out: he always has six checks coming in or none. One day in August, 1957, I was owed $300 by the New York *Mirror*, $1750 by *Good Housekeeping*, $250 by *Gourmet*, $500 by *Cosmopolitan*, $500 by *Playboy* and $250 by a man for whom I'd done a research job; I had less than $70 in the bank, and no chance whatever of laying hands on any of the money I was owed until the editors or the accounting departments were ready to part with their money. I have never been able to save any money; the instant I get some into a savings account, it's income tax time or I have to go somewhere to do some research or just to get the hell away. And, as Heilbroner has said, even the expert, practicing professional never knows where his next assignment will come from, or indeed if he ever will get an assignment. Once I went up to visit Ray and Mary Marshall in Westfield, New York, all set to finish off *A Murder in Paradise*. I spent Sunday setting up a desk in the garage, and Monday morning I settled down to work. At ten o'clock the telephone rang. It was my agent, telling me that O'Connell of *Cosmopolitan* wanted me to go immediately to the west coast and write three stories. Somehow I had accumulated money enough to last out the two months it would have required to finish my book, and I had been promising myself that luxury for nearly a year; but I was afraid if I did not snap up O'Connell's offer, he would never ask me again. I packed a bag and left the next day. Another two months passed before I got back to work on my book.

The position of the short story writer is even more uncertain than that of the non-fiction article writer. A short story man can never be sure that his output will be bought. For one thing, the market has shrunk considerably (four magazines that published short stories all went out of business in 1957; others have cut down the number of stories per issue). John D. McDonald and Charles Einstein are the two most prolific short story authors I know, and each has a fine collection of unsold manuscripts in his files. Stories may be turned down because the editor is feeling a little queasy or because he happened to buy a vaguely similar one the month before. (I knew one mercurial editor who rejected a wonderful story simply because the writer's typewriter's type-face annoyed him: "Anybody who uses a sissy type like that can't be any good," he said as he tucked the manuscript into the self-addressed envelope the writer thoughtfully had provided.)

The writer's pay never is as high as the public believes. The average free-lance article writer, at the top of his profession, gets around $1500 per piece. The annual income reported by the writers I polled ranged between $10,000 and $15,000 per year; a few, but not many, reported upwards of $20,000. Short story writers are better off; they can command slightly higher prices, and in addition, more things can happen to a short story—it can be sold to the movies or televised, anthologized, even expanded into a novel. Those things, and more besides, can happen to a novel, too—but only a few novels ever reach the best-seller list, and most novels today rarely sell out their first printing.

Every once in a while a writer does hit the jackpot. James A. Michener's *Tales of the South Pacific* was a short story collection that was breaking no sales records whatever until the Pulitzer committee awarded it a prize. Miraculous things happened to Michener after that. His first novel, *Fires of Spring,* which had been turned down several times, was published and became a best-seller. Rodgers and Hammerstein took a couple of the *Tales* and made *South Pacific* out of them. All Michener's books since have run up imposing sales records, including a rather esoteric treatise on Japanese prints. His reputation as a best-seller now enables him to command high prices for his magazine work.

For every Michener there are hundreds of writers who barely earn a living. Moreover, there are still instances of superb writers who write their hearts out and fail to catch fire. Nathanael West, perhaps the finest novelist of the thirties, has been enjoying a vogue during recent years; a publisher has brought out his four novels in one volume to overwhelming critical acclaim. Yet in a letter to Edmund Wilson, West wrote, "I once tried to work seriously at my craft but was absolutely unable to make even the beginning of a living. At the end of three years and two books I had made the total of $780 gross." West's solution was to go to Hollywood, where by working as a scenario writer he was able to earn enough money to give him time off to work on his books. Today Hollywood is no answer to any writer's financial dilemma; when I was there in March, 1957, a friend told me that of the 2500-odd members of the Screen Writers' Guild, only about twenty-five were under contract to studios.

Assuming that a writer is able to earn a decent living at his trade, he never knows how long he will be able to keep it up, or indeed if he will be resourceful enough to sustain his creative powers over a period of time. Nearly every writer is subject to what is called "writer's bloc," which means that the well has run dry, temporarily or even permanently. There is no overall rule that covers such slumps; they come from innumerable sources, most of them having to do with the individual's emotional problems. Nor is there any cure, except possibly psychoanalysis. A doctor named Edmund Bergler claims to have cured many writers of this distressing malady; he has written a book as testimony to his own success. Curiously enough, I know any number of writers who have been through anaylsis—again, it appears to be a prerequisite for the craft—and they still put in days when they are unable to write a line, let alone a paragraph. Some sit and stare at the paper in dumb misery. Others go to ball games or get drunk, or both. Others putter around the house, nervously breaking things, making ineffectual repairs, or giving their wives and children hell.

Fortunately for the writer in a slump, his time is his own—or is in most cases, anyhow. Therein may lie some of the appeal that the writer's life has for the non-writer. Whatever else he may be, the free-lance is his own boss (or feels as though he is). The writers I queried all held freedom to be one of the great advantages of their occupation. On the other hand, freedom can be a handicap. The very absence of tangible authority leads some writers into doing everything on earth but writing. "The hardest part of my job," one recently said to me, "is keeping myself on a schedule."

Alas, none of the disadvantages I've listed will keep the determined amateur from wishing to turn professional. No matter how black I've painted the picture, to the outsider it still will look as colorful as a Van Gogh. And if this were a conversation, the tyro would brush all my preliminary statements aside and ask, "How can I become a writer?" There is only one answer. A writer becomes a writer by writing. He becomes one by sitting down, writing something, rewriting it, retyping it neatly, and sending it off to a magazine. If it is good enough, it will be bought. It may not be bought first time out, but it will be bought. Maurice Zolotow once wrote that Grace Metalious made her fortune through an agent. That story will get agents much new business—and it will get the people who give them that business a lot of heartache and disappointment, for as any reputable agent will admit, no agent can be a substitute for talent and industry. Nor can any agent talk an editor into buying something he does not want. A beginning writer does not really need an agent. Editors are constantly looking for new talent. Every manuscript that comes into *Cosmopolitan* gets a reading, and the same situation prevails in all other magazines I know. There is always a chance that some gem will be lying in the "slush"—the editor's term for the pile of unsolicited manuscripts that flood in each day. Right here it ought to be mentioned that *Cosmopolitan* has not bought a short story out of slush since 1951 (although we have bought some articles).

There is a heartless practice being carried on by certain unscrupulous "agents" who prey upon the public's idea that an agent can mean the difference between failure and success. Some offer to collaborate with beginners; others say they will act as story doctors. They charge "reading fees" for inspecting manuscripts and sometimes, in the unlikely event that they sell a property, they take commissions higher than the 10 per cent all legitimate agents regard as a fitting return. I once knew a man in Tennessee who was shamefully robbed by a reading-fee agent. After selling over 150 short stories, he was still paying the agent not only a reading fee but also a 15 per cent commission. He could have sold his stories directly to the magazines, but he did not know that; he believed that the agent was working some sort of magic in his behalf. In fairness though, I should add that some legitimate agents also charge reading fees because of the heavy load of manuscripts pouring in on them. Aspiring writers will do well to beware of fly-by-night reading-fee agents, collaborators, and story doctors, and simply submit their work cold to the markets that seem likely. The way to find out which markets are likely is by reading the magazines themselves and by following *The Writer*, the only one of the trade magazines which I feel to be thoroughly professional in content.

It is comparatively easy to acquire a good agent—all of them are continually searching for new clients, and as soon as the writer has published one or two pieces he will get a note from an agent of repute asking permission to represent him. The young writer should not enter into such a relationship impulsively. It is no privilege to have an agent ask to work for one; the writer should always bear in mind the fact that the agent is his employee, and the employee should be selected with great care. All agents have client lists; the writer should first ask to see such a list in order to find out who his fellow employers will be. Then, if possible, he should meet the agent personally. Young, hungry agents with small lists of clients are best for young or beginning writers; the larger organizations have a tendency to forget about thc bcginncrs on their list in their natural desire to capitalize on the experienced professionals' work. The writer also should ask himself, *Do I actually need an agent?*

The agent's principal functions are (a) keeping the writer's price up to a certain level, (b) preserving his reputation, and (c) protecting him from the necessity of having to haggle with editors. Also, an agent sometimes can act as a critic—but not always, and, in my experience, not often. My first representative was a large, successful agency. A girl was in charge of "developing" new writers; she saw some work of minc in magazines, wrote me a letter, and I signed a contract with the organization. The relationship was a happy one. She introduced me to editors all over New York and stirred up a good deal of interest in my work. Then she left and was replaced by a woman who has become one of the most successful agents in the business. At that time she was less successful, but she was on her way; she naturally was concentrating most of her time on promoting the big-name, big-money-making clients on her list. I felt lost and buried and unhappy on her list, and she graciously released me from my contract. I then began to shop around. A friend told that a certain agent was a good man. I went to see him, liked him, and agreed to send him some stories. A week later I sent him three, and four days after that he returned them with a note assuring me that none was saleable. One was sold to the *Atlantic Monthly*, one to *Charm*, and one to *Collier's*. I have never since accepted an agent's criticism. There is an even more blood-curdling story concerning *Compulsion*, Meyer Levin's best-selling book. He showed the first third of it to his agent, who flatly refused to send it out in the form it then was in. Levin, incensed, took the book personally to Simon and Schuster, who immediately gave him a contract. It may be that if Levin had followed the agent's advice the book might never have become the sensation it was.

Some young writers go to agents in the hope that they can be taught to write. I have never known an agent who could teach, not even the ones who supplement their incomes by teaching in adult education courses at the various universities around New York. However, I have learned a good deal from my own agents, Wilkinson and his partner, Kenneth Littauer; but that pair came late to the agency business after many years as editors.

Books on writing are rarely worth the money they cost or the time it takes to read them (better get your money back for this one before it's too late). I have at hand a book called *How to Make $18,000 A Year Free-Lance Writing*, by one Larston Farrar. Its tone is modest enough, and its advice seems sound; but what works for Farrar certainly will not work for everyone. I might add here that although I have been reading all the major magazines for more than a dozen years and have the memory of a Teddy Nadler for writers' names and subjects of articles, I cannot recall once having seen the name Larston Farrar. Conversely, I am positive that although I have published nearly 400 pieces in the past eighteen years, I am certain that Farrar has never heard of me. As Heilbroner complained so wittily in *The Saturday Review*, the free-lance magazine writer works in almost total anonymity. I once had the impression that the only friends of mine who read my work were those with long hair and bad teeth. One month a few years ago I had thirteen pieces in thirteen different magazines, ranging from *True Confessions* to *The Atlantic Monthly*. I ran into my friend A. M.

Rosenthal on the street. Rosenthal owed his part-time career as a magazine writer to me; I had introduced him to Louis Ruppel, editor of *Collier's*, who had given him his first assignment. "What are you up to these days?" he asked. "Still writing?"

The sure-fire, get-rich-quick books on writing are bad enough, but unfortunately, even the more or less scholarly writing teachers and writing schools have no guaranteed formulae. During three years in which I supplemented my writing income by "teaching" writing at New York University, I attempted to tell my classes everything I had learned about it from experience, from reading, and from conversations with older and wiser writers. But I could find few absolutes or tangibles to communicate. Presently it dawned upon me that the students and I were wasting our time. Very few of them wanted to *be* writers; they were not willing to practice, as some might have done if they had wanted to master the piano. They wanted to know *how* to be writers, and they were convinced that because I had published, I knew some mysterious formula which would enable them to become professionals in the span of a thirteen-week course. It may be that I just was not meant to teach. Some teachers—Wallace Stegner, Paul Engle, John Crowe Ransom, David L. Maurer, to mention a few—have conducted college-level courses that have turned out many talented short story writers, poets and novelists. I still have the feeling that even those teachers' principal function was in giving encouragement and lending enthusiasm. I doubt seriously that any one would declare that any given course of instruction or any set of rules can constitute a foolproof formula. Not long ago, in his syndicated column, Jim Bishop listed the rules for writing taught him by his mentor, the late Mark Hellinger. They were as follows:

(1) Never write about something you do not understand; (2) use only short words; (3) all sentences should be terse unless you have a special reason for using a long one; (4) never begin a sentence with a hanging participle; (5) a writer is the eyes, ears and nose of the reader—the reader is his own brain; (6) before writing, always read a few hundred words of your favorite author; (7) pause to think of every aspect of the story before writing the first word; (8) the more spectacular the facts, the more you should undersay and underplay them; (9) the way to write a sob story is to be callous; (10) no one is all white or black—all men are shades of grey and should be painted that way.

Another set of rules I like is James Thurber's, concerning the writing of humor:

(1) The reader should be able to find out what the story is about. (2) Some inkling of the general idea should be apparent in the first five hundred words. (3) If the writer has decided to change the name of his protagonist from Ketcham to McTavish, Ketcham should not keep bobbing up in the last five pages. A good way to eliminate this confusion is to read the piece over before sending it out, and remove Ketcham completely. He is a nuisance. (4) The word "I'll" should not be divided so that the "I" is on one line and the " 'll" is on the next. The reader's attention, after the breaking up of "I'll" can never be successfully recaptured. (5) It also never recovers from such names as Ann S. Theptic, Maud Lynn, Sally Forth, Bertha Twins, and the like. (6) Avoid comic stories about plumbers who are mistaken for surgeons, sheriffs who are terrified by gunfire, psychiatrists who are driven crazy by women patients, doctors who faint at the sight of blood, adolescent girls who know more about sex than their fathers do, and midgets who turn out to be the parents of a two-hundred-pound wrestler.

There is only one possible objection to those rules: both sets are rules, and an important precept that every writer must learn, as I said before, is that rules should exist to be broken. It is difficult to think of what might have happened to Henry James if he had not broken Hellinger's Rule Three. One of the most troublesome aspects of the experienced writer's life is the desire, which rises like a tide in him each day, to find new ways of breaking the old rules. My own rule is: "There are no rules." This is not as easy to follow as it sounds. All writing gets harder and harder as the writer becomes more and more practiced. When I asked the writers I polled to name their toughest assignment, nearly every one said, "The one I'm working on now." That applies to me, too; this is the hardest piece I ever wrote in my life. And the next one will be harder still.

No writer I know—to get back to the theme—has ever discovered a way of making his life easier. A friend of mine of scientific bent a few years ago conducted a kind of time-and-motion study on his own work habits and concluded he was wasting fearful amounts of time and effort. He resolved to devote one week only to research and one more week to writing; that way he would be able, he figured happily, to turn out twenty-four pieces a year rather than twelve. It worked out fine in theory—except that most of the stories he did were unsaleable, and his income dropped appreciably.

It occurs to me that I am about as businesslike and disciplined as any writer I know, and yet I have never been able to work out any kind of sensible, efficient system. Nor do I ever hope to be able to. My day begins between six and eight A.M., depending upon how late I have been up the night before. Some writers maintain that they are at their best late at night. What I write late at night sounds as though it was written late at night. As soon as I am out of bed I lurch to the typewriter, roll in a sheet of paper, and force myself to write a page of a book I'm working on. That is the only way I get a book finished. I do nothing else until I have done that daily page—and after three hundred and sixty-five pages, a book is about finished. (That was how I wrote this one.)

After my page, or pages (some days I write two or three, if I am lucky), I get a cup of coffee. Now the day's work really begins; I regard my book-writing as a hobby, because none of the last five I've published has ever brought me much more than the satisfaction of knowing that I've published a book again. I get out the article I am working on and begin plugging away at that. Ordinarily, for a reason I will presently explain, I have two or three articles going at once. My choice of the one to work on is determined by deadline or whim. If a deadline is approaching, I naturally work on the article that must meet it; I sometimes persuade myself that editors are more interested in a writer's hitting a deadline than in the work he turns out (a noted editor once said to me, "So-and-so isn't very good, but he's prompt, so I buy him"). If no deadline looms, I turn to the article that interests me most that morning, or the one which for some reason is uppermost in my mind.

Often I will begin to write automatically out of some remembrance of the previous stint at the machine. A writer's occupational anxiety now and again comes out in the form of dreams about the pieces he is working on. Times immemorial I have pitched about in my bed all night long, my subconscious trying to get through a paragraph in some story in progress. Other times I have successfully dreamed leads, transitions, or endings for articles—passages I might never have thought of if I had been awake and sitting at my machine. Article ideas have come to me in nightmares, some good and some not so good.

Many writers I know begin an article by reading over their notes, thinking about them, and then sitting down and writing the lead and subsequent paragraphs in rough draft preparatory to polishing and refining the prose. I wish I were that methodical; I am about as organized as a band of Philippine guerillas. Before I begin to research an article, and while the research is in progress, I keep in mind both the preliminary conversation with the editor when the assignment was made and my own ideas of what the piece ought to contain. I continually look for material which the editor has indicated ought to turn up in the finished story. Gradually some of it begins to take shape. Or it does not—it may develop that the story as it is bears no resemblance whatever to the editor's preconceived notion of it. If it materializes in compelling form, I set it down almost immediately, no matter where it is to appear in the finished article. I do that with a good deal of material, and before long I have formed a good mental outline of the shape the article will take eventually. I get to a point where I could almost outline it aloud, paragraph by paragraph—which I seldom do, since I have found that telling a story is a good way to destroy any freshness it may have when one goes to write it.

The trick, once I have the article fairly well in mind, is to make each paragraph as lively, entertaining and informative as I can manage to make it. Long ago I discovered that my own work has a tendency to run downhill—that is, to start off strong and get weaker as fatigue sets in. I try to avoid that by writing any story in a disjointed, disorganized, helter-skelter order. Many times I have written an ending months before I even began the first paragraph. I write anecdotes, descriptive passages, considerations, etc., as they occur to me, operating on the dubious thesis that they will be fresher if I do them that way. Sooner or later I then have before me a pile of fragments which ultimately can be tied together into a coherent—I hope—piece.

I work until noon, or anywhere between four and six hours. Then I go uptown to meet either a friend or an interviewee for lunch—or, on some occasions, an editor. In the afternoons, I either interview people, look in at the office of *Cosmopolitan*, or go to the library. (When I have a writing bloc gripping me, I don't do any of those things; I loaf.) The uptown part of my day ends around six; I then go home, have dinner, and face the evening. I like to work in the evening, but not always. The fact is I am usually too tired to write. So I watch television, play records, speak to friends on the telephone, or read.

In a sense, reading is part of my work. Subjects for articles come mainly from my reading; I read all the New York newspapers and a few out-of-town ones, the newsmagazines, and most of the general and men's books. I rarely read the women's periodicals because I seldom work for them and feel no deep need to know what kind of stuff they're running. Not all my ideas for pieces come from my reading. Some come directly from editors; they say "Do a piece about jazz," or "Are you interested in stamp collecting? If you are, write us a story." Exasperatingly enough, assignments are often made in just such a casual manner—but stories seldom are bought so casually; a writer has handed in "a piece about jazz," the editor invariably thinks of fifty questions he should have thought of when he assigned the idea in the first place.

All this is only part of the story. I have neglected many sides of the writer's life, both intentionally and out of pure carelessness. But I have reached the end of my space. I cannot talk about Wild Editors I Have Known, Writers' Neuroses, Proper Conduct In Dealing With The Internal Revenue Men, or many other basic concerns that the new writer should know about before he becomes not-so-new. I can do nothing but sit here and wish I had an ending for this piece. And I have one: I have this

Post Script: The above piece, done for the mass audience of *Cosmopolitan,* was of course not originally intended as advice, although some did slip in—and I have added more in the expanded version.

Originally, I could not think of a lead paragraph for a mass-magazine piece about the business of being a writer; the lead that appears above is not the one that I used in *Cosmopolitan.* That original went as follows:

Once upon a Time, as the late George Ade might have Put it, there was an Editor who said to a Contributing Same, "Write a Piece about the business of Being a Writer," & so here I am on the terrace of this overpriced & underheated New York apt. I live in, wishing I knew how to begin such an article & also wishing the ampersand were regarded in magazine circles as a proper substitute for "and," since it would mean two less typewriter keys to poke. It is not regarded as proper. I don't know why. I don't know why I am thinking about it, either, except that thinking about it is a good excuse to keep from getting to work on this assignment. One of the principal ways in which writers occupy their time is devising methods of dodging work. I have been working away (or *not* working away) at this piece more or less continuously for six months, and I must now face a deadline and hand it in . . . I cannot stall any longer. I have to think up an opening, which, come to think of it, I have just done in this paragraph; and about four thousand words from now I will have to devise an ending, a problem I will untangle when I get to it. Here goes.

Then I went on with what is now the second paragraph of the piece.

I frankly don't know why O'Connell, the editor, permitted me to get away with that lead. It was, patently, a trick: a confession of inadequacy which, aided by a few feeble jokes and some sprightly (well, fairly sprightly) language, served as the adequate lead I needed. It did have the effect of plunging the reader directly into one of a writer's problems—the finding of a method of starting a story. Because the piece was about writers and writing, that was all right. But in the long run, I think, the opening would have benefited if I had written it "straight"—started it, perhaps, at the second paragraph. More about leads later on.

This piece demanded no research—I knew everything in it long before I began writing it. It did require some checking of facts and spelling, and I did send out a questionnaire to fifty free-lance writers listed in the Society of Magazine Writers. Most of them, by the way, painted as dark a picture of the working writer's life as I did. Grousing about one's lot seems to be another writers' occupational disease. I will bet, however, that if I had asked those writers, "Would you change your occupation?" I would not have received a single affirmative answer.

The fact is, I should have emphasized more strongly that while writing is hard work, and while it is frustrating to an agonizing degree, it is also fun. It brings one into touch with all sorts of fascinating people, as the old saw says; I number among my acquaintances and friends so many movie stars, Broadway stars, jazz musicians, scientists, athletes, thieves, government officials, ex-convicts, editors and other writers that when I return to my home town I have to watch myself in ordinary conversation with the people I grew up with—if I refer to the people I know and meet in the course of my everyday work, I sound like a name-dropper of the worst sort. The travel is fun, too; I get to Europe at least once a year and to Hollywood four or five times, and the rest of the year, when I am not holed up finishing off a book I am traveling to other spots around the country. Even the writing itself is fun, much of the time. The only thing that is not fun is the uncertainty of the income—but one gets used to that, after a time. (Well, perhaps not *used* to it, but at least accustomed to it.) In this book, while talking about the bad times, I also hope to communicate some of the good ones—and to set down, as best I can, the sum of everything I know about my work.

2 · *Waste Time Now — Write About It Later*

WASTE time, I suggested in the first chapter, because no time a writer spends is wasted. It has taken me a long time to learn that. If someone had suggested to me, while I was in the Army, that I was not wasting my time, I would have rolled on the floor in uncontrollable laughter. Yet, as the piece that follows indicates, the time I spent in one Army outfit was valuable—not at the time, but later, when I had a chance to think about it with some perspective. This piece was written after I had spent an evening telling some friends of the crazy behavior of the 13th Special Service Unit. Someone said, "You ought to write that stuff down," and others agreed. I was dubious, but the more I thought about it, the more the article began to take shape, and one day about a week later I wrote it in one sitting. The point is, I could not have written about it while it was going on; I needed nearly seven years to develop the necessary point of view. After that period, what originally had seemed tedious became funny.

It was not possible simply to string together a group of anecdotes; there had to be some excuse for them, first, and there had to be a unifying theme or a character. The excuse was simple: the 13th was an unusual outfit. I had only to explain that at the beginning. Then I found my connecting character in First Sergeant Edmonds, his exasperation with the men under his control, his humiliation, his decision to become like them, his ultimate triumph. Edmonds became a kind of framework on which I could hang the rest of the stories. He supplied me with a neat ending for a piece that easily could have fizzled out.

ARTICLE: "WHERE'D *YOU* FOUL UP?"

(From *Argosy*)

If another world war develops and they begin drafting fathers, I hope I get sent into an outfit similar to the old 13th Special Service Unit of Fort George G. Meade, Maryland, in which I spent several strange, unmilitary months during World War II. The prospect is unlikely. The Special Service Training Center, of which the 13th was a part, was the Army's first organization of its kind, and, if I know my Pentagon men, the last. Not that it didn't accomplish its mission. It did, in its day, in its own peculiar way.

At least 40 units of "morale-building" troops—actors, vaudevillians, motion-picture projectionists, Post Exchange clerks, athletic instructors and newspapermen—were dispatched from the SSTC, as we called it, while I was there, and I don't know how many more after I left. But even though the SSTC did what it set out to do, I'll bet the high brass breathed a sigh of relief when finally it was disbanded. All SSTC enlisted men happily shared one distinguishing characteristic; they steadfastly resisted and viciously resented any implication that they were soldiers. They wore uniforms, slept in barracks and ate in mess halls (well, some did), but they remained civilians in heart, mind, and—to the profane disgust of the regular Army non-coms whose thankless task it was to keep them in line—behavior. I've heard that some SSTC men got into combat, and although that was accidental, I'm sure they fought like Sikhs out of indignation at finding themselves in a soldierly situation. I've never been sure how this SSTC state of mind got started, but when I joined the 13th one cloudy December morning in 1942, it already was being displayed proudly and defiantly by every manjack.

When I got off the train at Odenton, the Fort Meade Station, I was met by a reedy, loafing corporal with dirty teeth and a nasty-looking chin. His face seemed familiar, and I was positive that I'd seen him before, but I couldn't think where, and he was so aloof at first—he waited indulgently while I carried my two barracks bags to his jeep—that I didn't dare ask him where we might have met. Outside of asking me if I was the one he'd been sent to get, he didn't say a word until he had started the jeep and we were well on the road. Then he turned to me abruptly and said, "Where'd you foul up?" (He did not actually say "foul," but I'm afraid I must.)

At that time I had been in the Army 13 miserable weeks, all in basic training. It was true that I'd never learned to make a bunk so tightly that a quarter dropped from a lieutenant's nose would bounce two feet in the air, but as far as I knew, I hadn't fouled up. "What do you mean?" I asked.

"Anybody gets sent to this outfit, he must of fouled up somewhere," the corporal said, emphatically. "Where you from?"

"Field Artillery, Fort Bragg," I said.

"Oh," he said, "the *Army*."

"Isn't *this* the Army?"

"This is Special Service, Jack," he said ominously.

The words had an ugly quality. They conjured up images of commandos who fought with bayonets between their teeth. I then weighed, on my best days, around 125. "Special Service?" I inquired, hesitantly.

He made no effort to explain. "Wa'j'do in civilian life?" he asked. Before I had a chance to tell him, he said, "I'as in burlesque myself."

Instantly I knew why he seemed familiar. "Why," I said excitedly, "I think I've seen you in—" but, embarrassingly, I couldn't recall where.

My poor memory didn't alleviate the brightness of the expression that flashed over his face. "You *did?*" he cried, delightedly. "Where? The Old Howard? Hey," he said digging me in the ribs, "remember *this?*" And before I could stop him—which I would not, of course, have considered—he went into a hearty chorus of *I used to work in Chicago, I worked in the Boston store*. I made a sound of appreciation when he finished.

"Killed 'em with that the other night at the Annapolis USO," he said. And then, warmed by the unexpected pleasure of meeting an old fan, Corporal Stacy (I am disguising all names here) went on to tell me everything he knew about Special Service. It wasn't much. Somebody in Washington, he said, had got the idea that soldiers ought to be entertained by other soldiers, so they had formed these two companies at Meade, the 13th and 14th, and a couple of others on the west coast. There were probably some others somewhere else, he thought, but he didn't know where. In fact, Corporal Stacy continued, nobody knew much of anything about Special Service. The units were under the direction of the Services of Supply (later, Army Service Forces), and there was a general in charge of the program in Washington, but as far as Stacy and his buddies could see, the program hadn't really got started. "So we give shows," he concluded.

"What kind of shows?"

"Oh, you know, shows," he said, shrugging. "We get some of the guys together and go out to one of the USOs around here, or one of the Service Clubs."

"What do you do during the day?"

"Sleep," he said, "or rehearse. We don't do much rehearsing, though, since most of us've been in the show business all our lives."

"What kind of training do you get?"

"Training?" he said, scornfully. "Are you kidding?"

A few days in the 13th convinced me that Corporal Stacy had not been exaggerating. There was no training to speak of, or to kid about, in those early days. The original directives from Washington apparently had been rather broad; the officers had been told simply to get their men in shape to build morale of other men overseas. Since the majority of the individuals in the 13th were entertainers, they presumably would build morale by giving shows. This meant that the officers, from Captain Roberts, the company commander, on down to Lieutenant Bruce, the unhappy mess and supply officer (I will go into his unhappiness presently), spent most of their time acting as booking agents. One of them, in fact, a Lieutenant Hock, had been a booking agent in civilian life. He set the pattern for the others. Soon after he joined the 13th, the rest of the officers took to smoking cigars, scattering ashes on their olive-drab shirt fronts, and talking on the telephone with their GI shoes propped on their desks. They called Service Club hostesses "baby," "sweetie," and, occasionally, "doll."

I was assigned to the Newspaper Group, which then consisted of three artists who put out an almost-weekly company magazine, "Chin Up," in a tiny room at one end of the mess hall. They were delighted to see me, simply because none of them were writers, and the captain had suggested a few days before that the magazine might be better if it had some text as well as pictures. Their leader,

Sergeant Werber, was an intensely practical man. "I am Czechish," he said to me the day I arrived, "and therefore realistic. Look at us here. We have all of us a rating. I am sergeant, Robinson there is corporal. Wolgren is corporal, too. I got sergeant by drawing a picture of Captain Roberts. Robinson got corporal by drawing Lieutenant Hock. Then we got to work and made this goddamn 'Chin Up' a magazine for the enlisted men." I took his advice and wrote a story about Lieutenant Hock. It said that Lieutenant Hock was a fine officer, which was not precisely untrue, and that before coming into the Army he had been a good booking agent (he had told me so himself). Sure enough, I made corporal about three weeks later. (There was an astonishing number of ratings available in Special Service. Promotions were published every two or three weeks. Men got promoted for giving good performances, and at least one man I knew was broken to private because he had somehow messed up a show.)

When Werber, Robinson, Wolgren and I set to work making "Chin Up" an enlisted man's magazine, we certainly did not lack for material. Almost everybody in Special Service was spoken of as a "character," and a newly arrived comedian once coined a phrase that summed up the 13th perfectly. "My," he said, listening to the ordinary barracks conversation, "there's a hell of a shortage of straight men around here." Special Service men griped, but not in the same way that other soldiers did. "That goddamned Lieutenant Hock's got it in for me, and that's for sure," Corporal Henry complained one day. "He always spots me right after Stacy. What the hell chance does a birdcall act have coming after a burlesque comic?" Pfc. Dolan, who had been a wild animal trainer, was constantly complaining because Captain Roberts wouldn't let him send home for one of his black panthers. The captain's argument was that the unit had no place to keep a black panther and that the supply officer probably couldn't get enough to feed it. Sergeant Loomis, too, had a gripe: he wanted to send for his trained dogs. The captain feared that if he gave Loomis permission, he would have to extend the same privilege to Pfc. Dolan; so the two wild-animal men used to sit disconsolately side by side on a bunk, passing pictures of their animals back and forth.

Everybody in the unit spent most of his time practicing his

specialty, which sometimes proved a little hard on the nerves of the rest of us who were not endowed with theatrical talents. Pfc. Talbot, a juggler, used to keep the air above his bunk filled with cleavers, butcher knives, and straight razors. Corporal Monte, a singer who had just learned to play "Ramona" on the guitar, sometimes played it as often as 25 times a night. Sergeant Stanley, an imitator, practiced his impression of Lionel Barrymore so assiduously that we all soon got to know it as well as he. He would stand up on a bunk, grab the sides of his shirtfront as though they were lapels of a frock coat, scowl like Barrymore, and then, shaking and nodding, he would go through a speech that began, "Ladies and gentlemen of the jury, are you going to sit there and let this poor boy die?" The rest of us, some in undershorts, some in pajamas, some fully clothed and some stark naked, would stand up and scowl, shake, nod and repeat the lines after him ensemble.

Our officers were so busy lining up engagements for Special Service shows that they left the operation of the 13th pretty much up to the noncoms. These noncoms had come from tightly disciplined Military Police companies, and most of them had been in the Army three or four years. No one knew just why they, who had no special training in, or inclination toward, morale-building activities, should have been assigned to us, but we all shared the same idea: i.e., they had fouled up somewhere. If the sourest, most vindictive personnel officer who ever lived had sat for 25 years trying to devise the cruelest possible slow death for a trained MP who had fouled up somewhere, he couldn't have hit upon a more diabolical method than sending him to us. Our officers had tried to explain to the noncoms that they were in Special Service, but the poor ex-MP's never quite understood that. They thought they were still in the Army. They continued to act like noncoms in charge of soldiers, and their life was one continuous frustration.

There was, for example, the matter of reveille. In the outfits that the noncoms had come from, and in most outfits in the Army, for that matter, reveille was at 5:30 A.M., and everybody fell out promptly, lined up in the company street, and sounded off when his name was called. In Special Service, however, there were shows nearly every night. They usually lasted until very late, and the men who worked in them were excused, by the officers, from answering roll call next morning. And since almost everybody, whether or not he was a performer, found some excuse to go along each night with one show or another (I used to get to go by carrying wigs), this meant that nobody ever showed up for reveille—nobody, that is, except the noncoms. I remember one time when I came back to camp from a pass to Baltimore around 5:30 A.M., and found the first sergeant, two staff sergeants, and the platoon sergeants and corporals holding a reveille formation. The strength of the 13th was then around 125. Seven or eight men had responded to the call; everybody else, having been on shows the night before, was sleeping soundly in the barracks. The noncoms outnumbered their men by at least four. Our first sergeant, whose name was Edmonds, was a fat, beady-eyed young man who pared his fingernails habitually with a mess-kit knife and looked as though he wished he could cut you with it. His voice, ordinarily, was a scraping, throaty challenge; he never asked for anything, he demanded it. He was generally despised. But in that foggy dawn, as I saw him standing there on the parade ground, wistfully calling the names of men who weren't there, I came very close to feeling sorry for him. He was a top kick without a company, and, as a matter of fact, without an officer of the day to report to. The O.D. also had gone on a show the night before.

The noncoms also had to cope with a uniform problem of considerable magnitude. Although each man had been given the same clothing issue, every one was, after all, an artist, at least by his own admission, and accordingly felt the need of expressing his artistic temperament in some way. It was not uncommon to see a man wearing a cloth-covered helmet liner, a field jacket with no shirt beneath, and khaki pants. Some of us wore fatigue shirts and dress pants, others wore dress blouses and fatigue pants. The imaginative costumes that turned up in the unit area would have made a spit-and-polish man, such as the late General Patton, go out of his mind in righteous indignation. Our noncoms, little Pattons to a man, regularly blew their tops, but it didn't do them much good. Early in the game, someone had figured out the perfect excuse for not wearing proper uniform. Special Service units had been issued large kits of equipment which were to be used in training and later in overseas areas. Among these was a theatrical kit, which contained costumes of the kind generally seen in plays put on by

Christian Endeavor groups in small towns—glazed chintz dresses, fright wigs, false noses and teeth and the like. Since our performers' acts were of a rather robust persuasion, having been designed exclusively for GI audiences, none of the entertainers had ever used this stuff. They had found that incongruous uniforms were far funnier to their audiences. So, in the shows, they wore mixed-up GI clothing, and they got so used to doing this that they seldom wore anything else, except, of course, when they were going off on furlough. The mixed-up uniform champion was a tap dancer named Sergeant Hermann, and he was the one who finally brought the uniform question to a head.

One morning Hermann went down the company street in his customary attire: a felt campaign hat of World War I vintage, an officer's shirt, blue jeans of the kind issued to prisoners in the guardhouse, white socks and Bass moccasins. First Sergeant Edmonds caught him as he was about to cross the parade ground.

"Hermann," Edmonds said, "where the hell you going in that rig?"

"Rehearsal," said Hermann.

"You're not going nowhere," Edmonds said, positively if not grammatically. "I been in this Army four years, and I never saw anybody as out of uniform as you are. Go back and get in your fatigues, and then go report to Sergeant Shore in the kitchen."

"But, Sergeant," said Hermann, "this is my *costume*."

A crestfallen look shadowed Edmonds' piggish face. "It is?"

"If I don't get over to rehearsal right away," Hermann said, "Lieutenant Banker'll be awful sore. We got a big show tonight at the Laurel USO."

Edmonds sighed. "O.K., go ahead."

The next day a notice appeared on the orderly-room bulletin board to the effect that all enlisted personnel, 13th Spec Serv U, would wear the *fatigue uniform only* between the hours 5:30 A.M. and 5:30 P.M. It was signed by First Sergeant Edmonds, and everybody read it with interest. The day after that, Hermann again started out across the parade ground and again was halted by Edmonds' grating voice.

"Didn't you read that goddamned notice?" Edmonds screamed.

"Yes, but this is my—"

"I don't care if it *is* your goddamned costume," Edmonds said, "I'm first sergeant here and nobody's going to make a goddamned monkey out of me. You goddamned actors don't fool me none—you don't need them goddamned costumes to practice in. You get your tail back there to them barracks and *change*."

Hermann went back, changed, and went in his fatigues to the empty building we used as a rehearsal hall. Something was missing from his performance in the run-through of the show. Even Lieutenant Banker, who was not perceptive, noticed it. Lieutenant Banker liked to think of himself as the producer of the unit's shows, possibly because he had been a movie-house assistant manager in a small West Virginia town in civilian life. He had not come to Special Service because he had fouled up somewhere; Personnel had. He had no more talent for theatricals than, say, First Sergeant Edmonds, but he was convinced that he was the Billy Rose of Fort Meade. The men allowed him to believe this; he could always be depended upon to get them out of uncomfortable situations as long as he thought he was an impresario.

"What's the matter, Hermann?" he asked.

"Lieutenant," Hermann said, "I don't feel right without my old campaign hat and the rest of those clothes I wear in the shows. I can't seem to get a beat for my dancing in these baggy old fatigues. I don't *feel* it."

Lieutenant Banker prided himself upon his understanding of the artistic conscience. "Well, then," said he, reasonable, "go back and change, Hermann."

"I can't, Lieutenant," Hermann said.

"Why not?"

Having gone this far, Hermann was disinclined to continue. He said nothing, an honorable soldier who never would have dreamed of ratting on his first sergeant.

Corporal Schlitzer, a musician, spoke up. "We can't wear the clothes we work in any more," he said. "That is, the clothes we *like* to work in. There's a notice on the bulletin board."

"Oh, there is, is there?" said Lieutenant Banker. "We'll see about that."

According to Pfc. Romney, the company clerk, who witnessed the incident and reported it to us later, Lieutenant Banker stormed into the orderly room and, in the vernacular of the company, chewed out Edmonds good and proper. The first sergeant tried to stand his ground. He fought gamely, Romney said. Edmonds said that he didn't see any reason why the goddamned men shouldn't wear fatigues while they were working—the fatigue uniform was the work uniform, after all, he pointed out—and furthermore, he said, he was never sure which one of these goddamned goof-offs was working and which one wasn't. Every time he tried to get men together to police the area, or work on the garbage detail, or go over to Post Headquarters for supplies, he could never find anybody who wasn't rehearsing. If you asked him, First Sergeant Edmonds said to Lieutenant Banker, it was one hell of a way to run an outfit. He wished he were back in the MP, where they did things sensible. Lieutenant Banker, who also understood the military mind, listened patiently and then explained that Sergeant Edmonds just had to understand that these men were morale troops. If they were going to build morale of our boys overseas, he said, they had to have high morale themselves. You couldn't expect them to behave like ordinary soldiers. If Sergeant Edmonds needed a detail to police the area, why didn't he just get some of his noncoms to do it? After all, said Lieutenant Banker reasonably, *they* didn't have to rehearse. Edmonds was entranced by this practical suggestion—so much that he was speechless.

From that point on, Lieutenant Banker was the hero of the company. Corporal Stacy was so overcome by his behavior that he made a singular vow: "I'd even play Scranton, if that Banker asked me to," he said.

The sergeant went into eclipse. We saw even less of him than we had before. Then someone reported that he had been sighted in the toy department of a Baltimore department store, pricing Gilbert Myst-O-Magic sets. "He can't beat us—he's going to join us," Sgt. Hermann said. "Edmonds, the boy magician. He'll wow them at the Service Clubs."

Earlier, I mentioned that the men in the unit resembled soldiers in that they slept in barracks and ate in mess halls. The latter half is not quite accurate. Food in the 13th was as good as Army food anywhere—which is to say that it was pretty bad—but most of the men were naturally opposed to eating in the mess. It was too military. Every day around noon there was a great commotion in the area: men rushing back from rehearsal, changing into dress uniforms, and dashing two miles to the Service Club for lunch. Afterwards they would run back to the barracks area, change back into their conventional (or, rather, unconventional) uniforms, and go back to, if I may be pardoned the expression, work. This was a source of the most intense puzzlement and pain to poor Lieutenant Bruce, the mess officer.

"Fellows," he would implore, "all that food is going to waste."

"So what?" a corporal would yell.

"All right," Lieutenant Bruce would say. "We'll just cut down on ordering supplies." He would put this off, however, for a few weeks, and then, finally, the cooks would be instructed to prepare meals for only 30 or 40 men. Inevitably, this happened around the last week in the month, when everybody was about broke. The company would then turn up for chow practically *en masse*, and Lieutenant Bruce would be beleaguered by the cooks' complaints that they didn't have enough supplies.

The food at the Service Club was not much better than that served in the company hall, but at least it was served in a somewhat less military atmosphere. The men thought that this was better for their stomachs. One man, Corporal Howard, often boasted that his superlative performances in the shows were the direct result of his never having eaten a single meal in our mess hall. He even put on his dress uniform in the mornings and went to the Service Club for breakfast.

Life in the 13th might have gone on indefinitely in that pleasant, relaxed way if it hadn't been for the message that arrived one day from Washington. The general himself was coming to make his first inspection. Instantly a new spirit gripped our officers. They began planning what was to be, in the exact words of Lieutenant Banker, "the most terrific goddamn show this outfit ever put on." Everybody in the company was recruited—even the motion picture projectionsts, who were then spending most of their time putting together and taking apart their machines, and those of us who were publishing "Chin Up." The program for the general's visit was to include a display of our equipment kits, a field demonstration designed to show how we planned to build morale overseas and finally, as a climax, the show. Two days before the big event, First Sergeant Edmonds lined us up and explained that it was generally the custom for an organization to police up its area extra clean and to get its barracks in apple-pie order when a general was about to arrive. He expected all of us to cooperate, he said. During the next 24 hours, everybody cooperated to the extent of asking Lieutenant Banker how we were going to police the area and get the barracks in shape and still have the show ready for the general. Lieutenant Banker was as puzzled by this as we were, and went to see Edmonds. The first sergeant managed to recruit a cleaning detail, mostly noncoms, and they did an admirable job.

The general turned out to be a tall, kindly, stoop-shouldered man who wore his star diffidently. He seemed vastly pleased with us. That morning we all had managed to turn out in regulation uniform, and it can be stated truthfully that we resembled soldiers as we lined up on the company street in front of our equipment kits. As the general came along, each group leader stepped out of file, saluted, and explained the uses of his equipment. "Well, well," the general said. "Think of that. Costumes and everything? Goodness," and so on. When he came to the Newspaper Group, he asked us how we liked our mimeograph, and we answered that it was one of the finest mimeographs ever made. "Goodness," the general said. "I see you carry paper and everything."

Unfortunately, the general had to get back to Washington around five o'clock, and so, to the pitiful disappointment of Lieutenant Banker, "the most terrific goddamn show this outfit ever put on" was never staged. We all felt, later, that this was a pity. If he had seen the show, we thought, the general might not have sent down the directive that arrived two days later. This document, in the most military language, stated that a new era was just dawning for Special Service troops. We were all to prepare to get our tails overseas on the shortest possible notice. Furthermore, we were to spend the major portion of each day in firing weapons, studying and practicing cover and concealment, caring for and transporting equipment, and—stiffest blow of all—brushing up on military courtesy. For a few days thereafter, most of us walked about as men dazed. The officers stopped smoking cigars and began drawing up training schedules. It was plain that they somehow could not throw themselves into this work wholeheartedly. The only person who responded to the directive with alacrity was First Sergeant Edmonds. At the first reveille—reveille was reinstituted the morning after the directive arrived—he was wearing his old service cap, and his voice grated with a conviction that had been lacking for several weeks. That afternoon, Sergeant Hermann was busted to private and dispatched to the kitchen for appearing in the company street out of uniform. The next day Corporal Stacy—who had been told at reveille that he would lead a garbage and area-policing detail—found some brightly colored bits of cardboard in one of the trash cans. They looked, he said, like the remnants of a Gilbert Myst-O-Magic set.

Post Script: The principal fault in this piece is that I failed to contrast the character of Edmonds as opposed to those of the other soldiers as dramatically as I might have. His astonishing behavior in buying the magic set should have been dealt with at greater length; that I did not do it well enough was proved when the article was in print, for the editor who worked on it actually cut the paragraph in which Edmonds went to the toy store. (This made the last line meaningless, of course, but nobody at *Argosy* noticed that.) Also, I believe I might have given the general a more clear-cut personality, so that there would have been intimations of the disaster to come in his seemingly ineffectual, gentle manner as he made his inspection.

This story has been included not so much because of the technical problems it presented, which were minor, as because it illustrates the fact that articles written out of true personal experience can be sold. The beginner, unless he has had newspaper experience, often has difficulty doing a piece of straight reporting that involves research, interviewing, fact-checking and other mechanical details. He will not get entangled with these things if he writes out of his memory—and the fact that his story happened to him will lend sincerity and accuracy. In my own case, I didn't begin to write this kind of piece until I had been working at my trade for seven or eight years; then it gradually dawned upon me that it was much less demanding on time and energy to sit at home and remember than it was to go to Hollywood and interview some such colorful, vibrant figure as Glenn Ford. Since then I have done five or six of these articles per year, on such subjects as the problem of parking a car in New York, my inability to screw screws in wood straight, the pleasures of eating pizza, the difference between optimists and pessimists, the art of loafing, and so on. As Maurice Zolotow has pointed out time and again, the best stories are often under a writer's nose. The trick is to see them, and that is a trick that anyone could master. Even Sgt. Edmonds.

The market for articles of this kind ranges from the magazines that pay the most, such as *Reader's Digest* and the *Post*, on down to the magazines published by religious orders, such as *The Sign*.

To return briefly to technique, the article ought to contain:

1. A clear statement of the reason for writing the story.
2. The introduction of the framework or the thematic character as soon as possible (another fault of mine was that I waited so long to bring in Sgt. Edmonds).
3. Lucid, yet casual, exposition and description.
4. Illustrative anecdotes—as many as possible, told as briefly as possible.
5. An ending hooked to the theme.

As it happened, everything in my article was true. But it is also possible to do similar pieces in which the truth is stretched a little, as the next chapter will show.

3 · More on Wasting Time—and Stretching Truth

BECAUSE, during my four years in the Army, I had sold short stories to *The New Yorker*, *Esquire*, *Collier's* and others, I saw no reason why I could not earn a living from writing after my discharge. I thereupon moved to New York and, to support myself while writing, took a temporary job with an organization known as Americans United for World Government. The executive secretary, Ulric Bell, needed someone familiar with the objectives of the atomic scientists, who immediately after Hiroshima had decided that this country's nuclear program should be taken out of the hands of the military and administered by civilians. Americans United was a pressure-group for people who advocated world law, but its directors viewed civilian control of nuclear fission as the first step toward that outrageous dream. I worked for Bell in the daytime, writing speeches, helping to compose newspaper advertisements and urging people to pay for them. At night I went home to an apartment on Tenth Street and did my best to further my career as a short story writer. It was two months before I sold my first story, to *Collier's*, and another six before it appeared. By then the McMahon bill (the first United States Atomic Energy Act) had been passed, and my work at Americans United was all but over. I had saved no money, but I decided to free-lance, for I was convinced that by devoting full time to my stories I could earn a fair living.

I was wrong. I sold nothing during those first few months but occasional short pieces to magazines that paid between $50 and $100. Then my short story appeared in *Collier's* and was noticed by Jerry

Mason, who was managing editor of *This Week*. He called and asked me to go in to see him.

"How much did *Collier's* pay you for that story?" he asked.

"Seven-fifty," I said.

"We might have gone a little higher," he said. "We're interested in you—we would have bought that story if it had been offered to us first."

Naturally, I was flattered; and, unnaturally, I could not think of any ideas to suggest at that moment. Mason was determined to get young writers into his magazine. He said, "I tell you what—I'll give you an article to write. Maybe you'll get some short story ideas soon, and if you do, we'll want to see them."

That sentence destroyed my career as a short story writer. A few days later Mason sent me out to interview an ex-prizefighter turned painter, Joe Gatto. I did a 2,000-word article on Gatto and turned it in; Mason bought it immediately. A few weeks later I offered him a suggestion about another artist, an ex-circus clown named Walter Philipp whom Hugh Stix, the founder of the Artists Gallery, had found working as a delicatessen waiter, hanging his paintings between the salami and liverwurst. Mason accepted the idea and assigned me to do the piece.

Foolishly, I thought: "This is a cinch. Short stories are much tougher to do than articles—and I'm not primarily interested in short stories anyhow. I can earn a living with articles while writing my novels."

Now I began to cast about for other article-writing assignments. Surely no writer ever went about the business in a more haphazard, impractical manner. I knew next to nothing about the craft of magazine article writing. I did not even know how to write an outline (I'm not certain that I know how today). I did not study the markets for which I was aiming. All I had to offer was enthusiasm, a certain amount of writing ability, a willingness to research a story thoroughly, and energy. I did blunder into a wise move: I aimed low to begin with—I decided that it would be easier to sell the magazines that could not pay as much as the mass-circulation books. Some of those magazines, such as *The Saturday Review, The New Republic, Theatre Arts*, etc., paid atrocious prices (I used to be delighted when I got a check for more than $12.50 from *SRL*), but they were scrutinized carefully by the people who worked on the editorial staffs of the mass markets. S. J. Perelman sent me into *Theatre Arts* to do a job they had asked him to do; I did it and became a more or less regular contributor (and irregular payee—the magazine never seemed to have any money). Norman Cousins made me an *SRL* reviewer, more out of kindness, I suspected, than admiration for my work (I was, of course, wrong about that, too; Cousins would never have hired me if he had not thought me capable of writing for him; no editor has ever been characterized by charity for contributors). Jack Weeks, then managing editor of *The New Republic*, gave me a job or two. It certainly could not have been said that I was doing well, but I was managing to survive. Meanwhile, I was plugging away at my first novel, a dreary autobiographical chronical which then seemed to me to be a grave and important statement of my belief in the spirit of man. (It never was published, thank God.)

While working for "little" magazines I continued to read the mass markets. One week, in *Collier's*, I happened to see a one-page piece by Corey Ford, a kind of burlesque of the Kinsey Report. What this piece contained is forever lost to my memory, but for some reason it moved me to write Ford a long answer which I sent off promptly. About two weeks later I had a note from him, asking me to come into the *Collier's* office. He said he wanted me to meet Gurney Williams, the humor editor. It was all I could do to keep from rushing up there that same afternoon, but I restrained myself to the extent of telephoning Ford for an appointment.

He met me in the *Collier's* anteroom. He said he had enjoyed my letter and had shown it to Gurney, who wanted to know if I might be willing to try a piece. Might be willing! I wanted to sit down and try one then and there.

Williams, a thin, amiable man, was most encouraging. He asked almost deferentially if I had any other ideas that might "work out" for the space he was trying to fill. Struggling to contain my eagerness, I said I would think it over. As I recall, I went straight home and wrote three pieces. One had to do with the problems posed in a veteran's home life by the unexpected appearance of old Army buddies. Having been an admirer of Perelman from about the age of fifteen, I naturally had unconsciously—or perhaps consciously—assimiliated something of his manner. A line by Perelman usually started out in a straightforward manner and then wound up far out in the field. I tried to do that sort of thing; as I recall, one line, telling of the visit of one of my old Army pals, went something like this: "He arrived carrying Scotch, gin, and bourbon; he carried these potables in his stomach, remarking that it just was not safe to trust them to the weak bottles being manufactured these days."

Looking back on that effort and others—or *not* looking back on them, for what writer can bear to read his work of a previous decade? —I realize they were not only imitative but feeble. Williams must have realized that, too, but he also must have seen some potential in my work—and he unquestionably was hard pressed for humor. This does not mean that editors will buy for the purposes of keeping a spark alive and fanning it. Both my ego and my knowledge of editors prevent me from saying that—and my sense of obligation to the beginning writer. Much as I may despise that work today, Williams would not have bought it if it had not measured up to the standards he then had set. I was competing with Corey, Park Cummings, and others who had been selling the big markets for years. No writer ever sells unless he is selling something the editor needs.

ARTICLE: "OLD BUDDY, STAY 'WAY FROM MY DOOR"

(From *Collier's*)

If I have my way, and I probably won't, I'm never going to run into any of my old Army buddies again. I have resigned from all the veterans' organizations, and I've ripped my uniform to shreds and sold it to a crone who makes patchwork quilts. When my old outfit's Newsletter comes this month, I'm going to stamp it deceased and give it back to the postman. I am growing a mustache and a Vandyke and cultivating a gutteral accent, and the next time somebody asks me what I did in the war, I'm going to reply thickly that I was a 4F or a home-front profiteer.

I'm not bitter: It's just that I've had so many old Army pals in my house during the past three years that my front room has come to resemble a small-town square on Memorial Day. They have drunk enough of my whisky to float an LCI; they have eaten enough of my food to keep an antitank company in fighting trim for six months. They have broken my furniture, burned holes in my rugs, ruined my plumbing and made love (unsuccessfully, I think) to my wife.

Most of all, they have *talked*. The men that I remember from my G.I. days were all morose, tight-lipped fellows who sat around sullenly on their bunks, wishing they were back home, and cursing the company commander. Civilian life has done something to this bunch, something rather terrifying. For one thing, it has made every man jack as garrulous as Gabriel Heatter. For another, it has wiped out any memory of any unpleasantness they might have experienced. To hear them tell it today—and just try to keep them from telling it!—the Army was nothing but one long, hilarious party.

Purely as a scientific study, I have been making notes on the behavior of these "friends" of mine, and I have divided them, for the sake of convenient classification, into a number of types. You're probably already familiar with them—and if you are, you have my sympathy.

Type One, *The I'm Sure I Know You from the Army,* is pretty repulsive. I always meet him at a cocktail party where most of the women are particularly unattractive. Just as I've cornered the one presentable creature in the crowd, this specimen appears.

"I'm sure I know you from the Army," he says, breathing in my face. "Weren't you in the old 12th MP Company?"

"No," I say coldly, turning back to the damsel.

"Wait a minute," he says, pawing my shoulder. "It was the 97th General Hospital, wasn't it?"

"No," I say, more frigidly. "As I was saying, Miss Borgen—"

"I've got it!" he cries. "The 312th Coast Artillery!"

I turn on him, furious. "No, it was not!" Then I stare at him pointedly, mutter, "Get lost, will you?" and turn back to Miss Borgen. She, of course, has drifted away.

This is just what my new old buddy wants. He now begins to tell me his entire Army history, from the time of his preliminary physical at the draft board to a day about a month after his discharge, when he met his old commanding officer, who had returned to his old job as a Western Union messenger, and punched him solidly in the nose.

Type Two, *The Gag Man*, is, thank your stars, rather rare. I've run into him only once, on the street, at which time he knocked me down. When he pulled me to my feet he shook hands and gave me a shock with one of those patented buzzers. Then the flower in his lapel squirted water in my face, after which he invited me to have a look at the passing girls through an X-ray tube. I did, and got a sooty eye. "Pretty funny, eh?" he howled. Before I could answer, he pressed his card into my hand. It read:

I am Cletus Dench
who the — are you?

The following evening, Dench arrived at my apartment, having gained admission by occupying the doorman with a double hot-foot. It appeared that he had bought out the entire stock of a novelty store, everything from flash powder to card tricks. While my wife and I yawned, Dench then put on a magic show which for sheer dullness rivaled anything I have ever witnessed. He had just drunk two thirds of a bottle of good bourbon, and had begun breaking raw eggs into my best hat, a preliminary to what he called "the greatest little trick in the world," when the doorbell rang.

Sometimes I feel that I am truly psychic, for something told me that the doorman, the superintendent, and a policeman would be standing outside. They were. Pausing just long enough for Dench to gather up his magic equipment, the five of us proceeded to one of our local precincts. I felt that the sergeant was unduly severe, and Dench, in turn, seemed to feel that I was somehow at fault. I mollified him by paying his fine, and out of deep gratitude he called me between 3 and 4 A.M. every morning for six straight weeks after that.

The third type, *The Carouser*, is by far the most dangerous. He arrives at my place without notice, carrying a great deal of whisky, gin and rum. He carries these potables in his stomach, remarking that it isn't safe to entrust them to the kind of fragile bottles they put on the market these days.

When I introduce this worthy to my wife, he leers disgustingly and says, "Well, Dickie, you always did know how to pick 'em!" Then, pretending to be puzzled, he adds, "But you never told me you were married."

Upon hearing this, my wife looks at Type Three with new interest. To divert her attention, I invite the old buddy to sit down. He lurches across the room, and, with the grace that can come only from years of practice, stumbles over an end table, breaking it to bits.

After he has settled in our sofa, putting his muddy shoes up on the new yellow slip cover, he further adjusts himself by deftly knocking a vase off a small taboret. As I am sweeping up the pieces, trying not to look at my wife, he launches into the inevitable reminiscences.

"Remember old Anytime Annie in Birmingham?" he cries, shaking his head. "What a chick!"

"I—ah—don't believe I do," I say, guardedly.

"Sure, you do!" he roars. "We used to meet her in front of the Tutwiler, every Saturday afternoon!" He looks at my wife. "You'd have loved Annie."

"I'm sure," my wife murmurs.

"I hear from her, every once in a while," Buddy says. "Says she writes to you now and then, too."

"Why, ah—" I begin—and then I stop. Further speech is useless. By now the little woman is halfway across the room, that home-to-mother look on her face.

"Anytime Annie, eh?" she mutters. "So *that's* what you do when you're working late." The door slams.

Wearily, I turn back to the old Army friend. He is now sleeping loudly on the couch, his mouth open. To make this picture of contentment complete, his cigarette has conveniently dropped out of his mouth, and is now burning a round, cozy hole in our rug.

These, then, are just three walking reasons why I wish to have nothing further to do with Old Service Companions. These days, whenever I see one approaching on the street, I either duck into a telephone booth or dive for the nearest manhole. If I'm too late to do either, and he's already seen me, I try to look as though I'm suffering from amnesia. It's hard to keep this vacant stare in my eyes, but it's worth it.

Post Script: Nearly every editor I know insists that he needs humor more than he needs anything else. Unfortunately, editors seldom agree upon a definition of humor—but most of them do say that the humor they print ought to have a wide appeal or ought to contain material with which the reader can identify. "Old Buddy" was printed at a time when many of *Collier's* readers were enduring unexpected visits from old G.I. pals they'd known only slightly. I had several letters beginning, "Let me tell you about the joker from my old outfit who showed up last week . . . etc."

This piece came off because I took a familiar situation, peopled it with familiar characters, and exaggerated both. I was not passing it off as truth any more than, say, Sid Caesar passes off his characterization of the animal psychiatrist as truth. Nevertheless, truth was at the core. Those old service pals were boring, and sometimes their antics were destructive and embarrassing.

Articles of this kind require no research on the part of the writer, except in his own memory. They need:

1. A beginning that states the theme, or problem;
2. Bright writing throughout (my writing was perhaps not as bright throughout as it should have been);
3. Some kind of solution.

The construction is substantially the same as that of a short story, even though the article, by dealing with the characters one by one, becomes more episodic than most short stories are.

As I remember, I wrote this piece rapidly in the first draft, simply setting down what I had to say. Then I went through it line by line and attempted to make each one funny or pointed. Reading it over, I notice several missed opportunities—but that is an experience well-known to any writer who reads his work after years have passed. Much of the humor is Perelmanesque, although none of it shows any of his skill or mastery of odd words. The ending is weak—my solutions are just too far out to ring true.

There are many markets for pieces of this kind in both the major and minor magazines, but the writer will not find them simply by sitting down and writing off something that has happened to him. He must choose a subject with a universal appeal, adopt a certain point of view (the point of view in the one above is that of hopeless exasperation), and be consistent throughout. The articles ought to be fairly short; it is hard to sustain humor over many more than 1,000 to 2,000 words (incidentally, the necessity for brevity applies to most humorous writing—it is hard even for the most enthusiastic fan of any humorist to read straight through a collection of pieces without interruptions).

In 1949–1950, I did a number of similar pieces for *Collier's* and other magazines. The subjects were varied: How women speak a different language from men (I later did that in different form for *Cosmopolitan*); how made-up words like "brunch" irritated me; how unexpected guests from the old home town could complicate my life (a variation on *Old Buddy*); how people seemed to be abandoning language in favor of gestures, etc. Most of these pieces apparently struck some chord of response in the editors and, apparently, in the readers. Pieces of this kind are not easy to write, but they afford good practice for the beginner because, in the actual writing, they train him in construction and the use of language. And as noted previously, there always seems to be a market for them in the men's, women's, and general magazines.

4 · *Mistakes I Made Ten Years Ago*

ALTHOUGH I was selling *Collier's* one of those domestic pieces every six weeks or so, I had to continue to look for other work; the more I plugged away at the novel I was writing, the more I was convinced that I really was not ready to undertake a task of that size.

Someone—Jerry Mason, I believe—told me that Carlton Brown, author of a fine novel called *Brainstorm*, had gone to work as editor for a man's magazine published by Martin Goodman, the comic-magazine king. I went up to see Brown, hoping for an assignment. He was cordial and kind, and set me up by saying he had seen some of my efforts here and there, but he explained, almost apologetically, that Goodman wanted pieces like "I FOUGHT THE ABOMINABLE SNOW-MAN AND LIVED." It seemed to me that I had nothing to offer him until I remembered David Maurer, an English instructor at the University of Louisville who was, according to S. J. Perelman, the world's foremost authority on criminal slang. Some years before, Perelman had come across a book of Maurer's, *The Big Con*, the definitive work on confidence games, and had been so impressed he had enlisted Maurer's professional counsel while writing a play about crooks, *The Night Before Christmas*. They had become friends, and Perelman had said to me several times that he thought Maurer would make a magazine piece for me. If Perelman had suggested that I do a piece on Mother Cabrini or someone equally far out of my line, I would have attempted it at once. I had made an outline on Maurer and had started it on the rounds, but no editor had even sniffed.

I told Brown about Maurer. He said he thought he might be able to use the piece. He said he would pay me $300—$150 down for expenses to Louisville, and the rest upon delivery of an acceptable piece. This was the first time an editor ever had shown sufficient faith to give me some money before I had put a word on paper, and I was off to Louisville by train the next day.

Maurer was understandably dubious about the desirability of having a story about him appear in one of Martin Goodman's magazines. He hesitated; he felt it might harm his professional reputation. Presently, more out of affection for Perelman than interest in my career, he agreed to cooperate. In the course of our interviews I managed to communicate some of my ambition (I managed to communicate that to everyone I met, I suppose), and after a day or two he generously allowed that there were two other possible article subjects in Louisville which he thought I might want to investigate. One was Fred Willkie, brother of Wendell and the operator of a distillery, who had some unusual ideas about a wedding between industry and education; the other was Charlie Farnsley, an eccentric scholar and politician who was mayor of Louisville.

Willkie turned out to be interesting but lacking in sufficient appeal for any of the magazines I was trying to hit. Then I met Farnsley and knew after the first half-hour that I could probably do a story on him.

I returned to New York and wrote the Maurer piece for Brown. He accepted it with some difficulty. He was trying to make the magazine into something a bit better than the bloods Goodman was in the habit of publishing. Goodman had had considerable success with his magazines; he saw no reason to attempt to elevate the taste of, or disappoint, his readers. He did not want my article, which he said was not lurid enough, but Brown talked him into taking it. It was published, long after Brown left Goodman, in a pinup-girl magazine called *Eye*, the chief distinction of which was that it was the first publication ever to feature a cover photograph and inside picture spread of Marilyn Monroe. The Maurer piece was the only text in the book. Maurer was justifiably furious. He told Perelman that I had betrayed him and damaged his academic standing. I may have been guilty of the former, unintentionally, but I certainly did nothing to harm his reputation. Nevertheless, this episode angered Perelman, which distressed me.

While finishing off the piece for Brown, I made an outline of the Farnsley piece. I went up to *Collier's* and asked Gurney Williams to introduce me to Walter Ross, the articles editor. Ross was interested in Farnsley and asked to see the outline. Realizing that I had told him more than I had put into the one I had written, I held off giving it to him, went home, wrote another that incorporated everything I knew about the mayor.

Two weeks later Ross called and said the *Collier's* non-fiction staff had agreed Farnsley might make an article. They were sending me back to Louisville. To my amazement, they also were giving me an advance for expenses. I felt that I had arrived at last. I returned to Louisville in a stew of pride and eagerness.

The Farnsley article was my first full-length job for a major magazine. I reprint it for its faults, which are discussed in the Post Script.

ARTICLE: "CONFUCIUS IN LOUISVILLE"

(From *Collier's*)

Last year, when Mark Ethridge, publisher of the Louisville *Courier-Journal*, heard that Charles R. P. Farnsley was the city's new mayor, he put his fists to his brow and groaned, "Now every day'll be like Derby Day!"

Ethridge was just about right. Charlie Farnsley, a relaxed, head-scratching, jovial eccentric of forty-two, has been in office less than 15 months. But in that time, acting on orders from the people, his administration has rebuilt or repaved most of the heavily traveled city streets; reshuffled traffic to make it move more smoothly than ever before; cut crime to its lowest ebb in the city's mottled history; reduced the smoke and soot which used to blanket Louisville; encouraged the repair and reconditioning of run-down schools; provided unheard-of recreational facilities for adults and children alike; he was instrumental in abolishing segregation in the main public library and on play streets; and activated a program of mass education and cultural activity second to that of no other municipal setup in the country.

As some Louisville people put it, Farnsley has "caused more commotion in town than anything since the famous flood of 1937."

Farnsley says that he is acting on principles handed down from Confucius, the 18th-century French physiocrats and Thomas Jefferson. Simply, his theory is: Government should serve the people.

One expert on municipal government has said that many of Farnsley's ideas may well set patterns for cities everywhere.

Farnsley likes to think that what he is doing in Louisville, a lively metropolis of roughly a half million, is the same thing that Confucius advocated doing in Chinese hamlets around 500 B.C. Confucius believed that the people should be almost wholly in control of civic affairs. So does Farnsley. "I'm gonna let the people tell me what to do," he said soon after election. "I'm gonna be in the aldermen's chamber in city hall ever' Monday, and the city officials're gonna be there with me. Anybody that's got anythin' on his mind, anythin' he doesn't like or wants done, all he's got to do is come in and tell us about it."

This was the beginning of Farnsley's Beef Session, more formally known as The People's Court.

Though the sessions are broadcast, Farnsley remains slangy and casual throughout, slumping in his chair, wriggling, rubbing his thinning brown hair, occasionally putting his feet up on the table beside the microphone. As originally promised, the city officials are right there with him. At a typical session last March, a Mrs. Delbert Butz stepped up and began, "Mr. Mayor, you're probably accustomed to having us Saunders Avenue folks down here, but—"

"Always nice to see you," said Farnsley.

"—but we're trying to get our street paved. We sent two men down here and they didn't do any good," she said, "so we decided to see what the women could do."

Farnsley beckoned to W. W. Sanders, city engineer. "Come on over, Tubby, and listen to this lady. Now, Mrs. Butz, what is it you want done?"

"Our street is half made," Mrs. Butz explained, "and they told us we'd have to get a petition to get it finished. I've brought one down."

Farnsley looked at Sanders, "How 'bout that, Tubby?"

"If I recall correctly," Sanders said, "the ordinance has been passed to get this work done."

"How soon can we do it?" Farnsley asked.

"Probably the latter part of the year."

Mrs. Butz' face fell. Farnsley shook his head. "That's a long time off," he said. "Can't we hurry it a little—let contracts and things like that? This lady and those neighbors o' hers out there need their street real bad."

"We'll do it as fast as we can," Sanders said.

"Put on an extra man or something, get things started," ordered Farnsley.

"All right," said Sanders.

"Thank you, Mr. Mayor," said Mrs. Butz.

"Thank *you,*" said Farnsley. "Come in any time."

Originally, people couldn't believe that Farnsley meant business. Then they began hearing of friends who had obtained action. Soon they were turning up in droves. Attendance now ranges from 50 to 200 each week. The crowds have brought some rather special problems to the mayor's attention. A man once asked for help in arresting his neighbor, who, he said, had stolen his cat. Farnsley helped him get a warrent sworn out but never learned if the cat was recovered. A woman living in a housing project where no telephone wires had as yet been strung needed a phone because her baby was sick. Farnsley got her one.

These Beef Sessions mark the first time that Louisville citizens have ever had a *direct* voice in their own affairs (the city aldermen, who must pass on all measures, are elected at large.) Political observers are convinced that the sessions will remain a part of future mayors' programs even if Farnsley is replaced by a fellow Democrat or Republican.

"It's an altogether new idea in city government," according to Roy E. Owsley, a Ph.D., who is considered one of the nation's top authorities on urban administration. Owsley was brought to Louisville by Farnsley to act as a consultant and to make a two-year study of the city. After watching Farnsley in action, Owsley said, "I've never seen anything like it!"

Old friends have not been particularly astonished at Farnsley's unprecedented conduct. He has always been unconventional (to put it mildly) in thought, speech, mode of life and, above all, in dress. At one time he wore clothes that had been made in the days of the Confederacy: swallow-tailed coat, brocade vest, planter's hat, congress gaiters and a string tie.

Soon after the 1937 flood, Farnsley appeared in a number of old-fashioned, pleated-bosom shirts, which he said the Boy Scouts had collected in a salvage drive.

Although he stopped wearing most of his Confederate clothes around 1942, when he left politics to go back to college, nothing could make him give up his black string tie. Always his trade-mark, it is now his badge of office and is being copied widely and sold in Louisville stores as the "Farnsley." When the mayor and his committee welcome visiting dignitaries, they present them first with a key to the city and then with a black string tie.

Alexander, Farnsley's older son, is probably the only six-year-old in the nation who wears a black string tie day in and day out.

"He won't wear anythin' else," Farnsley once said proudly.

Farnsley has not abandoned the Confederate traditions altogether. He is commander of Andrew Broaddus Camp No. 361, Sons of Confederate Veterans. He lives on a street called Confederate Place, and his telephone number is in the Calhoun exchange. When the city proposed to move the monument to the Confederate dead, that stands at one end of the street, Farnsley took up a musket and went out and stood guard. The monument is still there, and he likes to salute it every morning on the way to work. Occasionally, when traveling North, he carries a carpetbag, in defiance of the Yankees who carried carpetbags through the South during Reconstruction days.

In the thirties, Farnsley manufactured a blended 86-proof bourbon for himself and his friends. He called it Rebel Yell. But when he tried to make a whisky especially for his Northern friends, he ran into trouble. A federal board rejected his proposed brand name, Damnyankee, with the comment "bad taste." Farnsley named the whisky Bad Taste.

Farnsley's Confederate phase ultimately was replaced by his current, or Chinese, period. Confucius reputedly was a strong man for public-opinion polls. So is Farnsley. Soon after becoming mayor, he called in his friend Elmo Roper to find out what the people wanted most. In his first poll, Roper learned that the citizens' main desires were improved streets, more and better playgrounds and parks, better public-health services, increased salaries for city employees, more policemen, a better pension system for policemen and firemen, better traffic conditions, and more and better schools and educational facilities.

The mayor was willing to have a crack at all these things. Just one thing stood in his way—money. Accordingly, he put through an Occupational License Tax, which meant that every person earning an income from work in the city would contribute one per cent to the municipal government. Today, the tax is bringing in an additional $3,000,000 a year, expanding the city budget to $10,591,-054. People are accepting it because it has enabled Farnsley to carry out their wishes.

Appointing William Meyers as the new Director of Finance, Farnsley happily began to spend the money. He first got to work on the streets, many of which hadn't been fixed for fifteen years. The new budget, however, wasn't enough to include a complete resurfacing program. So Farnsley told the engineers to repave only on the driving lanes, leaving parking spaces as they were. His critics called the new street "band-aids."

"Maybe they are," Farnsley commented, "but those streets sure needed first aid."

To date, the city has resurfaced, restored or repaired more than 43 miles of streets. At this writing, engineers are working on 20 miles more.

Public Works Director Herman T. Meiners says that the mayor's system has saved about $1.60 per running foot, thereby enabling his department to build nearly 50 per cent more streets than was possible under old methods.

Farnsley next turned his attention to traffic. Experts had agreed that Louisville's problem was one of the worst in the nation. Undaunted, Farnsley sat down at a table in the Wynn Stay, a men's luncheon club that serves as one of his offices away from city hall, and marked up maps of the city with red, green and black pencils. Simply by making the best use of all available streets and reorganizing traffic regulations, he came up with a workable solution to the problem, synchronizing traffic lights, designating more one-way streets and establishing a belt highway encircling the city.

Farnsley next raised police salaries an average of $25 a month and started work on a new pension plan which will go into effect this year. To release male patrolmen for more active duty, he put 25 lady cops on the force to handle traffic at intersections near schools. (He had asked for 100 but settled for 25.)

The more active duty for which the mayor released the men was crime prevention. Louisville had long been considered, by many critics, one of the shadier cities in the nation. At one time its red-light district was ten blocks square. In 1948 bookmakers reportedly were doing an estimated annual gross business of around $20,000,000.

Late last year Farnsley authorized Safety Director David McCandless to organize a vice squad. Today, McCandless estimates that handbooks have been cut down by at least a third. He also says that there are no houses of prostitution in the city.

Farnsley did all these things because the people wanted them done—but, ironically enough, he was not elected by the people in the first place. He was put in by the aldermen, after the death of the former mayor, Leland Taylor.

The contest was a bitter battle between two camps of the local Democratic party—one headed by Mrs. Lennie McLaughlin, successor to old-time political boss Mike Brennan, and the other composed of Taylor's former allies. They had reached an impasse, when someone suggested Farnsley's name.

The McLaughlinites did not want Farnsley and fought his election bitterly, but the Taylor clan threw their weight behind Farnsley and picked up new strength from labor. In a stormy, drawnout public session on March 1, 1948, the aldermen elected Farnsley by one vote. But a state law provides that when the aldermen elect a mayor, he must run again in the next general election for a term which will extend to the next mayoralty election.

Farnsley ran again last November and proved that his whirlwind administration has been a success. Nevertheless, he must run once more next fall. This will make, counting primaries, the fifth time he has run for mayor. If he is elected and completes his term, he will have been mayor longer than any previous holder of the office.

Farnsley was born in 1907, the son of one of the city's oldest families. His father is Burrel H. Farnsley, a judge in Jefferson Circuit Court, Common Pleas Branch. His childhood was spent in a pleasant agrarian way of life at Saint Helens, just outside of Louisville. But as Farnsley grew older, he gradually broke away from his sheltered home.

At the University of Louisville, he organized his fraternity into a political machine from which all campus offices were filled. He also became intensely interested in Jefferson and formed the Jacobin Society of America to promote Jeffersonian thought. He ate well, drank heavily, and caroused around town in a 1921-model Rolls Royce.

Because of his notoriety from these college-boy activities, there was some question of how much he was dedicated to the public interest when he began his political carrer. While in the state legislature he passed out a good deal of whisky to thirsty colleagues. He was known as a steadfast machine politician. "I'm here to do just what Mike Brennan tells me," he told a friend in the legislature.

In 1942, when Farnsley found that he was ineligible for service in the armed forces, he went back to the University of Louisville to get his A.B. Inevitably he began to study Jefferson, his old idol, and finally arrived at the conclusion that Jefferson's democratic ideas did not come from Plato and the Greeks, but from the 18th-century French physiocrats. Then he went to Columbia to do some graduate work and learned, from a Chinese student, that the physiocrats had taken most of their ideas from China. Farnsley soon had a new thesis—which maintained that all true Western democratic thought had its roots in the East—and in the teachings of Confucius.

He is still busy trying to prove and document his ideas. He reads translations of Chinese philosophy constantly. Once, while speaking to some laborers at a political rally, he allowed some of his philosophy to creep into his speech. "I didn't understand much of what he said at the rally," a man said later, "but I liked it."

In order to put his Confucian principles of a people's government into practice, Farnsley sometimes has to fight the board of aldermen who, although they elected him originally, are not all ardent Farnsleyites. When he proposed that the city buy the Louisville

Railway Company, which operates the streetcars, to provide a source of revenue, the aldermen turned him down cold. He asked for an additional 12-cent tax to improve and repair city schools; again they said no. "But I'm gonna fight for the tax again next year," he promises.

Since Confucius and Jefferson both believed in cultural activity and mass education, Farnsley has made Louisville a cultural fanatic's dream. The Main Library broadcasts adult-education classes to its 10 branches. All 11 libraries are equipped with television receivers. People can borrow record players, records, motion-picture projectors and educational films from them. The Louisville Symphony this year has commissioned six composers to write original compositions and to conduct them in world *premières*. "Farnsley's idea," says Conductor Robert Whitney, happily.

Farnsley helped abolish segregation in the Main Library and on the 36 streets he has marked off to fill the people's demand for more children's play facilities. The city is now building a $250,000 public swimming pool. This year, he will supplement city-budget recreation money with a drive to be called The Louisville Fund, which will raise $100,000 to be distributed among the city's artistic groups.

Typical of Farnsley's frequent bursts of candor, which are the despair of his public-relations men, was a conference in which he was discussing Louisville's new city flag. Farnsley discussed one design and then went extensively into the designs of flags carried by the French kings. Suddenly he interrupted his lecture. "I don't just *know* this stuff," he confessed. "I went out yesterday and looked it up."

His humanitarianism often causes pain to the more practical politicians on the staff. An alderman once came in and said that a minor city employee wasn't doing his job and should be discharged. "Fine," said Farnsley. "Go ahead and fire him." Then he scratched his head. "Wait a minute—what'll we do to keep him from starvin' to death? Let's don't fire him until we figure out somethin' else he can do."

Farnsley is known to some of his associates as The Man Who Never Sleeps. He goes to bed, officially, only between 2 and 5 A.M., and catches catnaps in the daytime on a leather couch in his office. He works so avidly that his wife, an attractive blonde whom he calls Miss Nancy, once bought an old-fashioned motto and placed it on the mantel in his study. It read, WHAT IS HOME WITHOUT A FATHER? Farnsley met Miss Nancy in 1936 while serving in the legislature. They were married in February, 1937, and they now have four children—Sally (eleven), Ann (nine), Alexander (six), and Burrel (three).

Farnsley prefers to work at home, close to his books on city planning, achitecture, Jefferson and Chinese philosophy. When he uses his study as his office, his children swarm all over him. But Farnsley is never nettled by his family; possibly because Confucius believed in the institution, he does too.

Ambition is the big question mark in Farnsley's career. When he took office he gave up a law practice that brought him $15,000 more per year than his salary as mayor. He already has filed his papers to run again next fall. Some Louisville observers are convinced that this means that he does have ambition—that he intends to use the office as a springboard to higher things. Farnsley denies this emphatically.

"I may sound like I'm puttin' on an act," he stated, "but honest, all I want to do is be mayor o' Louisville. I think the gov'ment ought to help people in cities the way it helps farm people. We got county agents—why don't we have city agents? If we can make this city work and show that the people're happy and prosperous, then maybe other cities'll follow suit—and the day'll come when all men'll be brothers." Farnsley paused. "I prepared that statement, but it's true."

Although his critics still are skeptical, people who have known Farnsley for years are convinced that he means it. Adele Brandeis, niece of the late Supreme Court Justice and an editorial writer on the *Courier-Journal*, has known Farnsley since he was a child. "I think Charlie's telling the truth," she said, after hearing of his statement. "I don't think he wants to be anything but mayor." Then she reconsidered. "Unless maybe," she added, "he wants to go back and be Confucius."

Post Script: If I were an editor today and a young writer handed in this story, I would accept it—but for content rather than style, and for general interest rather than instructiveness. It is a typical young writer's effort. The writing is undeveloped and imitative, full of journalistic and public-relationsy phrases, such as "Ethridge was just about right," and clichés, such as "Soon they were turning up in droves." It has its lively paragraphs, but they are mainly direct quotes from Farnsley or transcripts of dialogues between Farnsley and others. It is hard to tell why the editors permitted it to go through in this form. *Collier's* was then in a state of utter confusion, it is true. Also, it is just possible that some of the editing was done in the Crowell-Collier printing plant, in Springfield, Ohio. Out there, if the makeup men had more print than they could force into forms, they simply pulled out paragraphs wherever their fingers happened to fall. It was not unusual to find a reference by last name, toward the end of a story, to a character who did not appear in the early part because he had been killed by the printers. "My God, those guys edit by brute force," Eli Waldron once said after reading over one of his short stories that had suffered the Springfield massacre.

There are two other reasons why the story seems so inept today. I had not yet begun to relax in my prose, and relaxation is the key to individuality of style. Also, I am nearly ten years older. "If you're serious about your craft," Merle Miller once remarked, "your standards get higher and higher and each job gets tougher and tougher." As I mentioned earlier, when in 1957 I polled fifty-odd members of the Society of Magazine Writers and asked each to name the hardest piece he'd done, all but eleven answered, "The one I'm working on now."

Here are the faults of this article as they leap out at me today:

Paragraph 1. The quote is not funny enough to justify the use of Ethridge. I should have put in Farnsley's full name, without the initials. The story should begin in Paragraph 2, with a clause after Farnsley's name explaining him.

Paragraph 2. The second sentence is probably much too long, and the sudden appearance of the phrase "he was instrumental" is jarring. I am almost dead certain that a *Collier's* editor put that "he" in there.

Paragraph 3. Lazy writing, that "As some Louisville people . . ." I should have quoted one individual directly. Also, the quote should have begun, "Farnsley has . . ." The quote is too stiff. "The famous flood of 1937" means little or nothing. (I believe this was *Collier's* fault, too.)

Paragraph 5. *What* expert on municipal government? Again, lazy writing.

Paragraph 22. The anecdote about the cat is spoiled by "but never learned if the cat was recovered." This is superfluous. The important part was Farnsley's helping him get the warrant.

Paragraph 23. "Direct" does not demand italics. I cannot imagine why I once used italics so frequently; I suspect I lacked belief in myself and my ability to write a sentence so that the reader could supply his own emphasis.

Paragraph 24. Where did Roy E. Owsley come from? His quote at the end of this paragraph loses its effect because we know so little about him.

Paragraphs 25–26. Should be a single paragraph.

Paragraphs 27–28–29. Should be a single paragraph.

Paragraph 30. How long did Farnsley stand guard in front of the monument?

Paragraph 32. How do we know that Confucius "reputedly" was "a strong man for public opinion polls" (ugh)? How did Farnsley and Elmo Roper become friends?

Paragraph 34. William Meyers should be explained, even if only with a short sentence.

Paragraphs 40–41. Should be a single paragraph.

Paragraphs 42–43–44. These should be a single paragraph, but more important, they should go into the Louisville situation in depth.

Paragraph 46. Since I did not put Farnsley's full name in the first or second paragraph, it should go here. Also, the full date of his birth is needed.

Paragraph 47. "He ate well, drank heavily, etc." tells us almost nothing that characterizes the man. An anecdote or two should go in here.

Paragraph 48. Brennan should be explained more fully—or should have been in Paragraphs 42–43–44.

Paragraph 49. We should find out why Farnsley was ineligible for service. Careless writing.

Paragraph 50. The reader wants to know what part of Farnsley's Confucian philosophy crept into his speech. Otherwise the laborer's quote at the end of this paragraph is pointless.

Paragraph 51. "Cultural fanatic," I hasten to put in here, is not my phrase. It is *Collier's*—the work of an editorial fanatic, I have no doubt. Also, the names of the six composers should be included.

Paragraph 52. How did he help abolish segregation? What "artistic groups"? Sloppy.

Paragraph 53. Unless I was a much worse writer than I now believe I was then (and I honestly don't see how I could have been), there must have been a paragraph between this one and the one preceding. If there was not, I should have had sense enough to have written some sort of transitional line, such as "Farnsley accomplishes all these things breezily and gaily, like a mischievous schoolboy playing at being principal. And he has a boyish candor which is the despair of his public relations men. A typical outburst . . ." etc.

Paragraph 55. There are so many things wrong with this I hardly know where to begin. It should have begun, I believe, "To the despair of his wife, whom he calls . . ." etc. Then the line about his being The Man Who Never Sleeps would follow naturally, and a line to the effect that it distresses both his associates and Miss Nancy would follow that. Also, the reader does not know Miss Nancy's maiden name or what she looks like. "Attractive blonde" is not enough. It does not say anything.

Paragraph 56. Sloppy reporting and poor writing.

Additional criticisms: There were not enough direct quotes from Farnsley. My phonetic rendition of his speech was careless; Farnsley never said "mayor," he said "murr." There should have been more scenes between Farnsley and his associates and his family. Somewhere nearer the beginning there should have been a stronger statement of his impact on Louisville and his potential influence upon municipal government in general. Farnsley does not come to life except in Paragraphs 6 through 21. I wish he would get himself elected again; I would like to go back to Louisville and do justice to him.

5 · *Louis Ruppel, a Great Editor*

THERE were two important influences in my life as a writer in the years immediately following World War II. The first was a group of young writers who were my friends; the second was Louis Ruppel.

At that time I was living on MacDougal Street in Greenwich Village (where else do young writers go to live?) in a rundown house once owned, it was said, by Dr. Bronson Alcott, father of Louisa May. There were at least ten of us in the neighborhood who were trying to make a living at writing—Eli Waldron, Hollis Alpert, Walt Grove, Eugene O'Neill, Jr. (who later killed himself) and others; we had been brought together by Donald Congdon, now a literary agent, who was an associate fiction editor at *Collier's* and as such had "discovered" Waldron, Grove and me. I forget exactly how Hollis came into the group, but he brought with him another occasional communicant, Morton Fineman, of Philadelphia. Josephine Herbst, who was living in Bucks County, sometimes visited and held us entranced with her stories of writers she had known in the preceding three decades. Marc Brandel would show up now and again, petulant and contentious, and J. D. Salinger frequently arrived from uptown. George Milburn was living nearby, and we saw quite a bit of him. We read our stories to each other and drank much too much, and our discursive and irrational arguments would last through the night until someone suggested going to the Fulton Fish Market for breakfast. A friendly liquor dealer who had a store down MacDougal Street, Harry Risetto, did more than sell us whisky. He knew that we were all broke most of the time. He would permit us to give him checks dated days ahead, which he could cash and then hold until we had money enough in our accounts to cover them.

One of my principal memories of those days of embattlement with the business of being a writer is Hollis Alpert's furious energy. He lived in a room on the third floor of my house. Each morning at seven his typewriter would begin to clatter nerve-wrackingly through the ramshackle place. It was nothing for him to write a 5,000-word short story before noon. When he finished he would rush downstairs to where Waldron and I were sitting around drinking coffee and wasting time, and ask if we cared to have him read it aloud. As soon as he had heard our opinions he would tear back upstairs, retype the manuscript, and streak to the mailbox to post it off to *The New Yorker*. Hollis had sold seven or eight stories to that magazine during the war, but he had yet to make a sale as a civilian. He was later to become an associate fiction editor on it, but in the time of which I write he had not yet trained himself to that restraint—that prissy, bloodless restraint—which the editors seem to demand of their fiction writers. The stories Hollis wrote all came back. He was never discouraged; he bottled up his disappointment and flung himself to the typewriter again.

Right here it ought to be stated that nearly every writer must become used to the idea, from the beginning, that he will be in for many, many disappointments before he sees his work bought and set in type. He must toughen himself against rejection slips—even pretend that they do not exist—and go on either to his next job or to the job of rewriting one that did not sell. Editors seldom give any indication of why a piece is unsatisfactory; they do not have time to do that. The writer must study his market and attempt to make his own analysis of why his work fell short. Above all, he must not permit his enthusiasm or confidence to falter. I remember Salinger saying in one of those late-at-night MacDougal Street sessions, "A writer lives mainly on his confidence." I am not entirely certain that I agree with that today—a writer needs more than confidence—but faith in his own ability certainly is an important component of the writer's personality.

Hollis Alpert never lost the conviction that some day, somehow, he would be a selling writer. But the behavior of Eli Waldron tried him severely. Eli worked less than any of us. He was a tall man with a long, haggard face; we called him The Cheap Jesus. He had been working on a newspaper in Chicago, and one Saturday night after he was finished he happened to see an airport limousine passing by a corner. On impulse he got in, went to the airport, and flew to New York. Don Congdon introduced him to us, and he holed up in a rooming-house a few doors away from my house. There he passed his time writing an occasional limerick or verses such as

Children, children, children
Although some of you may think it laughable,
Take, take, take
To your teacher
An affaple.

Another of Eli's masterworks was called, *When Beardsley Ruml and Rudolf Friml Got Drunk on a Bottle of Kreml.* He had weird fantasies. One day he came in and said, "The caffè espresso machine across the street just climbed off its counter and walked down to the San Remo and had intercourse with the machine in there. Such steaming and wheezing and whistling! Everybody in the street's too excited to work." Sometimes he would produce stories he had written; two of the titles I recall are *The Knocked-Up Arabian and the Umbrella Thief*, and *The Five Well-Mannered Fags and the Jocose Abortionist.* Hollis could not understand why Eli wrote such stories, none of which could ever hope to appear even in a magazine that was extraordinarily tolerant toward young talent, such as *Kenyon Review* (Eli had published a half-dozen stories in the latter). What was more puzzling to Hollis, and more exasperating, was something Eli did every six weeks or so. He would arrive in the morning and say, "Anybody got a pencil?" I would give him one. Then he would sit down at the kitchen table and, oblivious to whatever conversations were going on around him, begin to write in longhand on a lined yellow pad. After about three hours he would say, "I have written a story." And he would read it. Without waiting to hear what Hollis and I had to say, he would take it next door where a typist lived, and after she had finished he would go up to the *Collier's* offices and ask to see Kenneth Littauer, the fiction editor. On one of these occasions, Littauer read the story while Eli was still there and made it possible for Eli to get his money—around $900 —that same afternoon. Other times, Eli had to wait a week or ten days. No matter how long the delay between acceptance and check, the whole series of events drove poor Hollis nearly berserk. He knew well enough that Eli had thought the story out for weeks before sitting down to write—had, in fact, written it in his head—but the experience left its mark on him. But Hollis was determined; he kept on writing, and today he sells nearly everything he puts on paper. (He has just published a novel, *The Summer Lovers*.)

I have fond recollections of those days. Although none of us accomplished much, the time we spent together was nevertheless immensely valuable. We talked writing, writing, writing; we read each other's pieces and citicized them or made suggestions, and we listened eagerly to the opinions of older, more experienced writers. Little by little we each began to develop distinct, individual attitudes toward our work, and what had begun as several rather formless, youthful desires to write—to write almost anything, for the sheer joy of writing—gradually took the shapes of our own styles. Style is, after all, largely a matter of point-of-view and manner, and the two are often indistinguishable.

Because a certain amount of discussion with other writers must inevitably be beneficial for the beginner, if only because it encourages him to come to some conclusions about his own work, I would urge every hopeful to seek out his fellows and to meet with them regularly. (Unlike other businessmen, writers usually are willing to exchange trade information, craft secrets and technique; jealousy may exist, but it seldom shows as competition.) Writing classes and clubs are valuable for this reason alone, if for no other. Also, meeting with others of his own kind gives the aspirant something he may not get for some time to come—an audience. In one way, an audience of this kind is more worth-while than the unseen audience that becomes the ultimate consumer of the writer's product on the printed page: it is articulate and reacts immediately to what the writer has done.

Enter Louis Ruppel.

I had returned from my first *Collier's* assignment in Louisville with about three dollars to my name. Writing the Farnsley story took about five days. I had over-researched it; I had so much material I could not decide what to keep and what to discard. After two or three days I persuaded myself that the story should be done in two parts, and called Walter Ross, the articles editor, to inform him of this decision.

"Don't be silly," he said. "The story isn't worth two parts—not important enough. Besides, I don't want to throw cold water on your hopes, but there've been a lot of changes around here in the past couple of days. Haven't you heard? We've got a new editor, Louis Ruppel. He's not especially eager to buy anything that was assigned before he came in."

The words chilled me, but I knew I would be lost if I began writing that story with a nagging worry that it might not be bought. I therefore put everything Ross had said into some obscure corner of my mind and set to work to write Farnsley as a two-parter. The finished article ran forty typewritten pages. I put the piece away and turned to a book report for *The Saturday Review*. At the end of two days I could not bear the suspense any longer. I had kited a check for fifty dollars to Harry Risetto, and I had nothing else coming to me but the $12.50 the *SRL* would pay two weeks after my review would be published. Within seven or eight days I would be flat broke.

Taking out the Farnsley piece, I went through it and cut out everything that did not seem important. I got it down to twenty pages, took it in to the magazine and gave it to Ross. He read the first two pages and looked up. "This seems fine," he said, "but as I told you on the telephone, don't hope for too much. This Ruppel is a tough guy. He's got all kinds of new ideas—and he doesn't have much respect for what we were doing around here before he came in."

Out in the hall toward which I stumbled, I nearly collided with Oscar Dystel, then the managing editor. He did not recognize me; he was rushing along toward the editor's office at the end, an apprehensive expression on his face. Out of that office was pouring a series of raging shouts, like the trumpetings of an angry bull elephant. Dystel was ordinarily a calm, calculating man. He had been chiefly responsible for the success of *Coronet*, and Crowell-Collier had brought him in about a year before in an attempt to get some life into the dying *Collier's*. Walter Davenport, the columnist, held the title of editor, but Dystel was running the show. Davvy had been removed in favor of Ruppel. Dystel was still there, but from his look I surmised that he felt he would not be there much longer. He always had been cordial to me when I had been in the office conferring with Gurney Williams about my little pieces of humor; now, running down the hall toward the office where the explosions were taking place, he did not even say hello.

Even the New York newspapers had begun to chronicle the day-to-day havoc Louis Ruppel had been working at the magazine from the day he arrived. Kenneth Littauer, fiction editor for twenty-five years, had resigned at once. Seven or eight other editors had departed immediately thereafter; some resigned and some were fired. The great Quentin Reynolds, perhaps the most respected of all magazine writers, left after a fierce argument; Ruppel had accused him of laziness. Kyle Crichton, one of my boyhood idols, had joined the rush to the door. The only two staff writers who remained were Bill Davidson and Collie Small. The rest were out looking for jobs. New editors and writers were being brought in every day; A. J. Liebling, it was rumored, was coming over from *The New Yorker*. A former *Time* man who also had been wheelhorse on a number of newspapers with Ruppel, John Denson (now editor of *Newsweek*), was being brought into a position of authority.

Ruppel himself, it was rumored, was a rampaging tyrant. In his first two days on the magazine three secretaries had resigned because they could not bear his Marine profanity; he had smashed two glass desk-tops by pounding them as he screamed out orders.

After passing Oscar Dystel in the hall I went over to Tim Costello's saloon, where various friends told me most of the things contained in the two paragraphs above. I had an ominous conviction that Ruppel would never accept my Farnsley piece. I got drunk.

That was a Wednesday. I had hoped that I might hear something from Ross by Friday—but he did not call, and I faced the long, long week end. Nor did he call on Monday, or Tuesday. On Wednesday I could not stand it any longer, and called him.

"Well," he said, guardedly, "it got by all of us in the articles department. *We* liked it. Mr. Ruppel has it now, and you can't tell . . ." His voice trailed off; my stomach turned and pitched.

"I tell you what," he said. "I'll try to get an answer for you by tomorrow. Call me at one P.M."

"Walter," I said, my voice breaking, "do you think it's got a chance?"

"I don't know," he said. "The way things've been going around here, I don't know much of anything."

I called him the next day. His secretary answered the telephone. She said, "I'm sorry, Mr. Gehman, but Mr. Ross isn't with us any more."

Strangely enough, I had somehow known that it would happen; I had been hoping that it would not, but without any real belief. I had no money, no work and no prospects—and the chances were, now that this Ruppel had come in, I would sell no more humor pieces to Gurney Williams.

During the following weekend I tried to forget my crushing disappointment by working on article ideas, but I could not shake off the depression. I had been depending so much on that Farnsley piece—not only for money, which I desperately needed, but for the opportunity to do other pieces I had hoped it might afford me. The thought of giving up my crazy desire to write did not occur to me, but I cannot recall a single time before or since when I was more depressed—except possibly the time when the insufferable, incompetent Hunter got me fired off the newspaper.

On Monday I went uptown to see editors and to look for work. This is one of the most important activities in the free-lance writer's life. He must visit editors continually to find out what they are looking for. Even if he has an agent, he must do it; agents seldom have the time to keep abreast of all the markets. For this reason, most of the successful magazine writers live in or fairly near New York—or, if they live elsewhere, they make it their business to visit New York three, four or five times a year. The outsiders still are at a disadvantage. All but six or seven of the big magazines are published in New York, and the New York editors find it much easier to call upon a man they can reach readily than to send to some other state for him. In 1952 I moved back to Pennsylvania because I decided that I had become successful enough to work from there; I would go into New York, I vowed, only when it was absolutely necessary. Immediately, I found that I was getting less work than before. When I moved back to New York in 1954, my income doubled. The actual personal contact with editors does not have much to do with this state of affairs; nor does "salesmanship." I have never known an editor who bought a manuscript out of friendship. An editor friend of mine, Arnold Ehrlich, once said to another friend, "Dick knows how to sell himself." It was a nonsensical statement, as Ehrlich today would admit. One of the most active writers I know has one of the most repellent personalities I ever have encountered. He hasn't the slightest notion of how to sell himself, and would become enraged if anyone happened to hint that he does. It is availability and, of course, reliability, that makes it advisable for a writer to live near his markets. This does not mean that it is impossible for a writer living in another part of the country to earn a living as a free-lance. There are several who live outside New York who are among the top men in the field—Frank J. Taylor, Cameron Shipp and Dean Jennings in California come to mind, and Booton Herndon in Charlottesville, Virginia, Joseph Millard in Sarasota, Florida, and Frank X. Tolbert in Texas. But in the beginning it is almost imperative for the young writer to spend some time within striking distance of his sources of income.

So, on that dismal Monday—it was a cliché Monday, cloudy and grey—I made the rounds. I went to see Bernie Glaser at *Coronet*, who was cordial but whose requirements at that moment were the sort of articles (medical and inspirational) I did not feel qualified to do. There was nothing doing at *True*; I could not even get in to see Bill Williams. At *This Week*, Brooks Roberts said the magazine was overbought—"But keep sending us ideas," he said, pleasantly. At *Theatre Arts*, Sally Deutsch did give me a profile to write—but that magazine paid only $75 and usually was in such straitened circumstances one was lucky to get paid at all. Besides, its standards were so high that doing a piece for it usually demanded at least two weeks of research spread out over three or four months.

I took the subway back to the Village and let myself into my house. On the third floor, Alpert was banging away as usual; I thought of the many disappointments he had had, and of the other writers I knew who were struggling along and apparently not getting anywhere. I got up and drank what was left in a bottle we'd bought over the weekend, and then I went down the street to the Minnetta Tavern and spent the last six dollars I had.

At ten the next morning I awoke with such a hangover that it was some time before I realized that the ringing in my ears actually was the telephone. My first impulse was to let it ring, but after two or three minutes I got out of bed and answered it.

"Gehman?" a rough, scowling voice said.

"This is Gehman."

"This is Louis Ruppel, *Collier's*. I want to see you right away. Get up here soon as you can, willya?"

He slammed down the receiver. I sat there, trembling—and not from my hangover, which was awful. Then I got myself together as best I could, had a long shower, took three aspirins and two Alka-Seltzers, drank a pot of coffee, and went upstairs to borrow some money from Hollis to get up to the *Collier's* office.

"What's happening?" Hollis asked.

"The new guy at *Collier's* just called me."

I realized that I could not imagine what he did want. It occurred to me that he might have read the piece and wanted changes; that he might be taking it was too remote a dream even to consider.

"I don't know what's happening," I said to Hollis.

"Good luck," Hollis said.

As I was leaving the house, the telephone rang again. It was Oscar Dystel. "Louis Ruppel wants to see you," he said. "Stop in my office, and I'll take you in."

I took a cab to *Collier's* and gave my name to the receptionist. My head still ached and my hands were moist. In Dystel's office, I could scarcely sit still.

"What does he want?" I asked.

"I don't know," he said. "He just asked me for your telephone number and told me to bring you in as soon as you got here."

"Is—is it about the Louisville piece?"

"I don't know. Come on, let's go in."

Somehow I kept my knees straight. Ruppel was sitting at his desk, his head bent over a manuscript. He was scowling fiercely, shaking his head and cursing: "Sons of bitches, god*damn* sons of bitch-bastards." He did not look up. Dystel motioned me to a chair and I sat down gingerly. I had a chance, then, to size up the man. He was about six feet one and weighed around two hundred. He walked with a limp left over from a wound he'd picked up while serving with the Marines in World War II (he had gone in as a private and had become a captain). His face sometimes resembled that of an angry owl and sometimes that of a dyspeptic bullfrog—he had sharp, indignant eyes behind horn-rimmed spectacles, and a wide mouth. His hands were huge; he held his blue pencil in one fist and wrote in slashing, careless scrawls. His voice was harsh and sometimes rose to an even harsher whine: "Jeeeeesus Keeeeerist!" When he laughed, which he did almost as often as he scowled, he threw back his head and gave himself over to his delight. He was testy, guarded, and fiercely belligerent, but he was also warm and affectionate and unashamedly sentimental. If he liked you, he loved you; if he decided he did not like you, he did not hold a grudge—he simply wanted nothing further to do with you. "At all," he would say. "*Ever.*" He was, in many respects, a boy—but he was above everything a man, with lusty, demanding appetites and a charging, marauding vitality. While I sat watching him I found, to my surprise, that my timidity was vanishing. I don't know what there was about him—perhaps he made me think of Jack Martin, for they were alike in some ways—but whatever it was, I decided that I liked him and that we would get along. For I knew, from a subtle change I had detected in Dystel's manner, that what was going to happen was something good. Before, Oscar always had been pleasant enough, but now he was treating me almost with respect.

Ruppel jerked his head up violently (nearly all his movements were violent). "*Yeah?*"

"This is Richard Gehman," Dystel said.

He stood up, lunged around from behind his desk, and stretched out one long arm. "Hi. Ruppel. Nice to see ya." Then he stood back and put his hands on his hips and looked at me. I am five feet, eight; he towered over me. I stared back at him and said, in as strong a voice as I could evoke, "Nice to meet you." I had decided that I would not show my timidity no matter what happened.

"You a free-lance? Where you been working?"

Before I could answer, Oscar said, "He's been doing humor pieces for Gurney, Louis."

I started to tell him that Walter Ross had sent me to Louisville, but hastily decided that I might antagonize him by mentioning Ross' name.

"Good," Louis said, without waiting for me to answer. He went back behind his desk and sat down.

"We need good writers here," he said. "We got plans for this magazine. Who'd you vote for last?"

"Roosevelt."

"Good." He stared at me, as though trying to make up his mind about me. Suddenly he said, "You know this guy Boontch?"

I could not imagine who he meant.

"The man who negotiated the truce between the Arabs and the Jews," Oscar Dystel said, quickly.

I had, right then, only the vaguest notion of who Ralph Bunche was; from the time Ross had sent me to Louisville, through the writing of the Farnsley story, through my period of despair, I scarcely had looked at a newspaper. "I know of him," I said.

"He's comin' back," Ruppel said. "He gets in tomorrow by boat. I want you to go out on the cutter with the reporters and get to see him and tell him we want to print his story. You'll write it. By him as told to you. Now, he's gonna want to get paid. Try to get him for twenty thousand."

"We can get him for less than that, Louis," Dystel said.

"You shut up," Ruppel said, glaring. "Go higher if you have to," he said to me. "But get to him before anybody else does. Everybody's going to be after the son of a bitch. *You* get him, understand? I don't care how you do it. We want to run his story. Think of it! A colored guy goes over there and makes the Jews and Arabs sign that thing. What a story!" He began to pace. "And look: we got to have it right away. In a week if we can get it, understand?"

My spirits were surging. No magazine editor I had known ever had talked like this; this man was like a newspaper editor. He reminded me of tough, impatient old Earl Keyser in Lancaster. I was so excited I could not speak.

"Well?" he shouted. "You think I got all morning to stand here gassin'?"

I said, "What I was wondering was, what about the piece I did about the Mayor of Louisville?"

"What piece?" He looked blank. "Oh. Oh, *that*. Hell—we bought that yesterday. Now get out. Go draw some money if you need it. Let me know what happens with Boontch."

That was the beginning of our association. During the next two years, I worked for Louis twenty-four times. Twice I had two stories in the same issue, one under my own name and one under the name Martin Scott.

As it turned out, Ralph Bunche was unwilling to permit me to do an as-told-to piece. Unlike many people in public life, he did not want to sign an article that was not entirely his own. He said that eventually he planned to write a kind of autobiography, and he wanted to hold his own impressions of the peace settlement for that. I reported this reaction to Ruppel.

"Oh," he said, chewing his lip. "How much did you offer him?"

"I went to twenty-five thousand."

"I told you to go to twenty," he roared.

"You told me you wanted the story," I said, fearing he would throw me out of the office.

He nodded. "You done right. O.K. So can we get a straight piece about him?"

"He said I could follow him around for a couple of days—he said he would give me all the help he could."

"O.K. Well, what are you waitin' for? Get busy."

I trailed Bunche for four days. Each time he had a spare minute at his United Nations office, I slipped in and fired questions. Early each morning I went out to his house in Queens and waited for him to finish breakfast; then I would ride to the office with him and listen to him talk on the way. When he was tied up, I went around interviewing people at the U.N. who knew him, and I also did considerable talking to reporters who had been at the peace talks. I spent several hours with his secretary and several more with his wife. I wrote his grandmother, who had brought him up, and got in touch with people who had been friends of his long before he had become famous.

One day A. M. Rosenthal, of the *New York Times*, told me that there had been a report that Bunche was being considered for the post of Undersecretary of State in charge of Middle Eastern Affairs. That evening, riding home with Bunche, I asked if it were true.

"It's been mentioned," he said. "But I wouldn't consider it—I wouldn't live in Jim Crow Washington again. I wouldn't let my kids live there."

My voice shaking with excitement, I said, "Will you let me print that?"

"I'll give you a better statement than that," he said, and proceeded to elaborate on his reasons for deciding never to live in the nation's capital again.

It was all I could do to contain myself until I got home and wrote it down. Next morning I streaked into Ruppel's office and threw the paragraphs on his desk.

"Jeeeeesus Keeeeerist!" he cried. "Dystel! Denson! Get in here!" he banged the glass top of his desk. "Will he let us print this?"

"He said he would."

"I'm givin' you a bonus!" he shouted. "Denson!"

I was floating as I took the subway to the United Nations building, which was then at Lake Success, Long Island. My future was assured. Ruppel liked nothing better than a sensational story, and I had produced one for him first time out.

In Bunche's outer office, my spirits sank as quickly as they had risen. His secretary said, "Dr. Bunche wants to talk to you right away. You can't go in—he's in conference—but he'll speak to you on the telephone."

Bunche said, "I've been thinking over that statement I gave you—the one about Washington. There are several changes I must make. My secretary will give them to you at noon."

I passed the morning in the U.N. correspondents' bar, grimly reflecting that I had had the shortest magazine article-writing career in history. Bunche was backing down; he had thought better of his statement and would now give me something guaranteed to offend nobody.

Nobody, I thought, but Louis Ruppel. He would be livid with rage—not at Bunche, but at me. He would throw me out. I would never work for *Collier's* again. At noon I dragged my feet through the molehill corridors of the jerry-built structure to Bunche's office. His secretary ushered me in. Bunche, good-tempered and cordial as usual, handed me a typed statement. As I read it, my heart began to pound.

"Is it all right?" Bunche asked.

I broke into an hysterical laugh. It was phrased in stronger language than he had used the night before. If Ruppel had been excited about the first, he would go out of his mind over this. Then a thought occurred to me.

"Doctor," I said, "we'll print this exactly as you've written it. But may I ask a favor?"

"Certainly."

"In case no reporter asks you about the Washington job until this story comes out, which will be in about six weeks—just don't say anything about it, will you?"

His eyebrows went up. Then he understood. He grinned. "If nobody asks me any questions, naturally I won't volunteer any information."

We shook hands. My sensational beat was all but secured. But there was one thing more that had to be done. I went and had a drink with A. M. Rosenthal.

"Did you ask him about the report out of Washington?" he asked.

I nodded.

"Well, what'd he say?"

Feeling like Sammy Glick in Budd Schulberg's novel, I said, "He hasn't been approached directly. He knows he's been mentioned for the Middle East job, but no official overtures have been made."

"Will he take it? I mean, if it's offered?"

"No." I could not look at Rosenthal; I stared hard at the drink in front of me.

"Why not?"

"For personal reasons," I said.

"Well," Rosenthal said, "no story there, I guess."

I said nothing. All I could do was hope that neither he nor anybody else would happen to ask Bunche about the job. I sweated that one out for six weeks—but, thanks to the appalling lack of curiosity of the American press, nobody thought to check the Washington report, or, having checked, to ask Bunche why he would turn down the offer. When finally *Collier's* did publish the story that follows, it was a clean news beat. It made headlines all over the country.

ARTICLE: "RALPH BUNCHE, AMERICAN PEACEMAKER"

(From *Collier's*)

Ralph Johnson Bunche, a soft-voiced, patient, apparently indefatigable ex-college professor of forty-four, easily ranks among the top half dozen diplomats in America and possibly in the world. As the first United States Negro ever to become a leader in international affairs, he is a living demonstration that the processes of democracy can and do work. At the same time, he is a living challenge to democracy to work better.

Dr. Bunche's performance as Acting Mediator for the U.N. in the recent peace mission to Palestine was the climax to a career that reads like a present-day parallel to Booker T. Washington's famous Up from Slavery. His grandmother, who raised him from the age of ten, was born in bondage. He took menial jobs to work his way through public schools and college, and ultimately won his Ph.D. at Harvard.

Today he is recognized as one of the foremost authorities on colonial peoples and their problems; his work in O.S.S. aided in preparing for the successful invasion of North Africa in World War II, and he drafted much of the three chapters on trusteeship and colonies in the U.N. Charter. He won this year's American Association for the United Nations award, was cited by the One World Award Committee, and has been mentioned in newspapers as a candidate for the Nobel peace prize. Few Amcricans of any complexion can boast a similar record of scholarship and statesmanship.

Despite his distinguished background Dr. Bunche has lived constantly in the shadow of Jim Crow. Time and again he has been refused service in or admittance to restaurants, not only in Southern cities, but in Los Angeles (his adopted home town), Seattle and Washington, D.C.

Bigotry like this might conceivably someday deprive the nation of the full potentiality of his proven diplomatic abilities.

Soon after returning from Palestine last April, Dr. Bunche was mentioned by a State Department official as a likely appointee for a newly created job: Assistant Secretary of State for Near Eastern and African Affairs. When questioned, he told friends that he knew nothing more about this than what he read in the papers, but added that in any event he was not inclined to return to government service in Washington—in part, at least, because of his unwillingness to re-expose his family to anti-Negro conditions there.

The doctor clarified his position recently while relaxing on a couch in his small apartment in Parkway Village, the U.N. housing project on Long Island, New York, to which he and his family moved from Washington nearly two years ago.

"Frankly," he said, "there's too much Jim Crow in Washington for me—I wouldn't take my kids back there." (His two daughters, Joan, seventeen, and Jane, fifteen, attend a Friends school in Westtown, Pennsylvania; Ralph, Jr., five, goes to kindergarten at Lake Success.)

Dr. Bunche paused to light a cigarette. He is a chain smoker, usually getting through as many as three packs a day.

"I built a house in Washington while I was teaching at Howard," he continued, expelling smoke slowly. "It was in a section of the city in which the whites predominated at that time. The architect and the builders and I spent 18 months going over plans and putting it up. When we moved in, my daughters had to go three miles to school and I had to hire a driver to take them—even though there was a school for white kids just around the corner."

He paused. "When I was in the State Department, representatives of other governments, who knew nothing about race prejudice, would sometimes call me up and ask me to meet them at the Mayflower or the Wardman Park or some other place for lunch or cocktails, to talk over some business matter. My Negro friends and I had been refused service in many Washington public places so many times that I never knew what to expect—never knew whether to accept or decline.

"One time a foreign friend who was living at one of the better hotels was giving a dinner party and wanted to ask me. He asked the management if they would object to my presence. They said yes, even though my friend specified that I was a State Department man, as though that should have made some difference."

Dr. Bunche was the first Negro to hold a desk job in the State Department, which allegedly always has been off limits to minorities. If invisible barriers did exist, and they were lowered for him, he has no idea why; and he adds that his color, to his knowledge, never caused any incidents within the department. "If there were any doubters, I guess they must have decided that the government wasn't going to collapse, after all," he remarked.

Dr. Bunche crushed out his cigarette and lighted a fresh one. "Improving race relations is a long slow process," he continued. "One time Todd Duncan—I'd known him while he was at Howard—wrote me that he was coming to the National Theatre in the leading role of Porgy and Bess. Todd knew that the National was a Jim Crow house, and he was disturbed at the prospect of playing in his home town in a theater where his friends couldn't come to see him. He asked if there weren't something that we could do about it.

"I got together a committee from the teachers' union and we went down to see the manager. At first he was very tough—said it wasn't a personal policy, it was economic: White patrons wouldn't come if Negroes were admitted.

"He tried to pacify our committee by offering us complimentary tickets—said we could come 'to represent the community.' We didn't like that, either, so we threatened him. I was a representative in the Central Labor Union then, and I told him I could get a good many pickets out when Todd came to town. He finally agreed to change the policy for that one production; but just for that one. As soon as Porgy left, Jim Crow came back in."

Dr. Bunche leaned forward, his dark eyes intensely serious. "I have lived and worked in Washington for almost a score of years," he said. "Living in the nation's capital is like serving out a sentence for any Negro who detests segregation and discrimination as I do—and I know of few, if any, Negroes who don't.

"It's extremely difficult for a Negro to maintain even a semblance of human dignity in Washington.

"At every turn, he's confronted with places he can't enter because of his color—schools, hospitals, hotels, restaurants, theaters, bars, lunch counters and rest rooms, not to mention widespread job barriers."

The doctor paused for a moment, reflectively. Then he continued, "Washington isn't unique in this regard, of course—but after all, it is the nation's capital, and its racial practices have a great symbolic significance. The irony of it is that since the national government is there, the opportunities for effective attack on racial practices throughout the nation could be greatest there.

"For my part," Dr. Bunche asserted, "I have no desire to go back there—although admittedly, in a particular situation in the future, a sense of duty might be overriding."

Luckily for the cause of world peace, Jim Crow never edged his way into the Hotel des Roses at Rhodes, where Dr. Bunche and his staff received the delegates from Israel and the Arab states. Although the doctor's contingent of more than 700 people (Secretariat personnel and military observers) included a good many American Southerners, none seemed to object to serving under a Negro.

Soon after the first armistice in February, Colonel Mohammed Ibrahim Seif El-Dine, of Egypt, called Dr. Bunche "one of the greatest men in the world"; Dr. Walter Eytan, of Israel, said that the mediator's efforts had been superhuman. With characteristic modesty, Dr. Bunche gave full credit to the desire of both delegations for peace, and to the untiring efforts of his U. N. co-workers.

In response to this, one colleague declared, "The whole mission was a one-man operation. There were many times when most of us despaired of ever reaching a settlement. Ralph never despaired—or, if he did, he never showed it. He, and he alone, drove on to a successful conclusion."

At Rhodes, the Acting Mediator set a fantastic pace. An ever-present cigarette drooping from his lips, a sheaf of papers in one hand and a pen in the other, he often remained at his desk for a full 48 hours. Ordinarily he sleeps only five hours a night; at Rhodes he averaged three. A man who loves to eat—he weighs over 200 pounds—he often went without food for many hours. Even when negotiations seemed hopelessly stymied or about to break down, the doctor kept cool. Once an impatient Israeli delegate hurled a lead pencil across the table. It happened to hit the leader of the other delegation. Dr. Bunche reprimanded the Israeli in private, and insisted that he apologize, which he did.

Another time, the head of an Arab delegation refused to shake hands upon being introduced to the Israeli leader. Dr. Bunche rushed the meeting to a conclusion and then took the Arab aside.

"Look here," he said, "this is pretty serious. The Israelis have just said they're going back to Tel Aviv tomorrow to find out from their government if they should continue with the negotiations or not. If the proceedings are broken off just because you've failed to observe the minimum rules of courtesy, it's going to be your personal responsibility."

The Arab explained that he originally had been willing to shake hands, but that just before the meeting his delegation had voted against it. Nevertheless, he said he would meet the Israeli delegate in the doctor's hotel room that night. He was the first to arrive at the rendezvous. When the Israeli appeared, the Arab rose and shook not one of his hands but both.

"This time," the doctor recalled, "they acted like long-lost brothers. Pretty soon they started to speak Arabic—and then they apologized to me because they knew I didn't speak the language. I said, 'Hell, speak your Arabic—don't bother about me.' "

Dr. Bunche's negotiating tactics may well be recorded someday as a masterwork in the practical application of psychology. At the outset he was in a difficult position. The truce in Palestine was one of the first orders of its kind that the U.N. had directed to warring nations, and the world was waiting anxiously to see if it would hold. The doctor behaved as though he were completely unaware of this; he conducted the meetings, one of his staff later commented, as though he had been doing it all his life. "I never once saw him lose his temper," Mrs. Doreen Daughton, the doctor's secretary, said. "Whenever things got bad, he simply took a few minutes off and went down and played billiards. Then he came back and got to work again."

Of his method of negotiating, Dr. Bunche says, "We made the rules up as we went along." But in retrospect his procedure sounds immensely complicated. When each delegation arrived he would speak to the leading members separately in order to determine what kind of agenda he might draw up.

After this, he would call the first joint meeting, for the purpose of approving the agenda and signing a cease-fire agreement. "There was a double purpose in this," he later explained. "Primarily, it was to get both sides to meet—but also, I wanted them both to get accustomed to taking formal action, and to signing something. That way, I figured, the next step might not be so difficult."

The doctor soon found out that every step was difficult. Both sides at the beginning were always frigidly polite—not exactly hostile, but extremely reserved. No point in any agreement was ever signed immediately upon presentation.

"Whenever they got together," Dr. Bunche said, "you'd always find that there was still a gap between them. It was always a matter of timing, always a matter of finding out when it would be appropriate to reduce a discussion to a formal, written draft on one point. We never would throw a whole draft at them at the beginning—that would've scared them to death.

"Finally, after we had gone pretty far along, we'd give them the first draft of a complete agreement. That had to be modified over and over. It was just that you had to talk everything out with them beforehand, separately and together—a matter of their going back to consult with their governments, of compromises and more compromises."

Another of Dr. Bunche's strategic moves was to have the delegations formally elect him chairman of the mediation meetings. He would then use his position as his trump card. "Sometimes, when they reached an impasse, they'd ask me to prepare a compromise, which I did," he said. "If that didn't work, I would say to them, 'Well, I think this is a reasonable basis. If the negotiations fail because X side refuses to accept this compromise, X side will have to take the responsibility for this failure in the United Nations.' "

The doctor smiled in recollection. "It was pretty touchy sometimes—there was a crisis every day. Every time you blew your nose over there you'd offend somebody."

After 42 days of haggling, bickering and hairsplitting on a high diplomatic level, the Egyptians and Israelis signed their armistice last February 24th. Four days later the Trans-Jordan delegates arrived to negotiate with a new contingent of Israelis. Difficulty arose immediately. The members of the two delegations remained singularly aloof for the first five days. When Dr. Bunche finally brought them together he found them still cold. He shuttled back and forth between the two parties, compromising, browbeating. By March 11th he had achieved a formal cease-fire agreement, but he couldn't get them together to sign the armistice until April 3d. By then, the coldness had been melted by the force of his personality —melted to such an extent that the Trans-Jordan party invited the

Israelis to remain at Rhodes one more day for a party in celebration.

As though the delay in the Trans-Jordan meetings hadn't been enough, a similar incident occurred during the early days of the Syrian negotiations.

The Syrians were unwilling to come to Rhodes, and Dr. Bunche had arranged for their meeting the Israelis in no-man's land in Galilee. Occupied with other negotiations at Rhodes, the doctor sent his personal deputy, M. Henri Vigier, and his chief of staff, Brigadier General William E. Riley, to meet the two delegations in a trio of tents erected for the purpose. On the first day of formal proceedings a report came in that Israeli forces had crossed the border into Syrian territory. Negotiations were immediately suspended. Dr. Bunche flew to Beyrouth to appeal to the Syrians to hold off military action until he could talk to the Israelis. For 36 hours he begged and wheedled both sides by telephone, wire and personal visits. After two days the Israelis withdrew, and the doctor, wiping his brow, saw the no-man's land parleys swing into action once more.

The resolution of this incident was typical of Dr. Bunche's enormous restless energy. "He drove himself and his staff night and day," Bill Maschler, an administrative officer, said. The doctor's secretary was seldom able to go for a walk on Rhodes but that she was picked up by a jeepful of Marines, sent to bring her back to the doctor's office. One night she fainted from exhaustion, but was given brandy and propped up so that she could complete some urgent work.

If this makes the doctor sound like a stern taskmaster, members of his staff—even those who disagreed with him on points of policy—hasten to add that he never spared himself. "He plunged into every problem as though his life depended on getting it solved," one of the doctor's most severe critics says. "He has an uncanny ability for grasping a situation and sizing it up completely."

The details of the negotiations, step by step, can never be told. They are buried in the thousands of documents, drafts and counter-drafts, compromises and ultimatums, which were destroyed before the armistices were signed. Their effects linger, however, as circles under Dr. Bunche's eyes, as lines in his pleasant, earnest face, as tones in his soft, rather hoarse voice. At this writing, he is an exhausted man who has not had a leave from the government or from the U.N. since 1941.

Ironically enough, Dr. Bunche never intended to enter government service; still more ironically, he never planned to get into the Palestine fracas. He became mediator by accident—by accident and coincidence.

Last September 17th, on the Hill of Evil Counsel, along the upper Katamon road in Jerusalem, Count Folke Bernadotte, U.N. Mediator for Palestine, was returning in an automobile from Government House, which he had been inspecting as a possible headquarters for future activities. Suddenly, at a road block, the count's party was halted by an Israel army-type jeep painted cocoa brown, carrying five men.

One of them fired 20 blasts from a Sten gun. Colonel André Serot, a U.N. observer, was killed instantly. According to General Aage Lundstrom, then chief of staff, who was sitting in the rear with the count and Colonel Serot, he asked Bernadotte if he had been hit. The count nodded, and lost consciousness. He was dead on the car's arrival at a near-by hospital. Although the Israeli government promised full co-operation in tracking them down, the assassins got away and were never apprehended. All that has ever been learned of them is that they were members of the terrorist group known as the Stern Gang.

Fifteen or 20 minutes later, Dr. Bunche arrived at the place where the count's body had been taken. That he himself had escaped death was due to a series of uncanny delays. From time to time both he and Bernadotte had heard that terrorists were claiming: "We'll get No. 1 and No. 2." Colonel Serot's seat in the car at the time of the killing was the one that Dr. Bunche, as Bernadotte's right-hand man, had usually occupied. Some members of the party later said that they were certain that the terrorists had mistaken Colonel Serot, who was swarthy and rather stout, for Dr. Bunche.

The count and Dr. Bunche had planned originally to go to Jerusalem together. At the last minute, the doctor had to remain behind at Rhodes to complete a report. He prepared to leave to join the count the next morning, but the count's plane, which was to pick him up, was late. "That was the only time it ever developed any trouble," he told an acquaintance later.

There was another delay when he finally arrived at the Haifa airport. His secretary, Mrs. Daughton, who is a British subject, was held up by Israeli officials because of her British passport—the first time this had happened, too. The doctor was nearly three hours late when his party landed at Kolundia Field, near Jerusalem, for their meeting with the count. The party was detained once more at an Israeli sentry post in Jerusalem. Their names weren't on the approved list. Dr. Bunche produced his credentials, but to no avail. Finally he persuaded the officials to let him send to Bernadotte for help. While he and Mrs. Daughton and their party were waiting, a car came dashing up and an Israeli officer and some United Nations observers reported the assassination.

The death of the martyred Bernadotte was a crushing personal blow to Dr. Bunche. On its heels came the realization that he was now solely responsible for peace in Palestine. That night the Secretary-General of the U.N. ordered him to assume the post of Acting Mediator, and this action was confirmed the next day by an emergency session of the Security Council in Paris. He later told friends that he never paused to consider the extreme gravity of his assignment: "There was too much work to do."

Apparently he also never considered the element of personal danger. Immediately he began receiving notes like this: "You'll get what Bernadotte got." On one occasion a letter, from an ardent Zionist, read:

Dr. Ralph J. Bunche
United Nations Acting Mediator for Palestine
Sir:

Drop dead.

Your obedient servant,

Dr. Bunche and his party continued to move freely through the battle zones. Sniper fire was everywhere; he may have been shot at several times. "There were always bullets whizzing around," he said. "I guess it just wasn't my time to go."

He and his staff experienced air raids in Tel Aviv, Damascus and Amman. In Jerusalem they sometimes sat on the Y.M.C.A. veranda in the evenings and watched the Arabs and Jews taking pot shots at one another from the Old Wall and from entrenched positions in houses. His party was not armed. Dr. Bunche wore a U.N. arm band and his car displayed a blue U.N. flag; later he added a white one as well because the U.N. emblem looked too much like the Israeli flag at a distance. "The only safe credentials we had in no-man's land," he said later, "were the accelerators of our cars."

Including Colonel Serot and Count Bernadotte, the mission lost ten men.

Dr. Bunche's disregard for personal safety and his phenomenal drive are only two sides of a personality that often has puzzled even those who have observed him closely for long periods.

In one sense, the doctor's whole career has been paradoxical. Although he disclaims personal ambition, he has achieved virtually everything he has aimed for thus far; he always has plotted his career with great care. Yet even his opponents agree that he has no political aspirations.

Dr. Bunche's direct, purposeful manner is illustrated by his courtship. He met his wife in Washington in 1929. "He came in with some other fellows to meet some girls who had gathered at my place," Mrs. Bunche recalled. "We were all going to a party. I was sitting by the piano, and when it was time to go, he pointed at me and said, 'I'd like to take the one on the bench.' "

At that time the future Mrs. Bunche was teaching in a Washington elementary school, at $2,200 a year. Young Ralph, a fledgling instructor at Howard, was earning only $1,500. The difference didn't bother him. The Bunches were married in 1930 and spent their honeymoon at Harvard, where the doctor had begun his graduate studies.

Ralph Johnson Bunche was born in Detroit on August 7, 1904; his parents were Fred and Olive Agnes Bunche, one a barber, the other a musician. When the boy was about ten the family moved to New Mexico for the sake of his mother's health. When she died soon after, he went to live with Mrs. Lucy Johnson, his maternal grandmother. His father died when he was twelve.

Dr. Bunche has said repeatedly that Lucy Johnson was the strongest-minded woman he has ever known. Physically she was quite frail, weighing only a little over 100 pounds. A widow at thirty-five—her husband had been a schoolteacher in Indian territory—she not only provided for her own five children, but also took care of her grandson and his little sister, Grace, at her home in Los Angeles.

With his grandmother's encouragement, young Ralph earned excellent marks in school. He also found time to help out with the family income, by carrying papers and later working as messenger boy, carpetlayer and janitor. In high school, young Bunche played basketball and baseball and was on the football and track teams. In 1922, while out for spring football practice, he somehow got the tip of a grain stalk in his ear. This caused two mastoid operations, leaving him deaf on the left side. A blood clot that settled in his left leg was another result of the operation. Although the leg has given him trouble ever since, in college he was a star guard on a basketball team that captured the Southern California Conference title for three consecutive years.

The real nature of the problems facing the American Negro was brought home to him following his high-school graduation exercises, at which he was valedictorian. After the ceremony the principal shook his hand and said he hated to see him leave. "I've never thought of you as a Negro," he added.

"He meant that in a friendly spirit," says Dr. Bunche, "but it made me realize how deep-rooted and unconscious prejudice can be."

The incident may have been a factor in his decision to devote his life to studying and aiding colonial peoples. He literally breezed through the University of California at Los Angeles, where he majored in political science, and maintained an A-minus average all the way. He went there on a scholarship, the first in a long series that enabled him to obtain his entire education without paying a cent for tuition.

"Ralph always wanted to excel in everything he did," his aunt, Miss Nellie Johnson, has written. "If he had one outstanding characteristic as a boy, it was self-confidence. I remember one time that he was with his grandmother on the occasion that Oscar De Priest, a Negro congressman from Chicago, visited Los Angeles.

"A large delegation was waiting at the train to welcome Mr. De Priest, and Ralph said laughingly, 'Well, Nana, you can't tell—perhaps someday they'll meet me with a brass band.'" (This may well be the cast if the doctor ever decides to go back to Los Angeles. Both the city and the state of California have passed resolutions commending him for his service to the nation.)

Dr. Bunche graduated *summa cum laude* in 1927, and from

that point on he skyrocketed in the academic world. The following year he took his M.A. at Harvard, still in political science, despite the advice of older friends who thought he should concentrate on becoming a lawyer, doctor or minister. He joined the teaching staff at Howard in 1928, became assistant to the president in 1931, and finally became full professor in 1936. He has been on leave from the university since 1941. Meanwhile he went on with his studies. He earned his Ph.D. at Harvard in 1934 and later studied at Northwestern, the London School of Economics and the University of Cape Town in South Africa. He was granted the Ozias Goodwin Memorial Followship at Harvard, a Rosenwald Field Fellowship; and the Social Science Research Council post-doctoral fellowship; his Ph.D. thesis won him the Toppan prize as the best essay in social sciences.

He was never simply a book student. He spent all the time he could traveling and observing firsthand. He lived in Africa for long periods with natives, and once traveled around the world. One African tribe made him an honorary chief.

In 1941, when Gunnar Myrdal, the Swedish sociologist, began work on his book, *An American Dilemma,* a monumental study of the American Negro, he chose Dr. Bunche as one of his assistants. Together they made extended field trips in the South, and they were chased out of three towns for asking too many questions. In the course of this work he prepared more than 3,300 pages of manuscript material which was later worked into Myrdal's book.

When World War II came, Dr. Bunche was tapped by General Bill Donovan to head the O.S.S. African section. (His deafness and bad leg kept him out of active military service.) Donovan later remarked, "Why, the man's a walking colonial institute." This reached the State Department, and in 1944, Dr. Bunche was made associate chief of the Division of Dependent Territories. He attended the San Francisco Conference to draft the U.N. Charter as an adviser to Commander Harold Stassen, and there his work came to the attention of Dr. Victor Hoo, of China.

"He was the fastest draftsman I'd ever seen," Dr. Hoo said. "He would listen to a discussion, no matter how complicated, and right away he would make a draft of it—adding his own ideas, which were always good."

When Dr. Hoo became head of the U.N. Department of Trusteeship and Non Self-Governing Territories he offered Dr. Bunche the post of director of the trusteeship division, which he accepted. Later, when Dr. Hoo went to the Holy Land as a member of the U.N. Special Committee on Palestine, he took Dr. Bunche along. The latter's ability in draftsmanship never served him better. He worked on both the majority and minority reports.

This experience in Palestine led to his being appointed head of the Secretariat when Count Bernadotte was named Mediator. Dr. Bunche flew to join the count in May, 1948, on two hours' notice. From that point on, he never let up in his efforts to assist in making peace between the Israelis and the Arabs. At times he was criticized harshly by both sides—but, as the negotiations went on, those who came to scoff remained to praise.

Dr. Bunche came home from Rhodes determined to get a little peace and quiet, and to get reacquainted with his family. Before he had been back a week his desk was littered with more than 150 requests for lecture engagements. He was offered several first-rate posts with leading universities. He appeared on the radio five times in three days, and reporters from magazines and newspapers dogged him constantly. The only comment he would make on future plans was that he wanted to live, for a while, "in a state of complete anarchy," with his wife and children; and that ultimately he wanted to get back to teaching, his profession and first love.

In the course of the interviews he granted, the question of what makes Dr. Bunche go came up time and again. Inadvertently, perhaps, he supplied a clue to the answer. At that time Paul Robeson, the singer, was sounding off in Paris at the World Congress of the Partisans of Peace—a meeting attended widely by Communists and fellow travelers. Among other things, Robeson declared that American Negroes would never fight the Soviet Union—that they would never go to war for the United States, where they had been oppressed, against a country in which they had been elevated.

This struck many people as incongruous. Here were two of America's foremost Negroes, both in the headlines at the same time, both having risen to eminence the hard way, both having had experiences with Jim Crow custom—and yet they were as far apart as democracy and Communism.

Dr. Bunche was asked what he thought of Robeson's statement. "Paul should stick to singing," he said quietly. "I've known Paul since 1927. He's had some very unpleasant experiences here, as all of us have had. He's resentful of the injustices, as all of us are. I know that when he went to Russia he was very well received, and that may have influenced him to follow the party line.

"He's entitled to his opinions, of course, but I think he's radically wrong. His statements represent the attitude of very few Negroes indeed."

Speaking soberly, now and again rubbing his broad jaw with one thumb, Dr. Bunche continued, "The American Negro is an American citizen. Except for his racial problem, his reactions are the same as those of any other citizen. That's equally true of his patriotism.

"The Negro is a better American than most when he insists on the realization for all Americans of the ideals as set forth in the Constitution. Because he believes in these things, he would certainly fight to protect the country and its ideals. He's always done so, and I think he always will.

"But it's the responsibility of the Negro—and of every citizen, regardless of color—to keep insisting on the privilege of enjoying his birthright which is equality of treatment and opportunity.

"With very few exceptions, the Negro has no separatist or nationalist aspirations. His struggle hasn't been for a state or for a separate existence, but to become a full and first-class American. This has been denied him; his birthright has been denied him; and violence has been done to the Constitution.

"In my opinion, the first objective of the Negro is full integration into the main stream of American life. Every Negro is involved in the struggle—and the extent to which the Negro can find the fullest place for himself as an American is his contribution to the struggle."

There is no question that Ralph Johnson Bunche has found his fullest place; that he has contributed to the struggle; and that his efforts have brought all Americans, of all colors, closer to integration in democracy.

Post Script: Louis Ruppel died suddenly of a complication of ailments in 1957, just as he was about to quit the job he was then holding—he was an associate editor at *The American Weekly*—to write his autobiography. He was fifty-four. He was going to call his book *Never Marry a Newspaperman,* a title with which his wife would have disagreed. It's too bad that he never got to do it, for it would have been a wonderfully individualistic book, as everything he did was. It would have been full of sweeping, pugnacious statements, grammar that would just get by (and would get by only because he shouted down the copy editor), great stories about newspapermen he had known, implacable opinions, and warm tributes to old friends and enemies. When Louis hated, he hated as a boxer does—with a respect for his antagonist that bordered on love. He loved the same way; he could become almost apoplectic with anger toward his closest friends. It is hard to believe that he is dead. Every once in a while I half-expect the telephone to ring and to hear that bellow. He and I did not speak for nearly two years after we had a dispute that led him to stop publishing me in *Collier's,* but in 1953, when he went to Philadelphia as editor of the *Daily News,* our friendship was resumed. From that point on we saw each other all the time; he came to my house frequently —for the sole purpose, I sometimes thought, of keeping my other friends stirred up. Louis loved to set up people against each other and to hear them fight over some political or personal matter. He thought that argument was a strop for the wits, and he was impatient with anyone who was not sharp as a razor at all times.

Louis never stayed long in one job, and he always left because staying would have damaged his principles. Born in New York, he started his career on the *Daily News* and eventually became its Albany correspondent. In Albany he became acquainted with Franklin D. Roosevelt, then governor, and he remained a Roosevelt Democrat for the rest of his life—although not one who would blindly support any man because he happened to be for Roosevelt. Occasionally he supported Republicans he admired. In 1935 he went to Chicago to become managing editor of the *Times.* In three years he doubled the dying newspaper's circulation, and when he left in 1938 it was selling at the rate of 400,000 copies per day. He did it by exposing corruption and fighting prejudice and bigotry wherever he smelled them. That was the way he ran his jobs, and that was why he invariably got into trouble. Someone on the side of management would ask him to soft-pedal his policies or pull his punches, Louis would tell management to go to hell, and if he was bothered further, he would resign. He went from job to job; I cannot begin to set down all the jobs he had. Whenever he went into a new job he would send for the men he knew were reliable—first, usually, for John Denson, who was as quiet and mannerly as Louis was noisy and rude. Denson became managing editor of *Collier's* when Louis was called by Crowell-Collier in an attempt to rescue the magazine for its stockholders. Denson was the only man Louis trusted completely, I am sure (although he greatly respected the judgment of John Lear, his articles editor). The two men were so close they seldon had much discussion of the directions their policies would take. Sometimes this led to utter confusion. Once, as I was taking off for Chicago to do a story about a restaurant, Louis said to me, "While you're out there, you might look into that lawyer who got the guy out of jail." This was the celebrated case of false imprisonment that later became the motion picture *Call Northside 777*.

In Chicago I ran into Merle Miller. "What are you doing?" he asked.

I told him.

"That's funny," he said, "I'm doing a piece on that lawyer myself—that's what I'm here for."

"Who're you writing it for?"

"*Collier's*," he said.

We finally learned that Denson had assigned him the piece first and that Ruppel had forgotten that. What was even worse, Ruppel had forgotten that he had told me to investigate the story. Two nights later we ran into Irv Kupcinet, the columnist, who told us he'd just had a letter from Louis asking *him* to look into the story.

"It looks to me as though they're going to put out a whole anthology of pieces about this man," Merle said.

Such incidents were rare. Louis seldom missed a trick. He had an old reporter's memory and an unerring sense of detail. Once he sent me out to Kelly's Island, Ohio, to do a story about old Gus Sun, the vaudeville impresario who was known a half-century ago as The Daddy of Small Time Vaudeville. Mr. Sun, in retirement, was still spry and cheerful; he was eighty-three, I recall, but he drank a good stiff shot or two before every meal and had an appreciative eye for girls. I loved him. I stayed much longer on the story than I should have, for he had an inexhaustible stock of anecdotes. When I got back I went in to see Lear and told him I thought the piece would work out better as a two-parter. "No, write it in one," he said. "We're too busy with these exposés of Louis' to devote that much space to an entertainment piece." I wrote it and handed it in a week later. A day after that, Lear called me.

"Louis wants more work on the story," he said.

"How comc?"

"I don't know, exactly. He says his father knew Gus Sun, and this isn't the way his father described him."

"But I'm not Louis' father," I said, indignantly.

"Maybe you'd better go see him," Lear said.

I went in. "Lousy piece," Louis growled.

"What's the matter with it?"

"I don't know. It just doesn't sound like the old Gus Sun my old man knew." He scowled. "He used to tell such great stories about the old man—maybe that's it. You need more warmth in there. You ought to give him the feeling of being one of the grand old men of the theatre."

I went home and attacked the piece. It seemed to me I already had put warmth in it—I could not put any more in without making it treacly. When I handed it in, Louis still wasn't satisfied. "I don't know what's the matter with it," he said, "but if it was right, I'd know it."

That was part of the quality that made Louis a great editor. He did not know exactly what he wanted until he saw it. The remark has been made of editors before, but I doubt it ever was made with more justification. He was a most sensitive man who affected the language of the streets and the Marines, but he had first-rate taste—and his striving to get his writers to exhibit work that would satisfy that taste made them work all the harder, and thereby improved their work.

Louis had very definite ideas about writing (as he had about everything). He communicated them to me in a series of conversations we had at various places he liked to eat in—the Men's Bar at the Waldorf, Toots Shor's (for the companionship more than for the food), and the steak joints on 45th Street. He would begin more often than not with a compliment about some piece I had done, and I would glow; and then he would turn his glare on me and, hoarsely, say something like this: "But just because I liked *that* piece, don't think you're a great writer yet. You're not.

"Lemme tell you about writing. I doubt you even know the rules.

"Write briefly. Don't take five paragraphs to tell what you could say better in two. Some old joker—who was it? I think it was Ben Franklin once wrote a long letter to a friend and apologized at the end because he hadn't had time to write a short one.

"Don't show off. If you know a long, obscure word and want to use it, use it in a way that's logical and necessary—in a way that makes me restless until I go and look it up. Don't use big words, foreign words, obscure words just for the sake of showing the poor suckers who pay fifteen cents for this magazine that you know a lot of big words. You're a reporter and writer first and an entertainer second, and I'm mainly payin' you to be the first two. If I want some goddamned entertainment I'll go to a cooch show or turn on the television set.

"Don't try any tricks on the reader. If you come to a part of the story where there are some facts you ain't sure of, go and look them up, or call up and find out about them. Don't try to write around them and hide the fact that you don't know what you're talkin' about.

"Don't lead the reader up an alley and leave him there. That story about the Chicago steak restaurant you handed in—it was supposed to be a story about a Chicago steak joint. I assigned you that story to do, and that was what I wanted. Instead you spent the first fifteen paragraphs talkin' about a guy who eats there. All right, he's an interesting guy. I know him myself and I like the son of a bitch. The reader don't know him. The reader thinks the story's about him, but as soon as he gets interested in the guy you turn right around and drop the guy and start writin' about the steak joint. That's a false lead. The reader's bound to feel a little cheated, and maybe the next time he sees your name, if he's noticed it in the first place, which I doubt, he won't start readin' as fas as he did before.

"I don't want no dirty words or cuss-words in your stories unless they're absolutely necessary—and then you got to make out a damn' good case for the sons of bitches bein' in there. This is a family magazine.

"Don't write down. Don't stop and explain everything unless it's something you're absolutely sure the reader don't know about. Then explain it briefly. If he's readin', he probably went to school the same as you did. He probably had more education than you had. Writin' down is for the jerks in radio and television and in the movies. We're putting out a magazine for people who pay attention —interested, alert, informed people.

"Don't grind an axe unless you can do it in a way that the reader isn't offended by it. You did it just right in the Boontch piece. You told how this guy didn't want to live in Washington because they don't like the colored there—but you had *him* say it. You didn't grind the axe yourself. You're not sellin' anything but information, boy.

"Get color into your stories. Don't get so goddamned much color in that it crowds out the facts, but color it up as much as you can while still stickin' to the truth. If you're writin' about a man, let the reader see him in action. If you're writin' about a man's office, or his house, or his car, any goddamned thing like that, *show* it to the reader. I don't mean you have to spend paragraphs describin' things. That don't go today. But you can describe something in a sentence or two and *show* the reader exactly what it was like.

"Now, another thing. Be consistent. If you're writin' in the first person, which is all right as long as you don't get too much of yourself into a story that's about somebody else, stay in the first person. If you're writin' in the third, stay in the third. Don't all of a sudden after sixteen paragraphs in the third, put "I" into the story. It puzzles the reader. I notice some of the manuscripts that've been comin' in of late have this damn-fool habit of bein' a mixture of third-and-first, and I don't like it. I bounce 'em right back and tell the writers to be consistent.

"The last thing is this. Listen to what your editor tells you. When he's makin' an assignment, he's got a fair notion of what he's lookin' to find out in the story. If it turns out he's wrong, and what he's interested in ain't there, then go in and discuss the story some more with him, or write him a letter, or in some way let him understand that you weren't asleep when the two of you were talkin' out the idea in the first place. You'd be surprised how many pieces I send back for revision because the writer didn't listen to what Denson and I were sayin' in the first place. You got to remember that the magazine ain't your responsibility. It's the editor's. But you also got to remember that your responsibility is to the editor and what he wants and what he tells you to get. Don't be afraid to go and discuss a piece while it's in the process of bein' worked on. If you get stuck, go to the editor for advice. Keep in touch with him. He'd rather be bothered than have to go to the bother later of sendin' back a piece because you didn't listen or didn't let him know what was goin' on with it.

"Be prompt. I got some guys around here, they think when I say 'I want it Tuesday' I mean I want it Wednesday. I don't want it any time but Tuesday. Every time a piece is late I feel like bouncin' it on general principles. I give my writers plenty o' time to work. I give out reasonable deadlines. So do most editors in this lousy business. Do yourself a favor, and the editor, and meet your deadlines.

"The last thing. You ain't the greatest writer in the world. But that don't mean you can't be. And I want you to write every last goddamned piece as though you're tryin' to be."

Post Post Script: Reading over the Bunche story today, I find many things I would change—but I believe if I were doing it now I would not touch the form. I have reduced it to an outline:

1. Opening, which describes Bunche and tells who he is. Three paragraphs.

2. News-peg. Bunche still a victim of segregation, which may deprive country of his services. Eighteen paragraphs. These paragraphs also used to characterize Bunche further; I took his statement and put it into his mouth as he sat in his home, smoking.

3. Story of negotiations. Twenty-four paragraphs. Anecdotes from the peace talks. Additional sidelights on Bunche's character from people who know him.

4. Background. How Bunche came to job of U.N. mediator. Story of assassination of Folke Bernadotte. Seven paragraphs.

5. More anecdotes of peace talks. Four paragraphs.

6. Transition to get to his background—"In one sense, the doctor's

whole career has been paradoxical . . . Dr. Bunche's direct, purposeful manner is illustrated by his courtship." Three paragraphs.

7. Brief biography, making up remainder of story up to ten paragraphs from end.

8. Final statement from Bunche in which he gives his opinion of Paul Robeson. Another lucky news-peg. (This, incidentally, was Ruppel's inspiration—Robeson had just sounded off again, and Ruppel thought we might get two newspaper breaks out of the article if Bunche answered him.)

The article was chosen as one of the ten best non-fiction pieces of the year, more for content, I believe, than for style. Its narrative faults are obvious and need not be gone into here. I am reprinting it for the same reasons, substantially, that I included the three articles preceding. It seems to me, to recapitulate, that articles of this kind make good starting-points for the young writer. At the risk of being repetitious, I will go over my thoughts on the writer starting out in an earnest attempt to make a living as a free-lance. He ought to:

1. Write stories of personal experience. But he should be selective in material—he should try to choose universal themes.

2. Write stories of personal experience that stretch the truth—again, trying to choose universal themes and subjects.

3. Begin in the "second-class" markets—that is, the markets where the pay is lower, where the established professionals write only out of necessity, either financial or moral.

4. Concentrate on factual articles with news-pegs, such as Farnsley and Bunche. Farnsley was news because he was waking up Louisville and because his program could have served as a pattern for other cities. Bunche was news because of what he did at Rhodes. It is true that Bunche was handed me by an editor, but he would not have given me Bunche if I had not done Farnsley.

The news-peg article is, in the long run, easier to write than the straight article about the man who is interesting only in himself—the man who simply exists. It is easier because the writer does not have to justify the newsworthy man. Justifying a subject is a job that should be attacked only after the writer has had considerable experience in writing and selling articles. A professional can get away with an article about a man who carves wooden birds for a living, or a man who makes weird costume jewelry, or a man who operates the only shop in America that sells materials to Indians who make authentic Indian beaded bags. The tyro probably can't. He can sell an article with a news-peg as well as any professional.

The beginner may ask, "How do I get to the sources of news?"

If I wished to be flippant, I would say, "You go to them." That is what I did when I set up my interviews with Bunche. I went out to Ambrose Light on the Coast Guard cutter with the other reporters who were meeting the incoming liner, and when I got aboard the steamship I asked where Dr. Bunche's stateroom was, went to it immediately, introduced myself as a correspondent from *Collier's* and told him what I had in mind. It is not always that easy, of course. In that case, Bunche was trapped; there were no secretaries or public relations men shielding him.

Nearly all people in public life these days have press representatives—either private individuals on their own staffs, or organizations that handle several clients. Once a writer has a tentative sign of interest in an article from a magazine editor, it is perfectly proper for him to go to the p.r. man or organization and ask for an interview or a series of interviews. As a matter of fact, the writer does not even need a "pale green light" (the phrase of Max Wilkinson) from an editor to do that. He can simply go and say, "My name is so-and-so, I am a magazine writer, and I believe I can sell an article about your client." Or he can write direct to the subject, who will then turn the letter over to the p.r. man or organization. Or he can take an oblique approach and begin interviewing people who know the subject. Presently his activities will come to the attention of the subject himself, and he may be summoned.

Joe Laitin, a writer who works out of Hollywood, once was assigned to do a story about Marlene Dietrich, long regarded as one of the most unapproachable of all film stars. He knew it was useless to seek out an interview with her; she seldom saw any members of the press, even the old established ones like Louella Parsons. Joe thereupon began interviewing everyone he could find who knew anything about her. He went about this methodically. He spent at least an hour with each interviewee, and impressed every one with his sincerity and throughness. One day his telephone rang and a voice said, "This is Marlene Dietrich. I hear you have been asking questions about me. What do you want to know?" Joe had a date with her that afternoon.

Many celebrities hire public relations men or organizations for the sole purpose of keeping reporters at a distance. I have had infuriating experiences with outfits of this kind. A p.r. man who represented a client I wanted to do a story about once took me to the west coast, promising me an interview with my subject, without the slightest intention of delivering him; it happened that he had another story he wanted done, and he thought that by dangling the bait of the first he could get me to do the second. The big movie company press agents are exceptionally adroit at warding off writers. Two years ago I did three stories about Natalie Wood. Last year I had an assignment to do another. Natalie had become a friend of mine and I anticipated no trouble. Meanwhile a new public relations team had moved into the Warner Brothers lot. Natalie had said some frank things in our interviews, and they were eager to keep her quiet—or to supervise her interviews. They refused to give me her telephone number, meanwhile promising their full cooperation. I had only a limited amount of time in which to do the story. On the day I was leaving Hollywood, they finally told her that I was trying to see her. She called me and said, "I didn't even know you were in town. When can we get together?"

Joe Hyams, who calls the movie press agents the sup-press agents, ran into the studio wall as soon as he was sent to Hollywood by the *New York Herald Tribune*. Every time he asked for an interview, a press agent stalled him. Presently he decided that the only way he could make his mark in the colony would be to go direct to the people he wanted to see. He began accosting his subjects directly. He would politely ask for interviews, and in most cases he would get them. If he was asked not to quote something that was said, he would sometimes argue about it and talk the person into agreeing; if he could not do that, he would oblige. Before long the stars began to trust him. He was the only working newspaperman who came and went freely in Humphrey Bogart's house; because Bogey respected him, others began to. Katharine Hepburn, who almost never grants interviews, permitted him to visit her on the lot where she was filming *The Desk Set*.

Hyams and I have had many conversations on the subject of

how to interview a celebrity. His method is to simply meet the person as an acquaintance, to talk casually, and to wait for something interesting to develop. Jennifer Jones once exclaimed to him, "Why, you're not like a reporter at all!" Hyams thought this one of the greatest compliments he ever had received. The method works for Hyams because he does a daily 850-word piece in the first person —rather, in the "editorial we," which his newspaper requires—and because even if nothing happens he still has enough material for a column. The method works for me if I know I am going to have several interviews with the subject. Usually I know I am going to have only one or two, which means that I must make the most of my allotted time. I prepare for the interview carefully. I read everything I can find that has been written about my subject, and I talk to as many of his friends or associates as possible beforehand. I specify that I want a half-hour, or an hour, or an hour and a half. Sometimes I say, "I want twenty minutes," or "I want ten minutes." At the end of my specified time, I say, "I asked for twenty minutes, and time's up," and rise to go. Usually the subject is just getting warmed up and asks me to stay. Arthur Godfrey is a notoriously difficult interview. Once, doing a piece on Pat Boone, who was singing on his show, I asked Godfrey's secretary for ten minutes. Charlie Andrews, Godfrey's producer, interceded for me. I was ushered into the great man's presence. He was affable and voluble; it was one of his good days. At the end of my ten minutes, I stood up.

"Where you goin'?" he asked, in surprise. "Sit and chat for a while." I was with him for more than an hour.

Preparing for the interview beforehand by reading the clips on a subject also gives the writer a clue or two as to how to open the interview. Nearly every subject is vulnerable in terms of his special interests—his family, his sports car, his boat, his pet charity, etc. Once the subject has warmed a bit, the interviewer can get on with his more businesslike questions.

Again let me warn that none of this should be taken as the last word. There are methods and methods, just as there are rules and rules for writing itself. The writer will have to discover through experience what works for him.

6 · *Making the Outline*

In one respect, working for Louis Ruppel brought my development to a temporary halt. Although I learned an incalculable amount from him, John Denson and John Lear, they neglected to drill me in the art of making an outline, which is perhaps the first requirement for the budding article writer. They outlined a job in a few words and told me to go do it, and when I handed it in they either accepted it or suggested revisions. Ruppel usually left the suggestions for revision to Denson. Ruppel operated mainly on feel and intuition; if a piece pleased him, he would grunt or utter some gruff congratulatory oath—but, feeling grateful to the writer for doing the kind of job he wanted, he would communicate his pleasure by talking with violent enthusiasm of one of his interests, which were as diverse as the contents of the *Britannica.* I can see him now, striding about his office, pausing to gaze fiercely at the map of the world on the wall (Louis challenged the world) or to hitch up his pants (Louis' pants were always falling down), letting the words flow in an oral stream-of-consciousness, switching from one subject to another in a manner that would have made James Joyce itch to put him on paper. If a piece did not please him, he would sneer or, depending upon what else had irritated him in the preceding hour, bleat like a Minotaur. Jackie Gleason's portrayal of the emotionally mercurial Ralph Kramden in *The Honeymooners* could have been copied directly from Ruppel. He was a man of wholehearted and extravagant emotion; as William J. Slocum said in a memorial piece written after Louis' death, "He either loved you or hated you, and you felt the same way about him." Sitting at lunch with Louis in Toots Shor's was like trying to enjoy a meal on a smouldering pile of explosives. He had a tremendous appetite, and food and drink stimulated him to further excesses of emotion.

Denson acted as a kind of safety value for Louis, and Lear translated Denson's notions into instructions to the writer. A. M. Rosenthal once said that he felt that Denson bought pieces by weight. A writer would take a job to Denson and hand it to him; Denson would read carefully through the first three or four pages to see how the lead went. Then he would heft it in his hand for a moment, as though to find out how heavy it was; if the weight pleased him, he would throw it into a basket and say, "Looks like you got a piece there," or "I don't think that's a piece." Later, if there was something wrong, the methodical Lear would call in the writer and carefully and clearly explain what Denson wanted done. Lear was disliked by some writers because of his intense seriousness about his work and because his shyness made him seem cold; actually, he was most sympathetic and considerate, an extraordinarily likeable fellow, and a valuable editor because of his passion for clarity and detail.

From those three men I took more knowledge of my craft than I can calculate; but I did not learn to write an outline. I tried in vain for eight years to sell Sam Kramer, and finally sold him to the *Saturday Evening Post.* I probably would have sold him sooner if I had known how to make an outline, as the Post Script will explain.

ARTICLE: "SAM KRAMER JEWELRY? GEE! WOW!"

(From *The Saturday Evening Post*)

In the unlikely event that an international congress of odd ducks should ever assemble to proclaim a king, a black-bearded New York silversmith named Sam Kramer probably could win without trying. Sam has dedicated nearly twenty of his forty-one years to being eccentric—in manner, dress, tastes and living habits. Even his vocabulary is startling—it is a mixture of an intellectual's polysyllables and such teen-ager's expressions as "Gee!" and "Wow!" Most of all, Sam's work is strange. Sam makes jewelry out of blobs of silver, gold and other metals, combining them with materials that only a gifted African savage might think of using, and producing ornaments in the shapes of amoebas, kidneys, embryos and prehistoric monsters. During the past fifteen years, for example, Sam has been making silver earrings set with taxiderists' glass eyes, golden bracelets studded with moose teeth, copper necklaces festooned with the quills of giant Uganda porcupines, and platinum cuff links set with old buttons from subway motormen's uniforms.

He also has used, in conjunction with metals, the tusks of rhino and narwhal, antique Czechoslovakian beads, coral branches, ivory nuts, trilobites—fossilized sea insects—ancient East Indian coins, rare hardwoods such as grenadilla and Gaboon, buffalo horn and stag-horn crown, Victorian shoe buttons, giant black pearls, nacre—iridescent shell—and some oval pieces of quartz which, Sam insists, were once the eggs of antediluvian reptiles.

Sam finds such stuff by scouring junk and curio shops and by patronizing a man he calls "an old pack rat of a dealer." He keeps this man's name secret for fear rival craftsmen will find out about him. Sam particularly reveres the dealer for his ability to turn up little-known hunks of rock. Whereas Sam's fondness for bizarre materials is a fixation, his love for rocks and stones is an absolute obsession. He has made jewelry from such unusual rocks as jasper, Oriental girasol, fluorite, malachite, chalcedony and bloodstone, as well as ninety-odd other obscure ones identifiable mainly by mineralogists. "If it's stone, I'll use it," Sam has said.

He attempted to prove this statement when his wife, Carol, went to the hospital for a gall-bladder operation. Sam kept begging her to save the gallstones. She mislaid them, presumably on purpose, and Sam was upset for days. "I was going to make them into a bracelet for you," he said.

So unrelenting is Sam's passion for stones that his collection now numbers nearly 500,000, ranging from pinhead-sized spinels up to a 2500-carat smoky topaz as large as a goose egg. Sam carries the topaz around in his pocket, fingering it lovingly. He also carries a couple of handfuls of faceted zircons, tigereyes, moss agates and other stones. Some of them he sells to fellow jewelry makers, but always with reluctance; and when he does sell some, he immediately buys more. Many of his lots he buys sight unseen. Abe Brown, a dealer, called him one morning and said, "Sam, I got a mess of funny-looking rock, but I swear I don't know what it is."

"Wow!" Sam cried. "Bring it around, Abe! I'll take it all!" His reckless decision was rewarding: the ore contained rare crystals of titanite known as sphenes, which Sam immediately began setting into silver.

The jewelry Sam makes from his outlandish substances is often strikingly beautiful, but it is undeniably weird. His favorite adjectives for it are "tortured" and "massive." It is certainly the latter; a ring he made for the columnist, Mel Heimer, weighs a half pound, and his necklaces have scaled three or four. Also, some of his pieces do have a kind of tortured, agonized feeling, like the rough-brushed paintings of Georges Rouault. Sam likes to pretend that his work is a painful struggle between himself and his materials. "I twist and pull my objects out of raw silver and convulsed rock, using nothing but my bare, bruised hands and a few rusty, creature-like tools," he once explained. Sam talks that way all the time.

Other-worldly though the jewelry may be, it is the work of an artist, as Sam, who takes a refreshingly objective view of himself, readily admits. "I was the first to take the forms of modern abstract art and adapt them to human decoration," he claims. He may not have been the first. Futuristic silversmithing has long been popular among the residents of Greenwich Village, where Sam dwells. It looks easy, the overhead is low and it beats working. Few craftsmen, however, have been as successful as Sam. His pre-eminence is attested to by his income (around $25,000 per annum) and by the twenty-odd museum and university art galleries that have exhibited his work.

Viewed in museums, Sam's things sometimes are mistaken for ancient handicraft, for, although he is a modernist, he is also heavily influenced by the primitive. A waggish friend once took a Kramer ring to a museum curator and asked if it was Egyptian or Etruscan. "Unquestionably Etruscan," said the antiquarian, "and a fine example too."

Not everyone is similarly enthusiastic. A timid lady once ventured into Sam's shop, glimpsed a brooch, uttered a little cry and fled. This brooch resembled a pterodactyl cradling its young in one bony wing, and moved a second lady to exclaim that she had never seen anything so repulsive. "She was really disturbed," Sam recalls with real satisfaction. "Wow!"

Sam unhesitatingly declares that his stuff is not for all people. "In some cases," one of his leaflets states, "buying is actually discouraged." This does not deter Sam's admirers, who are warm in their praise. "Your work is metameric, diphasic and polyvalent," wrote Dr. Boris Kronenberg, an eye specialist, adding somewhat anticlimactically, "I like it very much." Another customer, a student of the architect Frank Lloyd Wright, told Sam in utter seriousness, "Your objects make me feel separate from the great man swarm of aimless living." Other correspondents have been less psychoanalytical and more direct. "Dear Sam," a woman once wrote, "I am crazy and would like to buy some of your crazy jewelry."

Sam makes, or torments, his pieces in a second-floor walk-up at 29 West 8th Street, diagonally across from The Jumble Shop, a Greenwich Village landmark and grogeteria, wailing wall for Bohemians. From Sam's window a painted red eye glares at passers-by. Next to it is a silvered plastic bas-relief of a protoplasmic figure asleep on a half shell. This freakish construction is wired with colored lights that flash on and off at night, frightening Village winos into rescue missions and sobriety. The doorknobs of Sam's shop are two cast-bronze hands; the outside one wears a pigskin glove in winter. As the visitor enters he is likely to be unnerved by the naked, peering plaster head of a female deer which a taxidermist once had planned to encase in skin. Sam had bought seventy-five pounds of glass eyes from this taxidermist; then had asked if he could take along the head too.

"Whatever for?" the taxidermist asked.

"I don't know," Sam said, "except that it looks mysterious and unusual, and I like it."

The other furnishings are no less mysterious or unusual. A faceless stone angel leans against a gnarled stump. The walls are hung with abstractions by Village Picassos, old Chinese swords, fencing masks and some tremendous Sam Kramer neckpieces which no one has yet had the courage or money to buy—Sam asks $400 for some. The front half of the shop is selling area, furnished with rickety showcases. A plump girl, leaning on a case, once put her elbow through the glass; Sam left the hole there for years because he liked its curiously splintered shape. The rear half of the shop is split in two. On the left is work space, heaped with Sam's tools and unfinished jewelry. On the right is a combination office and salon, furnished with Sam's desk and a number of chairs for friends who like to drop in and chat while Sam is battling his silver.

These friends are hard pressed to avoid the stacks of rosewood and ebony which stick out from beneath the counters, and the boxes and bags of African fetish beads, miniature ivory skulls, petrified bone and stones, stones, stones that are strewn all over the floor. Sometimes, finding no place to sit down because Sam has piled the visitors' chairs with materials, they perch on a safety ladder that stands astride one showcase. The ladder is a favorite roost for Sam's Space Girls, two dancers whom he hires by the night to wander the streets of the Village and distribute handbills. The girls wear black tights and color their skin a luminous, unearthly green. They have been asked to leave any number of night clubs on the ground that they were alarming the patrons, but much to Sam's disappointment, they have yet to be arrested. One night a policeman did decide that the Space Girls were disturbing the peace. He brought them back to Sam's studio and said that he ought to run them in. "Fine," Sam said eagerly, thoughts of priceless publicity dancing through his head. The policeman gazed at Sam for a long time. Then, without a word, he departed. "Well," Sam said to the girls philosophically, "better luck next time, kids."

Sam's clothes are not so shocking as the Space Girls' uniforms, but they fit in well with his shop. He designs them himself, in heavy tweeds; a friend has said that he always looks as though he's just back from a tramp on the moors. Sam's jackets have extra pockets, inside and out, the better to carry stones. His pants are also pocketed on the outside, like Army fatigue trousers. For a time he was addicted to black Mexican cowboy—*charro*—pants with red fringe at the sides. His attire causes comment when he ventures uptown; Mrs. S. J. Perelman recalls a night when Sam's arrival at a Broadway restaurant threw that spot into turmoil.

In the Village, his dress is comparatively commonplace. Once, going to a masquerade party, Sam dressed in a swallow-tailed coat, the *charro* pants tucked into red boots, a ruffled shirt and a diplomat's sash. Then he covered his face with white-lead clown make-up, which made an arresting contrast with his black beard and hair. Leaving his shop, he confronted the doorman of the night club next door. The doorman, accustomed to his neighbor's costumes, did not bat an eye. "Good evening, Sam," he said.

Part of all this is pose, designed to attract attention and, accordingly, customers, but part of it is also a deep and genuine dissatisfaction with the ordinary. Sam has been fighting convention since boyhood. At sixteen he grew his first beard simply because nobody else his age had one. He has worn it ever since, except for two brief periods when he decided it might be more unconventional *not* to have it.

Sam was born in Pittsburgh on November 22, 1913, son of Benjamin Kramer and his wife, Minnie. The father was an unsuccessful produce merchant who loved to gamble. He strayed away when Sam was small and never returned; much later the family learned that he had killed himself. Mrs. Kramer took odd menial jobs to make do. Sam's boyhood was miserable. He hates to discuss it. He attended public schools, and his one pleasant memory of those days is a jewelry-making course he fell into. He produced some fair pieces, but had no thought of converting his innate ability into a career.

Minnie Kramer's fortunes gradually changed. A friend counseled her on investing tiny sums she had managed to scrape together, and when Sam was seventeen she was able to help send him to the university. After two years at Pitt he transferred to the University of Southern California; his mother had decided to move west for the benefit of Sam's little brother, Jack, who had a rheumatic heart.

A friend recalls Sam as the most picturesque figure on the U.S.C. campus. He lived in a shack, wore dock hand's clothes and spent hours poring over modernist paintings and *avant-garde* books. He was planning to be a writer, but as a senior he took jewelry-making with Glen Lukens, a ceramist. Lukens praised his work, but he still had no idea of making a living at it. "My designs were in no sense unusual," he says.

Upon graduating he worked briefly on the Santa Monica *Topic*, but covering female club meetings quickly disenchanted him. "What can you write about three hundred women?" he inquired of the editor, who shrugged and sent him to another meeting.

Brother Jack had improved, meanwhile, and the family had moved back to Pittsburgh. Sam and his older sister, Lee, followed along with a St. Bernard named Paula that Sam had acquired. They followed a typical Sam Kramer route—through Florida, where he stopped off for several months. Sam spent this time reading every book on stones that he could find.

In Pittsburgh he took a job with Dave Helfer, a manufacturing jeweler with headquarters in a building that Sam describes as "a veritable catacombs" of the business. "I stayed three months, learning a lot of crass, mechanical, realistic, technical knowledge," Sam says. Other workers thought he was crazy, but they answered his questions patiently. It was here, he says, that he learned to work silver, principally by watching the masters toil with platinum. "They taught me a muscular approach," he has said.

Presently he tried a few pieces of his own. He opened a tiny shop, but closed it within a few weeks. "Pittsburgh was full of morbid industrialism," he now says. "Nobody there seemed to dig me."

Late in 1938, his pockets full of a collection of stones and ancient coins he had accumulated, he besieged New York. He took a nine-dollar-a-week room, enrolled in a course in gemmology at N.Y.U., and soon was selling off the stones and coins for food. He showed his handiwork to anyone who would look, but except for some charitable musicians in Guy Lombardo's band whom he had met through a college pal, everyone was spectacularly uninterested.

Ultimately he decided that he could not succeed without a showroom. One day he happened to take a bus to Washington Square, the center of Greenwich Village. The square was then bounded on the south by a row of studios in the charge of Papa Strunsky, a legendary landlord whose motto was, "You aren't an artist if you pay your rent." Sam convinced Strunsky that he was unable to pay any rent whatever, and was given a studio once occupied by Eugene O'Neill.

Even though his surroundings were now more in keeping with his character, Sam's luck worsened. The St. Bernard, which he had brought on from home because he was lonely, was an added burden. Sam often went without food in order to feed her. Yet he was comparatively content. "I was learning about life," he says. "Gee!"

One day a tall, striking model from Brooklyn, Carol Enners,

wandered into his shop. "She must have liked me," Sam says, "because I had a telephone. She didn't know the company was planning to kill my service." Miss Enners took to spending more and more time with Sam as he worked. Her calls from the modeling agency came more and more infrequently. Pretty soon she began to try her own hand at jewelry making, and one day when Sam was out spending their last dime for coffee, she finished a ring. "Wow!" cried Sam when he saw it. "You have real talent!" They were married a little later, and now have two boys, Johnny, fifteen, and Kieran, six. Carol has continued to work at her craft, and recently opened a branch shop on East 57th Street.

With marriage, Sam's fortunes took a turn for the better, and he was emboldened to move into the 8th Street shop he occupies today. For a time he and Carol lived behind a screen at the rear, cooking on a hot plate and sleeping on collapsible cots. Sam used to wait on early customers in his pajamas.

The customers had begun to drift in almost as soon as Sam opened his new shop. Many were drawn by his talent for self-exploitation. He adopted a drawing of a mushroom as his hallmark—"Because," he said, "a mushroom grows in dark, gloomy places, and my jewelry is often eerie and mysterious." He gave his suppressed writing talent an outlet in his advertising: "Some of my pieces," he wrote, "seem to cry out in hysteria." And he treated his customers as though they were as wacky as he. "What sort of psychological block or complex is preventing you from buying this lovely, vicious brooch?" he once inquired of a lady who could not make up her mind. He lengthened his beard, brightened his clothes and dressed Carol on occasion in necklaces that reached to her knees, and in rings that looked like silver vampires feeding on her hands.

All this crafty salesmanship paid off handsomely. Today Sam gets orders from as far away as Africa and India. Of all his customers, his favorite has always been a self-styled voodoo priest who asked him to make a wedding ring embellished with some voodoo markings. Sam set to work with relish. The priest was so delighted with the result that he asked Sam to be a witness at his wedding. Sam, full of visions of sacrifices, devil masks and native incantations, was half wild with excitement. He was disappointed to find that the ceremony was held in a Presbyterian church on Fifth Avenue, and that the usual Presbyterian service was read. "Still," he said, "it isn't everybody who gets to stand up for a voodoo priest!"

Of late, Sam has been prospering at a greater rate than ever and branching out. Experimenting with new ways to punish silver, he has hit upon a fusing process. He holds the silver under a pointed torch flame and lets the droplets form their own rough designs as they melt and fall. Also, he has developed his own method of "caging" rough, uncut stones; he wraps them in silver wire and hangs them from necklace chains and earring clasps. This method is so simple that any amateur can do it. Finally, he is designing a line of jewelry for a well-known leather-goods firm.

This new commercial success does not mean that Sam has gone commercial or conventional. He remains rigorously slavish to his Bohemian way of life, and would die rather than arise before noon. He prefers to eat in The Jumble Shop, where he is surrounded by other creative screwball friends. He will still accept any jewelry commission, the odder the better. Last year, when the CBS-TV show, Omnibus, was presenting Macbeth, a prop man called him and asked if he knew where they might get a poison ring.

"A *poison* ring?" Sam cried in delight. "Why, I'll make you one! Gee, a poison ring! Wow!"

Post Script: Writing an outline is the first step in selling an article. In these days of editorial committees, the outline has taken on more importance than ever before. No matter how carefully a writer explains an idea to an editor, the latter usually asks for an outline before giving out the final assignment; I have even known cases in which an editor made an assignment directly and then added, "Make me an outline before you go ahead." Writng the outline is inescapable, and the beginner will do well to learn how to write one early in the game.

There are some writers who prefer the formal outline, which opens with a general statement of what the piece is to be about and goes on to list the points to be made in order. Others—and I am among them—prefer the letter-outline, which is less formal and permits more freedom. Long ago I decided that the best way to do an outline was to write a letter to my agent which he could then send along to prospective buyers. To write a letter to a specific editor is a waste of time, even if one does not have an agent; if the editor declines the outline, it must be recopied before it can be sent on to another editor. It is only when I have an idea that I feel will do for only one specific magazine that I take the risk of writing the editor directly.

The ideal outline should contain:

1. A general statement or two about the story and why it would interest readers.

2. A statement of how the writer proposes to treat the story.

3. Some anecdotes from the story, told briefly.

4. Additional pertinent information, preferably the kind that will make the editor eager to buy the story.

5. Warmth and enthusiasm, indicating that the writer is anxious to do the story.

An outline need not be long. I have made several sales on the strength of outlines as brief as this:

Dear Max,

Ever since I met her in London last year and subsequently saw her throw a temper tantrum in the lobby of the Savoy Hotel because her dog was not allowed in her room, I have wanted to do a story on the volatile Maria Meneghini Callas, the most colorful opera singer of our time. Miss Callas has developed her temper as well as her voice; she is a throwback to the old prima donnas. She was fat and shy as a child, the daughter of Greek-American immigrants who apparently gave her, intentionally or not, a driving will to become the best in her field. She still has the drive. She literally made herself what she is—with the help of a husband twice her age who happens to be very rich. She has been in the news for the past year. I have been collecting material on her all that time, and I am reasonably certain that I can get a couple of interviews with her. *Time* had her on the cover, but there is much, much more material than they included in their profile. I hope we can get a go-ahead on this.

Coronet bought that one, first trip out. At the risk of sounding arrogant, I must point out that it would be dangerous for a young writer to submit an outline as short as that; I suspect *Coronet* gave me the assignment not only because they wanted the subject badly but also because they knew my work. It is better for the young writer to go into more detail, and to indicate that he has done a little preliminary work on the story.

As I mentioned in the introduction to this section, I failed to sell Sam Kramer for eight years, simply because I had not learned how to make a selling outline. The first one I did was in the form of a letter to Donald Congdon, who was then my agent:

Dear Don:

It occurs to me that Sam Kramer, along with his wife, Carol, might be a good bet or bets for an article. I'm attaching pictures of both—you can see that they're photogenic; I won't waste time in description.

What makes Carol and Sam interesting is that they are jewelry makers who utilize all manner of strange things to make pins, brooches, rings, earrings, tie clips, barrettes, and other items. Some of the odder materials they use are tiger's teeth, the jawbone of an ass, coral (because it looks like brains, Sam says), fossils, stag's horn, fluorite and other ores. He also uses glass eyes occasionally, and has perhaps the largest collection of them in New York—*seventy-five pounds*. He uses stones that most jewelers wouldn't touch, including such rare ones as the sphene.

Kramer's jewelry is as fantastic as the material he uses. He'll make earrings in the shape of kidneys or spleens, pins in the shape of some strange primordial bird suckling its young, and a necklace that looks as though its links were made from diseased corn. He once made an earpick in the shape of a nude woman. He has done jewelry for such people as Jose Ferrer, Sono Osato, S. J. Perelman, Jerome Robbins, Nora Kaye, Leo Cherne, Frank Buck, Zero Mostel and many other celebrities.

Once a friend of Kramer's took one of his rings, as a joke, to a museum in Pittsburgh. "I think this is Egyptian," he said. "Can you tell me if I'm right?" The curators took the ring for three days and examined it carefully. At the end of that time they returned it to Sam's friend. "You're wrong," they said. "It's Etruscan." Oddly enough, Kramer does use an ancient wax casting method for working silver. Everything he does is by hand—"We torture the metal with our bare hands and a few rusty implements," he says. He once designed a ring for a South Carolina voodoo high priest. The man was so delighted that he asked Sam to be the best man at his wedding.

I've talked to Kramer about this and he would be delighted. So, needless to say, would I.

Thine,
Richard

That outline was turned down by sixteen magazines. It simply did not tell enough about Sam and his work, and it failed to convince editors that Sam might make an entertaining piece.

The second outline, which got me a go-ahead from the *Post*, went as follows:

Dear Max,

You'll recall that after our last lunch with Sam Kramer, the eccentric silversmith and maker of jewelry, we agreed that a full-scale piece ought to be done about him.

Sam makes jewelry out of material that few other craftsmen would ever consider: stag horn, coral branches, tusks of rhino, and narwhal, taxidermist's glass eyes, trilobytes (fossilized insects), old buttons from subway conductors' uniforms, ivory nuts, some pieces of quartz which he believes were once prehistoric reptile eggs, and such little-known minerals and semi-precious stones are peridot, fluorite, lapis, obsidian, agate, amethyst quartz, malachite, chalcedony and sphenes.

Once his wife went to the hospital for a gallstone operation. Sam kept begging her to save the stones: "I'll put them in a bracelet for you," he said. His wife mislaid the stones, presumably on purpose. Sam was upset for days.

He uses these odd materials in silver settings to make really lovely and artistic jewelry. His work has been exhibited in many conservative museums, and is sometimes mistaken for the work of craftsmen of many hundreds of years ago. A friend of Sam's, as a joke, once took one of his massive rings into the Pittsburgh Museum and asked the curator if he could identify it. The man kept it four or five days, then finally rendered his verdict. "It's unquestionably Etruscan," he said.

Sam is recognized by jewelers' associations as one of the first craftsmen to successfully take abstract art forms—such as are found in the paintings of Picasso, Miro, Arp and Yves Tanguy—and make ornamental rings, bracelets, and earrings embodying the ideas. The making of jewelry has been perennially popular in Greenwich Village, where Sam has his shop. It looks easy, the profits are not inconsiderable, and it beats working. The turnover, however, is rapid. The shops quickly fail. Sam is one of the few ever to make not only a comfortable living at his craft, but an excellent one. He nets around $25,000 a year—from his jewelry, and from the stones he sells to other craftsmen.

It would be gross understatement to describe Sam as a nut on unusual materials. Every time a jobber gets hold of some stuff he can't unload anywhere else, he goes to Sam, who happily buys it. One morning a dealer called him up and said, "Sam, I've got some rock down here, I swear I haven't any idea what it is." "Bring it around," Sam said. He bought the man's entire supply. The material contained sphenes—rare crystals found mainly in Switzerland.

As you know, Sam makes a fetish of being original and different—not only in his jewelry, but in his personal life and in his surroundings. The doorknob to his shop consists of a bronze model of a hand—on which he draws a pigskin glove in winter. The walls are festooned with old duelling swords and fencing masks along with some Chinese armor and a plaster cast of a fawn's head which a taxidermist originally had planned to surround with skin. Sam bought this the same day he bought the seventy-five pounds of glass eyes he keeps on hand for his jewelry. "It looked mysterious," he said, "and I liked it."

Sam's appearance is something to conjure with; he wears a beard that makes him look like a Barbary pirate, and he designs his own clothes. They are usually made of heavy, massive tweeds—and, as you said, he is the only man ever to lunch in Shor's who looks as though he's just back from a tramp on the moors. For a long time he wore black charro (cowboy) pants with a red, fin-like fringe at the sides. His strange costumes are by now commonplace in the Village. One night he and I were going to a fancy-dress party at Sono Osato's house. Sam wore an old-fashioned swallow-tail coat, his charro pants tucked into red boots, a pleated shirt he had obtained from Brooks Costume with enormous difficulty, and one of those sashes that diplomats wear at state functions. This did not quite satisfy him. He thereupon covered his face with white-lead clown makeup. It made an arresting contrast with his black beard and black hair. As we were going out, we saw the doorman of the club next door. He did not bat an eye at Sam's outlandish rig. "Good evening, Sam," he said.

Part of this is pose, designed to bring people into his shop. Part of it, also, is a genuine dissatisfaction with the ordinary, the commonplace, and the commercial. Sam's entire life apparently has been a fierce struggle with the status quo. His mother runs a bowling alley in California. He came from middle-class Pittsburgh, attended school restlessly, and finally struck out for New York. He opened a studio on Eighth Street, sharing it with an enormous St. Bernard dog someone bequeathed him. Sam is an extraordinarily kind man; the dog always ate better than he did. For a time he was so broke he could not afford an apartment; he used to set up a cot in the john behind his studio, and he often greeted early-morning customers in his pajamas.

Sam first began attracting attention with his original advertisements. "Tortured and massive jewelry," one of them said. "Don't come in if you're a slave to convention," said another. And another: "We work these strange things out of raw silver, using nothing but our bare hands and a few rusty, creature-like tools."

People came, but they did not always buy. Once a lady came into the shop, looked at some of the jewelry, and ran screaming into the street. (There were witnesses.) A student of Frank Lloyd Wright, Robert McKelvey, was so overcome that he went home and wrote a fifteen-page critique, which he presented to Sam the next day. It said, rhapsodically, "Your work made me feel separate from the great man-swarm of aimless living." Once a woman wrote him, "Dear Sam Kramer: I am crazy and would like to buy some of your jewelry." Kramer's favorite customer of all time was an honest-to-goodness voodoo priest from South Carolina who came in and asked him to make a wedding ring. Shown the finished product, the priest was so enthusiastic he asked Sam for some of his fingernail parings and a bit of his beard, presumably for the purpose of using them in some weird rite. Sam obliged eagerly. Then the priest invited him to be best man at his wedding. Sam could talk of nothing else for days. "Gee, I'll bet it'll be a wonderful experience," he kept saying. He was terribly disappointed when he found it was being held in a Presbyterian church.

Customers began coming in more and more regularly. Many famous people turned up. Sam would not sell those who came merely to make fun. "In some cases, buying is actually discouraged," he wrote in his leaflet, and meant it. When selling to someone he likes, however, his technique is superb. I have copied down some of his better lines over the years. He once said to a woman, "Look at the heavy, agonized feeling in this piece—it actually cries out in hysteria." Another time, "You look as though you might like something vicious, like this."

Sam hates the daylight, I feel. He keeps his shop open until nine-thirty or ten. Then he goes off to one of his favorite restaurants, which are as strange as the other things in his life. Then he goes and sits around with writers, artists, dancers, actors and other people he admires and respects. He is one of the happier people I know. And, as you know, an exceptionally nice, warm guy. I have only scratched the surface here. I have known Sam for ten years and have been haphazardly collecting material on him for eight. I think we would have a funny, anecdote-crammed piece, and I hope you can get up some interest in it.

Best,
Richard

The reader will note that the outline contains nearly everything that went into the finished article. The first two paragraphs tell who Sam is and describes the materials he uses. Sam's character is pointed up by the third paragraph, which is an anecdote. The fourth paragraph makes clear that he is an artist of some merit, and adds another anecdote. The fifth paragraph "sets" him. The sixth returns to his mania for unusual materials, and the seventh shows how his approach to his work is carried out in his approach to his life. The eighth tell more about that, and the ninth takes a hard look at him, implying that some of his peculiarities may be rooted in commercialism. The tenth tells of his funny advertisements, and the eleventh of customers' reactions. The final paragraph tells more about him as a person.

This outline ran to three single-spaced typewritten pages. (There is some dispute among writers as to whether to single- or double-space outlines; I prefer single-spacing since it keeps the outline from seeming too depressingly bulky.) That is about the proper length. If one writes anything longer, he might as well go on and finish the article. A longer one, too, might take the freshness out of the finished product. I have had that happen time and again. In making an outline on the subject of Harry Kurnitz, the writer, I went to four and a half single-spaced pages in which I told most of Kurnitz' jokes, which were to form the body of the story. The *Post* said they wanted to see the article, and I wrote it. When I submitted it to them, the jokes were all familiar to them, and they rejected it promptly (it later was bought by *Playboy,* to the editors of which the jokes were fresh).

The outline must never promise anything that the article does not deliver, and it must never leave any doubt in the editor's mind as to what he may reasonably expect. About a year ago, after a conversation with Eddie Condon, who had a terrific hangover, I concluded that it might be fun to write a piece about monumental hangovers friends of mine had endured. I wrote Wilkinson the usual letter indicating that I wanted to do just that. He submitted it to *Playboy,* and after a few weeks they gave me a go-ahead. I wrote the article exactly as the outline had said I would write it. It was little but a collection of yarns about hangovers that I had picked up from Jackie Gleason, Toots Shor, Lee Meyers, Robert C. Ruark, Lew Parker, Paul Douglas, Prince Mike Romanoff and other sufferers. *Playboy* bounced it. Somehow the editors had got the notion that I had planned to go into the physiological and psychological details of hangovers, and they had been expecting a serious piece with some anecdotes to brighten it up. The fault was mine. I had not made my intentions clear in the outline.

Making an outline requires research—not as much research as the writer will devote to the finished piece, of course, but enough to enable him to present a comprehensive and fairly detailed picture of what he has in mind. A day spent in seeking out the high spots and some relevant details usually suffices. Indeed, since time is of such importance to the writer, it is probably not economical for him to spend more than a day at this chancy business. Some writers, approached by public relations men or organizations to do stories about their clients, permit the latter to finance the research, and some have even been known to accept fees for investigating a story. This practice is frowned upon by editors—most editors, anyhow—and is rather unethical. For one thing, it puts the writer in debt to his subject. For another, it destroys his objectivity; naturally, the p.r. people are going to present only those aspects of their client that they wish to put before the public. Once I proposed an idea to Jack Alexander of the *Post* as follows:

"Three airlines are now running regular flights from California over the pole to Europe. The flight has become a kind of milk-run. I'd like to do a story about those polar flights, and Pan-American will pick up my ticket."

"If we're interested in the story," Jack said, "*we'll* pay your expenses." (As it turned out, they weren't interested.)

Most stories I've done in the past few years have come as direct assignments from editors, which saved me the trouble of making outlines. It has taken me a long time to get to this happy position, and it is seldom that a beginner ever approaches it. It behooves him, therefore, to learn to do an outline early in his career—and to learn about research, which is the subject of the next chapter.

7 · Research

ONE AFTERNOON in the summer of 1956, as I was hanging around the Beverly Hills office of Irving Paul Lazar, the little king of the lone-wolf literary agents, listening to him shout at the late Harry Cohn, head of Columbia Pictures, over that special telephone-amplifier which permitted him to talk without holding the instrument to his face, it struck me that he would make a fine subject. To my recollection then, nobody ever had written a piece about a Hollywood literary agent (I was wrong; the late Alva Johnston had done a three-part series for *The Saturday Evening Post*). I asked Lazar if he would object to my essaying such a job. He debated at least a second and a half until his sense of public service triumphed over his innate modesty. I made an outline later that day and sent it off to Max Wilkinson, who wired back two days later, "POST INTERESTED LAZAR."

Now began what eventually evolved as both the toughest and easiest job of research and writing I have ever been up against. Lazar, in his own way, was a celebrity—even though, until my *Post* piece appeared, the general public had never heard of him. Moreover, he was a celebrity who collected celebrities and was, himself, collected by them. And he was—and is—an ingratiating egomaniac. Never before had I had such cooperation from any subject. While I was in Hollywood he would call me five or six times each day to remind me that Billy Wilder, Bogie, Harry Kurnitz or any one of fifty or sixty different people had interesting things to say about him. When I got back to New York he cut down the calls to one a day, but each lasted at least fifteen minutes. Lazar was endlessly interesting to himself, and he saw no reason not to share his interest with the world. When I attempted to explain that my article was to be somewhat shorter than *War and Peace* he was unperturbed. "Just trying to help, dear boy," he would say, jauntily.

In the three months that researching the Lazar piece required I interviewed more than seventy people and wound up with a stack of notes nearly four inches thick. Unquestionably, my story was over-researched; although for a time I entertained the notion that the *Post* might print a two- or three-parter, my editor there, Stuart Rose, quickly disenchanted me. Yet I kept getting better and better stories about Lazar, and livelier and livelier quotes. I could not seem to stop my investigation into the character of this fascinating, revolting little man.

There are writers who believe that any time over a week spent in researching a single full-length article is time wasted. It is true that very extensive research is apt to be uneconomical in terms of time; a writer is likely to be paid as much for a piece that takes three days to research as one that takes three months. (The three-day ones come all too infrequently, alas.) I lean toward the Maurice Zolotow school of research. Zolotow, one of the most skilled of all the magazine article writers, stalks his subject like a great predatory animal. He spends days tracking down a single obscure rumor, seeing scores of people in the process. He usually winds up with so much material and in such a state of exhaustion that he has to take two or three days off before he can even begin to think about the actual writing. He becomes passionately involved with the personalities of his subjects; if they are females, he may fall halfway in love with them. He once went to do a piece about Grace Metalious and later compared her to George Sand. "He means George Zaharias, doesn't he?" one of the *Cosmopolitan* editors inquired. He did not. Describing an outfit once worn by Gloria Vanderbilt—purple stockings, as I recall, a blue skirt and an orange blouse—Zolly said, "On any other woman, it would have looked a fright." It looked a fright on Miss Vanderbilt, too, but not to his inflamed eyes. Alfred Lunt once offered him some cookies he had baked. Maurice wrote, "They were the most delicious cookies I have ever eaten in my life." It is this very enthusiasm, plus his obsession to set down every detail, that makes Maurice Zolotow the fine writer—and before that, the wonderful human being—that he is.

I don't research as thoroughly as Zolotow does (no other writer does, for that matter), but I try to cover all aspects of every story, and to see as many people involved in it as might be helpful. I try to write down quotations as accurately as possible, and I listen carefully to what the interviewee is saying, even if he is saying something trivial, in an attempt to catch the cadence and idiom of his speech. I make notes on observations of my own, I scribble reminders of additional people to be seen, I jot down descriptions and minutiae. Before I set about writing a piece I attempt to make certain that I will not have to make any last-minute telephone calls (I have almost never done a piece that did *not* demand that I make last-minute telephone calls). Some writers type out their notes before setting to work. To me this is time-consuming. It also takes too much time to transcribe tape recordings. Some writers use a tape machine with great success. It certainly guarantees accurate quotes—but it also guarantees unnecessary quotes and much additional unnecessary dialogue. I used a tape recorder when they first came on the market, but I gave it up after about six weeks. For one thing, it was too heavy to carry around; for another, it made the subject nervous and self-conscious (there are some subjects who get uneasy even when they see you writing down something they've said; and there are others who insist that you write everything down). Joe Hyams has solved the problem by using a recorder the size of a transistor radio, with a tiny microphone strapped to his wrist, like a watch. This is handier to lug around, but the trouble of transcribing remains. I think the old method of taking notes is still the best.

Besides, I seldom look at my notes once I begin to write. I was taught this by Daniel Lang, a reporter for *The New Yorker*. Lang came to Oak Ridge shortly after the first atomic bomb was dropped. I dogged his footsteps, trying to learn everything I could about how a great reporter works. I asked him question after question, and in the course of our conversations he told me he never referred to his notes while he was writing except (1) to get a date or a figure correct, or (2) to get the exact wording of a quotation. "After I'm finished writing the first draft, I go back and check the notes," he said. I tried this on my next piece and was astonished to find that I remembered nearly everything I had put down while taking the notes. I have done it ever since.

All this has been a crafty method of easing the reader into the realization that I am now going to reprint some of the notes—only about a third, I hasten to add—I made while researching the Lazar piece. I am doing this for two reasons—to give Lazar the opportunity of seeing his name in print a few hundred additional times, and to give the aspiring writer some notion of the kind of work involved in researching a full-length article. Here they are:

IP LAZAR TELEPHONE CALLS ONE DAY

Hume Cronyn
Bob Fellows—re Elinson & O'Brien property CAPPY
Cole Porter
Mike Connolly
Peter Larkin—re his doing sets for "Les Girls"
Daniel Fuchs
Ralph Blane—re contracts—rko—"the girl most likely"
Hugh Martin
Mrs. Bogart
Frank Patty—stock broker
Milton Pickman
Luther Davis—"Grand Hotel"
Sid Luft—for Judy Garland
Robert Blees
Spewacks—"The Great Sebastians"
Leland Hayward
Mrs. Richard Brooks
Bernard Smith—Hecht-Lancaster
Walter Wanger
Ivan Goff

---

3 brothers—Murray, an associate in Richlar Enterprises
James, prop shoe store White Plains, NY
Henry, salesman with US Rubber

HARRY KURNITZ

Lazar never stops looking for clients. Once Harry Kurnitz took him to see Gian-Carlo Menotti's *The Medium* and *The Telephone*. "Lazar paid no attention whatever to the operas," Kurnitz says, "but he was impressed by the large audience. He asked me if Menotti had an agent. I told him I was sure he had, but didn't know. Somehow he got hold of Menotti's telephone number and called him up. Menotti didn't have an agent, and he was flattered by Lazar. He told Lazar to go ahead and represent him. Lazar sold him to Hollywood right away."

LAZAR OFFICE

3 signed Marc Chagall prints, one showing a man heels over head (appropriate)
2 original Oliver Smith drawings for sets he did for Okla movie
green and tan provincial wallpaper
Suite III—"Richlar Productions, Ltd."

Italian Provincial desks, plus a plywood cover for the telephone bells
silver cigarette box saying Moss-Kitty-Irving
in office an antique barometer
oil painting by Noel Coward of Jamaican scene
3 Bernard Buffets, incl a self-portrait
air conditioner
Ital provincial desk
picture by Milton Avery
an original Dufy
a Caffe showing priests at play
tray on breakfront
picture of father in a silver frame also on breakfront
silver cigarette box:

Colonel Wilson Loves you,
Flackmeyer loves you,
and I love you
Moss
November 20 1943

also one like a bible:

Lazar is our shepherd,
we shall not want
Ginny and Quent

silver frames
autographed picture of Louis Dominguin
one of Charles Vidors and Billy Wilders at Tia Juana
from Kaufman—"With love, plus admiration for his chutzbah," George Kaufman
"To Irving from the only French writer in his stable," Irwin Shaw
color photograph of Lazar holding a matador's cape
"For Irving with best wishes from his fan," Cole
another color photo of Irving making pass at a bull signed pic Dominguin —"From one bullfighter to another"
on tray—Citrocarbonate
Clover air spray
bufferin
a copper pitcher

BILL DOLL

(A Broadway press agent who knew Lazar in *Winged Victory*)
I don't know anybody who did as much for the e.m. in the Army. Darn near everybody from WV amounted to something: Pete Hayes, Mario Lanza in chorus.
Lazar went and involved Moss.
He was a lieutenant when I first knew him.

The officer in charge was Ben Landis, I think; he must be around NY.

(call him)

It was WV as much as anything else that kicked off his career.

(talk to Bob Breen)

He put the whole show together.

Joe Bushkin	Eugene Connelly
David Rose	Don Taylor
Red Buttons	Eddie O'Brien
Keith Andes	

Damn near everybody in it's a name today.

Opened in November and ran through to April & made the picture in Sept and toured a year.

IRVING'S DIRECTORY

Service Calls, Studios, Airlines, Restaurants, Hotels, Properties, Writers (Literary), Writers (music), Dance Directors, Set Designers, Girls (Las Vegas), Girls (New York), Girls (Los Angeles), Girls (Europe).

3″ thick

GEORGE ROSENBERG

(A Hollywood agent)

Lazar is far superior to Frank Orsatti. Of course the latter had a good friend in a fellow named Mayer and I don't think Lazar has a good friend. He's tolerated a lot of things that I wouldn't but basically he's a nice fellow.

(See Herb Baker at Fox)

"PRINCE" MICHAEL ROMANOFF

(Celebrated impostor, now going straight)

I am thinking of leasing him my crown.

LAZAR ON HIMSELF

M Pickman intro me to Sonny Werblen at MCA.

Very small office, they had bands.

A client they sued, get the winner said Jules Stein.

They were suing a juggler for commissions; he didn't want to pay; I rep him and beat them; get the winner, said Jules; Jules said, get him to work for us; I went to work for MCA in 1933.

I went to California & made deal Eddie Cantor & sold him 2 writers, Joe Quillan & Izzy Elliman. To get there I told Cantor I needed three transporation; he said, I'm only buying two writers & I told him they won't come without their agent.

I liked it here, rented an office in the California Bank Building to be an agent. Went back to NY & told Werblen I was going to be an agent; meanwhile had another writer, named Morey Amsterdam, now a comedian, sold him to Metro to write jokes; Werblen offered me $350 a week, so I stayed with them for 10 years.

Bands, acts, night clubs. Traveled everywhere.

Enlisted in 1942, went to OCS—AF Adm in Miami, then 2nd Ltcy, then sent Mitchell field latter part 1942, heard that Gen Arnold wanted an AF show as good as "This is Army."

300 submissions by various officers to Washington

I had a show that couldn't be done, I planned it all out. Was to be written by Rodgers and Hammerstein, the music, sketches by George S. Kaufman and Moss Hart, & I would get Gable for it, he in AF then.

I didn't know any of them. I was sent for by Arnold. Can you do this? Sure. Go ahead. I walked in the Plaza, somebody pointed out Moss Hart. He thought I was kidding. I called Hap Arnold's aide & said send him a wire. Moss & I went to Washington. Moss said: Every AF base in country lining up talent. Don Taylor, DePaul of the choristers, Basehart (Richd), Pete Hayes, Red Buttons, Gary Merrill. It opened in 1943, stayed w/ it to 1945, we made a million for AF emergency relief.

Lt Benjamin Landis

Building contractor

1945 discharged. Came out here for MCA, ran studio for Eagle-Lion for a year, 1945 quit and went Europe for a year. At that point Moss staying with Zanucks & asked me to rep him—got him $150,000 for ten weeks, highest price up to that time.

I get up at 9:30, breakfast in bed, check everything with the boy, 8:30–9:00 make NY or Europe calls, go to office at one—rarely go to studios.

I don't want any nervous clients. I go away a lot. I avoid them. There's no one they can talk to but me.

(This interview was conducted in Romanoff's. Mike came up to the table and said a pretty girl, a friend of Lazar's, was having dinner in the bar. She was alone. Lazar was off in the middle of a sentence. He came back and told me I ought to talk to the girl: "She knows me well," he said. I later talked to the girl, June McCall. She had met him only once, at Sinatra's house. She said she thought he was a funny man. She wondered if he could anything for her in pictures. She said, "This is my birthday. To hell with him." She would not talk further about him. I bought her a champagne cocktail and put her in her automobile and she drove back to the San Fernando Valley, where she lived.)

Lindsay and Crouse, I handle. Ben Hecht I've handled, John Patrick.

I did a good job with the pros, it kind of all came.

Shaw gave me 24 hours to get a job for him for $50,000. I got him $5,000 a week for ten weeks.

Got Odets.

I got Moss $150,000 for a screenplay, "Gents Agmt."

Got Shaw $10,000 a week for five weeks work on War & Peace, an editorial job.

KENNETH MCKENNA

(MGM executive in charge of story properties)

"Swifty"—the uppercrust social set in which he moves call him.

Colorful stories are hard to come by.

Handles a lot of properties.

Good, two-fisted tough negotiations. I don't find him hard to deal with—he's a good negotiator without being onerous to deal with.

He operates out of his hat; most agents have a setup; he's got a very able secretary.

Swanson only comparable.

He is indefatigable, will handle anything.

He gets his contacts and gets a lot of business; he kept asking me to go out but I do all business in my office.

We bought "Gigi" recently.

He'll say he's got a price, but it won't necessarily be the right price—it may be 50 per cent higher.

These fancy prices, ha.

(Talk to Lew Wasserman of MCA)

Got his training in the agency business.

He has never acted as agent for us to my knowledge.

I don't actually work with the agents but the agents can't get that through their heads.

He's here once a week when he's in the country, drops in on me, Benny Thau, but never without appointment, although I certainly would see him if he happened to drop in.

Has many people who work here steadily.

Sold Brooks to us to begin with.

Very active, aggressive, tenacious kind of an agent.

Like to do business with a man on the ball.

He moves around the world & uses his ingratiating sociability to bring proper people into his stable.

ARTHUR FREED
(M.G.M. producer)

I knew him when he was in the Army yet, fifteen years, later generally William Morris office & went to MCA? I think.

He's a one-man show; the only other successful one is Victor Borge. A one-man show in business and personal life; never even got married.

He started most of his business in this office with Allen Lerner, Comden and Green—the Gershwin estate and Ira Gershwin deal, but I had that idea and told him to get it for me because I knew he was close to the Gershwins. He got more help in the Gershwin livingroom because Lee G sponsored him, but he did represent Ira and I'd had Ira before.

Publication of most figures have a tendency to be exaggerated.

Moss helped him a lot.

Lazar hated to be an agent. Once came to me and wanted to be my assistant, some time after the war. He hated the common connotation of agent.

He developed this personality; I think Moss made it up.

He threw away the Morris & MCA vocabulary & got a whole new one; one night at Gershwins, Ira a bug on words, Levant there, me, "eclectic" —Levant said to Lazar, you don't know what it means—Lazar said I look it up every week.

He started buying paintings and sold most of them at a profit. Or worked them in on deals.

He's a snob at heart, I say it in his favor because it's helped him to know important people—he would rather represent important people and split commissions than have 100 per cent of somebody unknown.

A very shrewd ear, Irving.

The article already has to be a valuable commodity before he'll be interested in it; he doesn't want them except when they've already arrived.

He came into the business at probably its toughest period. And took most of his clients away from other agents, but not in the usual way—more like Raffles with silk hat and gloves.

A lot of people he got actually through parties, whether he gave dinners or they did.

Irene Sharaff, Comden & Green

When Alan wrote Am in P Lazar wanted to read it; Alan (check spelling of Lerner name) glued some pages together & when he got it back from Lazar pages still glued.

Hypochondria is terrible.

(See Charles Lederer & Kurnitz)

OSCAR LEVANT

(Musician, actor, wit and associate of Freed)

On account of "eclectic" he learned another word on page.

I told him a girl had the key to the tranquilizing drugs.

In Paris he speaks every word in English except the last & that's in French.

Moss liked him. Moss is very generous.

Lee let him use her house—a convergingplace for a lot of talent.

Dick Brooks, he took to the Gershwins. People from all over the world would drop in there, it was a world of wonderment for him.

He took Brooks & Brooks called up William Morris & said he was quitting. What's the matter, don't we get you asgmnts? they said. He said Yeah, but I need companionship.

ARTHUR FREED: Oliver Smith, designer. I used to talk about Oliver—at Gershwins' one day Irving came to me & said do you mind if I represent Oliver Smith? He'd heard me talking, but didn't know him.

OSCAR LEVANT: Never heard of him.

ARTHUR FREED: He called the NY agent & made a commission deal. Now he's representing Oliver Smith. We made a deal. He was back in two weeks. When is starting date? I told him I didn't know. Two days later he was back. 20th wants Smith, he said. I said to him, You never heard about Smith until you heard me. Oh that's right he said. He's the only titled agent in Hollywood. He's like an earl or a duke.

(Gershwins is CRestview 12824)

OSCAR LEVANT: I think he's very amusing—not in my way, which is incomparable, but in a strange way.

One day he started to reminisce about his college days . . . I'll never forget that debate we had with Georgetown, he said. I checked with Milton Pickman who was there. He never debated.

ROUBEN MAMOULIAN (Director): A wonderful, wonderful agent and a very nice fellow.

COLE PORTER
(Composer)

I came out here to rest and then got into "High Society" for MGM—he's a great agent—he sold me into it, gradually—I wouldn't do it with ten songs but he was so persistent I finally said yes I would do it.

He sold "Can-Can," which people didn't like. They said it wasn't Cole Porter—and I was only trying to write typical music of the early nineties in Paris.

Whenever a show is opening he takes the trouble to go both to the out of town and New York openings—a great help to the studios, because he knows what the prospects are.

He said to me, "The trouble is you won't let me do any favors for you."

"He took us to Las Vegas like a package—Gene and Howard Feldman, Audrey Wilder.

He always uses a long word when he should use a short one.

Porter had not done a picture since "The Pirate" when Lazar lured him to Hollywood, nearly ten years ago.

I'm devoted to him now, Porter says.

MORE CLIENTS

Maxwell Anderson, S. N. Behrman, Nat Benchley, Vera Caspary, John Crosby, Daniel Fuchs, Charles Jackson, John Patrick, Quent Reynolds, Irene Sharaff, Miles White, Harold Arlen, Blaine and Martin, Ira Gershwin, Harold Rome, Howard Dietz and Arthur Schwartz
Always carries the telephone directory.

BUSINESS OUT OF HIS HEAD

Lazar also has an auxiliary head, which—as English ghosts are said to do—he carries about tucked underneath his arm. It is his private telephone directory, and is nearly as thick as the Los Angeles public one. Carefully indexed, it is studded with tabs saying etc. Once, on a weekend at Las Vegas, Humphrey Bogart and Frank Sinatra stole the directory and hid it in a refrigerator in Lazar's room. "He never thought of looking for it there," Bogart reports gleefully, "and he went mad for four days."

Propriete Bailenea
St Jean de Luz, BP
Aug 23, 1956

Dear Mr Gehman,

Forgive me for being so late with this letter. I've been working a lot and skipping all correspondence. I hope whatever I can tell you about Lazar can be of use to you and is still in time for your deadline.

He's been my friend for a long time—since 1946 or 47, when he used to appear every Sunday at my house on the beach on the Pacific and where he first won my admiration by joining in a rough game we played of riding the long, big breakers in on a rubber raft, which often tumbled in the surf, hurling bodies in all directions. The rest of us were approximately twice his size, and practicing athletes—but when we saw disaster coming and abandoned ship on the crest of a particularly mean wave, Irving hung on with maniac courage, buffeted hideously by the waves, but courageous to the end. Once he had to be fished out, drowning, from under the boat, and another time he came up with some cracked ribs (not disclosed till later in the week by x-ray), but some grim sense of honor kept him at his place in the boat, solitary and defiant, to the end. He was not my agent then, but since nerve is as important to agents as it is to burglers, I remarked him favorably for the future.

At that time MCA were my agents, but a series of changes, chiefly the departure of Leland Hayward to more elegant work, made me restive with them. Still, when Lazar called me one October to ask me if I would accept a job he had suggested me for, I told him that I was bound by contract to MCA till the end of the year. He hung up with expressions of friendship, and waited until January second of the next year, to call me in New York from Hollywood, with an offer. The offer was a fair, round one, and I took it, and Lazar has been my agent ever since, to everyone's satisfaction, with the possible exception of MCA.

Incidentally, there is no contract between us, and our entire business arrangement, which has endured for more than five years now, was sealed merely by a handshake.

Physically, he is small, round, and shiny, like a new kind of beach-toy turned out by an expensive sporting-goods store—say Abercrombie and Fitch. He is full of energy and rotund phrases, possibly due to his early legal training. He is a hypochondriac with a huge case full of all the latest varieties of pills, but when asked about his health, always answers,

"Great!" He is a fanatic on the subject of cleanliness and has been known to travel around Europe with a box of Dreft in his luggage, for doubtful hotel bathtubs. He will only use a towel once and is constantly involved in long discussions with chambermaids and hotel managers in his unending effort to keep a fresh supply pouring through his rooms. In St Jean de Luz, after the chambermaid, misunderstanding his primitive French, had put a wet bath mat back on the edge of the tub twice in a row, he irritatedly heaved the mat out of the window onto the driveway below. In London, once, feeling that the representatives of an airline company had wronged him by cancelling him off a flight he had booked, he demanded to see the manager. When he was told that the manager could not see him, he kicked in a large plate glass window. The manager then saw him. He was on the next plane out. He loves cables, long distance telephone calls, bullfights, traveling, wearing small Irish tweed caps, and making deals. He loves going over lists of stocks and bonds—both those he owns and that he has bullied his clients into buying. He can get tickets for anything. He never admits to losing at the races or at a casino. He stubbornly refuses to move his office, which is a small, two-room, airless den, at the bottom of an airwell, cluttered with scripts, clients, two secretaries, and post-impressionist paintings. He sleeps with blinders, ear plugs, pills, and has his telephone cut off until ten in the morning. He likes pretty girls and mistrusts them and is a confirmed bachelor who dotes over the wives of his friends. Like all good agents who do well for their clients, he is occasionally the object of vituperation by the heads of studios. He enjoys money, giving parties, eating at a showy table in Pavillon. He is learning to ski, because Peter Viertel and I, both clients of his, spend our winters in Switzerland, and he visits us there.

He is loyal, tactful, and kind, and does not repeat the malicious things he hears about you in the course of his dreadful rounds in the studios, and when storms arise, he lets them rage around his head, not yours.

As you can see, I'm delighted he rode all the way in those Sunday afternoons on the rubber raft at the beach at Malibu.

I hope the piece comes out fine.

Sincerely,
Irwin Shaw

DAVID BROWN

(Twentieth Century-Fox Executive)

"Lazar writes candid, brief, non-apple-polishing notes in regard to business—not like some agents who affect a tone of supplication." When a studio owes a client something, he actually duns the studio.

And add Arthur Freed: "Lazar actually puts some studios on suspension. Won't work with them."

Dave: His technique with underlings at studio is to pretend he's protecting them. He will call an underling and say, Jack already knows this, but . . .

Always tries to get a job for someone who's not working.

Represents not only his own clients but other agents' clients, too.

Also Dave Brown: He's very forthright and candid and uses indignation beautifully.

Always shouts on the telephone.

Lazar's will leaves everything to the wives of:

Billy Wilder, Leland Hayward, Irwin Shaw, George Axelrod, Humphrey Bogart, Martin Gabel, Moss Hart, Augustus Goetz, William Goetz and Arthur Hornblow. Also, Mrs. Charles Vidor.

SOMETIMES HE SELLS ABSENT-MINDEDLY

Talking to Milton Sperling about two writers to do additional dialogue for Melville Goodwin, U.S.A. "I got two kids," Lazar said. "They're television writers, very funny. Their show's off the air for the summer. They could work for you for four weeks."

"Are they funny?" Sperling asked. "Can they work fast?"

"These guys," Lazar said dramatically, "can not only work fast but they write funny and original."

"How much do you want for them?"

Lazar assumed a deprecatory tone. "Oh, not much. Maybe like twelve hundred a week apiece."

"O.K.," Sperling said.

"Okidoke," Lazar said. He turned off the telephone and turned to a visitor in his office. "I had Nat Benchley on that screenplay before," he said, "then Charlie Lederer, and now these guys."

Truman Capote once asked Lazar to represent him.

"I thought you didn't like me," Lazar said.

"I've decided that if you can't beat them join them," Capote said.

LEW SCHREIBER

(Executive at Twentieth-Century-Fox)

No agent is hard to deal with.

But he's very ingenious in digging up things, more personal service, a good hustler.

He'll try to move in with the principal and make it look as though he's recommended or suggested a project.

They try to circulate legends about themselves but it's never there.

Orsatti had L B Mayer as a personal friend.

Besides being a very intelligent businessman, he's a good friend of mine, but I've said to him if that's the way you do business, I don't want to do business.

(Tie this to Dave Brown story and Arthur Freed's story)

But you have business arguments with anyone.

Don't see him socially much.

We first met him when he came out as an officer w/WV.

Very, very military but had a run-in with officer in charge & we heard they were going to ship him out.

Smart enough to make contacts for future relationships.

He was plugging them without representing them.

The Gershwins adore him.

On Brooks story (companionship): peculiarly enough, it makes sense; it's all personal contact.

He won't hesitate if Peter Viertel is in Europe and has a problem; he'll get right on a plane and fly over; that makes an author feel that they have a personal contact, having everything done for them.

I used to needle him. I would let him get to the door and say by the way you're fat aren't you? What do you mean? he would say.

I'll tell you a story. We in Paris—he there—called my wife and me, insisted we go to a cafe. Let's call, I said. When we got there, Lido, crowded, he got incensed, they can't do this to me, he gets up, gone about ten minutes, they move us to a table right on the floor, I ask him what he did, he said I said to the waiter this man owns Fox & if you don't treat us right he'll tell all the execs not to come here—and besides, I gave him a couple thousand francs.

Lazar stopped representing acting talent in 1947. When Frank Sinatra's career was going into the decline that reached its nadir just before he made "From Here to Eternity," he literally begged Lazar to represent him. Lazar is extremely fond of Sinatra, but he refused. Next to Sinatra, he is fondest of Humphrey Bogart. The latter's career has never been on the wane, but at one point he decided he could benefit from Lazar's representation. Lazar got wind of it, and refused to speak to Bogart on the telephone. Bogart called several times; Lazar always was out. Finally Bogart took an advertisement in one of the trade papers to inquire how he might get hold of Lazar.

GLORIA ROMANOFF

(Wife of Mike Romanoff, Hollywood restaurateur)

"An agent's word is never binding."

About girls: I know what he tells me, but some of us suspect he's basking in Sinatra's reputation.

Zanuck on sleeper flight, took a pill, groggy in a.m., Lazar in turkish slippers w/turned up toes, Mandarin style coat: "Good Morning, Darryl—I had this made at Sulka's."

He speaks of his time in the service endlessly.

He says, "I did it like anyone else, with grace and a certain amount of charm."

He's nuts on bathmats.

No girl could be fastidious enough for him.

He's maddening and endearing.

I think he wants to accomplish this thing in a social sense.

We enjoy him.

Big thing about not buying his way.

We tease him about the monogram; we ask him if he's afraid he'll lose his things.

He works so hard to endear himself to you it's hard to tee off on him.

"My servant" or "the boy."

I don't think he would dare relax to the point of being completely himself.

Going first class very important.

When Beaton did his photograph he sent copies to everyone.

At the Screen Writers' dinner they did a satire & apologized to him. I was sitting with him all through dinner & he was jittery. He said, I told them I think you should invite me up after the skit—what do you think, Gloria? Then he did go up and took a bow.

This must be part of his charm for us, the wives—we're flattered by his asking our opinions.

He said his mother was beautiful.

He periodically sends checks to restaurants in advance; always has a credit balance.

Lazar liked the Screen Writers' bit.

He's a snob about TV.

He's done fabulously well and is very well liked.

Building himself into a character.

He's a little bit silly.

Biggest sucker in the world for a rib.

Always tells how much he's made.

I think his business is largely five per cent.

He exaggerates *so much.*
If not invited to a party he'll go to New York so he would be able to say I was asked but I was in New York.

(Hayes Goetz, Martha Goetz)

IRA GERSHWIN
(The lyricist)

"Egregious." Ira: where'd you learn that word? L: I looked up "eclectic." How come? I look it up all the time

Lazar at track: only bets even money. Odds went from 7 to 5.
Lazar: My God, I'm playing a long shot.

PAUL STEWART
(An actor)

I was trying to get in the Army, very important to me; Lazar was an officer. I went down to Grand Central and was turned down, 4-F. I was very disappointed. Lazar called me that afternoon. My wife said I was out somewhere, and I had been disappointed. Lazar: "Why'd he go down there by himself? *I* could have got him in the Army."

LAZAR: The only thing we should expect from friends is predictability.

BETTY BACALL

A wife would encumber him socially. Also, how would he ever find a girl clean enough?

Once at Romanoff's with a girl he ordered caviar and specified that he did not want onions.
"I love onions," the girl said.
"My dear," said Lazar, "Please don't have onions."
The girl insisted.
"Very well," said Lazar, "eat all the onions you wish—this is the last dinner you're having with me."

He needs affection badly.

If you happen to drop ashes on the carpet of his limousine, he nearly faints.

He never will get married; he's too meticulous; a wife would drive him crazy

After every hors d'oeuvre he takes out a wash-n-dry thing and wipes off his face and hands

Lazar is a fearful hypochondriac. When Bogart was in hospital Lauren went there and Lazar called for her. He had to wait two minutes in the corridor and was green, said she, when she came out.

Harry Kurnitz says, Whenever I think of Irving, I think of what S N Behrman said of Oscar Levant—"If he didn't exist, you couldn't imagine him." Arthur Freed, the MGM producer, goes further. "I don't believe Irving is real," he says. "Moss Hart wrote him."

KURNITZ

(Screen Writer)

Like most agents, Lazar likes to think big—usually bigger than reality. This not only applies to properties—SOMEBODY says that he always jacks up the announced prices of properties he has sold—but also to things that concern him personally. Harry Kurnitz once bumped into him at a racetrack and asked him how he was doing. "Not so good," Lazar said, "I'm a hundred or eighty dollars behind." "Most people," Kurnits said, "would have said eighty or a hundred. Not Irving."

Lazar is single-minded about his work to the point of absurdity. Introduced by Leonard Lyons, the columnist, to Nancy Berg, a beautiful model, he stared rapturously into her eyes and said, "If only you could write."

10370½ Wilshire Boulevard. On one side lives Kay Starr, the singer; on the other lives Joan Harrison and Frank Sinatra.

Alan Jay Lerner: I put scotch tape on four or five pages of the script for "An American In Paris," then gave it to Irving. He was on the telephone next day—"It's a brilliant script, dear boy, no contest . . ." When the script came back, the tape was still on it.

Fritz Lowe: Lazar is the best-smelling man in Hollywood.

MIKE TODD

Irving Paul Lazar and Charles Kenneth Feldman, says Mike Todd, explaining parenthetically that he is a middle-name-dropper, "are the two greatest agents in Hollywood."

I go back with him to "Hot Mikado."

He was an agent in 1938, he had a guy named Bob Parrish, a colored guy, cast him as Nanki-Poo in "Hot Mikado."

He sells acts because he sells himself (put this in social section).

Very alert guy, ears to the ground all the time.

He can listen to an idle conversation and make a deal. He's always got a bug out—but he never appears to be an agent.

He becomes a willing stooge for his friends—Sinatra and Bogey threw him in the pool once at Palm Springs.

Bill Doll interrupted: We had a colonel trying to railroad him out of "Winged Victory"—ask Moss about that.

He was the sharpest-looking soldier in the Army.

Doll says when he reported Irving threw him a card and said, you got to see newspapermen, meet the press—here, go get yourself some tailored uniforms.

Todd again: He represents everybody who's not signed up with somebody else and many who are.

He's one of the few agents who has ideas. He can cook up things.

He's a semi-literate Frank Orsatti. He could sell the telephone directory. All he would want to know first is how many they printed.

Orsatti was a great literary agent here who never read anything at all. "You know if I read it, I can't sell it."

(This ties into a J Lerner's joke)

I think Axelrod invented him, Mike says; anyhow, he found himself through Axelrod.

I first knew him with William Morris office.

Soon after Lazar joined the Gershwin inner circle, says Oscar Levant, his vocabulary began to change; Ira Gershwin is a great student of words, and Lazar strove to keep up with him. Tell word joke. "Today," says Cole Porter, "he always uses a long word when he should use a short one."

Billy Wilder once watched Lazar spread towels and bath mats on the floor between bathroom and bedroom. "Why do you do that, Irving?" "Why," said Lazar, "who wants to walk on a dirty rug? How else could I avoid walking on that dirty rug?" "Well," said Wilder, "most people would wear bedroom slippers."

SECRETARIES IN NEW YORK
Patricia Lynch BU 8-4264; Ellen Mathers
also has secretaries in Paris, Rome and London

Lazar is so fanatically neat that when he appears in public the creases are so straight, the neckwear so faultless, and the scalp so shiny he seems like a large mechanical toy.

MOSS HART
(Playwright, director)

I was having a drink in the Plaza and this man came up. Irving in civilian clothes is most impressive, but in uniform he was ludicrous. He asked me if I were Moss Hart and then he asked if I would do a show for the AF.

I have a formula for bores. If you say no, they'll sit down. If you say of course, they go away. I said of course. He went away, and I never thought I would hear from him again.

Four days later he called and said, will you come to Washington? I said only at the invitation of General Arnold. By God, two days later there *was* a telegram, so I went down escorted by Irving.

Washington at height of war effort. We sent to Arnold's outer office, and an aide said, you have ten minutes, perhaps it was fifteen. Please don't take any longer.

Arnold's office was as long as Mussolini's. I walked the length of it. General asked what is this all about?

Irving stepped up, came to desk, saluted and launched into an MCA sell. He handed the general a dossier containing everything I'd ever done—all my shows, the notices. And he talked continually. I listened goggle-eyed. The General wasn't much of a playgoer, I don't suppose, and Irving made him feel that was his mistake. In that moment of crisis, instead of being befuddled, all those years of selling talent came to his aid.

I was *very* impressed.

They gave me a plane and a crew, took insides out of plane and put an office and a typewriter in it.

Meanwhile Irving lining up talent while I visited all installations gathering material.

I was grateful to him. When war was over, I said, don't go back to New York to the band agency business. I'll be your first client. I said that although I'd never had an agent in my life.

Sam Goldwyn offered him a job & I advised him not to do it.

I went to Cal to do a picture & introduced him to the Gershwins—their house like the Lincoln tunnel, where he would meet all vehicles.

Introduced him to the Martin Gabels & all around.

I did the MCA pitch for Irving to Cole.

It isn't kind of me to say, but before the Gershwins he always spoke in that curious William Morris patois.

When Kitty and I first were married we were the house guests of the Zanucks & he asked me to do Gent Agmt. Very hard to talk terms with your host, so I called Irving. I told him to concentrate on literary clients—that's what they need, literary people, I told him.

He's a good agent but he has no other life whatsoever. The others have wives, girls, children or some hobby—Irving has the can of Zonite and his agency which of course explains his enormous productivity.

I owe him something like $10,000 in commissions for "A Star Is Born."

Cole never had had an agent.

Someone once said that Irving's great claim to fame is that he has Moss Hart and can't deliver.

He's terribly on to himself, aware of his field in which agents are not beloved.

When he comes to town Kitty and I say, "Irving's here and the livin' is easy."

I think he always levels with me and he is an endless entertainment for me.

He's got a red light that flashes whenever I do anything.

Additional people interviewed: George Axelrod, Lenore Gershwin, Irving Mansfield, Willard Alexander, Monte Proser, Buddy Adler, Leonard Lyons, Lew Wasserman, Sam Jaffe, George S. Kaufman, Ruth and Augustus Goetz, Murray Lazar, Henry Lazar, Max Wilkinson, Adolph Green, Howard Lindsay and Russell Crouse, Abe Burrows, E Y Harburg, Harold Arlen, John Patrick, Truman Capote, Toots Shor, Vincent Sardi, Jr., Johnny Mercer, Gene DePaul, Arthur Laurents, Bennett Cerf, Richard Simon, Herman Levin, Sol Siegel, Mrs. Leland Hayward, Florence Wyatt, Sydney Chaplin, Billy Rose, Quentin Reynolds, Kitty Carlisle, Clifford Odets, Charles Lederer, M. Ashambeau of A. Sulka, Manager of Gotham Hotel, Darryl Zanuck, Harry Cohn, Nathaniel Benchley, Billy

Wilder, Ezio Pinza, Garson Kanin, Frank Tashlin, Jayne Mansfield, Charles Jackson, David Kaonohi, S. N. Behrman, Samuel Goldwyn, etc.

LETTER—SUE FOSTER TO R. G.

Dear Richard:

IP called me yesterday and asked me to give you the following:

"I meant to tell you I get the Herald Tribune and New York Times every morning, which I read before I read the trades, because they don't come in until about 11 o'clock.

Also, be sure to talk to Harry Kurnitz and Frank Sinatra."

Best,
SUE

ARTICLE: "SWIFTY"

(From *The Saturday Evening Post*)

Irving Paul Lazar, whose friends call him "Swifty," seems destined to go down in history as the most preposterously successful Hollywood literary agent of all time, and as one of the most delightfully preposterous characters in a community where preposterousness is well-nigh obligatory. A literary agent is a person who represents writers in the sale of their material. *Variety* has stated that Hollywood is currently controlled by four agencies. Two—William Morris and Music Corporation of America—are large organizations; the third, Charles Feldman, also maintains a staff and is as much a producer as he is an agent. Lazar, the fourth, is a one-man show, and although he keeps an office in Beverly Hills, attended by two harried secretaries and four continually-jangling telephones, his real office lies underneath the snub-visored Irish tweed cap that seems to grow like a patch of fuzzy mold atop his baby-pink head. Lazar is a small, round, shiny man, standing about 5′3″ in specially built-up shoes made for him by Foster of London; his friend and client, Irwin Shaw, says affectionately, "Irving resembles a new kind of beach toy turned out by an expensive sporting goods store." His elfin appearance is accentuated by tiny cobbler's spectacles. He is frantically dandified; he will not carry cigarettes lest the package bulge and spoil the faultless line of his jacket. He is also a hypochondriac who never travels without an enormous collection of pills, soothing potions, patented cleansing cloths and, above all, bottles of disinfectant. Perhaps as compensation for his small size, he comes equipped with ferocious energy and what in Yiddish is called *chutzbah* (i.e., audacity and courage) which has enabled him to consummate fabulous deals in Hollywood and on Broadway for the clients he represents, some of whom are Moss Hart, Ira Gershwin, George S. Kaufman, Cole Porter, Noel Coward, Howard Lindsay and Russell Crouse, George Axelrod, Alan Jay Lerner, Bella and Samuel Spewack and, as they say in Lazar's adopted home town, a host of others, some of whom he technically does not represent at all.

Many of Lazar's deals leave clients not only rich but also awestruck and bewildered. The late Louis Calhern ascribed miraculous powers to him: "Lazar is my shepherd, I shall not want," he said. Another, George Axelrod, is convinced that Lazar is a modern manifestation of The Old Nick: in Axelrod's *Will Success Spoil Rock Hunter?*, the devil is a broad caricature of Lazar named Irving Lasalle. Other amazed, amused but ever-grateful clients, sitting around their swimming pool patios, telling Lazar anecdotes by insect-repellent candlelight, have made him into a living legend, a miniature Paul Bunyon of Hollywood's stucco and plastic wilderness. Harry Kurnitz, the writer, contends that Lazar actually is a giant: "He's dehydrated," Kurnitz says, "and if you add water, he swells to enormous size." M.G.M. producer Arthur Freed goes further. "Lazar isn't real," he declares. "He's a character Moss Hart wrote." Hart agrees that there may be some truth in that. "Lazar is an invention of mine," he says. "Other men have hobbies, motor boats, racing cars, gambling—my innocent pastime is Lazar."

Lazar invokes such comment because he is indefatigable—his close friend Humphrey Bogart says he has never seen him when he isn't working—and because of his methods, which are revolutionary. Hollywood agents customarily take a ten per cent commission from properties they peddle. So does Lazar, customarily; but because he thinks nothing of, and indeed relishes, bargaining for clients who "belong" to other agents, some of his commissions are split—five per cent for Lazar, and five for the original agent. Some, too, are doubled and redoubled. Lazar has been known to represent, and collect from, the buyer of the property as well as the seller, and from assorted souls sold to work on it. This infuriates other agents, principally because they did not think of it first. Lazar perfected the technique with George Axelrod's first hit, *The Seven-Year Itch.* Axelrod had had an offer for the screen rights to the play from M.G.M., and in discussing it with Kenneth MacKenna, the studio story chief, mentioned that he hoped Billy Wilder would direct it. MacKenna passed on this bit of information to Lazar at a party. Lazar went to Wilder and offered to represent him, agreeing to split his commission with Wilder's agent. Coincidentally, the agent Charles Feldman told Lazar he was representing Twentieth Century-Fox, hoping to buy the play as a vehicle for Marilyn Monroe. "Good," said Lazar. "If I can get it for you, Billy can direct it." He flew to New York, introduced himself to Axelrod, and said he could deliver Billy Wilder.

"Suddenly," Axelrod recalls, passing a hand across his brow, "he was also representing *me.* By the time he got finished, he made more money out of the *Itch* than anybody did."

Lazar takes an ebullient pride in thus working both sides of the street. "One thing I do frequently is represent studios and producers in the acquisition of material," he says. "Paramount owned an F. Scott Fitzgerald story, *Babylon Revisited.* I heard that M.G.M. wanted it and told them I thought I could buy it. Then I told Paramount I thought I could find a buyer. I took it and sold it for $120,000. I've also represented such producers as Sam Goldwyn, Harry Cohn, Bill Goetz and Hal Wallis."

And, Lazar might add, he has played one producer against another when it seemed advisable, a statagem now regarded as legitimate by Hollywood agents. The coming of TV, the emergence of the independent studios, and the trend toward stars producing their own films has caused as many changes in the financial structures of Hollywood as the San Andreas fault, the mother of earthquakes, has wrought in the land itself. Big studios are no longer as powerful as they were ten years ago. Competition for story material is keener than ever before. It is a situation made to order for a shrewd trader like Lazar, who gleefully takes full advantage of it—as he did last spring when he was selling Irwin Shaw's novel *Lucy Crown.*

Like all Lazar's clients, Shaw is the beneficiary of Lazar's intense personal interest. Lazar is not content merely to sell; he also likes to advise clients on financial matters and, sometimes, to advance them considerable sums. "His secretary has standing orders to give us anything we need," says Quentin Reynolds. "Once when Irving was in Europe, I had to have $5,000 in a hurry. 'I'm wiring it to you today,' his secretary said." Some time later, Charles Jackson needed money to finance the writing of his novel *The Outer Edges*. "I locked him in a room in Ira Gershwin's house until he finished a screen treatment," Lazar says, "and I sold it twenty-four hours later for $50,000." Jackson, now an advertising agency executive in New York, says that is not entirely accurate. "He didn't lock me up; I went in voluntarily," Jackson says. "When I finished the scenario, he sold an option on it to M.G.M. for $50,000. A year later, when they failed to pick it up, he sold another option to Robert Rossen for $35,000." Lazar's lapse of memory may be forgiven because he makes so many deals of this kind; on current affairs, his mind is quick, incisive, and all-embracing. He gives his clients little rest. From time to time he pops in on them unexpectedly, partly to see how they are getting on and partly because he loves to travel; he seems restless when forces to stay in one country for more than a week at a time. Late in 1955 he flew to the south of France to visit Irwin Shaw, who was finishing a new novel. Shaw said he had no real hope of a movie sale; he feared the story, which concerns a mature woman's affair with a very young man, would never get by the movie censors.

Lazar returned to Hollywood and, in the most casual manner imaginable, began spreading the word that the new Shaw novel was a natural for pictures. By the time Shaw had finished it and the publisher, Bennett Cerf, had sent galley proofs to Lazar, several producers were eager to read it. Lazar shifted into high. He sent proofs by messengers to five studios simultaneously, noting in identical covering letters that he regarded $150,000 as a fair, decent price.

David Brown, story chief of Twentieth Century-Fox, called Lazar that afternoon. "We're interested," he said, "and we may be willing to go a little higher—if you'll close immediately and no monkeying around."

"How high?" Lazar demanded. "Say, $175,000, plus $25,000 for the publisher to exploit the book?"

Brown allowed that his studio might go that high.

Lazar immediately got on the telephone to Harold Hecht, of Hecht-Lancaster, Inc. "Hal," he said, "Twentieth has made a firm offer for the Shaw."

Hecht, before joining Burt Lancaster in the firm that produced the Academy Award-winning *Marty*, had been an agent himself. He knew that if Lazar had mentioned Twentieth by name, he was telling the truth. Unfortunately, he had not yet read the galleys. "We're still considering it, Irving. Don't close until you've heard from us."

"I'll give you twenty-four hours," Lazar said.

Hecht, Lancaster and their associate, Jim Hill, stayed up all night, passing galley sheets from one to the other. At 8:30 A.M. they went out to Lazar's duplex on Wilshire Boulevard. One of his Filipino boys—he has two, one who comes on duty at six A.M. and a second who relieves the first at six P.M.—informed them that the small master had not yet regained consciousness. The trio settled in the living room and, to pass time, began admiring Lazar's collection of paintings, which includes a Picasso, an Utrillo, a Vlaminck, two Rouaults, a Braque, a Gris, and a Dufy (that is Lazar's downstairs collection; his upstairs collection is equally impressive, and so is his office collection).

Presently Lazar descended, affecting astonishment at seeing guests so early in the morning.

"How much do you want for it?" Hecht asked.

That is the kind of question Lazar likes best. "Around $250,000," he said, his eyes gleaming behind his cobbler's spectacles.

"We might go that high," Hecht said.

"Plus $25,000 for Bennett to advertise the book," Lazar said, "plus a percentage for Irwin."

Hecht hesitated, wishing to confer with his associates.

"Excuse me," Lazar said, and rushed back upstairs to telephone David Brown. "David, dear boy," he began, using a familiar greeting he previously had appropriated from his client Noel Coward, "Hecht-Lancaster is offering $250,000."

Brown snorted. "Irving, that's absurd."

"I know it is," said Lazar, as though helpless. "I hate it when it gets this way."

"I'm sure," Brown said, sarcastically. "Count us out."

"Don't count yourselves out, dear boy," Lazar said, hastily. "I'm not sure Irwin will want them to have the book." He tumbled back downstairs. "I think," he said to Hecht, "we might do business."

As a diversionary tactic, Hecht remarked, "This is a nice collection of pictures you've got here, Irving."

Lazar, David Brown has said, is a price-tag with legs. Seeing an opportunity to send the ante up even higher, he said, "You like the pictures, Hal? I tell you what I'll do—for another $100,000 I'll throw in the whole entire collection."

Hecht did not buy the pictures, but he and Lazar did come to terms for the sale of the novel. According to the best estimates available, the figure will ultimately amount to something like $350,-000, a record pre-publication price for a book, and one which may stand for some time to come—or at least, one producer has remarked with understandable bitterness, until Lazar wangles a higher one. Hecht was well pleased, and even more so later when David Selznick offered him a $50,000 profit on his purchase. Lazar, too, was pleased. A few months later, he was panic-stricken. On a plane going from New York to Hollywood, he happened to read the first review of *Lucy Crown* in a news magazine. It was decidedly unfavorable. He got off the plane in Chicago and called his secretary.

"Has Hecht-Lancaster sent the *Lucy Crown* check?"

"Not yet," she said.

"Send a messenger over for it," Lazar said, "before they see that goddamned magazine and change their minds."

No one was more surprised by the sale than Irwin Shaw, who later told a friend he was certain that Lazar had never read *Lucy Crown.* If he had read it, Shaw said, he might have agreed that it was unsaleable. Nearly all of Lazar's clients believe he never reads the properties he sells. Alan Jay Lerner, who with Frederick Lowe wrote *My Fair Lady,* once tested Lazar by taping together three or four pages of his script for the M.G.M. movie *An American in Paris.* "He was on the telephone the next day," Lerner says, "full of praise—'Great script, dear boy, no contest, they'll love it at the studio, I assure you.' But when he sent the script back, the pages were still stuck together." Michael Todd, the producer, says that Lazar's habit of seldom reading anything is actually a great advantage. "Reading might distract him from trying to sell it," Todd says.

"Also, it would take time. Because he doesn't read, he could sell the telephone directory—all he'd have to know is how many copies did they print."

"Irving doesn't have to read," says George Axelrod, "because he's got an occult sense about saleable property. If this minute a Chinese coolie is sitting in a rice paddy working on a novel with a good sound plot and a strong sex angle, Irving will somehow know about it and get on a plane to sign him up."

Lazar, when pressed by chiding clients, insists that he does read. Pressed harder, he owns that there have been times when he has had only a sketchy idea of what a property was all about. When he was offering Sloan Wilson's *The Man in the Grey Flannel Suit,* all he had to go on was a brief verbal synopsis he had heard some weeks before from the book's publisher, Richard Simon. This did not prevent him from accosting Darryl F. Zanuck, then production chief at Twentieth Century-Fox, one night in Romanoff's restaurant. "Darryl," he said, "this could be one of the greatest pictures you've ever made. Why haven't I had an offer from you?"

Zanuck said he wanted the book, and named a figure. Lazar said it was not high enough, but promptly began quoting it to other producers in an attempt to get a better price. When he could not get one, he closed with Zanuck. The exact price has never been published; it was probably around $150,000. Lazar likes to intimate that it was closer to $350,000. "Swifty always jacks up prices," says Harry Kurnitz. "It's his nature. Once I bumped into him at a racetrack and asked how he was doing. 'I'm a hundred or eighty dollars behind,' he said."

"Prince" Mike Romanoff, the restaurateur, had listened to Lazar bargaining with Zanuck in amazement. "It was the first time I'd ever seen Zanuck doing business outside the studio, and what's more, the first time I ever saw an agent approach him while he was dining," Romanoff says. Lazar saw nothing extraordinary in his behavior. Like many small men, he appears to operate exclusively by aggression. He conducts his telephone conversations—about $1,000 worth of them each month—at a pitch just below a bellow. "He is forthright and candid and uses indignation beautifully," says David Brown. Also, Arthur Freed adds, "Lazar is the only agent who puts studios on suspension—just won't sell them anything."

Nor will he be intimidated. Once he was involved in negotiations with L——, a producer with a notoriously short fuse. Lazar and this man occasionally met for a gin rummy game each day at six P.M., and had been friends for some time—but in this deal, Lazar pushed him too far.

"Get out of my office!" L—— screamed. "Get out before I throw you out! I'll tear you apart! I'll have you banned from this lot! If you ever set foot in here again, I'll kill you, I swear it!"

Lazar hastily retreated into the outer office. Seconds later he stuck his head back in the door. "Gin at six, L——?" he asked.

L——'s temper collapsed at this display of fearlessness. "O.K., Swifty," he said.

Buddy Adler, production chief at Twentieth Century-Fox, who describes Lazar as "a great, great agent," says that Lazar sometimes gets carried away by his own *chutzbah*. One afternoon last summer, Lazar called Adler and, without preliminaries, demanded, "What about the girl?"

He was referring to Jayne Mansfield, the generously-endowed blonde star of *Will Success Spoil Rock Hunter?* Adler had signed her to a long-term contract soon after the play opened in New York; but previously, Jule Styne, the producer, had secured her consent to stay in it for its entire run. Now Lazar was trying to do one of two things: either to get Adler to release Miss Mansfield so that Styne could produce a movie version, or to get Adler to buy the play and produce it himself.

"Well, what about her this time?" Adler asked.

"Buddy, I've been thinking," Lazar said. "You could probably make *Rock Hunter* for around $350,000."

"Irving," said Adler, patiently, "I've been thinking myself. That play makes fun of the movies in a nasty way. We don't want to make a picture out of it. We don't want to make it if you give it to us."

Lazar had heard all this before, but he pretended surprise at Adler's attitude. He tried a new tack. "Suppose *we* made it outside somewhere. Will you lend her to us?"

"No," Adler said, flatly.

"If we made it," Lazar persisted, "we could make the girl a star."

"We're *going* to make the girl a star, Irving," Adler said. "She's going to be a big property, big as Monroe. We're putting her in *Wayward Bus* as soon as she gets out of that play. *Wayward Bus*—a Steinbeck story, an 'A' picture."

"All right," Lazar said, agreeably, "suppose we give her to you right now—will you lend her back to us for *Rock Hunter* later?"

"*Give* her to us?" exclaimed Adler, incredulously. "Irving, how can you give us something we already own?"

Lazar decided to withdraw, temporarily. "Call you later," he said.

Adler put down the telephone and addressed an acquaintance. "That's the twenty-fifth time he's tried to make that deal," he said. "There isn't the slightest chance we'll buy *Rock Hunter* or lend out Mansfield. But he won't give up. He never gives up."

Lazar now proceeded to prove Adler's final comment. First he approached Frank Tashlin, a writer-director-producer under contract to Adler, whose arrangement permitted him to work on independent jobs occasionally. Tashlin agreed to do a *Rock Hunter* script and to direct it.

"Tashlin is dying to do it," Lazar informed Adler.

"The answer is still 'No,' " Adler said.

Now Lazar got into touch with his client and friend Richard Brooks, who was in Africa making *Something of Value*. Brooks and Lazar are partners in a producing firm, Richlar, Inc. Brooks agreed to produce *Rock Hunter* if Lazar could get financing. Lazar quickly found a bank ready to put up the money. Then he flew to London. In the course of four days, he sold the writer Peter Viertel to a British company to do a script at a high figure, sewed up the rights to represent Peter Ustinov's play *Romanoff and Juliet* in its American production, and finally got Anita Ekberg to say that she would be delighted to play Miss Mansfield's part in a movie production of *Rock Hunter*.

One week later, Buddy Adler bought *Rock Hunter* for $120,000.

"I fixed it so they had to buy it," Lazar says, with a fiendish chuckle reminiscent of that of Irving Lasalle in *Rock Hunter*. "I got Tashlin—*their* man—and Brooks and Ekberg. I had the money. Jule Styne was willing to go along. Back in New York, I happened to mention to Jayne Mansfield that Ekberg would play the part Jayne had created. She got on the telephone and raised such hell they had to do something to pacify her. So they called me and said they were buying it. I said, 'You can't have it for the price I was asking'—which was $100,000. So they went to $120,000 and I gave it to them."

Miss Mansfield later denied that she had either raised hell or even spoken to Adler or anybody else at Twentieth. But she admits that her agent may have.

Twentieth, possibly to save face, denied that Lazar had anything whatever to do with the arrangement. "We simply discovered a way that we could do *Rock Hunter,*" David Brown said. "Also, we were very anxious to put Jayne into another picture, *Do-Re-Mi,* and that seemed to be the only way we could get her. Lazar stepped into the situation and capitalized on it."

Lazar, naturally, extracted an impressive commission from the package, which gave him some pleasure, but perhaps not as much as he derived from the maneuvers themselves. Today he is rich—from his commissions, which are considerable (last year he sold properties amounting to around $3,500,000), and from his stock investments, which are astute. He doesn't seem interested in money any more. George Rosenberg, a rival agent, adds, "Irving's real fun these days comes from cooking up things. He likes to start things and stir them up. He likes to go where the action is, and if he can't find it, he makes it."

Lazar has been this way all his life. He inherited some of his forging instinct for trading from his father, Samuel Lazar, a German immigrant who settled in Stamford, Connecticut, and became a commission merchant in the butter and egg business. Lazar, born March 28, 1908, was the first of four sons of Samuel and his wife, the former Stari Schacht. In these days when it is fashionable to blame all examples of notable energy on childhood unhappiness, it may startle some to learn that Lazar's home life was warm and stable. The family was always in comfortable circumstances. There was no necessity whatsoever for young Irving Paul to go and sell newspapers, haul ashes, jerk sodas, which left him plenty of time for extra-curricular activities in school. "Irving was president of every class he ever was in," says his brother James, who owns a store in White Plains, New York. "He had a terrific sense of organization. Although he was small, everybody recognized him as a born leader."

Samuel Lazar moved eventually to Brooklyn, where he founded a small-loan company. Irving graduated from Brooklyn's Commercial High School, class of 1926, and entered Fordham University to prepare to study law. Later he transferred to Brooklyn Law School, where he was an active debater and, as usual, president of his class —three years in a row. He was also editor of the school yearbook, *The Record*, which said of him upon his graduation,

"We shall never forget the farewell speeches of Irving Paul Lazar, which were always masterpieces of inspiration and originality."

Some years later, a friend said jokingly, "Irving, you wrote that yourself."

"It's possible," Lazar admitted, cheerfully.

Law school provided Lazar with his first opportunity to sell on commission. Harold R. Medina, later to achieve fame as the federal judge who heard the interminable trial of the Communist leaders, was giving a series of law-review lectures at Columbia University to students about to take the bar examinations. No comparable service existed at Brooklyn Law. Lazar persuaded a professor named Jay Leo Rothschild to give a series of similar lectures. He lined up students and took a small percentage of the fee each one paid. The courses were immensely popular. Quentin Reynolds, a fellow student of Lazar's, says, "Irving must have made $5,000 a year from those lectures." Lazar says, "It must have been more than that—later I took Rothschild on the road to other schools."

Once he himself had passed the bar exams, Lazar set up a small office on Broadway, determined to become what he called "a show-business lawyer"—principally because he felt there would be more color and action in that field. Through a friend he met Ted Lewis, the high-hatted orchestra leader, who in turn introduced him to Sophie Tucker, the singing comedienne, and by acquiring those two as clients he was able to get a few others. His real boost, however, came from the rapid-fire comic Henny Youngman ("Wanna drive a guy nuts? Send him a wire saying IGNORE FIRST WIRE").

Youngman was then working mainly in Catskill summer camps and small nightclubs; whenever Lazar happened to mention that he represented him, which he happened to mention ten or twenty times a day to anyone he met, the response inevitably came, "Henny? *He* needs *a lawyer?*" Youngman's principal contribution to Lazar's career was to introduce him to Lindy's, a Broadway delicatessen restaurant where the sandwiches were as thick as the help were surly, and where all kinds of show business people gathered every day. One day, as Lazar was eating a corned-beef sandwich with absent-minded fastidiousness but actually straining to catch every word that went on at a nearby table where agents and bookers congregated, he heard that Monte Proser, a nightclub impresario, was in town from Chicago to open a new tropical spot, The Beachcomber. A bit later, Proser himself stopped by the agents' table to find out if any of the boys knew where he could get a Hawaiian bandleader. None did. Proser was going out the door when he felt a tug at his sleeve.

"Excuse me, Mr. Proser," said Lazar, who had just set a new Lindy's record for totally demolishing a corned-beef sandwich and paying the check. "My name's Lazar—L, A, Z, A, R. I'm a show-business lawyer. I handle Henny Youngman."

"Henny?" said Proser, incredulously. "*He's* got a lawyer?"

"I've got a Hawaiian bandleader for you, Mr. Proser," Lazar persisted.

"What's his name?"

Lazar hesitated, Proser later told an acquaintance, only for one wild, panic-stricken second. "His name," he said, with consummate confidence, "is Johnny Pineapple."

"Send him to see me," Proser said.

Lazar did know a Hawaiian named David Kaohoni who was then playing bit parts on the Phil Baker radio show. He streaked to the telephone and called him. "Listen, David," he said, excitedly, "from now on you're a bandleader. I got you a job in Monte Proser's new club. You're going to be famous. There's just one thing. From now on, if anybody asks you, remember—your name is Johnny Pineapple." Kaohoni rounded up a few other friends, auditioned for Proser, and got the job. He is still a bandleader today, and his name is still Johnny Pineapple.

Lazar's industry gained him a small repuation in Lindy's. Performers of every kind began going to him for legal advice or assistance. One, a juggler, was being sued by Music Corporation of America for back commissions. Lazar can't remember the juggler's name, but he remembers that he won. He also remembers hearing that Jules Stein, head of M.C.A., said to one of his minions, "Get the man who beat us." Lazar took down his shingle shortly thereafter and went to work for M.C.A. as an agent. He has not practiced law since, but his training still serves him in writing contracts between his clients and people who buy their properties. However, he does not have a contract of his own with any of the writers he represents. "A handshake is contract enough," he says. The clients all agree. "I wouldn't trust Swifty an inch if I were a producer," one says, "but as a client I know he's absolutely trustworthy. None of us has ever known him to go back on his word."

Lazar first regarded M.C.A. only as a bridge to the west coast, where he felt there would be more action. Soon after joining the agency, he sold two writers to Eddie Cantor. "They'll need three transporations to California," he said in closing the deal. "Why three?" Cantor demanded. "These fellows," said Lazar, "are very insecure—they won't go anywhere without their agent." Cantor gave him fare to the coast, where he ran into Morey Amsterdam, then a writer but now a comic, and sold him to M.G.M. to write "additional" dialogue. Flushed with success, he rented an office and set up as an independent agent. Sonny Werblen, of M.C.A., got wind of the move and offered him (Lazar says) $350 a week to stay with the organization. That was a considerable increase. Lazar remained nearly ten years, traveling all over the country, booking big-name bands and performers of various kinds. In recalling those days, Lazar gives the impression that they were fraught with danger: "The clubs were run by The Mob," he says, "and many a time I had to run for my life." Willard Alexander, who was then with M.C.A. but is now the biggest of the big-name band agencies, says it actually was the other way around. "Lazar's persistence drove the nightclub managers nuts," Alexander says. "We had a band in a spot on 52nd Street that wasn't doing so well. We weren't getting our money and sent Lazar around to collect. Two nights later the manager called up and said, 'For God's sake, get him out of here. Every time I turn around he's got his hand in the cash register taking out the M.C.A commission.' "

Lazar explains that he was only trying to keep one of his co-workers from collecting and taking credit. Billy Goodheart, the chief of the band-booking section at M.C.A., liked to keep his four lieutenants

—Lazar, Alexander, Sonny Werblen and Emanuel Sacks—in cut-throat competition, and they were continually attempting to outwit each other. "Once there was a deal cooking to put Count Basie's band into The Famous Door," Lazar recalls. "It was my deal, but I hadn't been able to close it. Goodheart told me he was sending Mannie Sacks in. I went to Mannie and asked him to go along to Philadelphia with me—his mother lived there. I said I had a deal cooking at the Philly Ritz. When we got there I told him to go along and visit his family, and then I got on the train back to New York and made the deal at The Famous Door. For all I know, Mannie Sacks is still sitting there in a hotel lobby waiting for me."

Lazar enlisted in the Army in 1942 amid hoots and cries from his Broadway buddies, all of whom thought his small stature would keep him out. He promptly showed them up by getting himself accepted for Air Force Administrative Officer Candidate School—"I was not only the smallest man in my class, but the smallest *ever* to graduate a second lieutenant." Assigned to Mtchell Field, Long Island, he heard that the Air Force was hoping to produce a show that would rival the Army's *This is the Army*. Lazar sat down and wrote a memo. "I outlined a show that couldn't have been done," he says. "I said my show would have songs by Rodgers and Hammerstein, sketches by Kaufman and Hart, and would star Clark Gable and Jimmy Stewart." That he knew none of these people was of secondary importance. The names impressed the Air Force officials, and he was told to go ahead.

His next moves are best described by Moss Hart. "I was sitting in the Hotel Plaza bar, having a drink with friends," Hart says, "when this lieutenant came up. Irving in civilian clothes is most impressive; in uniform he was small and ludicrous. He asked if I were Moss Hart, and then he asked if I would be interested in writing a show for the Air Force. I have a formula for bores. If you say, 'No,' they'll sit down. If you say, 'Of course,' they'll go away. I said, 'Of course,' and he went away. Four days later he was on the telephone asking if I would go to Washington to discuss the show with General Hap Arnold. I said I would go at the invitation of the General. By God, two days later there was a telegram—so I went down, escorted by Irving. An aide said, 'You have ten minutes—please don't take any more time than that.' We were ushered in. The General's office was about as long as Mussolini's. I walked the length of it. The General said, 'What's this all about?' Irving stepped up, saluted, and launched into a real M.C.A. sell. He handed the General a dossier containing all my shows, the notices, everything. He talked continually. I listened goggle-eyed. The General wasn't much of a playgoer, I suppose, and Irving made him feel that that was his mistake. In that moment of crisis, all those years of selling talent came to his aid. It was a superb performance. I was very impressed."

General Arnold responded to Lazar's pitch by giving Hart a plane and a crew to visit all Air Force installations to gather material for the show, which was to be called *Winged Victory*. Lazar was ordered to New York to begin recruiting talent. "Lazar ran the office like a branch of M.C.A.," says Irving Mansfield, then a press agent but now a TV producer. "Every man was required to put in at least forty missions at Lindy's before he qualified for a good conduct medal." The regular Air Force colonel in charge was driven to distraction by the high-pressure agency methods of Lazar, who was by then a Capt. The colonel tried continually to have Lazar transferred, and was continually frustrated. Lazar's cast included Mario Lanza, Don Taylor, Edmond O'Brien, Red Buttons, Keith Andes, Joe Bushkin, David Rose and Peter Lind Hayes. They played on Broadway for a year, toured for a year, then went to Hollywood and made a movie. "All told, *Winged Victory* raised more than five million dollars for the Air Force relief fund," Lazar says.

"Irving went into the Air Force an artists' representative and came out an artist," says Irving Mansfield. Credit for the transformation is mainly due Moss Hart, who kept insisting that Lazar must not return to M.C.A. After his discharge, Lazar did return for a time, to the Hollywood office. He was listless in the job and endured it for only a year, then threw it up and went to Europe on vacation. When he returned to Hollywood, he was called upon almost immediately by his mentor, Hart. "My wife and I were staying with the Zanucks," Hart says. "Darryl wanted me to do the screenplay for *Gentleman's Agreement*. It's difficult to talk terms with your host, so Irving negotiated for me." It was the highest price ever paid for a screenplay—$150,000.

Hart also did one other important favor. He introduced Lazar to Ira and Lenore Gershwin. "The Gershwins on Sunday afternoons," Hart says, "was a kind of Lincoln tunnel—I knew Irving would meet all passing vehicles there." It was a way station, Oscar Levant adds, for talented people from all over the world. Lazar quickly realized that his previous existence had been nothing but a warm-up. He became one of the regular Sunday guests at the Gershwins'. "We found him amusing," says Levant, "although not, of course, in my way, which is incomparable, but amusing enough." Arthur Freed, another member of the Sunday *klatsch,* says, "Irving threw away the old M.C.A vocabulary and got a whole new one. He began speaking in a new accent—half Brooklyn, half Oxford." Lazar's speech delights his Hollywood associates. They are constantly trying to trip him up on the words he uses. One night at the Gershwins' he used the word "egregious." Ira Gershwin, who collects words the way some old ladies collect dolls of all nations, pounced upon him. "Where'd you learn that word, Swifty?"

"I learned it when I looked up 'eclectic,' " Lazar said.

"How come you looked up 'eclectic'?"

"Oh," said Lazar, "I look up 'eclectic' all the time."

Lazar utilized the Gershwins' Sunday afternoons both to cement relations with clients and to acquire others. Soon after he introduced a young writer, Richard Brooks, into the group, Brooks called his agent and announced that he was going over to Lazar.

"But why?" the agent screamed. "I've been getting you good assignments, haven't I?"

"Yes," said Brooks, "but Lazar gets me companionship."

Some of Lazar's deals were passed to him like little sandwiches. Arthur Freed and Gershwin had been discussing a projected musical, *An American in Paris,* to be built around the compositions of Gershwin's late brother, George. Gershwin asked Lazar to represent George's estate in negotiations with M.G.M. Lazar then sold Freed his client Alan Jay Lerner to do the screenplay. Weeks later, Lazar heard Freed mention that he hoped to get Oliver Smith for the production.

"Who is Oliver Smith?" Lazar asked Oscar Levant.

"He's one of the most talented designers in the New York theatre," Levant said.

"Do you mind if I represent him, too?" Lazar asked Freed.

"If you can get him, go ahead," Freed said.

Lazar contracted for Smith to work for M.G.M. "Two weeks later," Freed recalls, "he came to me and asked when Smith would start on *American*. I said I wasn't sure. Two, three days later he was back asking again. 'What's the hurry?' I asked. He didn't bat an eyelash. 'They want him at Twentieth,' he said. I reminded him he'd never even heard of Smith until I said I wanted him. He said, 'Hurry it up, will you, dear boy? This Smith is a very important client of mine and I want to keep him busy.' "

Lazar was given one other client as a present. "What do you want for Christmas this year?" Moss Hart asked him in 1954.

Lazar knew exactly what he wanted. "Cole Porter," he said, without hesitation.

Hart called Porter and gave him, he says, "a real M.C.A. pitch." Porter had never had an agent, but agreed to give Lazar a chance. Within a short time, Lazar wrapped up what he termed "a million-dollar package" and sold it to M.G.M. It involved screen rights to Porter's *Can-Can*, plus his services to write music for two movies, *High Society* and *Les Girls*. Last summer Porter complained, "I came to Hollywood a year ago to rest, and Lazar's had me busy ever since."

There was one other inconvenience, involving a secret vice of Porter's. The most sophisticated songwriter of our time is hopelessly addicted to radio soap operas. "Cole," says the actor Martin Gabel, "knows every dreadful thing that's happened to Helen Trent since she first went on the air." Lazar also has a vice which is less secret, since he likes to practice it when people are visiting him in his office. "Get me Cole," he will bark at Susan Foster, his secretary, or "Get me Noel," or "Get me Dore." Soon after Porter and Lazar shook hands, their vices clashed. "Lazar was so pleased and proud at having Cole for a client," says Gabel, "he couldn't resist calling him up all the time. Finally Cole called Moss. 'Look here, Moss,' he said, 'isn't there some way of getting him to lay off? He calls me so often I never find out what happens to Our Gal Sunday!' "

Lazar takes an intense pleasure from the new life that was conceived in the Gershwins' living room. He loves to discuss it as though he were gossiping about someone else. Some people drop names; he spills them like jellybeans—but whereas most namedroppers blight gatherings, Lazar only amuses his friends. They love to josh him about his social activities. Harry Cohn, of Columbia Pictures, has taken to calling him "The Society Agent." "What are you doing this week end?" Cohn asked Lazar one Friday in midsummer.

"I'm going up to Las Vegas with Betty Bogart, Cole and the Romanoffs to see Judy Garland," Lazar said.

"You really go with the big time, don't you?" Cohn said. "You'd never go out with a couple of bums, would you?"

"Harry," Lazar said, solomnly, "I find going out with people who are rich, famous, successful simply divine."

On many occasions Lazar's gregariousness has brought him clients without his having made any noticeable effort. "He first won my admiration," says Irwin Shaw, "by coming out to my house and joining in a rough game we played of riding the long big breakers in on a rubber raft which often tumbled in the surf, hurling bodies in all directions. The rest of us were approximately twice his size, and practicing athletes—but when we saw disaster coming and abandoned ship, Irving hung on with maniac courage, buffeted hideously by the waves, but courageous to the end. Once he had to be fished out, drowning, and another time he came up with some cracked ribs . . . but some grim sense of honor kept him at his place, solitary and defiant. He was not my agent then, but since nerve is as important to agents as it is to burglars, I marked him favorably for the future."

Some time afterward, Lazar heard that Leland Hayward, who was then Shaw's representative, was planning to leave M.C.A. to devote all his time to production. Lazar knew that Samuel Goldwyn had a script on which Shaw could work; he persuaded Goldwyn to postpone the job until Shaw became his client. When Shaw's contract with M.C.A expired, Lazar immediately called him. "How would you like to be my client?" he asked. Shaw said, "I tell you what, Swifty—if you can get me a $50,000 job immediately, I'll do it." Lazar called Goldwyn and told him he could have Shaw for ten weeks at $5,000 a week. Goldwyn complained, but accepted. "Lazar has been my agent ever since," Shaw says, "to everyone's satisfaction, with the possible exception of M.C.A."

Other clients—John Patrick, Arthur Laurents, Betty Comden

and Adolf Green, Johnny Mercer, Ruth and Augustus Goetz—trooped happily into Lazar's stable. "Almost single-handed," one producer says, "Swifty made Hollywood into a writer's market." Not content, he began to turn his attention increasingly toward Broadway. In the 1956–'57 season, seven of Lazar's clients or teams of clients will have plays opening in New York. Most of these clients are writers, but a few are directors, choreographers or composers. Lazar does not like to handle performing talent; although he represented Louis Calhern when the latter was down on his luck, he refused to handle his close friend Frank Sinatra even when the latter's career seemed at an end. "I knew Frank would come back," Lazar said.

Lazar now has so many hot clients that other agents cannot understand how he manages to keep track of them. The answer, says Moss Hart, is simple: "Other agents have lives of their own. Irving has none—all he's got is that agency and a bottle of disinfectant." Moss is referring to Lazar's abnormal passion for cleanliness. He will not even enter his own limousine—a high, old-fashioned Cadillac, a gift from Mrs. William Goetz—without making certain that it has been recently sprayed with a perfumed antiseptic. He keeps his own bed-linen in hotels where he stays habitually, and pales at the idea of using a towel more than once. His scrupulous neatness is carried out in his clothes, which are all made to order and monogrammed with an I.P.L. device of his own design; even his socks and underwear are monogrammed.

"Swifty is so clean," says Lauren Bacall, "I don't believe he'll ever get married. Where could he ever find a girl neat enough for him?" Lazar appears to want to get married, nevertheless. Like the ghost of Anne Boleyn that walked with her head tucked underneath her arm, he never goes anywhere without an auxiliary head, a fat private telephone directory, the size of the Manhattan one, indexed GIRLS-HOLLYWOOD, GIRLS-LAS VEGAS, GIRLS-NEW YORK, and GIRLS-EUROPE. He seldom appears in public without a dazzling girl on his arm. Lazar's girls all have two things in common: they are all a head or two taller than he, and all—says George Axelrod—send food back in restaurants ("One night I was sitting in Cherio's and saw a big plate of steak going back to the kitchen," says Axelrod, "and I said to my wife, 'Swifty's in town,' and sure enough, there he was in the front with one of his girls."). The girls have a third characteristic in common: none has been able to hold Lazar's interest for long. His real loves are the wives of his friends and clients, for whom he is an ubiquitous extra-man, limousine-sender, and escort. Lazar has written his will to leave every cent to these wives—Mrs. Axelrod, Mrs. Irwin Shaw, Mrs. William Goetz, Mrs. Augustus Goetz, Mrs. Billy Wilder, Mrs. Charles Vidor, Mrs. Moss Hart, Mrs. Ira Gershwin, Mrs. Martin Gabel and Mrs. Humphrey Bogart. The will states specifically that at the time he dies, all the wives are to be flown into the Beverly Hills Hotel, where they will be put up in grand style for three days, during which they are to throw a monster party. Lazar, with his customary penchant for detail, has even planned the menu for the principal dinner at this marathon. "It ought to be one hell of a do," he remarked not long ago to a friend. He looked a trifle wistful. "I wish I could make it myself."

Post Script: The first draft of this story ran to forty typed pages, or about twenty pages more than the longest single piece I had sold to the *Post*. Wilkinson was disinclined to send it off at that length. I thereupon cut it to twenty-eight and begged him to send it. He agreed, but as he had expected, it came back immediately. With it was a note from Stuart Rose that said,

The piece is full of amusing stuff, but it is too long, extremely hard, at times, to follow and not understandable to the layman, who hasn't the faintest idea of what a writer's agent does. I find myself constantly explaining the functions of literary agents to lay friends, who listen to my explanations with vague incomprehension and then stride away, shaking their heads.

"What Dick will have to do, then, is to cut this to eighteen pages. The early pages are most confusing and a great deal of the cutting should be done in that area. Dick quotes too many people about Lazar and the effect is to roughen the style. Many of the anecdotes are told in an elliptical way, as if the author were addressing the subscription list of *Variety*. He isn't. If Dick will undertake to do all this and then, pretty far up front, explain in simple, declarative sentences the function of an agent, I think he'll be able to get a piece out of this. Some years ago, we published some articles on the Hollywood ten-percenters by the late Alva Johnston. I'm sending tear sheets of these articles, so that Dick may read them, as they are models of what articles of this sort should be. The manuscript goes back to you, herewith, for further work.

I was crushed. I did not see how I could cut ten more pages out of the article. Also, I did not agree with Stuart's contention that the average reader does not understand the function of a literary agent. I had explained it clearly, near the beginning.

The piece was returned to Wilkinson on a Friday. Saturday morning I sat down to begin cutting, and got nowhere. I went out to lunch and returned to have another go at it. Again I got nowhere. Then I had an idea. I called A. B. C. Whipple, an articles editor at *Life.* I told him I had the piece, did not want to cut it, and wondered if he would like to have a look at it over the weekend. He said, "I'd like to see it, but it's four o'clock and I'm just now leaving for Grand Central to catch a train." I said, "I'll meet you at the Information Desk." He read it on the train. At seven P.M. he called me and said, "Ordinarily we would buy this at this length—the length is not important. But I checked with the guys at the office just now, and we've got another piece about a big operator. It's Ezra Goodman's story of how Mike Todd cajoled the stars into working for him in *Around the World in Eighty Days.* The general operations of Lazar and Todd are too similar. So I'm going to have to say No." I thanked him for his kindness and sat down to cut ten pages out of the piece. This time I pretended that someone else had written the story. I sacrificed some of the best material—many of the quotes about Lazar that appeared at the beginning, and the stories about his days as an agent for bands. Then I attempted to clarify the lead. I gave it to Wilkinson on Monday and he sent it immediately to the *Post.* It was eighteen pages long. On Tuesday Ben Hibbs, the editor, wrote a note saying, "Since Stu Rose is in New York today, I am writing to say that we are accepting the Lazar piece." I was pleased, but it was rather a hollow pleasure. I would have preferred to have seen the piece at its original twenty-eight-page length, which is the way I have reprinted it above.

Post Post Script: Until recently, I used separate notebooks or composition books or folded wads of copy paper for the notes I took on each story, then threw the notes, along with clips and bits of writing and allied material, into 9″ x 12″ envelopes that fit into a file-drawer. When I went to Europe in April of 1958, I found myself, as usual, researching a number of jobs at once—and I also found that what with passport case, cigarette case, keys, coins, address book, daily expense book and wallet, not to say a little notebook for each story I happened to be working on in a single day, I looked like someone who had just robbed the notions counter in a department store. It must have been vanity, then, that prompted me to begin using my present system, which is to buy one notebook and use it for various stories, appointments, telephone numbers, lines that I want to remember, etc., until it is full. When that happens I make a list of the contents of the notebook, date it, paste the list to the cover, and throw the book into my briefcase with books I have filled previously. This means that any given book may contain notes for four or five stories. The system's disadvantage lies in the fact that a single story may be spread over five or six notebooks, all of which I must keep at hand. Conceivably a story could be spread over as many as twenty or thirty notebooks—I find I use up one or two a week—especially if I continue to gather material on a long-range basis, as I have done in the past and as I have every intention of continuing to do.

The notebook dated April 1, 1958, contains the following material:

Page 1. GAMBLING IN FRANCE. Observation of men queued up to buy lottery tickets.

Pages 2–9. FIRST INTERVIEW WITH FRANCOISE SAGAN. Notes and quotations.

Pages 9–18. INTERVIEW WITH ALAIN BERNHEIM, SAGAN'S LITERARY AGENT. Notes and quotations.

Page 19. Single note on GAMBLING IN FRANCE.

Pages 21–22. NOTE TO INTERVIEW HELAINE LAZAREFF, EDITOR OF "ELLE," WHO KNOWS SAGAN. Additional notes and quotations from Bernheim.

Page 23. ONASSIS STORY. Note to check rumor that Aristotle Socrates Onassis' wife bought twelve Christian Dior dresses on a single afternoon.

Page 24. SHORT NOVEL. In France I began writing a short novel, and one night in a cafe, as I was sitting thinking about it, I had an idea for a scene. Outline of this scene.

Page. 25. STEPHEN GRAPPELLY STORY. Copy of menu in place where he works.

Pages 27–32. INTERVIEW WITH GRAPPELLY.

Page 33. ANOTHER SHORT NOVEL NOTE.

Pages 34–51. SECOND INTERVIEW WITH GRAPPELLY.

Page 53. DIRECTIONS ON HOW TO GET LES TROIS MAILLEZ, NIGHT CLUB

WHERE MEZZ MEZZROW IS PLAYING IN ORDER TO INTERVIEW HIM FOR SATURDAY REVIEW PIECE.

Page 54. RANDOM NOTES FOR THE BOOK ON MAGAZINE ARTICLE WRITING. (This book)

Page 55. Name of man reputed to be Onassis' press agent. Name of brand of mascara a girl asked me to bring back. Address of Jack Elliott, old pal from America.

Page 56. Name of lens a friend wants me to bring back from Germany. Two books to send Nancy, the helpful librarian in the *Herald Tribune* morgue.

Page 57. Time of arrival of Onassis at Orly field following Saturday.

Pages 58–73. INTERVIEW WITH KENNY (KLOOK) CLARKE FOR PURPOSES OF BOOK I SOME DAY PLAN TO WRITE ON LIFE OF CHARLIE PARKER.

Page 74. List of articles completed thus far on trip.

Page 75. INTERVIEW WITH BERNARD VALERY, PARIS NEWSPAPERMAN, ON SAGAN.

Pages 76–91. SECOND INTERVIEW WITH VALERY.

This notebook covered about four days' activity. Now that I have been using this system instead of my old one, I find it works much more efficiently.

Post Post Post Script: Thus far I have not said anything about the mechanics of research. Perhaps I have been avoiding it deliberately, for the process is different for each story. Some stories, like the Lazar piece, demand many conversations with many people; others can be done by talking to one or two individuals. Some require a good deal of technical knowledge on the part of the writer. I have found that it is wiser to stay away from the stories that are not in fields with which I am familiar, because I waste too much time in researching them. Once I had an as-told-to piece to do for *Collier's* with Dr. John Stewart, an astrophysicist at Princeton, who had definite ideas on how the United States Weather Bureau could improve its accuracy and efficiency. In order to be able to talk intelligently to Stewart, I had to read books about the weather—and, later, I had to re-read many chapters in each one. I wound up with more knowledge of the weather than I really cared to possess. I also wound up with a saleable article, but the price I got for it was not worth the amount of time expended. That was an exception. In most instances it is far better to over-research and to decide later what to use and what to discard. Furthermore, one never knows when the "overage" may come in handy. Maurice Zolotow and I sometimes trade notes on subjects that one has done and the other has recently been assigned to do. I did Marlon Brando for *Cosmopolitan* five years ago; two years ago, Zolly did him for *American Weekly*. Much of the material I had collected, I had not been able to use; I gave it to him, he checked it out, and incorporated it into his own series.

Another good reason for researching overzealously is the likelihood of stumbling upon another piece. Zolotow and I have found that one piece almost invariably leads to another. Once I did Abe Burrows for *Theatre Arts*. He was then appearing on a TV panel show produced by Irving Mansfield. I talked to Mansfield about Abe, and in the course of our conversation concluded that he might make a good subject. I sold him to *Esquire*. Mansfield then had a new comedian he was pushing, Sam Levenson. I sold Sam to *Theatre Arts*. A couple of my interviews with him were held in Sardi's theatrical restaurant, which ultimately resulted in my first non-fiction book, *Sardi's: The Story of a Great Restaurant*. During the Sardi's research I became acquainted with Leonard Lyons, the columnist, who since has proved a first-rate source of information, and through Lyons I met Monte Proser, later an advisor to Eddie Fisher, about whom I did several stories. Fisher's manager was Milton Blackstone, who also handled Grossinger's, the celebrated Catskill resort. I met Phil Silvers at Grossinger's—and Red Buttons, and Milton Berle—and later did pieces about all three. I could fill this book with this kind of chain of meetings and events.

To return to mechanics, I have no standard operating procedure —except to attempt to avoid those pieces the research for which I know will not come in handy later on. (The piece with Stewart about the Weather Bureau was a disaster; I have never once been able to use any of the material I could not use in the article we turned in.) After I get my assignment, I first procure all the clippings about the subject that I can find and read them through thoroughly. Frequently I do not have to send out for back-issue magazines or newspapers, because I always maintain a back-of-the-mind file of ideas I might take on at some future date, and I collect material on these ideas over long periods of time. Right at the moment, for example, I have at least two dozen back-of-the-minders in my hopper: Bean Soup, George London, Oscar Levant, Harry Cohn, Strange Edible Creatures of the Sea, Gambling in Paris. Finders Inc., Twins, Lee Myers, Cooperatively Owned Restaurants, George Axelrod, The Gabor Sisters, Steiff Toys, Rome Movie Colony, Pee Wee Russell, etc. I have no idea when, if ever, I will do these articles, but I continue to collect information about them. More of this later.

After I read the clips I generally have a talk with either the press agent of the person involved or someone who knows a good deal about the person or the subject, if it is an impersonal subject. In this conversation I try to find out names of other people who have information that will be helpful. I may also have talks with two, three or even a half-dozen additional people. Finally I am ready to interview the subject—or to tour the shop, if the piece is about some industrial or business organization. If the piece is a profile, I attempt to see the subject at least three or four times. If I can live with him, so much the better; sometimes a subject will say, "Come off on a trip with me." (Two hours after I met Mike Todd, who was not only a great, warmhearted man but a reporter's dream, we were on an aircraft heading for California.) After all this I go back and check up on facts I heard in the interviews. If additional reading is required, I go to the library. Then I make sure I have seen everybody, and I start to work. Many times, during the work, I make telephone calls to check on facts of which I am not certain.

How long all this takes is difficult to estimate. Some jobs take months; others take a few days. I can never say exactly how long any given job takes because I usually am working on several simultaneously. I believe my record was set in a piece I did in the winter of 1958 in London for *True*. I researched it one morning and wrote it in the afternoon; it was five thousand words long. On the other hand, it took me a year to collect the material on the article about the submarine sandwich, which I sold to the *Post*. The question of how much time one spends on any given story was best answered by Eli Waldron in a class I was conducting haphazardly at New York University a few years ago. Eli was my guest speaker, and we agreed that it might be effective if he were to read one of his stories and then tell how he conceived it and constructed it. The story was well-received. One student raised his hand timidly, and I acknowledged him.

"Mr. Waldron," he said, "how long did it take you to write that story?"

Eli was then thirty-two.

"Thirty-two years," he said.

8 · *More on Research*

THE AVERAGE article writer can do about twelve full-length, fully-researched pieces in a year. So the professionals declare. Some, in fact, say they cannot do that many. Although nearly every notable writer in history has been prolific—I need mention only Dickens, Balzac, Dostoievsky, among others—in recent years there has been a tendency in certain cliques to run down the prolific writer simply because he is one. I know of one writer who, having written two novels which were to be published in a single year, went to the trouble of putting a pen-name on the second in order to keep the critics from accusing him of being too prolific (it was an empty gesture, for the publishers, running true to form, let his real identity be known before the book came out). Because it is bad hat to be prolific, most writers these days refuse to announce their real production. I maintain that twelve per year is low. I also maintain that those writers who do only twelve per year do not know how to organize their work—or, rather, their research.

The piece following represents three years of research. I first met Red Norvo, the subject, in 1951, when he was playing at The Embers, a New York club. I met him at a Chinese restaurant, Confucius, run by an amiable gentleman named Joe Mah who liked jazzmen and would serve Scotch whisky in a teapot after the official curfew of four A.M. Eddie Condon and I used to go up there after Eddie's place closed: "Let's go up and see Joe," Eddie would say, "and get some of that slant-eyed booze." Red was on the wagon, but he dropped by Confucius to eat nearly every night. The two of them would get to reminiscing about their days in Chicago during the late twenties and early thirties, and I would prod them with questions that sent them into further explorations of their youths.

Red at that time was playing "modern" jazz. Eddie was clinging stubbornly to the same sort of thing he and his friends had played. So were the rest of the Chicagoans, although Dave Tough had attempted to make the transition to the new music. Eventually it dawned upon me that Red was phenomenal. He was the only one of the old-timers who had become a modernist—indeed, a modernist admired by the younger generation of jazz musicians. I decided to do a piece about him, and this is the one I did—three years after our initial meeting.

ARTICLE: "RED MEANS GO"

(From *Esquire*)

In Las Vegas, Nevada, it is axiomatic among the managers of hotels, night clubs and gambling salons that anything which distracts patrons from the tables is a major disaster. Musicians therefore are instructed to play as pianissimo as possible, in order not to attract attention. One night a few years ago in the Sahara Hotel, Red Norvo, the vibist, and the two men who comprise the Red Norvo Trio were following this unwritten rule meticulously. Norvo and his bassist and guitarist customarily play softly, so softly, in fact, that a listener must strain to catch every deft, subtle nuance, but this night they were keeping it so low that, as Red later said, "It was like we could hardly hear ourselves; it was like *dead*." Every conversation in the room thus came clearly to the bandstand, including one which gave Norvo pause.

A girl in her twenties had come in and was standing at the bar with an escort roughly her age. "Red Norvo," she said, wonderingly. "Why, I remember hearing him when I was a little girl."

"Yes," said the young man. "He sure holds his age for a man of sixty, doesn't he?"

Norvo, now forty-four years old, broke up in the middle of an elaborate cadenza he was working on his vibes. He is a man who laughs often, and explosively, and in this case, he flipped, or as he put it later, he *like* flipped (Norvo, in common with many musicians, has a great fondness for the adverb "like"). Yet the young man's comment served a purpose. It was a fitting, if somewhat left-handed, tribute to Red Norvo's durability.

There are many, many jazz masters still playing today who were going strong during the mid-twenties, when the music was in its Golden Age. Louis Armstong is blowing better than ever, some of his admirers believe; Eddie Condon shows no sign of losing his perpetual youthfulness; the Dorsey brothers are carousing as raucously as they did in their teens; and there are literally hundreds of old-hand sidemen still on hand. Most of the holdovers, however, have changed their styles little, except to get louder. The music one hears at Condon's Greenwich Village night club today is not much different from that played by the Mound City Blue Blowers or Elmer Schoebel's Friar Society Orchestra, circa 1929. Of all the old-timers, only Red Norvo, the man whose name sounds like that of an insecticide or possibly a rat poison, has gone onward and upward, expanding his musical personality, experimenting and keeping abreast of the newest developments in jazz. He is the only man to have bridged the gap between gutbucket and bop with any degree of success, and he has done it so successfully that even a die-hard like Condon, who likens bop at best to the sound made by a waiter dropping a tray of dishes, admits that he enjoys Norvo's music. Condon, however, is a Norvoite from antediluvian days; he once said, "There are two kinds of xylophone players—there is Red Norvo, and there are all the rest."

The fact is that Norvo singlehandedly made the xylophone, which he played before switching permanently to vibes, an object of respect among jazz musicians. It was a labor that required nearly forty centuries, all told. The xylophone is a member of the family of the marimba, which has been around almost as long as history remembers; there is evidence that it was being hammered in Burma, Siam and China 4000 years ago, and in Africa and Central America around the time of the birth of Christ. The Greeks had the xylophone, and in fact gave it the name, which means "wood voice" (most people pronounce it "*zile*-ophone," but Norvo and other xylophonists usually say "*zila*phone"). The instrument is nothing more than a set of wooden blocks placed over chambers, or pipes, of different sizes, which produce a resonant sound when the blocks are struck by mallets. In the old days, the mallets or hammers may have been made of bone; today they are constructed either of wood, tightly wrapped cord or yarn, or rubber, mounted on a slender handle. The xylophone differs from its parent marimba in that it is pitched higher, is less resonant and less mellow. The first xylophone virtuoso was Michael Joseph Gusikov, who lived in the early nineteenth century and was admired by Mendelssohn, the composer. Despite his regard for Gusikov, Mendelssohn never wrote xylophone parts in his compositions, and the instrument did not come into favor among highbrow composers until comparatively recently. It is now used often in the works of Stravinsky, Prokofiev and Milhaud. The fact is that the xylophone has always been something for the lowbrows. Its popularity reached a zenith in minstrel shows and in vaudeville and variety bills around the turn of the century, and the people who played it on the stage were a curious lot: phony Mexicans wearing painted sideburns and wide, rhinestone-studded sashes, and groups of pigeon-breasted, muscular-limbed girls led by slick-haired sheiks. Xylophonists used to tap-dance behind their instruments, sing, produce Teddy bears and bananas and American flags from the pipes, and tell lulus. Sometimes they would press hidden springs which caused the xylophones to fly apart or fall to pieces. This used to break up Chautauqua crowds. Some of the larger orchestras of the twenties and thirties, such as those of B. A. Rolfe, Jean Goldkette and Paul Whiteman, would now and again use the xylophone, but only in a tinkling arpeggio buried in a morass of brass and reed sounds. The drummer usually doubled on it. Norvo, whose background included a period in which he wore the sash and tap-danced in the breaks, changed everything. Although he plays vibes almost exclusively today, he is still thought of as a xylophonist, or rather, as *the* xylophonist, for it was he alone who took it into the smoky traps and barnlike recording studios where jazz matured, demonstrating that it could be as pure and pleasing a percussion instrument as, say, the piano or the drums.

Norvo's transition from xylophone to vibes began in the late thirties, and was gradual at first. Vibes differ in that the bars are made of metal, most often steel or aluminum, and the instrument has a sustaining pedal and is equipped with a motor-driven vibrato-producing mechanism. Contrary to popular belief, the word "vibes" is not the nickname for the instrument; it is the word used to cover all instruments of which the manufacturing-company trade names are "Vibraphone," "Vibraharp," "Vibrabells," etc. Norvo turned permanently to vibes around 1944, when he joined the Benny Goodman Orchestra as a member of the sextet. "The vibes seemed to like blend better," he says, adding that his new instrument is easier to play than the xylophone, principally because the sustaining notes are produced at the touch of a foot pedal, whereas in xylophone work they must be produced entirely by wrist action.

Aside from having marked his chosen instrument with distinction, Norvo is important for one other reason. In many respects, his life parallels the growth of jazz from disreputability to respectability, its rise from the gin mills and gonger-pads and rent parties up to the staid precincts of Carnegie Hall and the Library of Congress. In the twenties, jazz was mainly the music of people who balled—that is, people who got drunk often, smoked tea, caroused and stayed awake for days. Today it is still the music of those same people, God knows, but it is also the music of people like Winthrop Sargeant, Deems Taylor and even Arturo Toscanini. To admit jazz addiction is no longer to confess a vice; in some circles, in fact, it is a mark of the most accepted esoteric taste, like owning a neat little Picasso drawing or knowing which cheap wines aren't poisonous. In Norvo's youth, he balled with the best; although he was never much of a jam-session man, the xylophone being a rather too unwieldy instrument to tote about under the arm, he fulfilled most of the other requirements for the old-time dedicated jazzman. He practiced his instrument like a high-wire man getting into shape, he drank a lot, he experimented with the dread weed, he stayed up for long stretches and he sometimes vanished off the face of the earth for a day or two at a time. He failed to show up for jobs and was fired regularly, only to be rehired at once simply because there was no one else around who could match his skill with the hammers. He lived in a monstrous, amiable fog of forgetfulness. Once, while working for Stan Hubbard at KSTP in Minneapolis, he took a two-week vacation in Chicago, where he ran into Victor Young, then putting together a musical program for a washing-machine company at NBC. Young invited Norvo to try out. After hearing him in the band, Young asked him to stay on. Norvo agreed. A few days later Stan Hubbard came to town and met Young. They got to talking about hot musicians and Norvo's name came up. "We got him on staff at NBC," said Young, proudly. "That's funny," said Hubbard, "because we got him on staff up at Minneapolis, too." Young was ready to fire Norvo, but Hubbard generously released him from his KSTP job. The redhead was fired some months later. His Chicago NBC boss was taking an Eastern brass hat on a tour through the studios, and they came upon Norvo sleeping under a piano, a beatific smile on his face. The Chicago man shook him, but Norvo hardly stirred. "Not now, honey," he murmured. "Got to get to rehearsal in the morning."

Such episodes are relics of the past. As jazz has grown to be more widely accepted, Red has grown more conventional. Today he is on the wagon, and he would no more consider lighting up the lily of the Congo than would John Foster Dulles. He is a happily married home owner (in Santa Monica, California), the father of two small boys and a small girl, and the master of a scampering of dapple dachshunds. For a musician, he keeps surprisingly regular hours; he eats well and sleeps well. He is something of a health faddist, but what Californian isn't? He refinishes furniture and collects Bennington ware and pewter ("I dig that pewter," he sometimes says). This insurance-collector normality has not only not hampered his playing, it actually seems to have improved it. Today his work—and this opinion is shared by Benny Goodman, Woody Herman, Artie Shaw and even Lionel Hampton, one of the greatest vibists of all time—is nothing short of sensational. The Red Norvo Trio, all the critics agree, is the most exciting, imaginative and musicianly small combination extant.

There are those who say this is so because Norvo is a genius. Jazz musicians and enthusiasts thrive on hyperbole, of course; if anything is good, it is "the greatest," and if anything is so good it's far and away ahead of everything else, it's "the gonest." But if genius is the infinite capacity for work, for taking pains, and for other-worldly detachment, the word fits. No musician in the business works harder, and none is more of a perfectionist. In 1953 Norvo was at The Embers, a New York night club which he regards as home base, if only because he has played longer there than anywhere else. Although his guitarist and his bass man had played with him in several out-of-town engagements, Norvo insisted upon rehearsing three days each week throughout the five-week run at The Embers. The Trio worked in Red's room at the Hotel Woodward, a Broadway hostelry favored by musicians and entertainers. They got down to business at one each afternoon and did not knock off until it was time to go to work in the evening. Sometimes they spent two or three hours running through one tune, or a portion of one. Yet, strangely enough, they never *set* anything, much less wrote anything down. "What we were doing in those rehearsals, we were like getting to *know* each other," Red says. A month later they were called by Decca Records to make an album. Most musicians arrive for a record date a bit late, glance at the score, sit down and cut. The Trio rehearsed ten days for the sides.

Norvo's detachment is rather Einsteinian. Although he is something of a boisterous extrovert, with a laugh that bends him double even when he is mildly amused, he regularly falls out of any conversation into some mysterious inner world of his own on the average of twice every thirty-odd minutes. He gives the impression that he visited this planet temporarily. "Red's like off in music all the time," says Tal Farlow, who plays guitar in the Trio. "He's like always ahead of everything," says Jimmy Raney, who was replaced by Farlow. "That's right," chimes in former Trio member Red Mitchell. "With Red, it's always like The Future Department. He gets like impatient when he hears anything done the same as usual. He like wants to figure out right away something new to do with it, something different to play." (Norvo's musicians are as fond of the adverb "like" as he is.)

Norvo's detachment is never so strikingly noticeable as when he is playing. He holds his hammers, two in each hand, in twin X's, controlling them with his thumbs and the joints of his fingers; the stroke of each is motivated by the wrist, but it is not, Norvo says, really a stroke. "It's like you pull up," he says. "I get away from the bar, like the hammer was attached to a rubber band about six inches above the bar, pulling it back up." Norvo's arms move over the bars as though they were pivoted dollies. He crouches a bit, bouncing gently in light, easy rhythm. His face is something to see. It is that of a chubby elf at times, seraphic and at heavenly peace; other times it wears an expression of pain, even torture, that nevertheless conveys a feeling of ecstasy. People who like to get beaten with whips and birch rods probably assume a similar expression. Then there are times when the face shows wonder and disbelief, as though marveling at the rippling sounds the hammers are pulling up from the bars. As he plays, Norvo's face comes very close to speaking in understandable English. First he scowls mildly, his head cocked to one side, as though saying: "What can I like do with this?" Then comes surprise: "My God, what's this I've got here?" And then satisfaction: "There, that's it, now I've got it." And he turns either to the guitar or bass, the face asking, "Do you like dig it, boy? Are you with me?" When the boys dig and they are all together, it is as though they have become Siamese triplets. The three of them sing the music inaudibly as they play and, as Norvo says, "It's like we breathe together."

The music that comes from this threesome is sometimes unintelligible even to patrons of as fly a place as The Embers, simply because it is so far ahead of its time. But unlike the music of some bopsters, notably those of the Lee Konitz or the Charlie Ventura schools, who are either weepily vague or so frantic they can't return to the ground once they've got off, Norvo's music makes sense. After a while, the listener senses the pattern he's trying for, and although the melody is sometimes replaced by a creation of his own, the original elements are ever present. In his own way, Norvo is as imaginative as such classical Parisians as Ravel or Debussy. The fact is simple to accept, once one has heard him. It becomes hard to believe only when one looks at his background, which is so midwestern American it might have been devised by some latter-day Mark Twain.

The story of Red Norvo begins with the birth of Kenneth Norville, the fourth and youngest child of Joseph and Estelle Smith Norville, in Beardstown, Illinois, on March 31, 1910. Beardstown, which has a population of 6000-odd, is situated northwest of Springfield on the Illinois River, from which it is protected by a high levee. One of Norvo's earliest memories is the flood which arrived every spring with the melting of the winter ice; the river would break over the levee and, as Norvo says, the whole town would be like on the bottom. ("You'd be fishin' like out of a window," he says.) Beardstown had been settled first in 1819, as a ferry crossing; it was later a stopping-off point for riverboats, for it is the center of a fruit and farm area. The packet boats stopped there, and so did the showboats. Red recalls hearing jazz for the first time on those river steamers. One he remembers particularly was *The Capitol*, up out of St. Louis, with a band made up of the great Bix Beiderbecke on trumpet, Frankie Traumbauer on C-melody saxophone and Ray Ludwig on drums.

Young Kenneth was the only member of the Norville family with red hair; his father was a brunet, and his mother a golden blonde, but two aunts on his mother's side had been redheads. The family was comfortably off. Joseph Norville worked as a dispatcher for the Chicago, Burlington and Quincy line, and because he worked nights, Red never got to see as much of him as he did of Glen, his older brother. He spent his boyhood in the familiar pursuits—fishing off the levee, hunting birds with a slingshot, stealing apples and riding a pony that had belonged to Glen. Red had taken charge of this pony when Glen went off to the Missouri School of Mines. He kept it on the front porch of the Norville house on West Ninth Street, and it was his pride and joy. When Glen came home on vacation, he said to his little brother, "Tell you what—if you can ride him around the block, I'll give him to you." Norvo needed no further instructions. "Man," he says, "I was on him and *gone!*" He ran the pony so fast that his mother, alarmed, woke up his father, shouting, "Joseph, Joseph, the pony's running away with Kenneth!" A few minutes later Red completed the circuit of the block triumphantly, riding up to the porch tall in the saddle. Glen formally presented him the pony, thereby indirectly starting him on his musical career.

Howard, Glen, and Portia Norville all had shown marked musical aptitude early in school, and Joseph Norville had encouraged them to the extent of buying Portia and Howard a piano and Glen a violin. Their abilities, the father quickly learned, were stronger than their interest. All took lessons for a time and then gave up. Red, too, showed an ear for music; he was always going about singing such hits of the day as *My Sweetie Went Away* and *I'm The Guy Who Put The Salt In The Ocean.* When he was eight, his mother sent him to the same piano instructor who had taught Portia. Red took twelve lessons before the teacher realized that he could not read music. "I'd been takin' the lesson home," he says, "and I'd say, 'Portia, you play it for me,' and then she'd go over it once and I'd have it. When the teacher found out, she flipped. She like hit my hand, right across the knuckles, and that was enough for me. I never went back. Since then, everything I know I taught myself—I learned how to read and write music just doing it." When he was twelve, Norvo went up to Rollo, Missouri, to visit Glen and Howard at the School of Mines. There he met a young man who was playing xylophone in the local theatre. The xylophone fascinated Red and since the bars were arranged similar to the keyboard of a piano, he found that he could hammer out tunes. When he got back to Beardstown, he announced to his father that he wanted to learn to play it. "Nothing doing," said Joseph. "You'll do just like the rest—you'll play it for a while and lose interest." Red agreed, but he found as the weeks went by that he couldn't get the instrument's sound out of his head. He decided that if his father wouldn't buy him one, he would do it himself, and took a job on a pickup gang on the railroad. By the time the fall school term came around, he still didn't have enough money saved. His next step was a drastic one. He went down to the front porch, untied the pony, gave him a regretful look, took him downtown and sold him. His first xylophone cost $135 and took a fearful toll of his parents' nerves, for the experience with the piano teacher had convinced him that he would be better off instructing himself. It was a slow process. By his third year in high school, he was sufficiently expert to play the weekly assembly, but his repertoire was somewhat limited, consisting only of *Xylophone Rag* and *Mighty Lak A Rose*. By his senior year, however, he was able to play almost anything he'd heard one time previously.

Just before spring vacation in his senior year, Norvo was approached by a classmate named Dorothy Green, who invited him to join a small combination she was forming with the hope of taking it out on the Chautauqua circuit in the summer. Norvo, who didn't think much of girls as musicians, refused haughtily. When he mentioned this to his mother, she became indignant. "Of course you ought to go," she said. "Do you want to stay in Beardstown all your life?" Norvo began rehearsing with the Green group the next day. During the holidays they set out for Chicago with high hopes which, for the sixteen-year-old Norvo, rapidly turned to fears the instant he got off the train. The city frightened him, the hotel frightened him, the prospect of auditioning terrified him, principally because he had not yet learned to read music. "I was so homesick that first night," he says, "I like cried buckets." Next day he and Miss Green set out to make the rounds, winding up at the Fine Arts Bureau on Michigan Avenue. The bookers listened to their music and were unimpressed, but one called Red aside.

His name, he said, was Jack Tebo. He said, "I got a marimba band going out on the road this summer, and there might be a spot in it for you."

Norvo, thinking only of getting out of the big city and back to Beardstown, blurted out his secret. "I can't read," he said.

"Read, schmead," said Tebo, or midwestern words to that effect. "You could pick it up."

"I'll think it over," Norvo said.

Back home, Estelle Norville again gave him the encouragement he needed. Up until then, his principal inspiration had been the old Edison phonograph records of George Hamilton Green, the acknowledged grand-daddy of American xylophonists. His mother was aware that he had assimilated Green's entire recorded repertoire and there was nothing else in Beardstown. "How are you going to learn anything if you don't get out and play with others?" she asked.

In May, when Tebo wired him that there was an opening, Norvo packed up and left for Chicago. There, the booker took him immediately in hand. Norvo gives Tebo full credit for launching his career. The latter, a medical student, had gone overseas with the A.E.F. in World War I. In Paris after the war he had helped organize and produce soldier shows, and had become so hopelessly stage-struck that when he returned to Chicago he gave up his medical studies and became a talent agent. When Norvo met him he was booking attractions of all kinds, concentrating principally on musical acts. He put Norvo in a seven-piece marimba band called The Collegians. The leader was Forrest Hardy, of Terre Haute, Indiana, who made his boys wear striped blazers and white duck trousers. The Collegians played up and down the corn belt, in tents, in Grange halls, at festivals and carnivals, in parks where the farmers brought their families on Saturday nights. Because he still could not read, Norvo was used mainly in solo work. His break in *If You Knew Susie* became one of the mainstays of The Collegians' book.

In the fall, Norvo decided to give up show business. He enrolled in the University of Illinois, planning to be a liberal-arts major. He had scarcely tacked his pennants on the dormitory-room walls before Tebo wired from Chicago, notifying him that The Collegians were planning to tour in vaudeville. Norvo was on a train for Chicago an hour after the wire arrived. This time his mother was not encouraging. She thought he should stay in school, but nothing she said could change his mind. The Collegians had been augmented by a female impersonator, a song-and-dance act and a soft-shoe team. They rehearsed for weeks and broke in at dumps around Chicago. When they went out on the small time, they traveled as far west as Seattle and Portland. By this time Norvo had become the featured soloist, and on the tour he taught himself to read.

When The Collegians returned to Chicago and broke up, Tebo got his protégé an audition with band leader Paul Ash, who then had a big band in the Oriental Theatre. The first week with Ash was something of a nightmare. The production was called *Pianomania,* and featured a lady billed as Jerry and Her Baby Grands. It was one of those things far better imagined than described: four pianos on stands, sequins on everything, musicians waving horns, and Norvo and his xylophone high up on a platform in the middle of the stage, Norvo today does not wince when he tells of it; he acts as though it happened to somebody else. In the second week he had a featured spot, but somehow Ash could never seem to remember the name Norville. "Introducing that master of the zillaphone," he would say, "Red—ah—*Norvick!*" Other nights he pronounced it Norwarth. One night he hit upon Norvo and, presumably because it was shorter, he kept saying it. Norvo, resigned, began using it as his name.

After the stint with Ash, Red went out as a single. It is difficult to decide which period in his life causes him more pain in retrospect. The Ash job was bad enough, but as a single he had to wear the sash, the tight black evening pants and the full-sleeve blouse. To his credit it must be said that he refused to wear the painted sideburns, but he did end up his bit with a rendition of *Poet and Peasant.*

The pipes of his xylophone were concealed by a pleated curtain emblazoned with a glittering N. He played one number, *I Certainly Could*, in which he did a snappy tap dance in the breaks. He was big on the Orpheum time, and some weeks Tebo got him as high as $650. He went on that way for nearly a year—well, we all have our moments when young—and finally returned again to Chicago, where the energetic Tebo was producing a vaudeville show, *The Flaming Youth Revue*. Norvo went into it as xylophonist, tap dancer and, of all things, singer. It was out on the road for a year and a half, during which he again traveled to the west coast.

During that tour Norvo became disgusted with the music he was playing. It failed to satisfy him in any way. In his dressing room he kept the nerves of his fellow vaudevillians nicely jangled by playing the new, exciting records of the men who were making jazz history —Red Nichols, Condon and Teschemaker, King Oliver and Louis Armstrong and Earl Hines, bands like those of Fletcher Henderson and the Red Onion Jazz Babies. Whenever he returned to Chicago he sought out those musicians, and he constantly pestered Tebo to book him with a band. Tebo finally relented and sent him to Milwaukee as leader of a group working at the Eagles' Ballroom. He worked there through the summer of 1929, and in the fall, still disgusted, he decided to knock off the music business and continue the education that had been interrupted at Illinois. He enrolled at the University of Detroit and stayed four months—until the afternoon he happened to drop into a local speak-easy which was the hangout of musicians around town. The boys were buzzing with the news that the great Isham Jones was in town to take over and out on the road a band led by a local celebrity named Ocky Weslin. The talk of jazz and dance music ate Norvo to a point where he rushed to a telephone and called Tebo in Chicago. "I'm quitting school," he said. "Get me a job."

"Stay at that number," said Tebo. An hour later he called back and announced that Red had an engagement at the Marigold Ballroom in Minneapolis. Norvo's mother was coming in that evening. He met her at the station with his bags packed and put her on the next train back to Beardstown. Then he boarded the 11:00 P.M. for Minneapolis, realizing that his formal education was very probably over. He stayed a year (part of the time at KSTP) up where spiked beer was born and, as he later remarked in one of the most masterful understatements of his life, sampled a little of it. Then came the vacation in Chicago when he was hired by Victor Young.

Of those late-twenties days in Chicago, Eddie Condon has remarked, "We had nothing to eat but music, gin and ozone sandwiches." Red and his friends—Condon, Wingy Mannone, Bud Freeman, Gene Krupa, Benny Goodman—thrived on the diet. The boys had at first looked upon the xylophonist from Beardstown with some dubiety, but they quickly accepted him once they heard him play. "Life was like one long ball in those days," Norvo recalls. "We played and imbibed, played and imbibed. I was like $350 a week and broke six days of it." The life took its toll; his appendix gave him some trouble. A doctor told him he had chronic appendicitis, but it was nothing to worry about. By way of celebration over this sanguine medical bulletin, Norvo and David Rose, then a jazzman but later a leader of the stringy school, visited a speak-easy and stayed most of the night. Norvo wound up in the gut ward of a local hospital the next afternoon. So, eventually, did half the jazz world of Chicago, after they learned that Florence Nettleton, a dignified lady liquor wholesaler who used to make deliveries in a Roll-Royce, had sent Red three cases of hooch as a get-well-soon. This was a singular condition for Red to be in, this hospital stretch, for it was one of the few times in his life that he sat by and merely watched while his cronies marinated their complexes. "It was funny how everybody in the hospital—doctors, nurses, orderlies, people from the business office—came down to my room for like conferences," he recalls. Nothing could have delighted him more, for he had, and has, a high regard for medical matters. At one time, in his youth, presumably a time when he despaired of learning to read music, he entertained the notion of becoming a doctor. He has always had a good many physician friends, and there was one time when he used to carry about a small black satchel, from which he would dispense patent pills and unguents to ailing musicians.

When Red got out of the hospital he found that his career in the big time was just beginning. Paul Whiteman at that time was a consultant at NBC in Chicago, and he invited Red to play in his band on some shows he was putting together with Ferde Grofé and Roy Bargy. On these shows Red met Mildred Bailey, then singing on a network sustainer. Let us pause here in reverence. The late Miss Bailey was possibly the greatest white female vocalist of all time. Born Mildred Rinker in Spokane, Washington, she was the sister of Al Rinker, who with Harry Barris and Bing Crosby made up Whiteman's famous Rhythm Boys. Mildred, who was one eighth Coeur d'Alêne Indian, was a natural, effortless singer, with a high, sweet voice; people were often startled to hear such light, clear tones coming from a woman her size (she was overweight most of her life). Although she was older than Norvo, he was fascinated by her—both as a vocalist and as a woman. She, in turn, admired his music and his personality. They began seeing each other more and more, and before long they were married. When Whiteman took a band on the road and headed for New York, the Norvos went along.

Local 802, the New York local of the American Federation of Musicians, at that time had a rule which prohibited an out-of-towner from working steadily in the city until he had been in residence for a year. Norvo survived by taking one-nighters with small Meyer Davis combinations. Davis was—and is—king of society band leaders, and the music his farm-out groups played was not exactly the kind Red had been used to playing. He and Mildred had taken a house on Long Island, and on jobless days he would sit around and brood until he couldn't stand it any more, whereupon he would head for Manhattan to ball away the hours. Red Mackenzie, the singer and kazooist, was then in his finest flower, which is to say that no steadier patron of the grogshops was at large. Norvo describes this interval by saying, "Red and I became very close friends."

The boredom, the annoyance of working with Mickey Mouse bands, the unfamiliarity with Manhattan—all these took their toll. The Norvos' married life suffered as he and his wife engaged in a series of historical domestic skirmishes. Some of them were worthy of record and might be studied profitably by Dr. Paul Popenoe. One, a bit more vigorously demonstrative than the rest, was touched off by Benny Goodman, who came around one day and asked Red to go fishing. They set out early in the morning, headed for some unknown destination on Long Island.

"Where we going?" Red asked.

"We'll find a place, don't worry," said Benny. "I *know* Long Island."

The question was repeated, and the same answer given, eight or nine times that day. At four in the afternoon the Waltonians found themselves nearing Montauk Point, the extreme tip of the Island, more than a hundred miles from New York.

"I ought to call Mildred," Red said, worriedly.

"Aw, call her tomorrow," said Benny.

The place Benny picked was twenty miles from the nearest telephone. Red again suggested that he should call, but Benny was too tired to drive him to the telephone. Next day, after they'd got in some fishing, Benny was still too tired. Red started to walk the twenty miles. Benny's heart softened. He went after him and took him home. They arrived to find Miss Bailey in a Spokane swivet. As Goodman hastily ducked out the front door, she asked Red pointedly where he had been and why he hadn't taken her along. One word led to another—mainly her words, for Norvo has never been much of a debater. Finally, exasperated at her husband's silence, she rushed over to a table and picked up a $40 Cavanaugh hat he had bought the week before. He was very fond of that hat; it gassed him, as he later put it. Knowing this, Miss Bailey took it over to the walk-in fireplace and hurled it into the leaping flames. That was the trigger. Norvo rushed to his wife's closet, dehangered an expensive white mink stole, tore over to the fireplace and threw it in. Burning brands scattered about the room. Part of the carpet caught fire. Miss Bailey, watching her mink being devoured, hastened to another closet, procured her husband's topcoat, and consigned that to the embers. Red then took an expensive antique French love seat, his wife's favorite piece of furniture, and with much pulling and hauling got it across the room and into the fire. The mantel was burning, the rugs were burning, the hat, topcoat, mink stole and love seat were burning, and so were the Norvos. As they stood in the middle of the flames, just before the fire engines arrived, Red challenged: "If you make my weight, I'll lick you."

Spats of this kind, while not regular occurrences, more or less punctuated the Norvos' life together. As Lee Meyers, a friend of Red's, once remarked, the story of the marriage would make an ideal piece for *Ring*. Red and Mildred were divorced in 1941. Red later married Eve Rogers, sister of Shorty Rogers, a trumpet player he met while he was forming his own small band. Miss Bailey, who had a deep, lasting affection for her ex-husband, approved heartily of the union. Until the time of her death in 1951 she visited the Norvos often, taking presents to the children and acting like a godmother.

After he had become legal in the eyes of Local 802, Norvo stayed with Whiteman nearly a year. Then for four or five years he worked around New York, taking jobs wherever they happened to turn up. In the summer of 1934 to '35, he and a group of empathic jazz-hounds were booked into a Bar Harbor, Maine, spot where they opened under the name of Rudy Vallee's New Yorkers. Vallee never appeared on the date, which possibly was one of the luckier happenstances of his career. Most of the musicians in that band have since become famous: among the group were Toots Camarata, Herbie Haymer, Neil Reid, Eddie Sauter, Bill Miller, Dave Barbour and Charlie Peterson. They had a book of Fletcher Henderson arrangements, and according to Red they jumped like the famous Benny Goodman band in 1936. Nobody in Bar Harbor had ever heard anything but Meyer Davis' sallow, elbow-flailing music. There were continual complaints from the patrons, all ignored. Each night the boys set up their instruments and ripped into *Henderson Stomp, King Porter, Bugle Call Rag,* and the rest of the Henderson classics, having the time of their lives. They balled in the daytime, too. They had rented two houses, where they did a lot of jamming. They planted a patch between them. When they weren't jamming they cultivated the patch or went fishing for flounder or stole apples from a nearby orchard. Neil Reid had revealed that he was an expert piemaker and his skill, plus that of the fishermen in the group, turned out to be heaven-sent. After the third or fourth week the manager of the spot revealed that he was pressed for funds. He promised and kept promising—and the boys stayed on, subsisting on their Henderson music, flounder, apple pies and the aromatic produce from the patch.

Eventually Red wired Mildred for money to go home. Back in Manhattan, he formed a band with Haymer and Barbour, plus Don McCook, Pete Peterson and Stewie Pletcher, one of the finest trumpets of all time. They went into the Famous Door on 52nd Street and were socko immediately. The Street was bustling in those days, for that was the late dawn of the Swing Era. Norvo and his boys moved from the Famous Door to Hickory House to Jack Dempsey's on Eighth Avenue to the Versailles. They had a wonderfully bouncy, intimate little band, a perfect setting for Red's xylophonic coruscations. It presaged the band he formed in 1936 with Mildred, the ten-piece combination which they led as "Mr. and Mrs. Swing." Eddie Sauter, who had put down his trumpet to become an arranger, wrote the book for this band. In his compositions he first began using the ideas which later proved so successful in his work for the organizations of Benny Goodman, Woody Herman and Ray McKinley, and which make the music of the band he is with today, the Sauter-Finegan Orchestra, among the most stimulating now being played. The music Red and Mildred played was far ahead of its time and, as was probably inevitable, the public did not fully appreciate it. Their band's existence was one of the real milestones of modern jazz, and firmly established Red's reputation as an innovator.

The band jobbed around the country for two or three years, gradually accumulating a devoted audience. People used to drive five hundred miles to hear it on a one-nighter. Then, one night, Mildred fell ill on the stand. She was in a coma by the time she got back to New York, and her performing days were temporarily halted. After she retired (she later staged a comeback a year before her death), Red and his boys carried on for nearly a year, but then he broke up the group. As a leader, Norvo inspired an inordinate devotion in his men. Stewie Pletcher swore, during his Norvo days, that he would never work for another leader. He never did. Pletcher's trumpet played a brilliant part in the sides that band made. Unfortunately, few of them are available today, although the band may be heard on Columbia LP 6094, accompanying Mildred.

After his big band broke up, Red formed a small one. Then he joined Benny, working with the big band and the sextet. For a time he was with the Herman Herd. He was never very happy in the large organizations; he felt, as he says, "like drowned out." He formed his Trio five years ago. Today he believes that he has at last achieved some measure of fulfillment of the musical ideas that have been gnawing at him since he was a boy in Beardstown. He has always been more at home in small groups of men who are as forward-looking as he is, and in the two boys in his Trio, he feels that he has found two kindred spirits. The three of them are as articulate musically as they are inarticulate verbally. This state of affairs suits Norvo; he is not exactly satisfied with the work his Trio is producing, since he is a man with the soul of a watchmaker perfectionist, but he feels that his twenty-five years in the hot business have at last begun to amount to something. He does not know precisely where he is going, but senses that he is headed in the right direction. Recently he was discussing his present frame of mind with a friend. He spoke of Beardstown, the days in the tents and the bedbuggy theatres, of the balling in Chicago, of the years with Mildred and the big-band period. He said, at length, "You know, today it's like I found myself at last." And then characteristically, he like fell out of the conversation.

Post Script: There is an old, old joke about the government agency called—in the South—the W., P. andA. It concerns a man who called up to hire some W.P.A. men to cut his grass. They arrived next morning, a truckload of them, and promptly began digging a hole in the man's lawn. He protested.

"Don't worry, we know what we doin'," the leader said.

An hour later the man went out and found the workmen building an outhouse over the hole. Again he protested. "All I want is my grass cut," he said.

"Look," said the leader, patiently. "We can't just cut your grass. The way the W.P.A. works, we got two on, two comin', two goin' and two mowin'."

That is the way I write magazine articles. As a rule I have two or three in the process of being written, two or three being actively researched, two or three being haphazardly researched over a long period of time, and two or three being even more haphazardly researched over even longer periods of time.

Once, soon after I stopped writing for Louis Ruppel at *Collier's*, I submitted an outline for a piece on the magnetic recording industry to the *Post*. Stuart Rose told Wilkinson that the editors might like to read such a piece. He guaranteed nothing. The prospect of hitting the *Post* for the first time led me to bend all efforts for six weeks toward that single story. I traveled to Cleveland, Chicago, and California and talked to everyone I could find who knew anything about the subject. I wrote the piece. Stuart sent it back with this single line: "Sorry, just doesn't work out for us."

Whether or not it was a good piece—which it was not—is not especially germane. The real point is that no free-lance writer can afford to spend that amount of time on a single story if there is the slightest chance that it may be turned down (and there is always a chance that every story will be turned down). The free-lance must not think of himself as a writer of individual pieces. He must think of himself as a constantly-working writer of many pieces. He must gather material, throw it into his hopper, and use it when the occasion arises. He must look far, far into the future. If he does, he will find that he can turn out more than the accepted quota of twelve per year. After a time, he will find that he has gradually accumulated material enough to do, say, sixteen articles or more.

I divide my ideas into three categories:

1. Hot: those which must be researched and written at once.

2. Warm: those which can be researched and sold in, say, six months or so.

3. Lukewarm: those which will be written eventually, and therefore can be researched over a long period.

I keep a work-sheet on these categories, so I'll know where I stand. As I write this, my work-sheet reads as follows:

PIECES BEING WRITTEN
Pak Subuh (*American Weekly*)
Oscar Levant (*Coronet*)
Prince Philip (*True*)
Lloyd's of London (*True*)
Toots (*Saga*)
Beards (*Post*)
British Jazz (*Saturday Review*)
PIECES IN RESEARCH
Duchess of Kent (*American Weekly*)
Witchcraft in England (*American Weekly*)
Don Murray-Hope Lange (*Coronet*)
Hollywood writers (*Cosmopolitan*)

Thomas Wolfe (*Cosmopolitan*)
Sinatra (*Saturday Review*)
Bel-Air Hotel (*Good Housekeeping*)
PIECES TO BE REWRITTEN
The Hangover (*Playboy*)

In addition, I have—as I stated previously—at least two dozen, possibly more, ideas for articles for which I have been collecting material for varying periods. When I finally have accumulated what I feel is enough material for any one of these ideas, I make an outline and see if I can get an assignment for it. If I can't get an assignment and the piece still knaws at me sufficiently to make me want to write it, I go ahead and do it on the outside chance that someone will buy it.

The Red Norvo piece was in the latter, or lukewarm, category. I felt, after I had become acquainted with Red, that there was enough material in his life to make a good article. I began making notes on the conversations we had and throwing them into an envelope marked RED. Eventually, after about a year, I had enough material to convince me that I ought to do the piece. Nearly another year went by before I did anything about it, but I kept collecting material. Whenever I heard a Red Norvo record, for example, and thought of something to say about his style of playing, I would jot down the line and put it into the envelope. Whenever anybody told me a Red Norvo story, I did the same thing. I happened to become acquainted with George Simon, the music critic and recording-session producer. He had known both Norvo and Mildred Bailey, and gave me some anecdotes about them; I wrote them down and placed them with the rest of the material.

One day I was lunching with Frederic A. Birmingham, then editor of *Esquire* and surely one of the world's best luncheon or drinking companions. He said, "We need pieces dealing with jazz musicians—have you anybody in mind?"

I told him about Norvo, but added that I would not be able to deliver the story for some time. *Esquire* then was a second-class market, as far as prices were concerned; the pay ranged between $350 and a maximum of $1,000, with no expenses. I could not have afforded to work for the magazine if I had not been working on my system. So, I promised that I would write the story eventually, and I kept on collecting material. Approximately one year after my conversation with Birmingham—a year in which I continued to collect Norvo material—another magazine sent me to the west coast. I did the job I had been assigned, then sought out Red and began a series of more or less "formal" interviews. That took me three or four days. Then I had other things to do, later, in the east. I had to talk to some of Red's friends, and I had to assemble some material on the xylophone and the vibes. Paragraph 6 of the article is a condensation of five paragraphs on the history of the xylophone; Birmingham and I decided that I had gone too deeply into xylophone lore in those five, and when he asked me to put it all into one, I agreed.

When finally I sat down to write the article, I had so much material that it virtually put itself on paper. Here again I must emphasize the importance of extensive, exhaustive research. If the writer knows so much about the subject he cannot possibly cram it into 5,000 words, so much the better. He will be bound to put in the most important details. The reason Joseph Mitchell is the best nonfiction writer in the United States today is that he never begins to write until he has learned his subject so thoroughly that no man knows it better than he. Mitchell has been known to spend a year researching a single story (fortunately, he is paid a salary by *The New Yorker*, and therefore can afford that luxury).

The painstaking research can pay off in other ways. In London in the winter of 1957 with Eddie Condon and his band, I had a call from New York. An RCA-Victor executive was telling me that they were doing an LP by Red Norvo, and they wondered if I would be willing to do the sleeve notes. They needed the material at once. I began to think about Red and presently realized that I could have written my *Esquire* article almost word for word. I wrote the article in about three hours and posted it. The careful research thus had been justified—as it was one more time, a bit later, when I did a sleeve note on an album Red recorded for Liberty.

I recommend my system. It keeps one working constantly, it keeps one fresh, it keeps income pouring—trickling, anyhow—in. Once I saw Franchot Tone in an old S. N. Behrman play called, I believe, *The Second Man*. Tone played a writer. After a hearty breakfast, he sat down in a chair with a drawing board across the arms and clapped his hands together, as though summoning the muse. He scowled and sucked his teeth, and he clapped his hands again. The people behind me told me to be quiet. They saw nothing funny in these nonsensical preparations. I loved the play because it had so little to do with reality as I, as a writer, know it. I wonder how S. N. Behrman goes to work?

9 · *The Lead*

"YOUR lead paragraph," Jack Martin used to say to me over and over, "ought to contain the answers to the questions Who? What? When? Where? How? and, if possible, *Why?*" He drilled this statement into me so effectively that, years later, when it came time to write magazine article openings, I had a dreadful time getting it out of my mind. The Who-what-etc. lead must have been favored originally by newspapermen because they operated on the theory that their readers wanted to know the facts early. That accounts, too, for newspapers' habit of putting paragraphs in nearly all stories, except modern features and by-lined pieces, in descending order of importance. It also accounts for the drabness, over the years, of the vast bulk of newspaper writing in the United States (reporters' ingrained lack of curiosity, especially noticeable in the cases of wire-service writers in recent years, also is responsible for the newspapers' colorless prose—but that is another story.) The magazine article's lead does not have to set forth all the facts at once. It has one principal function—to get the reader interested, and to keep him reading on. It may be the most important part of a story, from the editor's point of view—for, these days, magazines must compete with a strong adversary, television, for the mass audience's attention. It is a simple matter for a person to lose patience with a magazine article and switch on the TV set.

I researched the article that follows over a period of approximately a year and a half. I can't recall how the idea came to me, originally, except that I began noticing submarine sandwich shops all over the eastern seaboard, and after I had talked to a couple of proprietors I concluded that I could eventually get an article out of the craze for subs. I made a hopper, marked it SUBMARINE, and began throwing in notes and items. Eventually I had enough material to make an outline, and the *Post* editors said they were interested but expressed doubts that I could bring off the piece. That was challenge enough. I had all my material by then—or, rather, nearly all; what I did not have was a lead. I could not figure out how to introduce this subject. Something like "All of a sudden, people all over the country are eating more submarine sandwiches than ever before" would not do. I had to have a lead that would indicate in some way that people who love submarines are a breed apart. Then I could go on from there and tell of the sandwich's newfound popularity.

Quite by chance, one morning, I saw a news items about a young man in Brooklyn who had been held prisoner by the Chinese Communists for thirty-three months. He was photographed in his home eating a submarine sandwich. In the interview he was quoted as saying that he had dreamed about the submarine all through his imprisonment.

There was my lead, made to order. I called him up and invited him to lunch (we went to Manganaro's, a submarine sandwich store). In our conversation he gave me several quotes which fitted into my lead nicely. Using those quotes, I got the story right off the ground, and the *Post* bought it two days after Wilkinson sent it in.

ARTICLE: "THE NOBLEST SANDWICH OF THEM ALL"

(From *The Saturday Evening Post*)

Not long ago I happened to see a newspaper account of the brave and resolute behavior of a young man from Brooklyn, New York, named Salvatore R. Conte. Held prisoner by the Chinese communists for thirty-three months, beaten and kicked and made to suffer incredible degradation and abuse, Conte nevertheless had refused to "confess" that democracy was a decadent philosophy. He was finally released in August, 1953. When he got back to Brooklyn, the first thing he asked for was an Italian hero sandwich, more popularly called a submarine. He was photographed eating one about two inches thick and eighteen inches long. He said, "The Reds were bad enough, but what almost drove me nuts was thinkin' about one of these." Aside from my admiration for Conte's steadfast resistance, I was interested in him because he and I share a liking, not to say a passion, for one of the greatest gustatorial creations ever devised. He and I are not alone in our admiration for the submarine. These days hundreds of thousands of people are equally enthusiastic. In some sections the sandwich has become a craze.

The submarine is a noble edifice built of meats, cheeses, fish—preserved and pickled—and fresh vegetables and greens, all stuffed into a whole long loaf of bread and laved generously with oil, herb-flecked vinegar and other delicious lubricants. It is the king of all sandwiches, and its kingdom is growing. Facts about it are hard to pin down, for as yet there is no National Association for the Preservation of the Submarine—but at its present rate of expansion, there soon will be. There are nearly two dozen sub shops in my home city, Lancaster, Pennsylvania. My wife once counted eleven in a three-block stretch in Wilmington, Delaware. I have seen and eaten subs in New England, in the South and in California. A restaurateur I know, Peter Palazzolo, proprietor of the Capri drive-in outside Cincinnati, recently estimated that there are between 3000 and 4000 places in the East and Midwest where subs may be bought. The shops I have visited—and I visit one whenever I can—sell anywhere from 200 to 1000 a day, ranging in price from twenty-five cents to a dollar. One does not have to consult Dun and Bradstreet to realize that, although the annual traffic in subs may be incalculable, it runs into the millions.

In its simplest form, the sub is made of two or three ingredients. In its most imaginative, inspiring and maddening form, it can contains as many as thirty, and more. The word "submarine" or its diminutive "sub" may be used for both the simple and the elaborate sandwich. The origin of the word is self-evident—the long loaf does roughly resemble an underwater craft. It also looks like an over-earth craft, so some people call the sandwich the Zep, or Zeppelin. It is even similar to an on-water craft; my friend Palazzolo calls his product the gondola.

Indeed, there are as many names as there are ingredients in a good-sized submarine. The names have no particular local significance. One would suppose that submarines would be called submarines in New London, Connecticut, where the Navy has a submarine base. Up there they are called grinders. This might be due to the workout one's teeth get while consuming a grinder.

Next to submarine, the most common name is hero, or Italian hero. There are two plausible explanations. One is the heroic size of the sandwich. The other is the heroic appetite required to finish one.

Another oft-used name is Hoagie, sometimes spelled Hoagy, Hogie, Hoggie or Hoggy—and right here the careful research that has characterized this piece thus far falls down like a thin man who has eaten a hoagie several sizes too large for him. None of the people who sell hoagies know where the name came from. It can be stated with certainty that the name does not derive from that of Hoagy Carmichael, composer of "Star Dust." That is about all I know. Jess Stein, managing editor of the American College Dictionary, confessed to me that he did not know the etymology. Neither did an editor of *Fountain and Fast Food Service*, a quick-lunch trade journal. My own guess, for what it is worth—about the price of an inexpensive hoagie—is that the word originally was hoggie, or hoggy—used derisively by people who confused hearty appetites with gluttony.

The list goes on and on. *Gourmet* magazine, regarded by many as a final authority on food, calls the sandwich the poor boy or po'-boy; so do many Southerners, who mistakenly claim New Orleans as its birthplace. The original poor boy did originate there, but the sub did not, as we shall see presently. *Gourmet* also uses the term flute, after the small French loaf of the same name. Last summer *Gourmet* published three poor boy-flute variations—Cinderella (a long loaf filled with cold chicken spread with curry mayonnaise); Rich Girl (lobster or crab meat in the loaf, with garlic-butter sauce); and Steak Flute (steak). I called up Ann Seranne, an editor, to ask some background on the names. "Oh," said she, "we just made them up for fun."

Several shops on the periphery of New York call the sandwich The Dagwood, after Blondie's husband in the Chic Young comic strip—Dagwood always has liked huge sandwiches. In Italian sections of large cities the sandwich is termed, with nice simplicity, Italian sandwich. Last year, outside Phoenix, Alizona, I saw a sign advertising it with even nicer simplicity: BIG SANDWICH.

My first encounter with the submarine occurred in 1946, when I was recently discharged from the Army and living, so to speak, in New York's Greenwich Village. My apartment was in MacDougal Street between 3rd and Bleecker, a block inhabited mostly by cheerful, industrious people from Italy. I was on short rations then, trying to live on a dollar a day.

The mainstay of my diet was *pizza*, that Italian pie made of a breadlike dough spread with runny cheese and tomato sauce, to which is often added sausages, anchovies, ground veal or pork, or anything that may strike its architect's fancy. A fresh *pizza*, baked to bubbling heat, is very very good, but it can get tiresome if it is eaten seven days out of seven. There was a place on Bleecker Street where seventy-five cents bought a *pizza* the size of a wheel on a child's express wagon, and I was its steadiest customer. That is, I was until I found out about the sandwich.

Down the street from my apartment was a grocery store operated by the Scarsi Brothers, who came from the Piedmont section of Italy. The brothers—Jack, Harry and Charlie—opened their store in 1906. Forty years later it was virtually unchanged. The floor was of tile covered with sawdust, the counter was marble, and the odor—a suffusion of hanging cheese and sausage, dried fish and pickling spices—was so wonderful I used to go in there for the sole purpose of sniffing.

One day as I was entering I nearly collided with a man coming out. The man was not watching where he was going. He could not. He was eating the biggest sandwich I'd ever seen. I asked one of the Scarsi brothers if he had made that sandwich, and he said proudly that he had.

"Would you make me one?" I asked eagerly.

"So," said he, "tired of *pizza*, eh?"

Mr. Scarsi took up a loaf as thick as his husky wrist and as long as his forearm and sliced it lengthwise nearly through. He spread both sides generously with a good stiff mustard. Then he took tissue-thin slices of *prosciutto* (an Italian ham which is smoked and cured with a demonstrative black pepper) and covered one side of the sandwich. On the other he placed thick slices of *provolone*, a smoky Italian cheese which is best when it is aged.

I began to get apprehensive, because I knew *prosciutto* and *provolone* were expensive. Now he was piling on *cappo collo*, a highly spiced pork-shoulder cut, also sliced thin. He followed that with lettuce leaves, crushed green and black olives, and a portion of the curd cheese called *ricòtta*. Finally he put on two kinds of *salami*. When he put the sandwich together it was three inches thick. I was sure it would cost more than the dollar I was limited to daily.

"How much?" I asked, trying to be casual.

"Thirty cents," he said.

I snatched the monster and ran home before he could change his mind. I went into my apartment and, a few minutes later, after my first bite, into another world, for there are few sensations comparable to the slow, ecstatic contentment that spreads over a man when first he begins to work on a sub.

From then on, I had no more worries about staying within my budget. Each noon I went to the store and got a sandwich from one of the brothers. They used the various ingredients in different combinations and sometimes added new ones—anchovies, tuna fish, pimentos, onions—anything that came to their gastronomically masterful minds. I became not a sub convert but an addict. I still am.

About two years ago, seeing the astonishing number of sub shops that were appearing all over the Eastern seaboard, I began to realize that I had plenty of company. At the same time I realized that I knew little or nothing of the origin or history of the submarine. I resolved to find out what I could, and forthwith embarked on an informal survey, in the course of which I gained a few facts and several pounds.

I began in Manchester, New Hampshire, where one day on Elm Street I saw torpedo sandwiches advertised. Thinking that this name might be the original, and that the proprietor might give me some information, I stopped in. Also, I was famished. Sam Grisaffi, the owner, sold me an excellent sub, or torpedo, made of boiled ham, sharp store cheese, hard *salami*, pickles, onions and lettuce. He said he was selling between 125 and 150 projectiles per day, but could not account for the sudden popularity.

Nor could he tell much about the name torpedo. "I brought it from Lynn, Massachusetts," he said. "I don't know who started it. The way I figure, one day a guy goes into a store to get some bread and meat and cheese to make a sandwich for his lunch. It strikes him it's a lot of trouble to make it himself. He tells the grocer to split the loaf and put the meat or whatever in. Other guys see him and get the same idea. It catches on."

Romolo Gaspari, who runs The Rendezvous, a sub shop a few blocks away from where I live in Lancaster, was no more scientific than Sam had been. He did not know who invented the sub, but he did give a reason for the current vogue.

"It costs seven, eight thousand to start an ordinary restaurant," Gaspari said. "It costs a thousand or less to start selling subs. The guy who services my juke box says Reading (thirty miles away) is lousy with them. He says they have about fifty. I tell you, subs are taking over."

Gaspari gets rid of 2500 subs each week. He has domesticated the ones he sells. "These Pennsylvania Dutchmen don't go much for hot Italian food," he told me, "so I use ordinary Bologna, a mild cooked *salami*, American or Swiss cheese, onions, tomatoes and hot cherry peppers if they want them, with oil and sage on top." Like almost all sub shops, Gaspari's also sells "steaks," a hot variation which contains only one ingredient. The filling of this sandwich consists of transparently sliced beef—from the hindquarter, shoulder or back—which is heaped onto an olive-oil grill and cooked until brown, with liberal dosages of more oil and water to keep it moist. When the meat is done, it is laid thickly on a sub loaf.

Gaspari said he had been prompted to go into the sub business by the success of several he had seen in Chester, Pennsylvania. To sub lovers, Chester is a pioneer town; a Mrs. Agostino Di Costanza has been making and selling subs there for nearly thirty years. A Chester bakery, Earo's, turns out 25,000 dozen sub loaves in a good week. Since Earo's territory covers only about forty square miles, this gave me a good idea of the extent of the sub boom. But nobody there could tell me of its origin or history.

Finally I decided I would go back and talk to the Scarsis in McDougal Street, and accordingly I made a trip to New York. Andrew

Scarsi, son of one of the owners, was in the store when I got there. He said he had heard of the sub upsurge but had not seen any evidence of it in his neighborhood. "People are eating as many subs as they always have," he said. "Funny that they should around here, since they don't eat 'em in Italy."

This was news. "They don't?"

"Not in Northern Italy, anyhow," said Andrew. "In my opinion, the sub is strictly American."

When I asked if he knew who gave this boon to the world, he thought for a moment. "The Hormel people might know," he said. "They make a lot of *salami*."

That seemed reasonable, since *salami* is one of the principal parts of the well-made sub. I called the Hormel Company, of Austin, Minnesota. A man there said Hormel began making dry sausage, or *salami*, in 1915, and now makes nineteen different kinds. The main ingredient is boned pork butt, flavored with garlic and black pepper. Hormel is pleased with the sub bonanza, the man said. Alas, he could not tell who invented the sandwich.

On my disappointed way back to Lancaster I remembered that once, in discussing the submarine with a friend from New Orleans, I found out that it resembled that city's famous poor boy. With this in mind, I got in touch with Mary Land, a New Orleans writer, authority on wildlife and conservation, and mistress of a pet lion named Charlie. When Miss Land is not ministering to Charlie, she is working away at her mammoth, definitive book, Louisiana Cookery. Miss Land responded like a real authority. She said the poor boy was invented in 1921 by two brothers, Clovis and Benjamin Martin, in their French Market Café.

"The Martins took the round family-sized loaf and reshaped it to a long loaf and filled it with cheese, ham and tomatoes," Miss Land wrote. "It sold for five cents. Now it sells all over New Orleans and costs anywhere from a quarter to a dollar. But the Martins were first."

This story would have ended right here if it had not been for the subject itself. Whenever my wife and I are in New York we stop at one of the markets in the 9th Avenue Italian district to buy stuff to take home for our own submarines. One day in early August we stopped there as usual, and quite by chance I walked into

Manganaro's, at 488 9th Avenue. There, at last, I found the solution to the riddle of the submarine.

It was noon, and Manganaro's was so crowded that I could scarcely get in. Without a single customer, the store would appear jammed; the front part is hung from floor to ceiling with sausages of every description, some of them five or six feet long. In the middle of the store round Parmesan and Romano cheeses, each as big as a snare drum, are stacked in rows on the floor, and immense *provolones*, some of them bigger than nine-year-old boys, are suspended from the ceiling. Many of these big fellows weigh 200 pounds, and the ceiling is reinforced to hold them.

During the lunch hour the packed condition of the store is compounded by the headlong arrival of about 1000 people of every age and description, all bent on getting one of Manganaro's subs. The store sells 1200 in a single average day.

Although this was unquestionably the New London of the submarine, when I introduced myself to Vincent Manganaro I had no real hope of finding out more than I already knew. By then I had concluded that the poor boy had somehow worked its way North after the Martins invented it, and that it had been adopted by Eastern Italians. Sure enough, Vincent, a husky, dark-haired lad, was not too clear as to details. "But come on," said he. "Mom will know."

I followed him upstairs to a comfortable apartment where, in the kitchen, a pleasant-faced lady was making sausage. This was Mrs. Nina Manganaro, who, with her brother, Louis, began operating the store around 1919. Her cousin, Ernest Petrucci, had established it in 1885. Petrucci and the Manganaros had come from Naples—and so, said Mrs. Manganaro, had the submarine.

"Sandwich is Neapolitan," she said. "There they sell little rolls in the shops, and they fill them up with meat, cheese—anything you can want."

Then Vincent and I went downstairs, where in transports at having finally learned something definite, I spent more money than I had planned.

The materials I carried off, though, enabled me to make the greatest submarine of my extensive career. My wife and I gave it to guests the next evening. I began with a loaf thirty inches long and eight inches wide at its broadest part, which I cut almost in two, lengthwise. Then my wife began pulling surplus bread out of the center of both halves. A sub of the kind we make gets too thick if you don't pull out bread; also, you can use the extra bread later for stuffing poultry or something.

While she was doing that, I mixed together two ounces each of Lucatelli olive oil, and some Regina wine vinegar. I spooned it lightly over the two plucked halves.

On the right half, my wife began laying down some of the stuff we'd brought from Manganaro's—slices of *prosciutto* and *provolone,* to begin with. I sprinkled this with a thin layer of white-hot Italian peppers preserved in vinegar.

A friend of our named Bob Fraunfelter arrived and set to work with us. My wife piled lettuce leaves on the right, and I put a layer of imported *salami* on the left, followed by some sweet peppers.

Fraunfelter was crunching cloves of garlic in a small hand press, and after we had laid in thinly sliced tomatoes and onions, on both sides, he sprinkled in his contribution.

Next we took down a jar of preserved artichoke hearts. They went on the right. On the left I laid the contents of an entire can of flat anchovy fillets, after which I poured on the oil. Capers, Spanish olives and crushed black olives came next; my wife dusted them with *orégano,* and Fraunfelter shook in some basil. Now we were ready for some *salami*—on the left—and some Lancaster County Swiss cheese—*au droit.*

"What have we forgotten?" my wife said.

"Nothing," I said, "except the pressed ham, the boiled ham, the *mortadella* (a spiced pork roll), the Gorganzola cheese, the summer bologna and the Lebanon bologna."

All these followed, and then we added a layer of *ricotta,* another of imported tuna fish, with its oil, some pimentos, some sliced pepperoni and salt and pepper. I spooned on more of the oil-and-vinegar mixture. My wife pointed out that we now had thirty-two ingredients. "We can do better than that," she said. She put on some of Manganaro's *cappo collo,* some American cheese, and a jar of tiny ears of corn, imported from France, which she had bought in a weak moment from Kilheffer, our grocer.

"Preserved mushrooms," Fraunfelter said, licking his chops.

"Smoked eel," I said.

Both were duly and ceremoniously added, and so were white pepper, cayenne pepper, celery seed and dillseed. That gave my wife the idea of putting in dill pickles, bread-and-butter pickles and some gherkins.

Fraunfelter, who had been peering into the refrigerator, held up a jar of preserved ginger. My wife objected.

"You can carry this too far," said she. "We've got forty-four things now." She looked at the sandwich speculatively. It was about four inches high. "I'll bet Mr. Manganaro would know of some things to add," she said.

"I'll bet old Ernest Petrucci is spinning in his grave," I said.

"I'll bet we'll all be spinning in our beds tonight," Fraunfelter said.

"I tell you what," said my wife; "next time we're in New York, let's stop by Manganaro's to see if we missed anything."

I agreed warmly. Agreed? I can hardly wait.

Post Script: The search for the fitting lead ought to begin as soon as the research is begun. Quite often, in the course of interviews about a subject, the writer will stumble upon the single telling anecdote that either sums up the character or illumines one facet of it compellingly. If that anecdote "feels" right, he ought to write it at once and put it aside for later use. Other times he may have to hunt a bit, and his lead may come from outside the subject.

I divide my leads into several overlapping categories—the direct statement, the oblique statement, and the unusual statement. The direct statement is the simplest and safest, but it also can be the dullest and the truth is, it is not much fun to write. Here is the lead to a piece I did for *Flair*, Fleur Cowles' beautiful and ill-fated experiment:

For the past two decades, give or take a year or two, a lithe, angular, tense-as-a-whippet tomboy named Katharine Houghton Hepburn has been a star of the American stage and screen. No other female citizen, with the possible exception of Anna Eleanor Roosevelt, has been so widely impersonated. An impression of Hepburn's strident, broad-A accent is as necessary to a night-club mimic's routine as calcium paint is to a circus clown. Wistful schoolgirls have stood secretly before mirrors, sucking in their cheeks, striving to force their facial contours into an approximation of hers. The personal philter that Hepburn has compounded has cast a spell as strong in momentary grip as that of, say, Canasta; but the magic seems almost as enduring as poker. At forty-one, Hepburn is still one of the golden girls. Last March, when Crown Publishers brought out *The Hepburn,* plainly labeling it a historical novel, some 525,000 copies were sold, many of them, according to booksellers, to people who believed the book a biography of Kate. In December 1949, when she opened in New Haven as Rosalind in *As You Like It,* sometimes accounted, despite its splendid speeches, as one of Shakespeare's undernourished efforts, theatrical sages predicted that she would never get it to Broadway. They reasoned that it had never previously been a hit in the United States. Hepburn, who likes nothing better than a challenge, rapidly set about proving the experts wrong. After playing it fifty-two times on the road to rave notices, she assaulted New York, where, despite the handicap of reviews that were not unanimously enthusiastic, she drove on by sheer force of personality through 148 triumphant performances. It was a spectacular record for *As You Like It* and, coincidentally, an imposing number in these culture-unconscious days for Shakespeare, whose luck has been running almost as low as Ibsen's. Not content with whipping the know-it-alls, Hepburn is currently at it again, this time in an enervating cross-country tour that upon closing will have taken her to twenty cities. "Katie is going to make people like *As You like It* if it kills her," a friend remarked recently. ("Not," he added a moment later, "that anything could!") If Hepburn has not already proved that the play can be a success, she at least again has demonstrated that she herself can. The women who were adoring teen-agers in the thirties are still turning up at stage doors, now as well-dressed, eminently respectable matrons who stand in eager reverence, waiting for a glimpse of Kate without her make-up. Many of them are accompanied by equally eager men. None of the newer stars has yet come forth with anything to match Hepburn's peculiarly distinctive quality. Perhaps for this reason, her most enthusiastic audiences are still those composed of sighing high school kids (which also has brought her the gratitude of teachers of Shakespeare who may be hard-pressed to persuade their charges of the Bard's real beauty). The fact is that Hepburn's free-wheeling, unfettered vitality appeals strongly to all ages and both sexes; and if there are some who claim that she is, as one of her close friends says, "rather strong medicine," at least they, too, are not unaffected by her.

Now, that is a fairly good lead. It tells who Kate Hepburn is (as though there were people who did not know) and it tells why she's important and it tells why the magazine is running a piece about her. It characterizes her in terms of her appearance and her energy. From the modern magazine editor's point of view, its only serious drawback is that it is one hell of a long paragraph. (Not long ago, when I did a piece on the pretzel industry for the *Post,* my opening ran to a page and a half, doublespaced. Someone—I think it was Robert Sherrod—wrote in the margin, "No paragraph should be this long." I disagree. A long direct statement slides the reader into the piece swiftly. He is absorbed before he knows it, I feel. But I could be wrong. Perhaps a direct lead such as the following is better:

By all modern standards for success, the firm of F. X. Zirnkilton, a seventy-five-year-old Philadelphia custom-jewelry-making establishment, ought to be a spectacular failure. Founded in 1880 by Franz Xavier Zirnkilton, a gifted Bavarian goldsmith who thought of himself as the spiritual descendant of the great Italian artisan, Benvenuto Cellini, the store is now operated by his sons, Franz, Jr., sixty-four, and Carl, fifty-eight. Moreover, it is being operated pretty much as it was in the early days. For example, the father never advertised, and so the sons do not. "If people want us, they can find us," Franz, Jr., says. The Zirnkiltons' pieces bear no identifying hallmark. "Our work is its own identification," says Carl. Compared to most manufacturing jewelers, the firm is tiny, consisting only of the brothers, a lady secretary-bookkeeper and five craftsmen. "We can't find workers to turn out our kind of work," the brothers explain. Although their pieces have been bought by the finest jewelry stores, the wealthiest families and by kings and maharajahs, the Zirnkiltons have always kept their customers' names secret. "We don't boast," Franz, Jr., says. Finally, the brothers appear totally uninterested in making high profits. "Money has always been secondary to us," Carl states. "We are mainly concerned with doing the finest work of which we're capable."

When printing that lead, the *Post* split the paragraph into three separate paragraphs. I think it works better as a single. Again the subjects are characterized, described, and quoted. The reader does not have to waste time finding out who they are.

The direct statement may be preceded, or supplemented, by a statement "setting" the subject. This is how I began a piece about Audrey Wood, the literary agent:

Within the past two decades the traditional relationship between the creative artist and his business representative, his agent, has somehow been reversed. The latter's position gradually has become the stronger, so that it is now not uncommon for a literary salesman to communicate the impression that his clients work for him. More often than not the impression is an actuality, which partially accounts for the generous festooning of the literary flower-market with wax and crepe-paper fabrications designed for quick sale and cursory inspection. Audrey Wood, a personable, firm yet gentle lady who possesses the enthusiasm of a girl half her age and the experienced judgment of a woman twice it, neither believes in nor approves of the prevailing arrangement. She is happily anachronistic, a young agent of the old genteel school who has dedicated herself to her clients' welfare.

For this reason, Miss Wood is already something of a theatrical legend. She is sometimes referred to as the woman who "made" the new playwrights Tennessee Williams, Carson McCullers, William Inge, Maurice Valency, and Mel Dinelli, and the young directors Daniel Mann, Martin Ritt, Dan Levin, and Alan Schneider. Nothing could annoy her more. "My blood boils when I hear that," she said recently. "I resent it because it's just not true. An agent has a definite place, but talent is always first and most important. Williams, for example, is a tremendous talent. I just *found* him. Any agent is only as important as his client." Miss Wood carries this attitude to a length that many of her competitors would regard as abnormal, if not indecent: "I'm just a part of the firm of Liebling-Wood," she told me, insistently. "Be sure you write it that way." (I promised that I would; here goes.) Miss Wood is just a part of the firm of Liebling-Wood, Inc. She is also the wife of the other part, William Liebling, actor's agent. And she is overly modest, as her husband, who refers to her either as "my favorite woman" or "The Great Wood," quickly attests. "She works too hard," Liebling, who is likewise firm yet gentle, remarked recently. "But it's that capacity for hard work, that wonderful perseverence of hers, that brings out talent."

That piece was from *Theatre Arts,* which was, at the time I was contributing to it regularly, a wonderful place in which to experiment. I did a piece every month or so in the year or two just before I went to work for Ruppel. The training was invaluable—which is why I suggest that the young writer will do well to begin in the second- and third-class markets (that is, those that pay second- and third-class rates). *Theatre Arts* paid me around $75 per article; I should have paid the editors for the experience.

The oblique statement is a dangerous lead for the young writer to attempt to use. Looking at it one way, it is a false lead—that is, it begins away from the subject, and may at first mislead the reader. Here is an example from a piece I did for the *Post*:

One day in 1951 a philanthropic bird lover named Hiram Bellis Demarest Blauvelt, a fuel-oil dealer and prominent citizen of Hackensack, New Jersey, decided to do something nice for his fellow admirers of our feathered friends. Some time previously, Mr. Blauvelt had ordained the Demarest Memorial Foundation, a museum to exhibit relics and mementoes of the Demarest family, one of the first to settle in the state. Mr. Blauvelt wanted to enhance the museum's wildlife section with some models of the Garden State birds. He therefore went to see John L. Lacey, an artist who carves birds from wood and calls himself "The Birdsmith."

There followed two paragraphs about Lacey, after which I brought Blauvelt back into the story and told of the stupendous order he gave Lacey. It numbered more than 350 different birds. I then told how Lacey took this in his stride and quietly set to work.

"The Ratcatchers of London" (Chapter 11) is another example of how the oblique lead may be used. In this instance I deliberately misled the reader into believing that the catchers were members of a gang of thieves. I thought this gave the story more "atmosphere." When the oblique lead is used, the subject still must be introduced as soon as possible. This applies also to oblique leads with anecdotes; the story ought to get to the point almost immediately.

Once when I was doing a story on the sausage industry for *Collier's*, I couldn't find a lead for weeks. There seemed to be nothing on which I could focus, nothing that would communicate my enthusiasm for sausage. My editor on that piece was Eugene Rachlis. He said, "Why don't you just say, 'There are five thousand different kinds of sausage being made in the world today'?" I tried a lead that said something similar. It was dull and colorless. I put the piece aside and brooded a bit more—perhaps three weeks more —and then, one night after I left Eddie Condon's saloon, I happened to stop by the corner of West Third Street and Avenue of the Americas, where Charles Caruso parks his sausage wagon. Charles and I are old friends. I bought a sausage sandwich from him—and there, as I was eating it, was my lead:

Charles Caruso is a hard-working Italian with a bearish, brusque voice that in no way resembles that of the great Italian tenor of the same last name. Nevertheless, Charles is every inch the artist that Enrico Caruso was. Nearly every day around noon, Charles goes into his studio on Carmine Street in New York's Greenwich Village and grinds up pork butts and scraps, seasons the grindings with salt and strong black pepper and a couple of other herbs—the names of which he will not divulge—and stuffs the resulting redolent mixture into an animal casing to make *salticcia dolce,* or sweet sausage.

By the time he has made about 50 pounds of short, fat sausages, it is nearly dusk. Charles carries his sausages, plus several gallons of stewed peppers previously prepared by his wife, out to a large roofed pushcart parked near the curb. Constructed of shiny sheet metal to his own specifications, this cart is Charles' pride and joy. It is equipped with a grill, compartments to keep the peppers warm, and a small stove to relieve Charles' accursed arthritis in the winter. He trundles the cart a couple of blocks north to the busy subway-stop corner of West Third Street and Avenue of the Americas. There he climbs into the cart, lights a fire under his grill, and places on it a succulent coil of *salticcia dolce.*

Within a few seconds the sausages begin to snarl, spit and buzz, sending out a wonderfully magnetic odor. A customer steps up and demands one. Charles cuts a single sausage from the coil, splits it neatly in half and pressed it down on the grill to brown its insides, then places it on a soft fresh roll. He adds a large spoonful of the simmering peppers, sprinkles the sausage with dried red pepper-seeds, wraps it neatly in a paper napkin, hands it to the customer and collects 35 cents. Meanwhile, the mingled smell of sausages and peppers attracts more people. It even draws some of Charles' neighbors up from Carmine Street.

It draws me, too. I am a nut on sausage. A long time ago I fell shamelessly in love with this ancient, delicious example of man's imaginative mastery of foodstuffs.

Sausage is man's meat—strong-flavored, full of character, honestly designed for hearty eaters. The beauty of sausage is that in its various forms it can be eaten almost any time—for breakfast, with eggs; for lunch, with sauerkraut and mashed or boiled potatoes; for dinner, in a number of excellent casseroles; and for the late at night poker game or pre-bed snack. And, of course, it can be eaten between meals in the form of the frankfurter. Babe Ruth, according to legend, frequently knocked off 10 or 12 hot dogs at a time.

(This story, incidentally, was bought by *Collier's,* then sold to *True* after *Collier's* went out of business.)

Leads frequently come from personal experience of that kind. In 1957 I was researching a piece for *Woman's Day* in Asheville, North Carolina. Again I had no lead. I went ahead and wrote the body of the story, then began to stew and fret. Presently I remembered a morning when I had awakened and looked out of my hotel room window, and there was my clue. The lead went as follows:

One morning I arose around six and looked out my window at the blue-green mountains, lying like serene giants in repose beneath a hazy blanket of gray and purple, touched at their tops by the brightness of the awakening sun: that kind of view is to be seen from nearly every second-story window and eminence in this small city. I stood there and thought how similar views must have stirred the young Thomas Wolfe, Asheville's most articulate (and most controversial) son, and how they must have moved him to pour out the emotions they invoked. Altamont, he called Asheville in his first novel, *Look Homeward, Angel,* and he wrote of its people and of his own family with deep pity and blazing anger and despairing compassion. And with a certain blindness to his own troubles and internal tremors, which kept him from becoming the writer he might have been. Some Asheville people have never forgiven him; one lady said to me indignantly, "Lots of us here aren't impressed with Tom Wolfe, *period.*" Lots of them are, nevertheless: Pack Memorial Library, on the town square, has assembled a comprehensive collection of Wolfe memorabilia, and the city now keeps up his mother's house, which he called Dixieland in his books. Asheville has done what Wolfe was never able to do: it has achieved maturity, and in the process survived and forgiven him, as though in tribute to his profound appreciation of its worth and beauty and of the distant soaring ranges, as he called them, which encircle the town.

The unusual statement in the lead, my third standby, must shock or arouse the interest of the reader at once—preferably in one line:

Mike Todd now owes more than a million dollars, but he still spends money as though it were owed to him.

The proprietor of a bar-and-grill on Jericho Turnpike on Long Island is a song-and-dance man named James Barton.

Ezzard Charles says that he fights only for money. "Glory, nuts," he said recently.

Queen Elizabeth has many problems before her—but her biggest is one she is not likely to solve.
Its name is Princess Margaret.

On some occasions I have used a question as an opening:

Who among us can point to the day on which his destiny was decided? A friend of mine named Demetrios A. Sazani can.

This lead then went on to tell how Sazani, a producer of street parades, saw his first parade at the age of six and became incurably addicted to the spectacles.

If a lead will not come when the writer first sits down to put his story together, he will be better off if he waits to write it until after he has completed the first draft. Many times I have stumbled upon my lead in the middle of a piece. John O'Connell once suggested that an ending I had put on a story was a far better beginning, and he was right. To sum up, the lead ought to:

1. Introduce the story gracefully.
2. Seize the reader's interest.
3. Tell enough about the subject to make the reader wish to know more.
4. Entertain.
5. Inform.

Post Post Script: The lunch I had with Sal Conte in order to get my lead for the submarine sandwich story also got me interested in Conte's own story. He had been held by the Communists in China for nearly three years, and for eighteen months he had been confined in a box roughly the size of a telephone booth. Here was a great personal-adventure story, and I invited him to stay at my house—I was then living in Pennsylvania—for a week. In four sessions of eight hours each the story came out—an almost unbelievable tale of one man's patient heroism. The Communists simply could not break Conte's spirit. We sold the piece—it was a 20,000-worder—to *Argosy*. One story nearly always leads to another. The writer who says he can't find stories simply isn't looking.

10 · *The As-Told-To Article*

ONE DAY in the summer of 1950 a press agent of the Baltimore and Ohio railroad was taking me to Balitmore to interview the line's president, who had some new ideas about dining cars and railroad food. I was writing a good many food articles then, and I thought I might get a piece out of the man. Before boarding the train I bought a *New York Herald Tribune*, and as I was glancing over the pages I noticed that Richard Crowe, a Staten Island bank employee who a couple of years before had suddenly run off to Florida with nearly a million dollars, had just been released from prison. Crowe's story had interested me principally because so few details had been printed. He had been a good member of the community, a fine husband and father, and he was a kindly and generous man. After he was apprehended, the sentencing judge had been deluged with letters from people who knew him, begging for mercy. I wondered what had caused him to commit his antisocial act, and I wondered if he had plans to tell his story. I wondered these things aloud, and the press agent, Martin Quigley, said casually, "That man is my next-door neighbor."

I lost all interest in the B. & O. story. "Can you introduce him to me?" I asked Quigley, excitedly.

"I don't know," Quigley said. "I'll see what I can do."

Now began some of that connivance that must characterize all free-lance writers' lives at one time or another. I had to meet Crowe; Quigley was my only hope. Quigley was very anxious to have me do the story on the railroad. Therefore, the idea was to make Quigley eager to please me—and to pretend that I was not altogether willing to do the railroad story. This, in turn, would move Quigley to do everything in his power to get on the good side of me. Throughout my interviews in Baltimore I expressed mild skepticism. On the train returning to New York I told Quigley that I was not certain that I could do anything about the B. & O. I had him. As we parted, he said, "Let's keep in touch—I'll see if I can't introduce you to Crowe."

Crowe came to my house a few nights later.

A half-hour's conversation convinced me that this would be the best story I had done to date. The trouble was, I didn't know whether he'd had other offers. I decided to bluff. I then had about three hundred dollars in my bank account, and was not owed a penny for any work. I said to Crowe,

"I believe I can sell this story—but I've got to have exclusive rights. Here is my check for $1,000, dated a week from today. If I can get an offer that suits you, we'll go ahead. If I can't you may keep the G and you'll be free to sell the story yourself."

"Fair enough," Crowe said.

When he left the house, I sat there appalled at my own temerity. I was not really certain that I could sell the piece, or that he would accept any offer I might be able to get him. And I had no idea where I would get the additional seven hundred dollars needed to cover the bad check I had given him.

Next day I called *Collier's*. "Not interested," said Ruppel.

"It's a great story," I said.

"Not interested, goddamnit," he said.

I called Stuart Rose at the *Post*. He said he would check with the other editors, and he called me back in fifteen minutes. "Afraid not," he said.

I called A. B. C. Whipple, at *Life*. Same reaction. Now I was beginning to sweat. Only *Look* was left—and I knew nobody there. I called the articles editor, introduced myself, and told him I had Crowe sewed up. He was interested, but he could not get anybody else interested.

Well, I thought, there goes a thousand. I cursed my foolishness. Now only the secondary markets were left, except for *Cosmopolitan* and *True*, neither of which I had sold. Herbert Mayes was then editor of both *Cosmopolitan* and *Good Housekeeping;* I did not know him, but I did know his young managing editor, John O'Connell. I called him and asked if he thought *Cosmopolitan* might be interested in Crowe. My voice faltered as I asked the question; I was certain Mayes would not be interested.

O'Connell said, "How much does Crowe want?"

I said, trying to sound matter-of-fact, "He wants $2500—and I want my price, $1500."

"I'll call you right back," he said.

He did not call right back; more than three hours went by before my telephone rang, three hours in which I tried desperately to think of someone from whom I could borrow money to cover the check I had given Crowe. Then he was on the telephone.

"How soon can you have this?" he asked.

"In a week."

"We need it before then. We'll put it on the cover—could you do it in three days?"

"I think so."

"Good." He paused. "Do you mind if your name isn't on it?"

I said, "Why?"

"Mayes doesn't like as-told-to's. Take my advice, Dick—do it as he wants you to. You may get some more work out of this."

I agreed. "I'll send Crowe's check down by messenger right away," O'Connell said.

Crowe came in that night and we set to work. Three days later we had finished the following article.

ARTICLE: "HOW I STOLE A FORTUNE"

By Richard Crowe
(From *Cosmopolitan*)

"You look thoughtful tonight, Mr. Crowe," the bartender said. "You worried about something?"

I laughed. "Something worry *me?* You know I never worry, Joe."

That was the way I was: I never let anybody know what I was thinking. In the banking business, you learn to keep your emotions to yourself. I guess if Joe had been able to read my mind, he'd have concluded I'd suddenly gone stark, raving nuts. Certainly the idea that had just come to me was spectacularly crazy. It was about six o'clock in the evening on Wednesday, March 23, 1949, and I had just decided to rob the 195 Broadway Branch of The National City Bank of New York.

How the idea came to me, I don't know. I was standing in Lawler's, a favorite bar of mine around the corner from the bank, feeling depressed and bitter—for reasons I'll explain presently—and, all of a sudden, I knew what I was going to do. The odd thing was that I felt better the instant I made my decision. I didn't stop to consider whether it was right or wrong, and I didn't even speculate on the consequences. I never gave a thought to my wife, our three children, my fourteen-room house on Staten Island, my position as a civic leader, or my career in the bank, to which I'd devoted twenty years of my life. If I'd stopped to think of all those factors I'm sure I never would have carried my wild scheme through. But I didn't stop to think. I didn't even stop to plan the theft—if I had, I might never have been caught. I might be in Europe or South America today, safe from the extradition treaties, living high on the fortune I stole. The Government bonds would have brought me around $5,000,000 on the European black market. The American dollars would have been worth a lot more than their face value of $193,666.

The harebrained idea that came to me that day in Lawler's ultimately resulted in my taking $883,660. I've been told that this was the largest robbery ever undertaken by a single individual. I'm not boasting—I'm not proud of what I did. I could have lived high on the money in some foreign country, all right, but I'm not sure that I could have lived with myself.

I remember one afternoon when my wife and some friends and I were sitting on our beach-front lawn, and the conversation got around to dogs. All at once, I wanted a dog. I got up, left without explanation, and bought a collie for thirty-five dollars. And that was precisely the way it was with the idea of stealing the money from the bank. The idea came to me, it enthralled me, and there was no question of doing anything but following it through. It got into my blood stream, you might say. It was compelling and exciting, and I found it irresistible.

Wednesday night I went home and had dinner with my wife and

family as usual. We had some friends in afterward, but I was careful not to let them see the excitement I felt inside; nor did I allow my wife to become aware that I was thinking of anything out of the ordinary. Actually, my mind was working hard, figuring out how I was going to do it.

The National City Bank, like most banks, has a system of "dual control" on its vaults. The system was devised to prevent crimes of the very nature I was planning. If I was going to be successful, I would have to figure out a way to beat it. It won't make the bank's officers very happy to know that I didn't have to do much figuring. As assistant manager of the 195 Broadway branch, one of four officers stationed there, I knew all the facts about dual control. The bank had one big vault in the basement that was opened by a series of time clocks, set by one officer and double checked by another person. Inside the big vault were six smaller ones, in which the tellers kept the funds entrusted to them. Two combinations were required to open each of those smaller vaults: the teller set one combination, and an officer set the other. Neither knew the other's combination. We four officers took turns for a week at a time setting the clocks and helping the tellers open and close their vaults. It was then my week. My first problem was to learn the tellers' combinations.

Next morning, Thursday, I appeared at the bank at 8:15, my regular time, and went with each teller to his vault inside the big one. First I spun the dial to my own combination, and then I stepped back to let him dial his—and to watch. Many people later asked me how I could remember all six tellers' combinations. Actually, it wasn't hard. I was a teller myself for years, and I knew that because a teller is a busy man with many things on his mind, he wouldn't choose an elaborate combination. He would make his numbers follow in simple, logical sequence. If the first was ten, the next would be twenty, and the next thirty. Or if the first was fifteen, the next would be thirty, and the next forty-five. If you can see the first number, in nine cases out of ten, you've got it.

None of the tellers thought there was anything peculiar in my standing behind him as he dialed his combination. And none of them noticed me watching him sharply that afternoon when we locked up. I was checking on my memory then. I found that I'd got all the combinations fixed in my mind that morning. It will probably surprise the tellers to find out here that three of them were using the same combination.

The custodian of the big vault was an old employee. He didn't work a full day, as a matter of policy: he always went home around three-thirty in the afternoon, just after the tellers and the officer on duty locked up their inside vaults. The big vault itself never closed up until five.

On Thursday, then, after locking up the tellers at three-thirty, I made sure the old man had gone home. Then I went back upstairs to my desk and worked until around four. At that time, I glanced around the room and made certain that all fifty-odd people were working at their jobs. Then I got up from my desk, a paper or two in my hand, and went over to the stairs to the basement. Out of the corner of my eye, I saw that no one was paying any attention to me. But even if someone had come downstairs while I was in the big vault, he would have thought nothing of my being there. After all, I had every right to be in the vault—for any number of reasons.

That was when I made my dry run. I tried all six vaults, using first my own combinations and then the teller's combinations.

Each vault opened as easily as a swinging door.

The excitement inside me seemed to mount. It was going to be easy, damned easy. When I went back upstairs, I had to force myself to keep my mind on my routine work until closing time.

One other important part of my scheme went off on schedule on Thursday. At midmorning, I told the manager I was going out for a while. I took a cab uptown to the air-lines terminal and bought a ticket to Florida on the plane that was to leave Sunday night at eight-thirty. I used the name Robert Crane.

Around nine-thirty Friday morning, I left the bank and went to buy a pair of glasses with thick horned rims. Then I went to a hardware store and bought a pair of cutting pliers and a stout crowbar. After that, I went around to see a leather-goods dealer I knew.

"I want a big, sturdy suitcase," I told the clerk. "Something with heavy straps."

He showed me two or three. The one I finally chose was about 8″ x 24″ x 16″, made of cowhide, and weighed around twenty-five pounds. The store was having a sale, but even with a twenty-five per cent discount, it cost seventy-five dollars. I put the crowbar and the pliers inside it and asked the clerk to gift-wrap it. Then I want back to the bank.

"What're you doing with the suitcase?" my boss, William Mead, the manager, asked.

There was no suspicion in his voice, naturally, but the question set my nerves on edge.

"Present for a friend," I said casually.

Mead's inquiry should have made me stop and think, I suppose, but it didn't. Once I'd made up my mind, that was all there was to it.

Friday afternoon in the banking business, everyone hurries. The tellers usually rush to get locked up before three-thirty, if possible. But that day, something happened to make them a little late. It seems, now that I look back, that time was against me all the way. The tellers weren't ready for me to lock them up until around three forty-five, and the old vault custodian was late in leaving. I went back upstairs and fidgeted at my desk. There was one factor in my favor: Mead had gone out to see a customer. Finally, at four-thirty, I went downstairs again.

The instant my foot hit the bottom step, I sprinted into the big vault. I opened each teller's vault and took out the money boxes. They were made of steel, measured about 30″ x 16″ x 12″, and each weighed about forty pounds. I carried them one at a time to a clothes closet situated in a customers' safe-deposit room outside the big vault. I knew it probably would not be opened for the rest of the afternoon.

My heart was pounding, and I felt as though I were sweating blood. If one teller had discovered an error in his day's calculations, he would have come down to the vault looking for me to help him open up. The whole game would have been called then and there. Once I thought I heard a footstep outside on the stairs. I turned quickly, and almost dropped the cashbox I was carrying.

It took me about eight minutes to hide the boxes in the clothes closet.

I started back upstairs, and halfway up I was struck by a thought. It was important to my vague plan that as much time as possible elapse before the bank could discover my theft. At five o'clock, I would be closing the big vault. There were three different clocks that controlled it. One had been wound at eight-thirty that morning to reopen the vault the following Monday morning at eight-thirty. I had wound the other two at four-thirty—that was my pretext for going downstairs—to reopen at the same time; that was part of the control system. At five o'clock, when the main-vault door was closed, the other checker would examine the clocks to see that they were set to run until Monday. I wanted to have those clocks appear as though they hadn't been tampered with, and yet to be out of commission. I was enough of a mechanic to know that if you pull a hairspring out of a watch, it can't run down. That was what I did. I went to the clocks on the big vault and, with my pliers, pulled the hairsprings out of the three clocks. It was a neat job, if I do say so. I had to smile, in fact, thinking of what Mead and the others would say on Monday morning when the big vault failed to open. (As a matter of fact, I heard later that the big vault didn't open until four-thirty Monday afternoon—and then only after experts had cut their way in.)

After pulling the hairsprings, I wiped my forehead with my handkerchief, straightened my tie, and went back upstairs. At five, I went calmly down with the checker and closed the big vault. He never saw that anything was wrong with the clocks. When I got back to my desk, I saw that Mead had returned. I sauntered over to him.

"My wife's in town shopping, and she's going to pick me up here around six," I said. "I'm going to catch up on some work."

"Fine," he said. "See you Monday."

Ten minutes later, I was the only person left in the bank.

I knew I had to work fast. The 195 Broadway branch is in the American Telephone & Telegraph Bulding, and the bank uses the building's cleaning facilities. The cleaning women usually came into the bank around six. It was then five-fifteen. I picked up the suitcase and rushed downstairs. The boxes I'd taken from the vaults were each secured with two locks: I had the key to one, the box's teller had the key to the other. The old dual-control system, I thought again, as I pried open each lock with my crowbar.

There was so much money in those boxes I knew immediately I wouldn't be able to take it all. I had to rule against singles and fives. Incidentally, I had a bad break (I thought at the time) in that there weren't very many large-denomination bills. I put about $5,000 in my pocket, but I didn't count the rest of the money I took. I don't know to this day exactly how much it was; all I know is the figure the FBI gave me. I must have left 50,000-odd dollars in singles and silver there on the floor. After I put in all the money the suitcase would hold, I grabbed a large brown envelope full of negotiable bonds and put them in, too.

Then I cleaned up. I took the money boxes, the wrappings from my suitcase, the tools, the wrappers from the money, and put them all in a near-by closet that old junk was stored in, one that hadn't been opened for nearly five years.

When I got back to the customers' room, I saw I'd put so much money in the bag it wouldn't close. I had to sit on it to get it fastened.

It was then about five forty-five.

Halfway up the stairs, one lock on the suitcase popped. One side fell out—I'd forgotten to buckle the straps—and all that money cascaded down.

It was then, for the first time, that I realized what a horrible thing I'd done. Boy, I thought, what a mess you've got yourself into. I began sweating, and for a moment I was tempted to run away and leave the money there on the steps and the floor. But I'd gone so far I couldn't stop. I stooped down and began cramming the money back into the bag, sat on it again, and got the locks closed. It was then just a few minutes to six. As I went out, through the lobby of the A. T. & T. Building, the cleaning women were just checking in.

The bag seemed to weigh a ton. I stopped into a bar—I'd never needed a drink so much in my life. On impulse, I put the bag on a penny scale near the door. It weighed 167 pounds. I had another drink and thought I'd better call my wife. The maid said she was at the country club with some girlfriends, and would I please pick up all the husbands and meet them there for dinner? I left the bar and tried to get a cab, but there was none in sight. Finally I had to take a bus to the Staten Island ferry. As I was getting on the bus, I had another chilling thought: Suppose a lock should pop again?

Fortunately, none did. I got off the bus and started toward the ferry. When I had gone three or four steps, I felt a hand on my arm, a firm, strong grip, like a cop's. Well, I thought, they've got me. I nearly started to run, but then I heard the voice, a familiar one.

"Well, Banker Crowe!" it said. The voice belonged to a fellow I knew quite well, whom I'll call Tom. "Here," he said, "let me give you a hand with that bag."

Before I could stop him, he'd snatched it from me. I tried to pretend I was grateful. "Boy," I said, "I didn't think I could get much farther with that heavy thing."

Tom grinned. "It's heavy, all right," he said. "What've you got in it, anyhow? Taking home some samples?"

For one frightful moment, I thought some of the money was protruding. Then I realized I was getting hypersensitive. I laughed off his little joke.

On Staten Island, the distance between the ferry and the place I habitually parked my car was about a half-mile. My friend Tom was going off in another direction, so it was up to me to carry the bag myself. I was exhausted. I put it down on a street corner and asked the cop on duty to watch it for me while I went to the parking lot. The FBI and other people who questioned me later couldn't understand why I left the suitcase—after all, there were hundreds of people going by that intersection, and the cop was too busy to watch it closely. My answer is that I wasn't thinking of the money in the bag as money. I was just thinking of *getting back at some invisible force that was weighing me down.* More of that later.

I drove back from the lot, picked up the bag, and threw it in the trunk of the car, principally because I knew I would have a hard time explaining a suitcase that size to my wife. Then I went and picked up my friends and took them on to the country club, where we met our wives and settled down for a pleasant evening. During the next few hours, I almost forgot what I'd done that afternoon. In fact, when I thought of it at all, it seemed dreamlike.

My wife's name is Honora, I call her "Hon." That night, driving home, I said to her, "Remember that customer in Buffalo I told you about? I've got to go up there and see him on Monday morning. I guess I'll leave Sunday night."

"How long will you be gone?" she asked.

"Not very long, Hon," I said vaguely.

Usually I play golf on Saturday mornings. That Saturday I had more urgent matters to attend to. First of all, I burned a lot of trash that had been accumulating in our garage (much to Hon's relief). Around ten, I went into the house and asked her to call George, a friend of mine, and ask him to meet me for lunch at the country club. When I had finished burning the trash, I told her I was leaving to meet him. Instead I drove to my parents' house. I live in the Eltingville section, and they live about five miles away, in Woodland Terrace. They were spending the winter in Florida, and I was in the habit of going around every week or so to see that the house was all right.

I took the bag out of the car, went into the house, and spread all the money out on the dining-room table. Previously, I'd procured some heavy brown envelopes, and I began putting various sums of money into them. I can't explain why. All I know is that I'd thought up a list of friends, relatives, and members of my wife's family, and it seemed important to me to send some money to each person on that list. I put several thousand dollars in each envelope, along with a note. One, I remember, said:

Dear———:

Here, have a nice vacation.

Give some of this to Hon someday.

Love, DICK

I can't remember the names of all the people I sent money to, but every cent was later sent back voluntarily by the people who'd received it. I also made up envelopes in the amounts of money due on notes of mine that various banks were holding. All told, the money I put into those envelopes, including the relatives' and the banks', amounted to approximately $30,200. When I had finished, I put the suitcase and money under the bed in my mother's room, left the house, and drove to the post office, where I registered and mailed the letters. That was a stupid thing to do, since nothing is easier to trace than a registered letter. But the whole thing was stupid: there was no reason connected with any of it.

Early Sunday morning I again went to my parents' house and made up more envelopes. I worked away for about a half-hour when I heard a knock at the door.

I felt like a trapped animal.

I hurriedly scooped all the money and envelopes into the suitcase and returned it to its hiding place under the bed.

The knocking continued insistently.

I washed my hands hastily, tucked in my shirt, and went to the door. Somehow, I thought it might be police. When I saw who it was, I breathed audibly in relief. It was a man I'll call Bill, a good friend of mine who was employed as a purser by a steamship line. He'd seen my car in front of the house and decided to come in and chew the fat a while. I shook hands with him and offered him a drink. He told me he'd just come back from a long ocean trip and was about to go out again in a couple of days.

A wild irrational idea came into my head. Why couldn't I spill the whole story to him, offer to cut him in for half, and let him arrange to get us out of the country?

"Bill," I said tentatively, "what would you say if—"

Something—I don't know what—made me stop abruptly.

"If what?"

I gestured aimlessly. "Funniest thing, I can't remember what I meant to say."

He left, finally: it seemed to me then that he had stayed for hours. I finished making up the envelopes. When I'd addressed the last one, I looked at all the money spread out on the dining-room table and realized I couldn't possibly carry it all. There was a considerable amount left over, although I didn't bother counting it. I went down to the basement and found an old Army-surplus ammunition box I'd once used to keep ice cubes in during parties, brought it back upstairs, and packed in as much money as would fit (around $50,000, the FBI informed me later; again, I didn't count it). Then, looking once more at the suitcase, I realized there was *still* too much for me to carry comfortably. So I took another handful—approximately $6,000, I later learned—and put it in a cardboard box I found in a closet. I went back down to the cellar and got a small shovel.

What made me drive to the cemetery, I don't know. It just seemed like the logical place to bury something. While I was there, digging in my father's plot, several people I knew passed and spoke to me. I answered them and went on digging. I don't know what they thought I was doing: planting flowers, I guess.

When I finished covering up the ammunition box, I realized I still had the problem of keeping my wife from seeing the big suitcase. I drove from the cemetery to Costello's parking lot near the ferry. There was an old man on duty.

"I'd like to leave this bag for a while," I told him. "Will you be here later, around five, say?"

"I think so," he said.

"Keep the suitcase for me, will you?" After tipping him, I drove back to our house, stopping first at a club I occasionally frequented, where I paid a monthly bar bill of eleven dollars—not with cash, but with a check from my personal account. Approaching the house, I could see my wife and some friends on the lawn in the rear. At my mother's, I'd taken the brown envelope full of securities out of the suitcase, and I didn't want her to see that. So I went in on the opposite side of the house and up to the attic. One side of the attic is finished off as a playroom for our children. I opened the door to the other side, and threw the envelope full of securities in there. There was still the cardboard box full of money to dispose of. I finally put that in the back of a linen closet on the second floor. Then I went down, greeted my wife and friends, and sat around with them on the lawn.

We had dinner around two P.M. I'd showered and changed clothes and packed a small bag; I was all ready to take off. Around four, my impatience got the better of me. I knew I couldn't wait any longer. I got up quickly and said good-by to Hon.

"Have a good trip, Dick," she said.

I couldn't face her; I wanted to get away. "Sure," I said. "Take care of the kids."

This time I took our smaller car, the Austin. At the parking lot I found—of all the damned luck—that the old man had gone home and locked the shack. Through the door, I could see my bag sitting in there. I went around to the back and tried the window. Locked. I was about to force it when I remembered something: the police station was right next door. Most of the cops knew me, but they might well have thought it funny if they'd seen me trying to break in—and there was a slight chance that they might have become uncomfortably inquisitive about the suitcase.

There was an emergency number posted on the shack's door. I called it from a drugstore. The owner's wife answered. The owner wasn't at home, she said, and she didn't have a key to the shack, nor did she know the name of the old man. "Try forcing the window," she suggested.

I went back again. It wouldn't budge.

I called the owner's wife a second time. "I've *got* to get that bag," I said. "I've got a plane to catch."

"You'd better break the window," she said.

Outside the shack, I picked up a rock, but as I was about to smash the pane I thought again of the cops. They surely would have heard it and investigated. So I kept heaving and tugging at that window. Finally the catch broke.

At home, I had packed a smaller suitcase. In the Austin, just before I got on the ferry, I transferred the clothes from the small bag to the large one. Then I left the Austin in the lot and boarded the ferry.

In New York, I hailed a cab and went directly to the main post office, where I posted the envelopes I'd made up that morning at my parents' house. As I was mailing the last one, it occurred to me Hon would need some money, so I took a handful out of my pocket —it was around $800, she told me later—and sent it to her. I'd been in such a hurry to get to the registry window that I'd left the suitcase, open, on one of the writing counters. The clothes were on top of the money, but if anybody had looked at it carefully, he could have seen the money.

At the air-lines terminal on Forty-second Street, I thought I should have something to read on the plane, so I bought a copy of *Dinner at Antoine's* by Frances Parkinson Keyes. Then I bought a little box of stationery, thinking I might write some letters during the flight.

At the Newark airport on the plane, I began to read the novel. I didn't read very far. The next thing I knew the stewardess was shaking me. "We're in Jacksonville, sir," she said.

Thus far I've attempted to tell my story matter of factly, because that was how it occurred. Even though it was an act of emotional release, as I will try to explain, I was still too deeply set in my manner of response to external stimuli to behave in any way but an extremely "conventional" one. I moved through the theft and its aftermath as though it were nothing more exciting than the act of brushing my teeth. It was only later that the reaction set in—that the guilt and fear took over.

Ever since my story first broke in the papers, people have been wondering what made me do it. Psychiatrists at Bellevue Hospital in New York tried to find out, too, after the FBI picked me up in Florida. (I spent nearly three weeks in Bellevue, and the doctors there ultimately decided I was not psychotic.)

I've wondered about why I did it as much as anybody. I had plenty of time to think about it—six weeks in the Federal House of Detention in New York, and thirteen months and two days in the Federal Correctional Institution at Danbury, Connecticut. And I've thought about it almostly constantly since I've been out of prison. I'm still not entirely sure why I did it, but I believe I'm beginning to arrive at the answer. The clues, I think, are buried in my early life, and in the kind of life I was leading for ten years prior to the time I committed my crime.

I was born in Staten Island on May 6, 1908, the only child of Helen (Henderson) and William John Crowe. My father was a fourth-generation Staten Islander, and he'd been with Dun and Bradstreet for thirty years before going to Florida in the mid-twenties to go into the soap business. As a child, I got everything I wanted, and I never got in any trouble—well, the usual scraps with other kids, the ordinary pranks, but nothing serious. I never stole anything or did anything particularly bad. After attending elementary schools, I went to Nazareth Hall, a military prep school in Pennsylvania. I spent four years there, and was an exceptional student: I made A's in most of my subjects and was a three-letter man on varsity teams for three years running.

I had been planning to go to college after prep school, but when my folks moved to Florida, I decided to work for a year. I got a job in the display-advertising department of the Miami *Herald*, and held it until the fall of 1925, when I matriculated at the University of Miami. In college, I was still an excellent student and still played basketball, football, baseball, and other sports. My father could have sent me through college, but I preferred to work my way. I'd had odd jobs in the summers during prep school, and I continued to work during college vacations. One summer I came North and got a job as a messenger in Varick Street branch of the National City

Bank. I liked the banking business from the very beginning—so much, in fact, that I was tempted to quit college and stay in New York. But finally I returned to Miami to study for another year.

I came North again in September, 1930. By then, I had decided definitely that banking appealed to me more than any other occupation, so again I went to the National City. They hired me as a clearance clerk. I can't remember exactly how much I was paid, but I believe it was around eighty dollars a month. Meanwhile my family had moved back to Staten Island, and I was living with them, paying board to my mother, not because she asked me to, but because I insisted upon it. I'd still kept up an active interest in the U. S. Volunteer Lifesaving Corps, I went to the Moravian church regularly, and although I took a drink once in a while, I certainly wasn't a heavy, or even habitual, drinker. You might almost say that I was a disgustingly well-behaved young man.

Around 1934, I met a girl named Honora Wall. She was a graduate of the University of Pennsylvania and was working as a dental hygienist in the New York school system. I took one look at her light-brown hair and blue eyes, and that settled it. The next thing we knew, we were talking about getting married. As I write this, we're celebrating our tenth wedding anniversary We've got three children—Richard, Jr., eight, Mary Elizabeth, seven, and William John, three. I don't believe I know of any couple more happily married. When the FBI was hunting me, the agents tried their best to find some other woman in my background. The laugh was on them. There never was anybody but Hon—there's not a woman in the world who could get me away from her, even for a date. And now, after she stood by me so nobly while I was in trouble, I'm just beginning to realize what good judgment I showed when I married her.

When I first ran off to Florida, the newspapers called me one of the bank's "fair-haired boys." I understand that National City officials later denied this statement. Well, whether or not I was a fair-haired boy, I know that I liked my job immensely and was pretty well liked. The thing that hurts now is that although the bank people have every reason to be sore at me—after all, I made a fool of their foolproof system—they still don't give me any credit for the twenty years I spent working as their trusted employee. I've heard, in fact, that they issued a directive—I don't know if it was verbal or written—to the effect that any employee caught speaking to or seeing me would be suspended. I haven't heard a word from my best friend in the bank—who was also my best man. The point I'm trying to make is that, on the surface, I had nothing against the bank. In those early days, I was interested enough in the business to take night courses at the American Banking Institute in New York. With the help of what I learned there, plus my own enthusiasm and ability, I rose fairly rapidly in the National City. From clearance clerk, I was promoted to teller, and then through note teller, loan teller, and finally to chief clerk. During that time, I served at various branches all over New York. I was learning the business thoroughly.

Around March of 1932, I was sent to Stapleton, Staten Island. The National City had bought the Bank of America, which had a branch there, and they assigned me to it because I'd grown up on the Island. I took the job of chief clerk at a salary of about $1,800 a year. Here I should like to mention that I'd made more than that in Miami working for the *Herald*, before I went to college. Salaries are never high in the banking business, and if you want my honest opinion, that's one of the reasons some people do the kind of thing that I did.

When I first went to the Staten Island branch, it was about a $780,000-a-year operation, losing money rather heavily. When I left it, in November of 1947, it was a $6,000,000 branch, and was earning a decent profit every year. I'm proud of that record. The bank was evidently pleased with it, too—and they rewarded me by steadily increasing my salary. When I finally was transferred from Staten Island to the 195 Broadway branch, I was earning around $6,000 a year. Later I was raised to $7,200. That was a good salary, but it wasn't enough—not for the life I was leading by then.

I don't want to blame the bank for what I did. Mostly, I blame the war. It may sound funny, but the way I look at it, I was just as much a war casualty as the man who was shell-shocked on the battlefield, even though I was deferred all through the war. And please understand here that I'm not trying to excuse myself; I'm just trying to state what happened.

When war came, a prominent lady on Staten Island began a drive to raise funds for the USO. Her husband called the president of the National City and asked him to recommend someone out on Staten Island to help her. The bank recommended me; then they called me to New York and told me of the importance of the job I was to do, and how it would help both the country and the bank. I readily agreed to help—after all, the only hobby I'd ever had was people. The lady managed to get an office in Borough Hall, and we launched the campaign. It was a great success.

Prior to this time, I'd like to emphasize, I'd been living a fairly modest life. The newspapers have made me sound as though I were living like a millionaire. They made much of my fourteen-room house, my speedboat, my two cars. The truth was that the house cost $20,000—and I'm still paying off the mortgage. It just happened to be a good, sound buy—and I got the down payment by selling a small house my aunt had given my wife and me as a wedding present. I'd turned the power boat over to the government during the war, and I later sold it at a modest price. The two automobiles I bought on time payments, like any other man with a modest income.

But once that USO campaign was over, the deluge began. Next thing I knew, I was mixed up in every conceivable kind of local cause and activity. I ran the War Bonds drive for Staten Island for the duration of the war. I was a director of the Community Chest, treasurer of the Red Cross, director of the Chamber of Commerce, co-chairman of the Salvation Army, Boy Scout committeeman, member of the Police Athletic League, director of the U. S. Volunteer Lifesaving Corps, president of the Staten Island Rotary, president of the Richmond County Bankers Association, and president of Group Seven of the New York State Bankers Association. I also founded and was president of the Stapleton Board of Trade. I organized the Staten Island Servicemen's Center and attended it once a week. I helped raise funds for the Catholic Youth organization and the Jewish Youth Center. Hon helped me in all these things, by the way. She kept as busy as I did—busier, in fact, considering that she was running the house and taking care of two small children (the third hadn't yet arrived).

I never took on any of these outside jobs without consulting the bank. They always told me to go ahead; encouraged me, in fact. After all, every time my name got in the papers, the bank's did, too. But sometimes, in connection with these volunteer jobs, which were supposed to help build the bank's good name, I had to take a party to lunch or dinner. The check would be, say, forty dollars. Sometimes I got the full amount back from the bank; sometimes I didn't. And many times I took a customer to an eight-dollar lunch and presented the bank with an expense item of about three-fifty—which, I knew well, was about all they would allow.

Don't misunderstand. I was living high and enjoying it to the hilt. I guess I got cocky and big-headed; the public-servant business went to my head. But I was never home at night—I had too many places to go—and when I was home, I was irritable with my wife and children. I suppose the out-of-pocket expenses were worrying me. They were terrific. Some nights, going to a formal dinner, I had to spend twenty-five dollars or more for flowers for the hostess, getting my tails and white tie in shape, cab fares, tips, etc. Before long, I had to begin borrowing (don't forget, during the war I was only making around a hundred dollars a week). At that time, too, I was trying to pay off the mortgage on my house. All told, when I ran off to Florida, I owed about $35,000, including the mortgage. If I had been sensible, Hon and I could have sat down and figured out a way of liquidating those debts. But I wasn't sensible; I was caught up in a maze of what I thought were important activities, and I was most concerned with keeping up that big front.

When the war ended, I felt as though I'd burned myself out. And I had—but, again, the reaction didn't set in until later.

The bank was evidently well satisfied with the job I'd done during the war. They called me in and asked how I would feel about transferring to a bigger branch in the city. The salary would be better, they said, but I would have to take a reduction in title. The plan was for me to go in as assistant manager, with the understanding that I would be made manager at some not-too-distant date. I agreed immediately. It seemed that I was getting somewhere at last.

After a year and a half at 195 Broadway, however, things didn't look so rosy. I'd got my raise, all right, but I found that it wasn't enough to keep my head out of the financial swamp I'd fallen into.

The manager there, moreover, was just about my own age. There seemed to be no chance of my replacing him, and it seemed unlikely I would be transferred to some other branch. Shortly after I'd gone to the Broadway branch, I'd begun to have spells of what my doctor called "bad nerves." I couldn't sleep nights—oh, I could get to sleep, all right, but I always awakened a few hours later. Some nights I went down and wandered the beach aimlessly. And all this time I was trying to keep up the front I'd established during the war. Hon and I had been asked to join the country club, and we were going around with people who had a lot more money than we did. (I resigned from the club after I ran off to Florida, to keep from embarrassing the members.)

So you can see what a mess I was in. And, after months of keeping everything bottled up inside me, I found out I couldn't do it anymore. One day—that Wednesday in March, as I stood there in Lawler's—everything exploded. I suddenly got disgusted with myself for leading such a phony life, trying to keep up with the Joneses. And I transferred the blame from myself to the bank—I somehow held the bank responsible for the situation I was in.

I thought, What am I going to do?

And then I thought, I'll fix their wagon, good.

And that was how I decided to take the money.

The sky was beautifully clear and the stars were shining brightly when I got off the plane in Jacksonville. I got a cab and told the driver to take me to the best hotel. He pulled up in front of the George Washington Hotel. It was almost full, but the clerk eventually found me a huge, barnlike room ordinarily rented to salesmen in town to display samples. When the clerk told me what the room was used for, I had to bite my lip to keep from laughing—I remembered what Tom had said to me on the ferry about taking home samples from the bank. I had plenty of samples to display, all right. I registered under the name of Robert Crane, the same monicker I'd used to get the plane ticket, and then I went upstairs and had a good stiff drink from a bottle of whisky I'd brought from home. After a while I had another. Then I got to thinking about Hon, and what a lousy trick I was playing on her, and I sat down to write her a letter. I kept it short. I told her I'd done a terrible thing, and said I hoped she would forgive me. "Try to understand —I can't seem to help myself," I wrote. "People have been coming to me with their troubles for years. They don't seem to think I have troubles of my own." (I suppose I should explain, here, that I never bothered Hon with any of my troubles; after all, she was concerned with raising the children—she had a tough enough time of it.) I wrote practically the same thing to my mother, who was then in Miami—but I mailed her letter to Staten Island, as I knew she was just about to leave for home. I went out and put both letters in a corner box. Then I went to bed.

The next morning was the first time I really began to grasp something of the nature of the trouble I was in. I put on the thick-rimmed glasses I'd bought in New York and went out and had some breakfast. I figured the sun would help disguise me in a day or two, and I planned to let my mustache grow. After breakfast, I went looking for a used car. Most of the lots were closed, but in one I saw a fairly new club coupé I liked, and I waited around until a salesman showed up. The price of the car was $2,350. I gave the man $1,000 in cash and told him I would go cash a check. I told him my name was Robert Franklin. When I returned, an hour later, the manager had arrived.

He seemed cordial, and suggested we go across the street for coffee and doughnuts while they were sending out for the license plates.

"What line you in?" he asked.

"I'm a salesman, in the printing line," I said. "I'm heading toward Sea Island, Georgia."

"What about the title to your car?" he said. "It'll take a spell for it to come from the capital, so you'd better leave me a forwarding address."

I thought fast. "Tell you what," I said, "—have them send the title to you, and when I come back through here in a week or two, I'll stop by and pick it up."

If he thought there was anything unusual about that, he kept it to himself. I thought he looked at me curiously, but I pretended that it was the most natural thing in the world. As soon as the car was ready, I hopped in and drove off. First I went to Jacksonville Beach, stopped long enough to buy some sports clothes, and then I drove on to St. Augustine. There the first thing I did was go to a barbershop for a crew cut.

I took a room in a little hotel on the beach, again as Robert Franklin, and for the next few days I didn't do much but make myself inconspicuous and let the sun help me with my disguise. I swam, saw some movies, had dinner in some of the nicer restaurants, and tried not to think about what I'd done. Every now and again I was tempted to buy a newspaper, but I kept myself from it. I'd bought a small radio, but whenever a news broadcast came on, I switched it off or tuned in some other station. The guilt was really beginning to work in my subconscious, I guess. Once, one afternoon in a bar, I played the horses, which I'd never done before. Ironically enough, I won two or three hundred dollars.

It was then, too, that I began to feel hunted. Before I went into a restaurant, I would try to look through the window to see if there was anybody inside who might recognize me. It was lucky I took that precaution—several times I saw close friends. I always got away fast before they had a chance to see me.

On Thursday morning, I came down to breakfast and there on the table before me was what I'd been dreading—a newspaper with my picture staring up at me. They'd discovered the theft—and, what was worse, they'd traced me to Jacksonville (naturally, they'd found out from Hon I'd written her from there). They'd also talked to the man who'd sold me the car. They were looking for me everywhere. A nation-wide manhunt was on—the biggest manhunt, I heard later from the FBI, since the nation had gone on the trail of the Lindbergh baby kidnaper.

That was the first time I was frightened.

I left the restaurant, got in the car, and drove into St. Augustine proper. There I parked the car and walked until I found a garage.

"I've got an automobile I want to put in dead storage," I told the attendant. "It belongs to a friend of mine, John Roberts—he's going to Japan for a year to work for an oil company."

"Bring it in," he said. He asked no questions. I paid him several hundred dollars, took the receipt, and left there fast. Later it was reported in the papers that he had immediately notified the FBI.

I walked down the street until I came to a new-car showroom. There was a light-gray job in there, brand new.

"I'd like to buy that car," I said to the salesman. "I'll pay cash, but it's got to be ready in an hour."

He said the car'd been promised to somebody else, but for a consideration—well, it's remarkable what cold cash can do. It took around $3,100 of the money from my suitcase. An hour later I drove back and parked within a couple of blocks of my hotel. I went in and got some clothes and the radio—I didn't want to take everything, as I didn't want them to know I was leaving—and I tried to walk through the lobby as though I were just taking some stuff to the cleaners. Outside I ran down the street to the car, got in, and headed out on the road for Miami.

On the way, I stopped and bought some papers. The news didn't make me feel any better. The authorities said they were closing in, and that it would only be a matter of time before they nabbed me. That was when I started to think seriously about covering my tracks. It had started to rain, and I thought I might drive the car into a lagoon and hitch a ride the rest of the way. Some motorist would take pity on me in the rain, I thought. Once I even drove right up to the edge of an inlet, but the water was too shallow to cover the car.

The sun was overhead when I pulled into Daytona Beach. I parked the car and walked several blocks until I came to a hotel called The Renee. The national swimming meets were on then, and the place was full of reporters and photographers. The woman at the desk said she had one room available; a reporter was in it then, but he would be checking out in the late afternoon. I got my stuff from the car and stowed it in the room.

Funny thing: of all the newspapermen in that hotel, none recognized me. The papers were very good to my wife and me all during our trouble—we'd asked them not to photograph the children, and none of them tried to—but, frankly, I've lost my respect for the reporters' powers of observation. All during the time I was hunted, and later, even after I got out of prison, they kept printing information so erroneous as to be laughable. That's one reason I'm writing my own story. I want to get the facts straight.

My next problem, after checking into The Renee, was to get rid of that gray car. I drove it back to Daytona proper, put it in a parking lot, and flagged a cab to go back to the beach. On the way back, it struck me that the parking lot was right across the street from a police station, and I remembered Costello's, back on Staten Island. I thought grimly, My life is just one damned parking lot across from a police station after another.

The next few days are all jumbled and twisted in my mind, like a nightmare I don't want to remember. All I did was go swimming and try to keep out of people's way. The Daytona Beach seashore is policed—every fifteen minutes or so a patrol car drives up and down. Whenever one passed me, I dove into the surf. My appearance had changed considerably by then, but I wasn't taking any chances.

I did a funny thing in those days, too, one I can't account for. Every morning, just after breakfast, I would take the bus into the city and saunter past that parking lot, looking to see if the car were still there. It was. It looked as though it hadn't been touched.

In the evenings, I was in the habit of going into Jack O'Clubs, a small night club and bar with a package-liquor store attached. I'd struck up an acquaintance with the bartender, and I used to sit in there and shoot the bull with him, talking about golf mostly. By that time I'd changed my name again, this time to Richard Franklin . . . I took my own first name because I'd found, while going as Robert Franklin, that I didn't pay attention when people I met called me Bob. I was afraid it might make them suspicious. I was jumpy as hell.

On Sunday, I awoke to find it raining. It rained all day. I went into town, checked on the car, and then, because I couldn't go to the beach, went to the movies. Early in the evening, after dinner, I went into the little night club. There were a few other people there, sitting at the tables around the room, and one or two others at the long bar. I must have sat there an hour or so before the blond kid came in.

He was tall and looked as if he were in his early twenties. He said to the bartender, "Where's the head?" The bartender motioned toward the back of the room. The kid went back to the lavatory and came out a few minutes later. I thought, as he passed me, that he gave me a long look. But then, in my state, I thought everybody was giving me long looks.

A few minutes later a big, elderly man came in and began talking to the headwaiter near the front door. When I saw him, I thought,

"Cop," but he never even glanced at me, so I put the idea out of my head. As I did, another young fellow came in and asked where the lavatory was.

By that time, the other people who had been sitting at the bar had drifted out. I was the only bar customer. Fifteen or twenty minutes later, another fellow entered. He was dressed neatly, and he seemed like a pleasant fellow, maybe lonely, who'd wandered in for a beer. There were thirty stools at that bar for him to sit on. He picked one next to me.

For a couple of minutes, I thought nothing of it. I bought another drink and went on joking with the bartender.

Now, I don't believe in telepathy, second sight, or anything like that. But I swear that as I sat there, drinking my drink, it suddenly dawned on me that something was up. I hooked together the two young guys who'd asked where the head was, the big man at the door with the headwaiter, and now this fellow beside me—and the hair on the back of my neck literally stood on end.

I thought, Let's see if I'm right.

As unostentatiously as possible, I got up and walked to the lavatory.

The instant I opened the door and went in, they seemed to come through the windows, the doors, everywhere. There must have been about ten of them, all with guns. The neatly dressed man who'd been sitting beside me was the first one after me through the door. He came in with his gun cocked, six or eight others right behind him, and that was where they got me, right there in that lavatory . . .

There's not much more to tell. They rushed me back to Daytona, stripped me, searched me, and then it dawned on them I didn't have the money on me, so they took me back to the hotel and picked up the suitcase. Later they counted the money while I stood naked in one corner of the room. Even then, my business sense came out. I kept yelling for a receipt for the money, but nobody seemed to pay any attention to me. The total, they said, was 54,000-odd dollars. That night they put me in a cell in Daytona Beach. It was the filthiest place I'd ever seen—all kinds of dirt and stool on the floor—but it was no worse than Bellevue Hospital in New York. Dirty as the Daytona Beach jail was, I just curled up in the corner and went to sleep.

Next day in Tampa, they arraigned me before the Federal commissioner, who assigned bail of $100,000. The rest of the story has been pretty well covered by the newspapers. Two days later, back in New York, they asked me if I wanted an attorney. "What for?" I asked. "I'm guilty as hell." They asked me if I wanted to see Hon, and I said I didn't—I just couldn't face her, after what I'd done. But they told me she'd been waiting all day, and I agreed to see her.

When Hon walked into that room, the whole thing hit me fully. I realized, just by looking at her haggard face, the enormity of what I'd done. She'd had every reason to turn her back on me, but, as far as she was concerned, there had been no doubt that she would stand by me. The same, incidentally, was true of my mother and father, and of Hon's family. They all behaved—well they behaved better than I had any right to expect. And so, by the way, did the people on Staten Island. Some of them even started raising a fund for my defense. Nobody could ever have asked for more loyalty.

When Hon came in that day in New York, I broke down. From then on, I began cooperating with the authorities. I helped them get the money back—from the attic, from the cemetery, and from all the people I'd sent it to. The only money that hasn't been recovered to date is the amount I spent in Florida, which includes the price of two cars—although they were confiscated by the FBI and, I believe, resold. There's one strange factor in the recovery of the money. When the FBI had me in that room in Daytona Beach, they counted—I think—$54,000 in my suitcase. Next day, in Miami, the count was only $49,000. I'm certainly not accusing anybody of anything, but as I said before, I kept asking for a receipt. They never gave me one, so I have no way of knowing if their figures were right in either case. It seems odd, to me at least, that there should still be $5,000 unrecovered. I'm pretty sure that all the money I spent or sent was accounted for—the FBI and I went over it time and again. Incidentally, the FBI men, one and all, treated me better than I had any right to expect. They were gentlemen; and from what I hear from Hon and my mother and father, the ones who interviewed them and searched the houses behaved the same way.

One thing I'd like to make clear. Ever since I stole the money, Hon and I have been getting letters from people who're still under the impression that we've got it. I suppose we've had nearly fifty letters from people asking us to help them. We don't have the money. We wish people would stop writing us.

On July 6, 1949, I was taken before Federal Judge Henry W. Goddard in New York. Previously, all my friends on Staten Island and elsewhere—and I'd never realized that I'd had so many—had written him to ask for leniency on the basis of my previous fine record. There were four counts in the indictment: embezzling moneys and securities from a member bank of the Federal Reserve System, entering the bank with intent to commit embezzlement, transporting stolen money in interstate commerce, and using the mails to transport stolen money. The judge sentenced me to three years each on the first three counts, the sentences to run concurrently, and to three years on the fourth, which was suspended—but I was to be put on probation for five years, to begin after the service of my sentences on the first three counts. I was lucky. Some legal authorities had estimated I might get as high as forty-five years, possibly even more. A few days later, I was sent to Danbury.

Now, after serving my time, I'm free once again. I was released on parole on August 7, but of course I'll be on probation until 1957. My wife, her family, my family, and our friends have forgiven me, but I know that as long as I live I will carry the guilt for the anguish and trouble I caused them. That's something I've got to live with. From now on, I know my work and behavior will give them good reason to be glad for the faith they had in me. I am working in a job—I had a number of offers while in prison—and I am working hard to rebuild my reputation and character.

As far as society is concerned, I feel I've paid my debt. I don't feel *justified*, of course, but I feel this way about it: All over the country, I know there are thousands of Richard Crowes. Men, that is, who are living the kind of life I was living before I let the tensions get the better of me, men trying to put up big fronts. If I've done nothing more than make just one of those men see the futility of his life, I feel my crime will have accomplished something constructive. I'm not setting myself up as a martyr, heaven knows. I did a stupid thing, and I'm ashamed of it. But I hope someone may profit from my mistake.

It's funny how the mind works. The things I remember most

clearly today are those that didn't really have much to do with the crime itself. For instance, when the FBI cornered me in that lavatory in the bar, the nicely dressed man, his gun pointed at me, flashed his FBI badge and said, "You look something like a fellow we're looking for. Fellow named Crowe."

"Yes," I said. "I'm Crowe."

"Do you mean it?" he asked.

And then, as I stood there with all those guns aimed at me, *he made me take out my wallet and show my identification.*

That's one thing I remember clearly. The second occurred in the Tampa jail, where they took me after Daytona Beach. They put me in a cell with two thugs who'd just been apprehended. I struck up a conversation with them, and ultimately we got around to trading names.

One of them whistled. "*Crowe?*" he said, in stupefaction. "You mean you're the guy who got away with all that scratch in New York?"

I confessed, shamefacedly, that I was.

"Man," he said, shaking his head, "you don't know how lucky you are."

"What do you mean?" I asked.

"The minute that story came out in the blutes," he said, "every heavy gee in the damn country headed for Florida, lookin' for you. That's how me and my pal here happened to be in the state. We came after that money you stole." He shook his head again. "Yes, sir," he said, "it's lucky for you, Crowe, the FBI got you. If we'd have run into you, or anybody else had, your life wouldn't've been worth a plugged nickel."

I guess I *was* lucky.

Post Script: If the subject is articulate and willing to talk freely, the as-told-to article is ridiculously easy to write. All the writer need do is ask the questions, prod the narrator's memory, then put the story into language that approximates the latter's and arrange it in logical or dramatic order. Crowe was an articulate man, and he had had a long time in prison to think about his theft. I had him tell me the story from the very beginning of his life, and I put it down on the typewriter as fast as he spoke, making certain that I put in his peculiarities of speech in order to make the story uniquely his. This first session required about seven hours. When Crowe left my house I took the notes and wrote a rough draft of the story—again, starting with his childhood. I knew, as I was putting down this draft, that it would not do for *Cosmopolitan.* A magazine story of this kind ought to start off with a bang. It could not begin with the crime, for I wanted to build suspense up to the point where he actually took the money. I therefore determined to start with the very day that the idea for taking the money had come into his mind. Then I cut immediately to Crowe's behavior in the period just before he committed his crime—this, in order to build some sympathy for him. The reader had to be shown that he was a deranged man; the episode of the sudden purchase of the dog established that.

During our second session I got Crowe to fill in details we had not covered in the first. His explanation of how he actually got into the vaults was not clear to me; I made him explain it over and over, then wrote it out and had him check and recheck it. By now I was well along with the article, but even though O'Connell had told me to take as much space as I needed, it was much too long. I therefore had to decide what to cut, and it seemed most sensible to eliminate the details of Crowe's boyhood. I left in only what was necessary. The trouble was, I had to cut some of the incidents in Crowe's early life that gave clues to his real nature—but I consoled myself that *Cosmopolitan* was interested in a story, not a psychiatric analysis.

The fact that a subject is articulate does not always guarantee that the as-told-to will work out. The most difficult subject of this kind I've ever had was Sid Caesar, the TV comedian. I had read somewhere that he had been in psychoanalysis and that he often stated that it had changed his life. I went to him and suggested that we might be able to sell a piece called *What Psychoanalysis Did for Me. Look* was interested, and agreed to pay Caesar $1500, which he then gave to one of his favorite charities and matched with an additional $1500. We sat together for six hours while Sid rambled on about his problems and how he had solved them or failed to solve them. The trouble was, he kept changing his mind. He would make one statement, then take it back; he would make another, then decide that the original was what he wanted to say. It was hard, exasperating work, made bearable only by his charming wit and his ability to laugh at himself. Finally I had enough material to do a draft, but when we sat down to go over it, I found that he had changed his mind several more times. The piece that ultimately appeared in *Look* was not as strong as the one we originally wrote; it did not really get under the surface.

The second most difficult subject was Ezzard Charles, the former heavyweight champion. Charles is an affable and intelligent man, but he does not say much. He responded to questions with "Yep," "Nope," or "Hell, I don't know." Presently I realized that I would have to phrase the questions myself, get his affirmation or denial, then pretend that the questions had come from him. Milton Berle was just the other way: he was so anxious to fill in details I had a tough time getting him to listen to my questions and stay on the subject.

The steps in writing an as-told-to are roughly these:

1. Read the clips on the subject.
2. Spend some time with him to become familiar with his manner of speaking.
3. Discuss the story in broad, general terms and make an outline.
4. Ask questions leading to details.
5. Make a first draft.
6. See the subject again for more details.
7. Write a second draft.
8. Sit with the subject and, if possible, read the story aloud, making notes of his corrections, alterations or additions.
9. Incorporate the changes.
10. Check with the subject again.
11. Get his initials on the manuscript—on each page, if possible.

Some subjects insist on being paid; others are satisfied only with the publicity they get and with the amateur's thrill of seeing his name in print. One will insist on sharing credit with the writer; another will prefer that only his name appears. The professional writer should not care, one way or the other. He is not going to make a reputation with his as-told-to's, except among editors, and they will learn from other editors some estimate of his ability.

11 · Telescoping Time

EVERY now and then a writer gets a story that proves so be so much fun it makes him forget all the drudgery, all the uncooperative subjects, all the travel on filthy trains and rough planes, all the dingy hotel rooms, all the bad food—and all the other things that so often make him wonder what in the name of God he is doing in the magazine-writing business. The story that follows was that kind. It was the inspiration of Spencer Klaw when he was an articles editor for a firm that was producing a section of *This Week*. Spence gave me the idea in these words: "I hear that Jackie Gleason spends several weeks, every couple of months, in a suite in Doctor's Hospital in order to lose weight. They say it's a madhouse because he produces his TV show from the room. Why don't you see if you can spend some time there and then write a piece—850 words, no more—about it?"

I called Dorothy Loeffler, the press girl at CBS, and told her what Klaw had in mind. She said she would get back to me. She didn't; Gleason did. Two days later, my telephone rang and a voice said, "Hello, Pal. This is Jack Gleason. I hear you want to do a story, Pal. What can I do for you?"

Sam Boal, who had done Gleason for *Coronet* some months before, had warned me: "Be prepared to drink a lot on this piece. Gleason's supposed to be on a diet, but he cheats every now and then."

Gleason closed our conversation by saying, "What kind of booze do you like, Pal?"

I went up to see Gleason a few days later, and the piece following was the result of that visit and several others.

ARTICLE: "THE HOSPITAL BIT"

(From *This Week*)

"How'm I gonna order scenery if I don't know what the scene is?" Jackie Gleason was shouting into the phone. "The scene isn't set yet, Pal. Right. Yeah. Call me back."

He faced his five writers. "You see? They're yellin' for the scenery. They got to build it. Here it is Wednesday already—we shoulda had this set by Monday."

The writers said nothing. They looked, if possible, even more glum than they had when I entered, and I will never forget my first glimpse of them. Opening the door to Room 901 of Doctors Hospital, I had been reminded of that climactic scene in "M," the German horror movie, when Peter Lorre, as a psychotic killer, suddenly confronts a jury of thugs and thieves. The comedy writers' 10 grim, merciless eyes had stared at me in accusing silence. Two more pairs, one belonging to a blonde secretary, the other to Jack Philbin, Gleason's First Assistant Personal Manager, had also regarded me coldly. If I had not seen Gleason's black, curly head bent over a script, I might have turned and fled.

"Sdown," Gleason had ordered me. "Want some coffee? Makerself-t'home." Then he had resumed his reading. The room was heavy with the writers' silence.

Gleason, a 37-year-old veteran of night clubs, "B" movies and the stage, is now the hottest comic in television. His temperature and audience-rating are both so high that CBS has guaranteed him $300,000 a year. In addition to being hot, Gleason is fat—a condition for which he holds television accountable. Nothing produces so many worries as a weekly television show. Some people lose weight when they worry. When Gleason worries, he eats. When he eats, he instantly gains. When he gains, he worries more—and eats more. Finally, with cries resembling those of a great wounded beast, he has one last dinosaurian dinner and packs himself off to Doctors Hospital, there to submit himself to a strict diet and the bewildered ministrations of a chattering of nurses. Unfortunately, CBS does not grant leaves to reducing performers, and because of this stuffy network rule Gleason must put together his show from his hospital room, which is what he was doing the day I visited him.

He threw aside the script. "You haven't got anything, boys."

The writers—a stout young man, a thin and harried blond man, a bald man with a cigar, a pin-striped man with a moustache, and a man who looked like a professor—all began to speak at once. They had been laboring since Friday to come up with a sketch for "The Honeymooners," Ralph and Alice Kramden, a fictional young married couple who live in Brooklyn. Gleason grew up in Brooklyn and his characterization of Ralph is drawn practically from life.

The man with the cigar jumped to his feet. "You don't get the pitcher, Jack," he said.

"The pitcher I get," Gleason said, "is they're waitin' down there for the scenery order, and we're up here with no script."

"Lemme give you the pitcher," said The Cigar. He began to pace, gesturing violently. "Ralph asks the traffic manager home to dinner. Alice knows the manager's single. She wants to get him married off. You know—"

The fat young man stood up excitedly. "My wife's *always* tryin' to marry people off. She's got thirty girl friends, all clams. But *clams* —horrible looking. She's always—"

"Willyalemmegawanplease, Mahvin?" The Cigar interposed.

"Sorry, Harry," said the fat man, subsiding.

"Ralph brings the manager home," The Cigar continued.

"This clam girl friend's there. Ralph helps her off with her galoshes. He pulls her off the chair on the floor. Terrific laugh! A *boff!* Like this—" Demonstrating, he walked to the door, ducked his head quickly and pretended to bump it, meanwhile giving the door a hard kick. "Terrific!" he cried. His colleagues' faces might have been carved from stone. "Well . . ." he said.

"The manager fires Ralph for producin' this clam," said the professorial writer, adjusting his thick-rimmed glasses.

"Nobody gets fired for a thing like that," said Gleason. "It's too terrible. It's not believable." He walked over to the window and stared out. The writers once more all began to talk at the same time.

The phone rang, and Manager Jack Philbin handed it to Gleason with one word: "Toots." It was Toots Shor, a restaurateur whose place is frequented by television people.

"Yeah, Toots," said Gleason. "Yeah, yeah. I was two-thirty when I come in week before last. Twelve off last week, maybe twelve this—and that's with cheatin'! I sneaked out a coupla times. Yeah. Yeah. See you, Pal."

A nurse appeared, noisy in a starched skirt, and handed Gleason two pills and a glass of water. He took the pills absently, and then swung around and faced the writers. "It's not right because it isn't honest. Maybe I got it. Ralph decides to butter up the manager by bringin' him home to dinner. The manager's engaged to a clam he doesn't like. The wife says she's got a girl for the manager. She—No. No, it won't do. Now how about goin' back and workin' on this 'til you get it?" The phone sounded. "Yeah, Bullets, I know," said Gleason. "Somebody always wants an endorsement on something. Non-caloric? Bring 'em up."

The writers were putting on their coats like condemned men. They shouted some more, with decreased vigor, and left.

"They're good boys," said Gleason. "They'll be all right. We've had worse things happen. Last Saturday three whole hours before show-time we threw out twelve whole minutes. It wouldn't play. We—"

A dapper little man, Gleason's tailor, burst in and began spreading swatches of cloth on the bed. "We beat that NBC All-Star Revue last week," said Gleason, thumbing over swatches. "They threw everything at us—Berle, Tallulah—and still we beat 'em on the audience ratin's. We got thirty-two point seven, they got twenty point zero. It's like football scores these days, television. Omnibus thirty-four, Kukla, Fran and Ollie twelve. Bishop Sheen twenty, Strike It Rich eighteen. Hit Parade thirty-six, Notre Dame thirteen. Maybe there's a sketch in that. Pat," he said to the secretary, "order my dinner. This noon they gave me a piece of stale Swiss cheese cut up in a hundred pieces. I never get anything I can chew."

"Jack," said the tailor, holding up a dark gray bolt of cloth, "I brought this one up special for you."

"Crazy," said Gleason. "I'll take one."

"I thought you'd dig it," said the tailor. He gathered his cloth together and left, nearly colliding with the girl bringing in Gleason's dinner. The comic regarded the tray sourly. It contained two thin slices of Swiss cheese, some cottage cheese, lettuce, carrots, peppers and celery.

"It makes you hate food forever," Gleason said. "I've done this a hundred times, this hospital bit. Once I came down from two eighty-six to one eighty-six. I'm like the guy who says it's easy to swear off booze; he's done it a thousand times. When it gets rough is nights. I'm lyin' there in bed and Horn and Hardart starts goin' by. The macaroni goes by and waves . . ." He smiled and waved. "The meat pie waves, the baked beans . . ."

Gleason shrugged. The phone rang and the secretary handed it to him. "Ah, boys. Yeah. Yeah. No. No beauty shop bit. It always winds up with an egg bein' broke on somebody's head. I did it once and hated myself. Listen, they're gonna call me about the scenery again. Get it finished, willya?"

The door opened, and in marched three tall men and one short, bald one. The short one was Bullets Durgom, Gleason's Number One Personal Manager.

"Here they are," said Bullets, grabbing a piece of celery from Gleason's plate.

"What do you need?" Gleason asked.

"Ice water," said a man with glasses.

The secretary brought a glass of water. One of the tall trio produced a tiny glassine envelope. He tore it in half, and shook two pills the size of aspirin tablets into the glass. The water turned red and begin to fizz. The man stepped back.

"Non-caloric?" said Gleason.

"Non-caloric. Taste it."

"It tastes good," said Bullets, spearing more celery.

"What's the selling point?" Gleason said.

"It's a soft drink which you don't hafta carry it in bottles," the tall man said, taking a carrot from Gleason's plate.

"Isn't enough," said Gleason. "You can't just sell it on no bottles to carry. I can't give my name to anything like that."

The tall men began getting their things together, utterly discouraged. Bullets copped another piece of celery, then a tomato. He looked sorry for the men.

The phone rang. "The writers," Jack Philbin said, handing it to

Gleason. He said to the tall men, "Sorry, fellows," and they started out the door, the last one taking a tomato.

"Ah, boys," said Gleason into the mouthpiece. "You got it, eh? Yeah. Yeah. But what's the finish? You got to have a finish." He slammed down the phone.

Two more men—Bobby Hackett, a trumpeter, and Sam Boal, a writer—arrived. Boal helped himself to a piece of Gleason's celery. The telephone rang again and this time Gleason answered it. He cast his eyes to the ceiling. "Yeah. Yeah. Call you tomorrow morning." He turned to Philbin. "The scenery again."

He looked at me. "This is where you came in, isn't it?"

"What'll you do?" I asked.

"Who knows? They got the sketch worked out, but they got no finish. Ralph's manager turns out to be engaged to this clam the wife brings in. Ralph has been apologizin' to the manager for his wife bringin' in this clam. Then the manager sees her and it's his girl. What's Ralph do? What's the finish? The way it is now, I'm standin' there with egg on my chin." He began to pace. "We'll get through—we always do. Main thing is, I mustn't worry. When I worry, I eat. When I eat, a marshmallow puts on ten pounds. Sdown, you guys. Hi Bobby, Sam. Mustn't be nervous, mustn't worry. You guys want some coffee? HEY! WHO ATE UP ALL MY FOOD?"

Post Script: The narrative technique used in this story is a simple trick that was originated, I believe, by *The New Yorker* in its "A Reporter at Large" articles. I spent nearly a week hanging around Gleason's hospital room, then took the best episodes, scenes and bits of dialogue I observed and heard and made them appear to have happened in the space of a few hours. At the same time I took a real problem—the working-out of the sketch—and ran it through the story to its logical conclusion. In an attempt to heighten the humor, I made it appear that Bullets Durgom had picked away at Jackie's food until there was nothing left. Strictly speaking, that was not true; but it was true in effect, for Bullets did snatch something from Gleason's plate, it seemed to me, whenever he came into the room.

At first glance this kind of article seems the easiest of all to write. Apparently all the reporter need do is set down what he sees and hears—or so one might assume. There is a good deal more to it than that. When I was finished with the research for this piece I had enough material to do an article five times its size. I began putting down the episodes as they had occurred, but soon found that simple reporting was not enough. The story had to be cast almost in the framework of the short-short, with an opening, a careful but not ostentatious delineation of Gleason and the subsidiary characters, enough action to keep the reader interested, and an ending that would satisfy him.

Several frameworks came immediately to mind. At first it seemed to me that Gleason's continual war with his doctor might be a good hook on which to hang the narrative. A bit later, I thought of using the three men who were trying to sell him the instant noncaloric soft drink—for they actually did turn up on three separate days when I was there. The war with the doctor was self-evident; the three men were ideal as characters adding to the confusion, ideal, but they could not carry the piece themselves. To tell how an entire script was constructed would have involved too much explanation and would not have allowed for the humor contributed by the people around the comedian. Finally I decided that a single sketch had to carry the burden—and that the sketch did not have to be explained in full. To hint at its complications was enough.

This worked out well enough—but it was twice as long as the 850 words Klaw had set as limit. I began going through the article, cutting lines, but even that did not help much. Originally I had the writers come in again toward the end, just after the departure of the three soft-drink salesmen. The scene took up too much space and wasn't funny. I therefore decided to throw it out and substitute the monologue by Gleason. He did not actually say those lines in sequence—but at one point or another he did say all of them, and the harmless deception of the reader gave me my ending.

Now the piece was approximately down to size, and to get it down all the way I began cutting words. Presently, it wound up in the form it appears above.

Some notes on technique in the story that occurred to me as I read it through while preparing to put it in this collection are as follows:

Paragraph 3. Would have been improved if I had been able to communicate more adequately the fact that all showbiz writers, hangers-on, flunkies are essentially unsure of themselves and their jobs, and that the writers' hostility stemmed from a vague fear that I was possibly a writer Gleason had called in to help, or replace, them.

Paragraphs 1–6. Gleason could have been characterized more accurately; I could have described gestures, expressions, movements or possibly his dress, which—as I recall—consisted of loud, flowered pajamas and a dark blue bathrobe.

Paragraph 7. I did not give the writers their real names for two reasons: (a) they only would have confused the reader, and (b) it would have been cruel to add to the tortures they already were suffering.

The three men should have been described more fully than "three tall men." Jack Philbin and Bullets Durgom also should have been given more substance. I suspect today that I cut the descriptions to the minimum for the sake of saving space, but today I would seek and find single words or short phrases that would fix the minor characters in the readers' minds. The same would be true for the characters Bobby Hackett and Sam Boal. Boal, incidentally, visited the room frequently while I was on this story—and not merely to sample Gleason's liquor. No writer ever enjoys himself as much as when he contemplates the spectacle of another writer sweating out a story.

12 · The Subject Who Won't Be Interviewed

It is sometimes possible, but almost never desirable, to write an article without ever having interviewed or seen the subject. Such a chore should not be undertaken without the full knowledge and approval of the editor. I have done perhaps a dozen such stories —but, more often than not, when I have learned that the subject has refused to cooperate, or has been unable to, I have given up and gone on to something else. Frank Sinatra once agreed to let me do a story about him from his daughter's point of view, and I flew to Hollywood with the blessing of Herbert Mayes of *Good Housekeeping,* not to say with his expense money. At about that time, Bill Davidson's profile of Sinatra appeared in *Look.* The singer was so enraged by Bill's candor that he refused to see any reporter from any magazine. After six days of waiting for him to change his mind, I returned to New York. It was then Mayes' turn to be enraged, and after he had his, I had mine.

It would have been possible to do the story about Sinatra without talking to him at length. Once, after a monthly had bought a long piece about him by a lady writer with a national reputation, I was called in to rewrite it; there was that experience, plus the fact that many of Sinatra's friends—Toots Shor, Phil Silvers, Bill Morrow, et al., were also friends of mine. Mayes, the frenzied and amiable martinet, would never have permitted that.

Some editors, however, have deliberately ordered stories to be done from clippings and talks to friends of the subject and other research. *She Plumb Give It All Away* was such a piece. Thomas J.

Fleming, the workhorse of the *Cosmopolitan* staff and one of the most capable of the factual-piece editors in the entire field, came across a two-paragraph item in the *New York Times* that told how a spinster bank employe in a small Southern city had made off with one of the biggest takes in the history of embezzlement. He sent it to O'Connell with the note, "Might make a piece for Gehman." O'Connell wrote "Agree" on the note and I took off for Norfolk, where the incident had occurred.

Before going there, I was reasonably certain that Minnie Mangum, the lady in question, would not talk to me. I went first to see her lawyer, who confirmed that; he was cordial but totally uncommunicative. Miss Minnie had yet to go on trial. The lawyer refused even to say how she intended to plead. I next went to the prosecutor. He was a bit more helpful but gave out no hope that I might get an interview. The people at the building and loan society shuddered when I mentioned her name; they liked to pretend that nothing had happened. The bank examiners were not much more inclined to chronicle her defalcations. Then, after a day or two, a reporter friend of mine named Croswell Bowen arrived on the same assignment. We compared notes. Neither of us had much information, but we traded what we did have (the magazines we were working for were not competitive, and Bowen and I were taking different approaches to the story). The next day I had a stroke of luck: I got an interview with Roy Phillips, who had been president of Miss Minnie's bank. At first he seemed as mystified by the whole thing as I was, but presently he began to talk about Miss Minnie in depth. I had two two-hour interviews with him, and gradually my story began to take shape. The day after that I went out to Miss Minnie's neighborhood and talked to those neighbors who would see me; they were not many, but from each I managed to get a bit more insight into her strange character. I went to her minister, to a man who sold her drugs and medicines, to some other tradesmen she had patronized. Little by little I began to build up some superficial knowledge of her personality.

Bowen, meanwhile, had been far from idle. He too had made some fringe investigations. That evening it became clear to both of us that we each had information the other did not have; we remained cordial, but when we discussed Miss Minnie we did it guardedly. I had decided by then that the only way I would be able to do Miss Minnie would be from a pseudo-sociological point of view, trying to set her in the framework of her times and viewing her with a certain amount of delight, awe and sympathy.

Then came an unexpected jolt of luck. I ran into a man who had talked to her at some length soon after she had been arrested. He told me as much as he knew. I went back to the prosecutor, confirmed some suspicions I had developed, made a number of telephone calls to other interviewees and then went back to New York, stopping overnight in Washington to collect some dirt—pardon, research—on the life and times of Richard Milhous Nixon, about whom I was doing a piece for one of the men's magazines.

If I were doing Miss Minnie today, I should do her from the same point of view as I did her in 1956. I attempted, in this one, to profit from and apply what I had learned from my appreciative readings of the tales of rascality that St. Clair McKelway used to write, but without imitating him. This one is reprinted exactly as it appeared in *Cosmopolitan*.

ARTICLE: "SHE PLUMB GIVE IT ALL AWAY"

(From *Cosmopolitan*)

Everybody in Norfolk who knew Minnie Clarke Mangum was fond of her; in that affectionate, respectful way some Southerners affect, they called her "Miss Minnie." They knew her as a fiftyish-sixtyish spinster with a homely face and a comfortable, restful manner, with a homely voice that drawled out homely phrases in the charming, slurring style of that section of Virginia. They liked to do business with her in the Commonwealth Building and Loan Association, where she had been working for twenty-eight years, most of that time as Assistant Secretary-Treasurer. And they liked what they knew of her: that she was a regular churchgoer who practiced her Christianity all week long by caring devotedly for her blind sister. What they never suspected was that Miss Minnie Mangum possessed a streak of larceny in her soul as wide as her ample back. Somewhere in that motherly bosom, like a time bomb sunk in a tub of cosmoline, a relentlessly efficient mechanism for embezzlement ticked away for two decades—and when it finally exploded on December 22, 1955, it rocked all Norfolk and scattered likenesses of Miss Minnie's soft face to the front pages of newspapers everywhere in the world.

The good, responsible citizen suddenly unmasked as a criminal has become one of the symptoms of the pervading tensions that shake our uneasy times. Miss Minnie is, however, more than just another news story, not only because of her personality (her only modern counterparts are fictitious—the sweetly murderous sisters in Joseph Kesselring's *Arsenic and Old Lace*), but also because of the enormity of her crime (she took off $2,884,957.06, as nearly as twenty-four Federal bank examiners could compute it), and finally because of what she did with the boodle ("She plumb give it all away," a neighbor lady later said wistfully. "Hoo-*ee*, I wish I'd known her better. I sure missed out on somethin' ").

When the statistics of skulduggery in the ulcerous 'fifties finally are compiled in the All-Crooks' Record Book, it may very well be that Miss Minnie will go down as having been retired with the ladies' title. Her spinsterly idiosyncrasy, embezzlement, is on the rise, the Fidelity and Deposit Company of Maryland reports in gloom and outrage. Last year industriously dishonest employees in banks and other establishments appropriated nearly half a billion dollars, or about $2,000,000 every working day, or $1,000 per minute. None of these hard working thieves was anywhere near as successful as Miss Minnie, who made monkeys out of Willie Sutton, the Brink's heisters, Richard Crowe (the Staten Island bank official who winged south with nearly a million) and in fact virtually every other present-day malefactor except a wily Californian named Gilbert H. Beesemyer, who in 1930 was accused of embezzling $7,500,000 from Guarantee Building and Loan in Los Angeles.

What distinguished Miss Minnie from all others was her method. She stole blandly, almost absent-mindedly, but above all, methodically, with the ruthless, passionless, apparently guiltless purpose of a horde of carpenter ants consuming a tree. By the time she finally was restrained from gnawing away at the sturdy, firm-branched Commonwealth, one of the most prosperous institutions of its kind on the eastern seaboard, it collapsed into a heap of shavings. "I didn't believe it, and I still can't quite get it through my mind," says Roy F. Phillips, former Commonwealth president.

It may be that the bewildered Phillips cannot bring himself to admit that he was totally taken in by Miss Minnie's approach to stealing, which was not merely not at all supernatural, but was actually the kind of fuss-budgety behavior one might normally expect of a lady in the declining half-century of life (assuming that one could accept the wild premise of her doing it at all). Miss Minnie stole like an amateur; but she had to have the inordinately capacious mind of a near-genius at mathematics and organization to keep track of her clumsy snitching. Also, she was blessed with a gargantuan run of luck that for twenty years kept the auditors, who showed up with the inevitability of seasons, blind to her connivances. Finally, at some point her brain acquired that cunning and courage which characterizes the master professional criminal and enables him to seal up, as if with cement, that part of his mind in which his conscience resides. If at any point Miss Minnie's Sunday School morality managed to seep through, she must have confronted and forced it back with the twistedly logical, prettily feminine excuses that must serve, because she admitted no others, as her motives: after all, she did not use the money for her own benefit—and after all, she gave it to people who were deserving, either out of tangible need or out of a need imagined by her vast matriarchal affection for them. A collection of ornaments on Miss Minnie's lawn included a plaster mother hen with a brood of plaster chicks. Some writers have viewed these statuettes as symbolizing Miss Minnie, and so have some of her neighbors. "She was just like that ol' mother hen," one has said. "That's the only way I can explain what she done."

It is no wonder that Miss Minnie's acquaintances were baffled. There are few clues to her outrageous behavior in her early life. She was born in a town with a name like a sneeze, Kershaw, South Carolina, on December 9, 1897, the fifth of nine children of John Joseph Mangum, a machinist, and his wife, Alice Victor. Mangum moved his family to Portsmouth, just across the river from Norfolk, when Minnie was three. For all Miss Minnie's friends have heard of her childhood, it was as uneventful as the growth of a mushroom; she appeared on the earth and swelled to maturity, and like a mushroom, she was unattended by the love all individuals need to achieve adulthood without neurosis. There were too many children, and not enough affection to go around. There was practically none from the father, who drank heavily, and little from the mother, who spent most of her time worrying about him. Minnie and her brothers and sisters lived in constant dread of the man's soggy moods and blazing whims.

At the time Miss Minnie was sentenced, State Probation Officer Elmer R. Jeter read to the court the report of an investigation made by him in collaboration with a Baltimore psychiatrist whom Minnie's attorneys had brought in an attempt to penetrate that casing of fatty defenses behind which her real self lived.

It said in part, ". . . the children . . . had few friends in the home for fear of possible embarrassment in case the father [would] come home inebriated and insult their company." And Dr. Manfred Guttmacher, the psychiatrist, using that bloodless language that keeps his breed strangers to the rest of us, concluded that her childhood was shaded over by a "marked affectional deprivation."

John Mangum worked on a railroad, and every Saturday, after receiving his wages, he would pay whatever bills he could manage, deposit a pittance with his trembling wife, and set out upon a bender. On the night of November 24, 1917, he went upon his last. Boozed up and confused, he tried to force his way into the Portsmouth home of a man named Claude Bradshow. The Mangums previously had lived in that house; the police decided John thought he was home. So he was, to Jesus; Bradshaw fired three shots, and two disposed of Mangum permanently.

Miss Minnie's strong sense of kindly familial responsibility, an attempt to buy the love she never had been able to get in the ways that most of us do, began to develop immediately after John's death. Later, when she began flinging the Commonwealth's funds about her like her father on one of his expansive pay nights, her principal targets were relatives. Nearly all have been accused of receiving tremendous sums, as follows:

Mrs. Lillian Eure, an older sister, and her family got $296,558.70. Miss Maude Mangum, the blind sister who lived with Miss Minnie, got $11,102.25 (jointly with Miss Minnie, officials said). Curtis A. Mangum, a brother, and his family got $49,081.44; Mrs. H. L. Vail, a younger sister, and her family got $132,265.78. The late

Jesse C. Mangum, Miss Minnie's younger brother, who died in the spring of 1955, also benefited; his wife, Mrs. Adele D. Mangum, got $209,562.59. Carlton and Kitty Mangum, Miss Minnie's favorite nephew and his wife, got $145,902.22. The only living member of Miss Minnie's immediate family who has not been accused is a sister, Mrs. Mamie Adams, a Norfolk saleslady. There were others, not in the family, who were treated as though they were. Next door to Commonwealth was a small restaurant, Crocker's, where Miss Minnie ate a simple lunch every working day. It was the kind of one-arm operation in which a hearty, filling meal could be had for less than a dollar. The proprietors, Mr. and Mrs. George S. Crocker, friends of Miss Minnie, could well afford to charge loss-leader prices: they and their son, George S., Jr., were accused of having received $94,162.67. Miss Minnie's affection for them was as nothing compared to what she felt for a backwater evangelist of Lynchburg, Virginia, Mrs. Coretta J. Mason, and her chicken-farmer husband, the late A. J. Mason. They were accused of receiving $134,840.90, presumably to help carry on the Lord's good work.

Miss Minnie was a long time preparing for her magnanimity—or *manguminity*, as a Norfolk wag has termed it. Like many super-crooks, she was wholly self-taught. She attended Glasgow Street School in Portsmouth until the seventh grade, and left in 1914. A friend of her school days has said that she kept to herself a good deal: "You never saw her walking to and from school with others." Her first job was with the J. J. Bilisoly Toy Company in Portsmouth, after which she became a clerk in a drygoods store. In 1918 she was hired by Hatch and Coolage, a haberdashery whose proprietors were so struck by her ability they sent her into Snaps' Secretarial School for five months. By then a fascination for figures already had her in its grip; she began studying a course in accounting by correspondence. That same year she went to work for a sporting goods store, Hutchins Brothers, in which she remained for eight years. In 1926 she joined the Portsmouth Stationery Company, and held that job until the company went bankrupt.

All this time she was a true homebody. She hurried home each evening to help out with the housework, and she appeared to have no outside interests except the church. While her sisters were getting married, one by one, she seldom went out with a man. The probation officer's report later said, ". . . she never has enjoyed many social affairs such as dancing or dating . . . there were only two men ever in her romantic life, but the responsibilities of the home were too great for her ever to become serious-minded with either of these men." Deprived of normal sexual activity, Miss Minnie took the course of many frustrated girls. She began to overeat.

Miss Minnie met her destiny in 1927. From the bankrupt stationery company she went to work as a clerk-typist for a group of promoters who were then organizing the building and loan association which was to be known as Commonwealth. When it was ready to open its doors, she was one of the first employees hired. In the early days she did nothing of significance except, as one official later remarked with acerbity, keep her eyes open. Whether or not she had stealing in mind then will never be known; there is a chance she had it in mind without realizing it, for as the years went on and the prospects of marriage receded, her life became even more barren, and the need to purchase love and affection rose proportionately. Certainly the bank personnel never suspected for an instant that she might be planning even a minor defalcation. Former president Phillips recently said that she seemed an ideal employee—hardworking, uncomplaining, trustworthy, accurate in her accounts, and willing to work overtime without compensation. This latter virtue was the very one which later brought Phillips and his fellow board members to grief.

After a few years in which Miss Minnie functioned as a teller, she was given additional authority. The treasurer of Commonwealth worked only part-time. He was the late S. W. McGann, a cashier full-time at the nearby Seaboard Citizens' National Bank.

As time went on, Miss Minnie assumed more and more of McGann's responsibilities. "She did his job," Roy Phillips later said wryly, "and a job of her own." Within four years, acquaintances began to notice a gradual but distinct change in Miss Minnie. She became more authoritative. She began to pay more attention to her dress (although she never was ostentatious in her clothes, and seldom wore any jewelry except a few strands of imitation or cultured pearls). She even tried to improve her grammar. Phillips recalls that she always said, "This is she," when someone asked for her on the telephone. Some of the girls in the bank would say, "This is her," and Miss Minnie always corrected them. Miss Minnie ultimately was put in charge of all girls who worked at Commonwealth. She hired them and fired them, discharging a few because they insisted upon violating her no-smoking-in-the-bank rule. She was finicky about the clothes they wore; in the summer, when the girls wore sheer seamless stockings, she would pinch them through their dresses to make certain they were following another of her rules, which said that all female employees would wear stockings at all times. Miss Minnie was prideful of the way she handled her girls. "I like to take them right out of business school and train them while they're eager to learn," she once said to a reporter. She might have added that she also liked them to be pretty. The clerks, typists, and stenographers at Commonwealth were all uncommonly attractive. Phillips and other male Commonwealth officials admired Miss Minnie's acumen in selecting such knockouts. Some told their wives solemnly that it was very good for business.

Miss Minnie herself was also good for business, everyone thought, little realizing that she was especially good for the business of Miss Minnie Mangum. Her work began slowly, on a modest scale. It began, as nearly as the auditors could reckon, in 1933—at about the same time, significantly enough, that people began to detect the subtle difference in her personality. She stole only $271,000 before 1946, according to a statement by John F. Harbison, chief examiner of the Fourth District of the Federal Home Loan Bank Board. She might well have stolen more before then if the times had been better, he added glumly, since the system she used worked better when Commonwealth had a good deal of money on hand. During the period of Miss Minnie's really energetic activity—after 1946—Commonwealth did traffic in huge sums. In an average month it would do business amounting to nearly $1,000,000. Miss Minnie's part in this imposing flow was not inconsiderable. She helped bring business into the bank, Phillips has said; her business friends liked her so much that on her birthdays they sent so many bouquets that, in Phillips' phrase, "The damn' bank looked like a funeral home."

Miss Minnie worked hard to achieve such esteem. Later, when the examiners were nosing through her private papers, they found a memo in her desk on which she detailed her duties:

"Keep general ledger and see that money is in bank each day," it said. "Open new accounts. Talk to public. Give payoff figures and assist Mr. Phillips in every way possible. Make all reports and see and check all loan papers before being filed. Figure dividends."

In other words, as the examiner Harbison later put it, "*Be* the bank." The entire business revolved around Miss Minnie. She was a well-paid axis, too: when apprehended at last, she made restitution to the amount of $100,000 worth of property, $25,000 in stocks and bonds, and $35,000 in cash. She had a salary of $9,000 per year (which made her the highest-paid female bank employee in Virginia), but because of shrewd investments she had made, mainly in real estate—she would buy cheap properties, let the rent pay for them, and sell them at a profit—her income at the time of her arrest was more than $2,000 per month.

It was not enough. A mere $24,000 a year could never satisfy those deepset cravings. And so, while Phillips and McGann and all the rest remained foolishly secure in their belief in her total honesty, Miss Minnie got busy.

To a banker, her operations were so simple that the chief mystery lies in the fact that they were not discovered sooner. To a layman, they are harder to understand. Miss Minnie cribbed mainly from savings accounts, which were posted on individual cards. These cards were kept in tubs. At the end of each business day, the tellers would take Miss Minnie all related records of their activity—records, cash, checks, and "posting cards" showing amounts deposited. She, in turn, would post these records in the general ledger. If a day's receipts amounted to $100,000 and she wished to take $50,000, she would—according to federal bank examiner William A. Patton—destroy, lose, or misplace the posting records to the amount of $50,000, and then post only $50,000 to the general ledger. That would give her the $50,000 she wanted, and she would credit to the accounts she wished to use. She mainly took from large, inactive accounts—trust funds and the like. She kept the cards of these accounts either in a small cabinet in her office or in her personal cabinet in the main vault.

If someone with whose account she had tampered came in to make a deposit or withdrawal and a teller could not find the card, Miss Minnie always was able to find it quickly. (The tellers often shook their heads in admiration at her firm grasp of the bank's accounting system.) When she did find the card, it always would be in perfect order. So would the general ledger when the auditors came around each year, as three groups of them did—federal, state, and a private firm Phillips had called in. The auditors customarily showed up without warning, but when they did, Miss Minnie's books showed one total, and the cards she permitted her visitors to see showed the same one. The auditors never did suspect that she might have some cards ratholed away. After Miss Minnie whimpered her plea of guilty at her trial, chief examiner Harbison said he thought she had "advance knowledge" of the times when the examiners would visit the Norfolk-Hampton Roads area. Commonwealth was never the first bank to be examined in that vicinity. Harbison's theory may possibly be true, but it is more plausibly an attempt to explain why the examiners were duped for so long.

Harbison's other alibi was more believable. He said that Miss Minnie's mischief could be blamed directly on the management of Commonwealth, "who allowed her to establish her own dynasty in which she had absolute control of all money accountability." She was the only one, he said despairingly, who knew anything of Commonwealth's interior operations. "If an adding machine tape was short of the controls [the general ledger], the only thing to do was to ask if there were any cards missing." When asked that question, Harbison added, Minnie would inquire, "How much are you short?" When told, she would bring forth cards from her hiding places, and everything would tally in a way that brought joy to the auditors' hearts.

In her thirteen years of indulging in her favorite pastime, Miss Minnie was visited at least sixty-nine times by auditors. They were not happy with what they found, but they were men of good faith: "We knew everything was a mess, but there was no reason to suspect stealing," William A. Patton has said, rather lamely. What is even more amazing, and may indicate that a special thieves' providence watches over the benevolent ones, is the fact that Miss Minnie survived two separate changes in the bank's overall accounting system. Each time the system was changed, Miss Minnie had to change her own false records—a massive book-juggling which would make the average embezzler give himself up. Miss Minnie simply gave herself over to additional work. She confided once to a friend, "I always work better at night." And her fellow parishioners in the Port Norfolk Baptist Church (to which, by the way, she contributed over $8,000 in a period of twelve years) remember that they grew accustomed to hearing her say, after services, on Sunday mornings, "I've got to go back to the office this afternoon." One later commented, "Miss Minnie just about lived in that bank."

So she did—lived there, worked under a picture of George Washington, and ruled like a medieval baroness. Girls who went to work for her learned the first day that she was never to be questioned, let alone challenged. They were not afraid of her—she was not a hard taskmaster, and she gave them all fairly expensive presents at Christmas—but they knew that nothing so upset her as objections to, or even inquiries about, her accounting. As the examiners later said, "Anyone who got too familiar with the procedure was not there any longer."

A Mrs. Esther Marie Cannon earlier had found out the truth of that statement. Mrs. Cannon was a Navy wife who had moved into the Norfolk area with her husband. Previously she had worked for a building and loan association in Waukegan, Illinois. When she applied for work at Commonwealth in September of 1955, Miss Minnie seemed impressed with her experience and hired her.

On November 3, five federal and two state examiners sauntered into Commonwealth and announced that they were there to audit the accounts. Prior to that time, Miss Minnie and Mrs. Cannon had had a trifling pussgrapple or two, but the arrival of the auditors brought the friction between them into the open. On the mornings of November 3 and 4, Mrs. Cannon had to go to Miss Minnie several times for cards requested by the examiners. On November 6, one card proved inordinately elusive. "I've checked everywhere, but I can't find it," Mrs. Cannon told one of the callers. Miss Minnie wrote the number of the card on a scrap of paper and headed for her office.

"Miss Minnie will find it," Mrs. Cannon said, confidently.

Without showing the slightest agitation, Miss Minnie several times shuttled back and forth between her office and the counter where Mrs. Cannon and the prying outsider were standing. On the third trip, with a great show of naturalness, she picked up a stack of cards in which Mrs. Cannon had been searching. She returned to her office. She remained there ten or twelve minutes. Then she came back.

"I just can't find that card," she said, helplessly.

Mrs. Cannon turned to the auditor. "If you look on the bottom of that pile of cards Miss Mangum has just put in the tub, you'll find it," she said.

Miss Minnie gave a small, hardly perceptible start, but held tight to her composure.

The auditor picked up the pile that Miss Minnie had taken and brought back. He riffled through it and located the missing card at once.

Miss Minnie denied having placed it there.

Mrs. Cannon is twenty-one years of age and the owner of a forthright disposition. "Miss Mangum, you are lying," she said, "because I saw you do it."

With a slight sniff, Miss Minnie turned and walked back to her office. The auditor and Mrs. Cannon looked at each other for some time, and then Mrs. Cannon was questioned by the head examiner. Mrs. Cannon said that she had seen Miss Minnie do that same thing several times before. Later that day Mrs. Cannon was called into Miss Minnie's office and advised, in tones that were shockingly cold for a Christian lady, that her services were no longer needed. Mrs. Cannon was urged to get her pay and go home. Still later, Miss Minnie appeared in Roy Phillips' office and said, quietly, "I had to let that Mrs. Cannon go. She was a troublemaker."

President Phillips later said, "I paid no mind to it. She was in charge—she could do as she pleased."

Well, she couldn't.

Someone wrote the federal examiners an interesting letter. It may have been Mrs. Cannon; she will neither admit nor deny it, for she is back in her job in the company that took over from Commonwealth after Miss Minnie wrecked it. Nor will the examiners reveal the name of the writer; one later said, with a confidence not entirely substantiated by the auditors' previous myopic conduct, "we would have discovered what Miss Mangum was up to sooner or later." In any event, the letter was received and acted upon. On December 16, at 5:59 P.M., twenty-four examiners marched in and took possession of the bank, an auditor stationing himself behind each clerk and teller.

"My God," said Roy Phillips, "you were just here in November!"

"Here we are again," said one auditor, inscrutably.

Phillips is inclined to sigh when he recalls this episode. "It took me over twenty-five years to build the company from a volume of $800,000 up to one of $24,000,000," he has said, "and between her 'n' them they took it all away in one afternoon."

It took the auditors longer than that: they worked from the day they arrived until mid-May, marveling at Miss Minnie's meticulously haphazard deeds and, one might suspect, their own previous ineptitude. But on that first day, evidence began tumbling into sight. "Everything we would pick up in her cubicle," said William A. Patton, "money would fall out: cash, coins or checks." Depositors' cards were everywhere in filing cabinets, desk drawers, even—one witness later attested—under the rug. So was currency. Patton at one point followed Miss Minnie into the main vault, where she nervously opened a file drawer and closed it. Patton then opened it and found a roll of money secured by a rubber band; around $4,000 worth, he later said.

Miss Minnie was visibly flustered, but struggling with every last one of her excess ounces to remain calm. Patton asked her for the key to the safety deposit box where she kept her cash. "It's at home," she said.

"We'll go and get it," Patton said.

"No," said Miss Minnie, "that's too much trouble." Seconds later she told him she had "decided" that it was somewhere in the bank. Presently she reluctantly located it and handed it over.

It was 1 A.M. December 17th when the auditors called it a day. Miss Minnie was then at least $6,000 short, and the auditors knew they were going to be busy for some time. "But we never suspected it was anything at all like it was," one said later.

Miss Minnie did not go to the bank on the following Monday or Tuesday. A sister called in and said she was ill. On Wednesday, four days before Christmas, Patton and an assistant determined to pay a call on Miss Minnie. With Phillips, they went out to Portsmouth, knocked at the Mangum door, and were informed that the lady of the house was still very sick. They unceremoniously walked into the house, found Miss Minnie abed, and told her she was needed urgently at the bank.

Miss Minnie's good manners did not desert her; she said, "I'll be delighted to come down and help you out."

On December 22, at the bank, Miss Minnie was questioned extensively. She signed a statement "freely and voluntarily." Soon afterward, word of her deeds leaked out—but whenever Phillips, the examiners, or other officials were questioned, they said nothing. The truth is they did not know what to do. Neither, at first, did the law enforcement officials. Lynwood B. Tabb, Commonwealth's attorney, felt that he ought in conscience to arrest her, but he was not sure that the case was within his jurisdiction. He called Shields Parsons, district attorney, and asked what he thought. Parsons said he would check into it. A little later he called Tabb and said he did not know what he could do, since no complaint had been made. He said he did not see a thing his office could do about it.

"Look," said Tabb the next day, "stealin' is stealin'—we got this woman runnin' around, and we got to get her off the streets." Parsons said he had checked further and found that Tabb had jurisdiction. Tabb then called the auditors to find out if they would testify in the event that he should take Miss Minnie to court. After careful checking, the auditors allowed that they would.

Miss Minnie, having made restitution to the limit of her ability, meanwhile sat and lay quietly in her little frame house on the edge of a Portsmouth dump, a house distinguished from its neighbors by the four air-conditioners protruding from its windows. She sat gazing, crying a little from time to time, at the photographs of her relatives and friends that festooned the living room. On December 29, after visiting her attorney, Max Broudy, she was arrested as she left his office, taken to headquarters and booked like any ordinary criminal. Her bail, $25,000, was posted almost immediately by the friend of a relative, a man who did not know her personally. It was the general attitude of most Norfolk people that the whole thing was a sin and a shame. "If a woman's that smart," a cab driver said, "she ought to get away with it."

Miss Minnie withdrew to the seclusion of her little home, where she refused to answer the door or see any of the many people who began badgering her. Soon afterward, Commonwealth was taken over by another company; its depositors were assured that their money was safe. Almost simultaneously, suits were filed against the relatives and friends who were said to have received Miss Minnie's love-payments. No one can yet determine if any of the funds may be recovered. Nor does anyone know how much of the sentence Miss Minnie, who pleaded guilty at her trial on May 16, ultimately will serve. On June 25 she was given ten years for stealing, ten for lying to the State Corporation Commission, and an additional twenty-two for forgery, giving false information, and embezzlement. Those latter sentences are to run concurrently with the first twenty years; the extra two years overlap other two-year sentences.

With time off for good behavior—and how could saintly Miss Minnie behave otherwise?—she will get out in five years. It is the kind of sentence that law-enforcement officers detest: they say it encourages other people to take bad notions into their heads. They say it makes some go and do likewise. Miss Minnie was not especially pleased with the sentence, however. She was worried about what would happen to her blind sister, Maude. As they hauled her off to the State Industrial Farm for Women at Goochland, Virginia, she displayed the first sign of emotion she had shown since her arrest. A single tear fell from her eye.

Post Script: In my initial conversation with Miss Minnie's lawyer, I had mentioned that perhaps someday she might like to tell her own story; I surmised that she had perfectly—to her—valid motives which would not come out either before or after her trial. I said to the lawyer that perhaps I could get her some money for a story told by her to me, and I gave him my address. Miss Minnie was tried and went to prison. One of the faults of my piece was that we had to rush it into print before we could print the full details, as they came out in court, of her methods. About a month after she had begun her bit, I received a curious letter from one of her relatives. The writer offered to discuss with me the possibility of doing the story I had suggested to the lawyer, and said that it would be possible to interview the nice little old lady. I never did reply; I was busy with other stories and could not get off to Goochland, Virginia, for the preliminary interview. I've always been sorry that I couldn't; perhaps I'll take up that offer some day.

13 · *Digression, or the Art of Not Sticking to the Point*

IN THE winter of 1957, when I went along with Eddie Condon and his orchestra on a trip to the British Isles, I happened to meet Robert Meusel, a United Press International correspondent stationed in London. Meusel said, "There are so many damned magazine articles lying around here with nobody writing them, it's a crime. For example, look at this," he added, taking a clipping from his pocket. The clipping concerned the Dalton family, who made their living catching rats. "If that ain't a story, I go to hell if I know what a story is," said Meusel, in the cultured accents of the veteran newspaperman. I agreed that there probably was a story in the Daltons. I suggested that Meusel might do the research and send it to me, and that I would write it and split the fee with him. A year went by, every week of which Meusel said, "I gotta go and see them rat catchers." He never did.

Before I left for Europe in March of 1958 I went to see Charles Barnard, managing editor of *True,* and told him what I had in mind. He allowed that the Daltons might interest his readers, and told me to go ahead and research the story. As soon as I arrived in London I got into touch with Bill Dalton, head of the clan, and the following article was the result of four days of interviews with him and his brothers.

ARTICLE: "THE RAT CATCHERS OF LONDON"

(From *True*)

Midnight. In a small, cluttered garage in a mews in Lambeth, a group of men are huddled around a packing case with a candle stuck on top of it. They are dressed in a variety of costumes that look Dickensian in the flickering light—chin-hiding mufflers that fall to their knees, tattered greatcoats, battered hats. The dominant figure of the group is a short, stocky man in a grey suit and a smudged black Homburg. He holds a sheet of paper in his hand, and is softly reading off directions in a Cockney accent. As he reads, pairs of men detach themselves from the circle and prepare to depart. They pick up a number of small mesh boxes and sling canvas bags over their shoulders. They check their pockets to make certain their tools are in place. They move like stealthy cats, even in the cramped quarters of the garage—like men who have trained themselves to walk without a sound. And they leave the garage like wraiths, vanishing into the murky London night. In a matter of minutes they will be slipping into buildings all over town to do their jobs, into private homes, restaurants and hotels, department stores and warehouses and banks. And in the morning they will return to the garage with their bags and boxes full of scores of squeaking, squirming, wriggling, vicious rats.

These are the members and in-laws of the famous Dalton family, ratcatchers of London and the British Isles, once Royal ratcatchers to Queen Victoria, wearers of the Rat Catchers' Belt. There are now eleven of them, proud and honorable and highly individualistic members of a line of rat catchers that goes back nearly 250 years. "We've been a remarkable firm in that if there's anything in the line of rats in England, we've always been consulted," says Bill Dalton, the eldest, the man in the black Homburg. "We want to meet the man who can tell us anything about our tip." The family is split into two firms, for accounting purposes; one, run by Tom and Joe, Bill's two younger brothers, does ordinary exterminating jobs, ridding buildings and residences of large families of rats, mice and pests such as cockroaches, bedbugs, fleas, flies and other insects. Bill's firm does that sort of thing too, but he specializes in catching live rats. "The man who 'ires me wants to see Mr. Rat still kickin'," he says, "so 'e'll know I've done me job and not rung in a dead rat on 'im." But Tom and Joe also catch rats live. The two firms share the garage in the mews, and they usually have two or three dozen live rats in cages there for sale to laboratories and hospitals which use them for experiments. In recent years, however, the demand for live wild rats has fallen off; the institutions prefer white rats deliberately bred for experimental purposes. However, the Daltons still do a good business in selling rats to film and television producing companies for use in realistic productions. But for the most past, the Daltons destroy most of their catch, either by swinging them by their tails and bashing them against the wall of the garage, by feeding them poison, or by flicking them between the eyes with a snapped finger (a rat's skull is so thin, and his brain is set so close to the surface, that a light tap between the eyes will do him in, Bill Dalton says).

For simple extermination jobs in which the object is to get rid of as many rats as possible in the shortest time, the Daltons use Warfarin, an odorless poison which they set out in trays along with food that rats prefer, such as new-baked bread. It causes internal hemorrhages. They feel a certain guilt about using it, for they are strong traditionalists: "If my dead grandfather could be woke up and told we was usin' this stuff," says Bill " 'e'd say, 'Boy, put the lid back on!' " The grandfather caught rats with his bare hands, and so do his grandsons, using stealth, cunning, ingenuity and an uncanny, almost instinctive knowledge of their quarry's habits gained through generations of experience. They also use a variety of curious traps the old man invented over 100 years ago. Highly secretive about these traps, they will not show them to outsiders; even when they take a new member into the band, which they do only after investigating and inspecting him over a long period of time, like members of an exclusive London club looking over a candidate for membership, it takes them a year or two before they make up their minds to instruct the newcomer in the use of the ancient devices. In fact, they are even reluctant to speak aloud of the traps. "My grandfather devised a trap 'e called The Shoot," Bill said to me one day, "and if 'e knew I was tellin' you its nyme, 'e'd turn right over in 'is gryve." He shook his head in awed recollection. "Oh, 'e was a clever one, the old man was. I've seen 'im catch rats with nothin' but *a sheet o' metal.* 'E'd put it outside a rat 'ole in a barn and cover it with grain, and 'e'd wait by the 'ole. Mr. Rat was somewhere in the room, the old man knew that, because 'e'd plugged up all the entrances except the 'ole. 'E was 'idin' in the grain, 'e was. So the old man would wait, and presently 'e'd make a noise. Now, a rat is a 'ighly tuned personage, let me tell you—he always knows what's 'appenin', and when he 'ears a noise, 'e makes a dash and asks the questions afterward. So Mr. Rat would dash toward the 'ole, and 'is little feet would begin to slip on the metal under the grain, and before 'e could say Corblimey, *whist!* the old gentleman'd 'ave 'im in 'is bag. Oh, 'e was a clever one, the old man was, rest 'is soul."

Bill is a clever one himself, by 'alf, as he might say if he were arrogant enough to brag, which he is not. In addition to the secret traps and the rat-bag he carries, he goes to each job equipped with a pair of carpet slippers, which he puts on just before entering a room where rats are believed to exist, plus a flashlight and a pocket full of odds and ends, such as screw eyes, string, and small bags of sand. He calls this pocket his "workshop." He says, "To catch rats, a man's got to improvise—and I improvise out o' me shop." First he examines the room carefully for holes from which rats are likely to emerge. Sometimes, he picks out a hole because there is rat dung around it or in a direct line leading to it. A rat always travels the same path in a room, a mystery of nature which even Dalton, with his immense knowledge of rats, is unable to explain. "The blighters *never* vary a tic," he says. "They get a path they like and they never swerve off it by so much as an 'alf-inch. It's one o' Mr. Rat's peculiarities."

Frequently there will be no clues whatever as to the proper hole —but Bill and his brothers will find it anyhow. They simply *know* because they have seen so many, many rat holes. They can no more explain this ability to detect holes than a rat could explain how he happens to travel the same path.

When Bill locates the hole, he sneaks around the room plugging up other holes that may be there with the sandbags he has brought. If he runs out of those, he uses newspapers or anything else he has handy, such as his handkerchief, his coat, or his hat. ("A jolly 'elpful fellow, the cap, 'e's helped me out many a time.") Then he is ready to begin capture-preparations. First he goes to the selected hole, which usually is located where wall and floor meet, and fastens a screw eye into the wall about three feet above it. A foot or two above that screw eye, he puts in another. Then he runs a string through the two eyes, and to the bottom of it he ties a small sand bag. He steps back, grasping the top end of the string, and pulls it until the bag is raised and poised just above the hole. He takes up his position then, and settles down to wait.

If Bill Dalton gets to Heaven, the prophet Job will lose his reputation. Bill is one of the most patient men who ever walked the earth. He can sit motionless, hand holding the taut string, for hours at a time. "There was one particular rat in an 'otel in Brighton," he says, "kept me sittin' for six hours. I've sat and waited for rats all over England, I 'ave. A rat is no respecter o' persons or classes—I've sat and waited in board rooms and I've sat in basements, in peers' 'ouses and in stables. When I'm after Mr. Rat, I can't move a muscle. Nothing must give him warning of my presence—I must find a chair that won't creak, or I must sit there on the floor where there are no loose boards. It's no work for a restless man, it ain't. You can't smoke, you can't suddenly decide to 'ave a cup o' tea. There's a certain amount o' personal inconvenience in catchin' rats." Many times, after Bill has got up from his vigil, he's fallen sprawling to the floor with a leg gone to sleep.

After what would be an unendurable length of time to anyone but Bill or his fellow rat catchers, the rat comes out of his hole. Half the time, Bill doesn't see him; but his ears give him eyes in the dark, and the second the rat emerges, he lets go the string in his hand. The little sand bag drops and the rat's last escape-hatch is plugged. From then on, says Bill, it's only a matter of finding the rat, grabbing him, and hurling him into a bag or a mesh cage. "A schoolboy could do that," he says. Well, a schoolboy couldn't do it, and very few men could do it. When the bag drops down, the rat takes off like a missile, heading for a place to hide. But Bill has carefully inspected the room beforehand, looking for places the rat might choose. When in danger, a rat will hide anywhere—in the pipes of a radiator, in folds of curtains, in the undersides of chairs and sofas, etc. He abandons his pre-established course to run for cover; but once the danger is past, he returns to the track that leads to his hole.

Quite frequently, Bill goes directly to the place the rat is hiding. "Rats are past masters at camouflage," he says, "but we know them so well, we can find 'em nine times out o' ten. I've often seen only one paw or a toenail stickin' out o' some place o' 'iding." Bill cannot begin to estimate how many thousands of times he and his brothers have outguessed rats and picked them out of their places of concealment within seconds after they've emerged and taken cover. Usually Bill grabs the rodent with his right hand, moving with incredible swiftness. He is bitten nearly every time; his hands, after a lively night's work, are covered with tiny needle-pricks. Once, when a rat bit him, he lost his temper, lifted the rat up, and bit him right back. "I 'ad two good front teeth on me then," Bill says, "and I made the blighter squeal, I did." Except when actually held in the hands, rats will not attack humans, Bill says. "A very desperate rat may gnaw a sleepin' person," he adds, "but that's *very* seldom. A rat keeps mostly to his own kind—'e don't want too much to do with the human world."

Bill's non-rat catching friends, most of whom regard his work with a certain amount of revulsion, are unable to understand why, over the years, he and his brothers never have contracted any disease from rats, which are notorious germ-carriers. The black rat has always been held responsible for the bubonic plague, and a British scientist to whom Bill supplied some rats for study later told him that a census of rat fleas turned up some twenty-seven varieties. Time and again, Bill has seen fleas leaving dead rats: "When the blood stops runnin', the little buggers know it at once," Bill says. "So they go to Mr. Rat's underside and jump off and go find themselves new 'omes." Bill himself often wonders why rats have never given him any disease. He believes he may be immune, but he also has a sneaking suspicion that the scientists may be wrong. "I'm not entirely sure in my own mind that rats *do* carry disease," he said recently. "Mr. Rat is a destructive fellow—he'll gnaw anything he can get his teeth into. He's the cause of many a fire and a dead, complete and unqualified loss to the commercial world. But does 'e bear the plague? Corblimey, I just don't know."

When Bill and his brothers are called in to rid a building of scores of rats, they adopt different methods from those they use when they are after small numbers—especially if the building is a restaurant, grocery, or some other establishment in which the use of Warfarin or other poison, such as arsenic, would be too dangerous. In the basement or the room the rats infest they construct a "harbor," using rubbish, newspapers, and junk of all kinds—old mattresses, broken chairs, kindling wood, baby carriage frames, etc. The harbor is horse-shoe-shaped and built up of layers, providing many crevices and crannies in which the rats can prowl and hide. It is also liberally sprinkled with garbage—orange peels, bits of apple and other fruit, coffee grounds and new bread. As a rule the brothers leave three or four openings in the harbor, clear channels through which the rats will dash when alarmed. They build the harbor one night and return the next, knowing the rats, having become curious and hungry, will be exploring it. Outside the room they put on their carpet slippers and get their cages and bags ready, and at a given signal they let themselves in. They head immediately for the harbor exits, and then they make noise. The rats tear out, right into the waiting bags and cages. One night the Daltons got 1600 rats out of a harbor—their record catch.

It used to be that in some buildings the rats were so numerous the boys did not bother to build a harbor. Back in the twenties, Bill Dalton invited a reporter from a London newspaper to go along on a rat hunt in a restaurant. They crept along a corridor to the kitchen, then suddenly burst in the door. The reporter wrote,

> Dalton flashes his hand torch on such a scene as I had never dreamed possible . . . For all around, on chair, table, mantelshelf, and peering from every nook and crevice . . . are rats. Rats, peering, startled, transfixed, quivering with fear, stupified by the beam of light. No panic, no movement. They are utterly hypnotized. "We'll have that fellow," says Mr. Dalton, pointing to a grizzly-looking chap ten inches long (not counting his tail), and in a jiffy his bare hand has pounced upon a terrified rodent, and with a couple of swings around by his tail the rat is in the bag held by one of the assistants. Rat after rat awaited Mr. Dalton's miraculous fingers, and after half an hour there were thirty huddled, petrified brown bodies, physically none the worse for their experience, in his bag. Once or twice Mr. Dalton shot out his hand in the pitch darkness without the aid of his torch and with a cool, "That's a big fellow" swung twelve or fourteen inches of slimy vermin into his bag. Sometimes a rat would give a chase. He would hide himself amongst the pots and pans or in the fastness of the kitchen range. Only then would Mr. Dalton become annoyed . . .

In those days, Bill went about his work in high good humor, talking to the rats: "Come on, me little chap . . . into the bag, me bucko. What, scared? Nothin' to be scared of, lad—into the bag you go!"

Actually, it has been years since Bill or his companions have been on such a rat hunt. "There just ain't as many rats as there used to be, there ain't," he says, a trifle regretfully. He blames this state of affairs on the fact that new buildings are rat-tight, on improvements in sanitation and garbage disposal, and on the fact that he and his fellow exterminators have made tremendous inroads on the rat population. Nowadays he is called upon more and more frequently to deal with a single rat or with one small family. This makes his work much more difficult. An individual, given the run of an entire house, can outwit an entire family of rat catchers for long periods—but not, says Bill proudly, for longer than two weeks. "There ain't a rat in England we can't catch within a fortnight," says Tom Dalton.

One rat, in a Soho restaurant, eluded the boys and all their paraphernalia for exactly fourteen nights. They named him Old Joe, and they finally got him with The Shoot (from hints that Tom and Joe have dropped concerning this top-secret weapon, I gather that The Shoot is a pole with a kind of noose, or perhaps tongs, at one end—something like those things grocery clerks use to lift boxes off high shelves). (The old man is fair turnin' in 'is gryve, 'e is.) Old Joe weighed a pound and a half and measured twenty-two inches. He was a monster, relatively speaking; the average black rat is about ten or twelve inches long and weighs a little over a half-pound; and the brown rat is slightly smaller. The boys stuffed Old Joe. Bill Dalton once saw an even bigger rat, one his grandfather caught in Tonkenhouse Yard. It weighed two and a half pounds. All the Daltons have heard reports of rats as big as dogs or cats, and all the Daltons scoff at them. "The Tonkenhouse Yard rat was the biggest my grandfather ever saw," Bill says, "and 'e saw more rats in 'is lifetime than any man 'o ever lived, 'e did."

Bill speaks of Old Joe and other elusive rats with fondness, especially those that made it necessary for him and his brothers to exercise all their rat catching ingenuity. Once he was called in by Madame Adelina Patti, the diva, who said that whenever she burst into song in the music room of her home at Castle Craig-y nos, a rat scampered around in the walls and so annoyed her she couldn't stay on pitch. Bill waited for two nights, but heard no rat. "On the third night, the gentleman finally showed up," he says, "but me trained ears told me 'e wasn't in the walls. 'E was in the rafters." This fact made Bill conclude that the rat was getting in somewhere just under the roof, climbing the wall to find a hole. Bill went outside and sprinkled flour all around the house, and next morning found a number of tiny paw-tracks leading to an oak tree.

"This proved," he says, "that Mr. Rat 'ad 'is 'ome in the tree, and at night he strolled across the lawn, climbed up the ivy on the walls, and let 'imself into the house through an 'ole I found in the bloody eaves."

That night Bill took up his position near the rat's track, and when he appeared, as Bill had known he would, made a dive for him. His foot caught on a root and he went sprawling on his face. Next night the wily rat chose not to arrive. On the third night, Bill made a grab for him, missed him, and took off in pursuit—only to run smack up against a tree in the dark.

By now he was determined to have that rat no matter what. He suggested to Madame Patti that the tree be dynamited, and she reluctantly agreed. When the tree fell he found a huge brown rat, one pound seven and a half ounces, dead in a nest. Also in the nest was a pearl necklace that had been lost several years before by a house guest. "Mr Rat'd thought it was some sort o' food," Bill says, "and took it right 'ome with him."

This was surprising to Bill, for rats seldom make mistakes about anything. One of the most marvelous abilities they possess is their uncanny feeling for electricity. They will never go near any electrical apparatus while it is alive, but will walk on it or play near it fearlessly when it is dead. Rats have often been seen sitting on the third rail in the London Tube after the last rain has gone by and the power has been turned off—but none has ever been observed near the rail when it is charged. Bill once knew a restaurant owner who devised his own trap, made of electrified copper plates on which he placed food. He kept the power off for four nights running, and knew the rats were taking the food because it was all but gone each morning. The next night he turned on the electricity, and returned an hour later fully expecting to find a quantity of dead rats. There were none; the food was untouched. Nor did the rats ever go near the plates when the power was on. Rats can also distinguish between pipes carrying gas and those carrying water; they will run freely on the latter and stay well away from the former.

Bill Dalton does not know why this should be so. He just knows that it is—that the rat is one of the most intelligent of all living creatures. "I'm a great respecter o' Mr. Rat," he often says.

So are most animal authorities, including Ivan T. Sanderson. In his book, *Living Mammals,* Sanderson says flatly, "Although Man is undeniably 'top-mammal' in certain ways, and the Elephant may be regarded as the most highly 'evolved,' there is little doubt that some rat, and probably the Brown Rat (*Rattus norvegicus*) is actually the finest—in every sense of that word and especially in efficiency—product that Nature has managed to create on this planet to date. Further, there are sound reasons for stating that, even if man eliminates himself entirely from the earth by the undue release of long-term radioactive materials or by other means, certain rats could survive . . . Rats preserve a much more practical balance between compassion for and indifference to their own kind than we do. While weaklings or cripples among their numbers may be left alone, 'fools' and 'criminals' seem often to be deliberately eliminated or killed outright."

These facts have always fascinated Bill Dalton. "Rats inbreed all the time," he says, "and usually, when you get inbreeding, you get weaklin's. Yet Mother Nature seems to look over the rat extremely well, and it buggers me 'ow she does it. I've never seen a poor lot of rats yet. Why is it a 'uman can lose a limb and die of shock? And yet nature has so looked after the rodent that if 'e loses a limb 'e's as sound as a bowl of brass and 'e can limp along on three legs rather than four. I've even met blind rats what could get about fair lively—I met one in an Italian restaurant in Limehouse one night, lost 'im then, but got 'im six weeks later . . . and 'e was just as smart, just as cunnin', as one with two good eyes in 'is 'ead."

One weakness Bill has detected in the rat is an inability to go without water for many hours at a time. A rat can survive without food for nearly a week, he estimates, but for barely more than a day without water. One of his favorite rat catching tricks is to eliminate all water from a house—to have his men fit new washers to taps that drip, to wipe all moisture from sinks and their undersides and from pipes, to tape down toilet-lids, and then to seal up the building so the rats cannot get outside to seek water. After that he sets out a small saucer of water in a room and simply waits for the thirst-maddened rats to congregate.

Another rat failing is sex. Rats are the Casanovas of the animal world. Bill has often thought that he could catch more rats if he could just grab a few females while they are in heat and put them into houses where there are large colonies of rats. "The boys would be after the girls at once," he says. Bill is possibly the only living human who has ever seen wild rats in the act of copulation. The female comes into heat for approximately four or five hours, he says, and the male works fast: "The lady may be by 'erself in an 'ouse, but some'ow a gentleman'll get wind o' her condition, and 'e'll travel a long way to introduce 'imself to her," Bill says. " 'E's on 'er and 'e's off 'er, and then he cleans 'imself up immediately thereafter." Despite their hospitable attitude toward the twenty-seven varieties of fleas they carry, rats are immaculate about their persons.

A healthy female rat, sometimes called a sow, but more often a doe, may produce seven or eight litters in a year. Her first pregnancy may yield only two or three babies, but after that she may throw as many as ten or twelve at a time. Bill once uncovered a nest in which there were seventeen young. (The female builds her nest of bits of string, material, paper, shavings—anything she can find. She gets no help whatever from her husband; indeed, once he has impregnated her, she may never see him again.) The large litters, and the frequency with which they are produced, accounts for the fact that, around the turn of the century, scientists estimated that there were 47,000 rats to the square mile in London (there are less than 20,000 to the square mile now, authorities claim). The gestation period is between 21 and 24 days. The babies are born hairless and sightless, but they begin to move about almost immediately, and their eyes are open by the time they are three weeks old. The doe suckles them, and miraculously enough, grows teats enough to accommodate each baby in the litter—Bill has seen females with teats running in pairs the entire length of their bodies, including a pair just under the jawbones, at the throat. A rat takes approximately three and a half to four months to mature. Bill is not certain as to the accuracy of Sanderson's statement that the adults kill off the strays and the fools, but he is ready to believe it. He believes that rats can talk to each other. He is absolutely certain that, from the moment her children are born, the mother rat communicates with them in some manner, warns them of danger, teaches them to run in habitual tracks, and shows them where food may be found. He also thinks that she shows them how to keep their teeth down by gnawing. If rats do not practice this habit, their teeth continue to grow; Bill has seen old, feeble rats, well up to six and seven years old (five years is the average age of a lucky rat who does not get caught), with teeth an inch and a half long. Rats' gnawing is what makes them so destructive and dangerous. They are indiscriminate. Once Bill caught a rat that had gnawed through the center of twenty-four fox fur pieces. Another rat he knew had gnawed all the fringe off the carpet in a large corporation's directors' room. Yet another, in the London mint, was working his way through large sheets of one-pound notes.

For some reason, rats are extraordinarily fond of chewing up insulation on wiring—and getting away just before they are electrocuted. Bill estimates that nearly twenty per cent of all London fires of undetermined origin are caused by rats. Some years ago a clever London arsonist, trapped by circumstantial evidence but not yet proved guilty, stoutly maintained that rats had caused the fires he was accused of setting. The prosecuting attorney sent Bill samples of the wires found at one burned building and asked if, in his opinion, rats had done the damage. Bill replied that the work was not that of rats. The arsonist went off to Wormwood Scrubs for a long stretch. Bill got three guineas for his expert judgment.

Not all rats are gnawers. Some are diggers, some are thieves, some are storers-up, like magpies. According to Dr. G. Gaylord Simpson, of the American Museum of Natural History, there are more than 550 forms of genus *Rattus* currently swarming over the earth. They are found just about everywhere except in the north and south polar regions—not because they can't stand extreme cold, which they can (there have been rats aboard ships on polar expeditions), but because there has been little opportunity for rats to get to those areas. The general term "rat" embraces such exotic types as the African Rock Rat, the Australian Water Rat, the Bamboo Rat, the Bandicoot, the Cane Rat, the Cloud Rat (no, Virginia, rats do not live in the clouds; Cloud Rats are large, long-haired creatures who live in the Philippines and New Guinea and the Indonesian archipelago), Darling's Mole Rat, the Fruit Rat, the Hamster Rat, the Kangaroo Rat, the Maned Rat, the Mist Rat, the Mole Rat, the Pack Rat, the Porcupine Rat, the Rice Rat, the Rind Rat, the Rock Rat (alas, there is no Roll Rat), the Sand Rat, the Shrew Rat, the Spiny Rat, the Strand Rat, the Veldt Rat, the Wading Rat, the Wood Rat, the —well, that is a fair sampling. There are hundreds of others.

Most rats were Asiatic in origin, Ivan Sanderson says. The two most numerous are the two the Daltons catch—the Black Rat (*Rattus rattus*) and the Brown Rat (*Rattus norvegicus*). Bill and his fellows call the brown rat the sewer rat, or the grey rat. They call the black rat the ship rat or, for no reason they can explain, "the snake." (For an equally unexplainable reason, they refer to mice as "chimneys"; they call their cages "slums.") The brown rat has a short tail and ears, and is sometimes greyish-brown and even black in color. The black rat has a longer tail, longer ears, a pointier nose and a glossier coat. The black rat, scientists believe, originally was an arboreal species native to Indonesia, and the brown a fossorial resident of the Central Asian plains. Sanderson states that the black rat began its emigration to the western world earlier—"Probably in Roman Times," he writes, "and probably did so primarily in ships and in cargoes of tropical fruits and other edible produce." When the ships hit port, the black rats ran ashore on ropes and began living in the tops of houses and in places where grain was stored. (Contrary to popular belief, rats are not good swimmers; they may be the first to leave a sinking ship, as legend has it, but they also are among the first to drown.) Sanderson claims that the brown rat came west with the Mongols that sacked Europe; rats always have followed man in his wanderings. The brown took up residence in the basements of buildings, primarily because it is a terrestrial animal and likes the ground.

Throughout rat history, the brown and the black have been engaged in a struggle for numerical superiority. The European sewage systems worked to the brown's advantage and put him ahead for a long period, but when concrete buildings, overhead cables and kitchens on upper floors came into popularity, the black rat gained in strength. "There are now more blacks than browns," Bill Dalton says. The twain never meets. Bill has tried to induce brown rats to mate with black, but without success. "I've never seen the two fight," he says, "but they won't make love, either."

Rats *will* fight each other, however, say the authorities—and they also will take on other animals, including dogs and cats, if cornered.

This fact was discovered early in the thirteenth century, when the black rat first reached Europe, and gave rise to the sport of rat-baiting, which at one time was more popular in the British Isles than cricket is today. According to Hamilton Mayhew's *History of the Blood Sports,* rat-baiting originated on The Isle of Dogs around the middle of the eighteenth century. Mayhew himself does not know what the earliest rat fights were like, but, British tradition being what it is, we may assume that the early rat-baiting contests were similar to those which were held in Bill Dalton's boyhood, nearly two hundred years later. The spectators gathered around a pit approximately three feet deep, a circular excavation about twelve feet in diameter with another circle, two feet in diameter, marked off in the center. Terriers were brought in and weighed, and each, according to his weight, had to kill a certain number of rats within a specified time. A twelve-pound terrier thus had to kill twelve rats in the same time required for a fourteen-pounder to kill fourteen rats. The terriers were put into the pits first, and then the rats were thrown in. After the terrier had finished his gruesome work, and time was called, all rats still moving were put inside the inner circle. Those that could drag themselves outside it under goading were declared alive, even though they were half dead. The number of dead rats inside the circle determined the dog's score. The sport was immensely popular among rich men, noblemen and even royalty. Bill Dalton remembers his father telling how King Edward VII, the roistering playboy monarch, often turned up as "Mr. Smith" at pits to which the Dalton family supplied rats. " 'E was a great man for the ladies and the rats, King Edward was," Bill says.

Rat baiting put the Dalton family into the rat catching business. Bill's great-great-grandfather was the first of the line, but strangely enough, considering the immense respect the British have for their antecedents, Bill never knew the first Dalton's name, nor that of the latter's son, Bill's great-grandfather. He does know that the second Dalton was awarded a coat of arms and a belt of office by a king—George III, he believes. (Bill still has the belt; it is a four-inch leather band, worn over his shoulder, studded with brass rats.) About all Bill knows beyond that is that the very first Dalton to become a rat catcher began operations in 1710. The grandfather, old John, born in 1825, was the one who made the family famous, mainly because he was the only one-armed rat catcher in history. He lost his left arm as a child of five, and in Bill's view this gave him the necessity for developing an inventive turn of mind, which subsequently enabled him to devise the secret traps.

Old John worked the London sewers, which ran with hundreds of thousands of rats. Bill, who scampered along at the grandfather's side from the time he was able to walk, will never forget the sight of him: " 'E'd walk along with 'is miner's bulls-eye lamp strapped to his belt, transfixin' the rats, with his bag slung over 'is left shoulder, and grabbin' off the rats with 'is right 'and." Some days, John worked the London parks, sending ferrets into holes after brown rats and using well-trained mongrels to chase them and bring them back alive. He was not paid for this work; he caught the rats for the sole purpose of selling them to publicans and other promoters of rat-baiting matches, and every Saturday the rat buyers would queue up outside his rattery, eager to take the rats off his hands. His reputation grew. In the mid-1890's, he was summoned by Queen Victoria to clear the rats out of Buckingham Palace, and for a time his establishment, in Southwark, which is the section of London celebrated in many books by Charles Dickens, bore the royal crest and the legend, "Rat Catcher by Appointment to Her Majesty the Queen." He de-ratted the London Lord Mayor's House, Scotland Yard, even the Tower. But after Victoria's death, rat catching was put in the hands of the Ministry of Public Works.

Old John had two sons, Jack and Bill, both of whom became rat catchers. Jack died in 1915, at ninety. Toward the end of his life he found it increasingly difficult to earn a living by selling his rats—the Royal Society for the Prevention of Cruelty to Animals began abolishing rat pits all over the British Isles. The last open rat fight was held in Soar-lane, Leicester, just after World War I, in 1918. Jack and Bill had been in the habit of taking 3,000 rats there for every fight. When the officers of the Society raided the baiting and hauled the promoters before a magistrate, Bill was taken along and fined two guineas. He went back to London gloomily convinced that he would have to go into some other line of work. His sons—the present Bill, the eldest, Tom, and Joe—were convinced they would never grow up to be rat catchers.

They reckoned without the prolific rats. Unaware that they were out of the danger of the pit, they continued to increase and to plague humans—and before long there was an increased demand for the Daltons' services. To their joy, they found that people now were actually willing to pay to be rid of rats. The family began to prosper as it never had before, even at the height of the rat-baiting craze. Old Bill was fairly well-to-do when he died at seventy-nine and passed the business on to Bill, Jr., Tom and Joe. Currently all three are still active. So are Bob, Peter, and Gerald, sons of Bill, and Tom, Jr., son of Tom. Then there is Tag Knowles, who married Bill's wife's sister; Charles Charnock, the brothers' cousin, and Charles' uncle, Alf Atterbury; and Charles' brother-in-law, Longboat Charlie Sumner. That makes eleven in all. The youngsters now take the jobs that require a good deal of traveling; Bill, Tom, Joe and the rest work London and the seaside resorts.

The in-laws were accepted into the Dalton craft only after they had been tried out over a period of time for ingenuity, skill, and above all, honesty. "A rat catcher's got to be as honest as a banker," Bill says. "In fact, rat catchers are more honest than bankers. I've 'eard of bankers goin' to jail, but never a rat catcher." (Bill himself did go to jail once, however—to clean the rats out of Wormwood Scrubs.) Honesty is an absolute necessity because the Daltons, as a matter of routine, are handed keys to the buildings in which they will perform their nocturnal labors. There is scarcely a bank in England to which Bill has not held the keys at one time or another. "I 'ad a cousin once who seemed a fair prospect for rat catchin'," Bill says, "until the night we was cleanin' out some refreshment booths. 'E 'elped 'imself to a couple o' biscuits. I told 'im to put 'em back. 'E wouldn't do it. I sacked 'im the next day. Good riddance, I said, I did."

One night, while working in a city warehouse, Bill and one of his former colleagues, the late Bill Bruce, surprised a couple of burglars, overpowered them, and turned them over to the police. They were later commended by the Lord Mayor of London, Sir William Pryk, and given a five guinea reward.

During World War I the Daltons discovered a source of income that had not previously occurred to them. The Chemical Warfare Branch of the Army ordered 500 rats to be used in experiments with poison gas. "They found," Bill says, "that the lung of a rat tested out the same as the lung of a man—a rat could stand up to about as much gas as a goat or any other animal." After that war, more and more laboratories began calling upon the Daltons for rats—until the business of breeding white rats, which were purer because they were raised in captivity, began to flourish. For a time the Daltons went into the rat-raising business and supplied thousands to experimenters. In World War II, there was another large order for live wild rats from a branch of the War Office, but Bill and his brothers did not find out what that batch was used for until long afterward. They learned eventually that the rats were killed by Commandos, stuffed with high explosives, and left during raids on the streets of French villages, as booby traps to lure Germans. "Mr. Hun came along, kicked Mr. Rat, and *bang!*" says Bill.

The Daltons are immoderately pleased when rats can assist mankind in the above-listed ways. The truth is, all three, and their sons and in-laws, have a genuine affection for their victims—an affection that even spills over into sentiment. One night Bill witnessed a rat performing an amazing feat. There was a loose floorboard, about a foot long, over a water tap. The rat came into the room and pried the board to one side with his head, then slipped under to get at moisture dripping from the tap. Bill caught him the following night by putting the board on hinges. The rat came in, lifted the board as usual, but as soon as he was under it, it fell back into place on the hinges and imprisoned him. Bill had him in a cage in a matter of seconds. At breakfast next morning, Bill found himself admiring the rat's marvelous ingeniousness, and all of a sudden he found that he was sorry. "Poor old cock," he said aloud, "I robbed 'im of 'is 'ome."

It is the intelligence of the rats that the Daltons principally respect. They become furious when they hear one human call another a "rat." "It ought to be a term o' praise!" Bill bristles. Rats can learn readily and can perform appalling feats of ingenuity on a second's notice. A scientist once told Bill about a rat in a cage who was offered a dog biscuit lying flat on the floor; without hesitating, the rat reached out his paws, turned the biscuit on edge, and pulled it through the bars. Such feats no longer surprise Bill. In fact, they delight him. He has grown so fond of rats over the years that sometimes, as he is sitting a lonely vigil in a dark room in the depths of this ancient city, he often begins to speculate uneasily over the future. "What I wonder," he says, "is this—suppose I'm a rat in the next world? What am *I* gonna do to keep away from the bloody Daltons?"

Post Script: This article violates several rules for article writing. It begins with a false lead, for one thing; it gives the reader the impression that the rat catchers are thieves. Second, Bill Dalton's dialogue is mainly reproduced as he uttered it, in his original Cockney, which—according to some editors, anyhow—is hard for the American reader to understand (many editors have as little respect for readers as TV producers have for their audiences). Third, the first three paragraphs are probably much too long. Fourth, an important detail—the exact nature of the secret trap—is held back from the reader (if the writer is not going to tell what something is, he should not discuss it at all). Fifth, the article stops dead in the middle while rats are discussed at length. Some of the rat information comes from Bill Dalton, it is true, but most of it comes from various reference books. This section was pure self-indulgence on my part. The more I read about rats, the more fascinated I became, and the more anxious to communicate what I knew to the reader. This is dangerous practice unless the material holds up. In this case it did. But before the writer digresses he had better be certain that his digression will hold his reader's attention. In my Red Norvo article, for example, I stopped near the beginning to put in a vast amount of material about the xylophone and marimba. The editor decided there was too much of it, and asked me to condense it. Thus the digression became an integral part of the story; if I had left it in its original, it might have driven the reader away. Later on in that article, describing the summer Red and some friends went up to Maine to play Bar Harbor, I told how they had planted a marijuana patch between the two houses in which they lived. This led me almost inevitably into a discussion of marijuana smoking among musicians. I wrote seven paragraphs about it, and as soon as I was finished with them I decided to cut them—first, because Red had only experimented with the weed, and second, because they would only have given the public the impression that tea-smoking is widespread and prevalent among jazzmen, which it is not. (And here is a digression: magazine readers, the majority of them, do not read carefully—which is another good reason for writing as clearly and simply as possible. Once, in *This Week*, I published an article about the lecture-dances held in Manhattan and Brooklyn each week. These functions are New York phenomena—the audience dances for an hour, listens to a lecture on Achieving a Sane Sex Life or some such interesting topics, then dances for another hour. In the first paragraph of that article I printed the names and addresses of four places where lecture-dances were held. I got 200 letters, each asking, "Where do they hold these lecture-dances?")

Before digressing, the writer should decide whether or not the digression is absolutely necessary. If it is, he ought to put it in—but he ought also to keep it as short as possible. And after he puts it in, he ought to have another look at it to decide if it is doing the job he has in mind. In an article for *Coronet* about gospel singers, I decided that the magazine's audience probably was not familiar enough with the history of jazz to understand the sources of present-day gospel. I therefore wrote six paragraphs outlining the course of jazz through the years. I later took them out because they simply were not needed. In an article about Jack Bleeck's restaurant for *True*, I put in eight or nine paragraphs about a character named Artie Hinchman. He was an habitue of Bleeck's who liked to be photographed with important people. Whenever he heard that Mayor James Walker was going to be photographed, he rushed to the ceremony and got into the picture just as the cameraman clicked his shutter. Strictly speaking, Hinchman should not have been dealt with at such length, since the piece was about Bleeck and his shebeen —but he was funny enough to stand up, so I kept him.

Toward the latter third of the rat catcher piece there is another digression—in the paragraphs about the Daltons' grandfather. This is a necessary one, first because he was the first in the family, and second because he was such an unusual character in his own right. This digression thus was justified.

14 · Cutting

JOHN J. O'CONNELL, editor of *Cosmopolitan,* once said that he had never seen the article that could not be improved by cutting, and I suppose that in general he was correct. Nearly all writers are windier than they need be. In the past ten years the average magazine article has shrunk from around 5,000 words to approximately 3500. I deplore the trend toward the short article, not merely because it is harder to write a short one than a long; it seems to be just one more indication of our national willingness to settle for the facts and ignore the important details. Headlines and picture magazines have made us lazy; intense competition and the desire for money have made us shallow. Today, when people say they don't have time to read (and everybody says that), they may be speaking the truth, but they also are voicing a standard evasion.

The longer one works on an article, the harder the job of cutting becomes. This next piece was four months in research. The last three weeks of those four months were spent in day-to-day research. The article was assigned by A. C. Spectorsky, *Playboy* executive editor and author of *The Exurbanites,* in a telephone call early in October, 1957. He then followed with a letter outlining exactly what he had in mind. I am reprinting the letter in full because it is a good example of what a writer has every right to expect from a conscientious editor who knows exactly what he wants (alas, letters of this kind come all too infrequently; few editors can express themselves so well). Here is what he said:

Dear Dick,
Here's the poop on the piece we want about *The Captain's Paradise.* I'm going to put it all in writing, in spite of what we discussed on the

phone. Then it's going to be up to you to let me know whether you think it's the right kind of piece for you, and up to Max to negotiate a price. If all this gets squared away—which I hope and believe it will, and in a hurry—I'll write to Morgan and tell him that he's going to hear from you.

First off, then, the team which had such success with the movie, *The Great Man*, i.e., Jose Ferrer and Al Morgan, is readying a musical version of *The Captain's Paradise*. Insofar as such things can be predicted, this should be a smash hit since even before the first word was put to paper, the New York showing was sold out from its February opening through the month of April.

Our idea is to do a blow-by-blow take-out on this production from conception of the notion through preliminary conversations, the writing of the script, the composing of the music, the casting, the cutting, the all-night rewrite sessions, the rehearsals, and so on, to the first public performance. Although work is already in progress, we have the advantage of the fact that Al Morgan has taped most of the preliminary conversation and will make the tapes available to you.

Morgan and Ferrer have been commuting back and forth between Beverly Hills and New York and Cape Cod, working together for spells, and then working separately. The book is just about done.

The team of Livingston and Evans (composers of "Mona Lisa," "Buttons and Bows," etc., and Oscar winners) is doing the music and lyrics. Abbe Lane is cast as the sexy wife—which means a walk-on part for Xavier Cugat, who won't let her out of his sight. Ferrer is playing the lead. No further casting has been done to date.

Ferrer will go to New York sometime in October. Rehearsals start November 18. There will be a New Haven opening on December 28. Following the New Haven opening will be three weeks in Boston and then on to the Alvin in New York February 4. Previous to that there will be one week of previews at the Alvin. What we hope to do is get this piece in our March issue—which means having just about everything ready so we can go to press immediately after the December 28th New Haven opening.

The idea is to have you spend some time with Morgan first and then with Morgan and Ferrer, and then with the casting director and the musical director and at casting sessions and at rehearsals—all with a view to getting a continuous story of the birth of a hit, a story which will have good reporting but will also be rich in the romantic atmosphere of the theatre and backstage doings and personalities as they work together and clash in the making of a hit.

What we were looking for in a writer, Dick, was someone who could spare the time to go interviewing and partying and casting and rehearsing with Morgan and Ferrer and who would still not have to abandon some full-time pursuit to do it. We wanted a person who was on a par with Morgan and Ferrer in the social-professional sphere (so that he could get to know them and would be a welcome guest) but perhaps above all, someone who knew something of the theatre and was not a complete innocent about it, but who still had a considerable love of it and could get the warmth of his feeling into a piece. We think you're the man.

This is a thing we will probably never do again and certainly have not yet done, nor have we ever seen it done right anywhere else, and we want it to have all the marks of your professionalism. There's going to be an investment in time, we know, but it should pay off if it's handled with insight, intelligence, sophistication and, at the same time, warmth and romance.

Cheers,
A. C. Spectorsky
Associate Publisher

This was a large order and, as it turned out, I wound up with more material than I knew what to do with. I am reprinting the piece as I sent it off to *Playboy* here. The magazine's cuts, set in italic type, can teach a valuable lesson to the beginner.

ARTICLE: "THE MAKING OF A BROADWAY SHOW"

(From *Playboy*)

What goes into the making of a Broadway theatrical production? Recently, the editors of this magazine asked that question of themselves, then assigned me to write a day-by-day diary of a show's conception, inception and reception that would not only chronicle the birth pangs of one specific show, but also be, in a sense, a portrait of Everyshow.

We picked a musical that was, at the time, little more than a gleam in the eyes of novelist Al Morgan and actor-director José (The Hose) Ferrer. The projected production was to be based on the clever and successful British film *The Captain's Paradise,* which starred Alec Guinness. Morgan and Ferrer, who had worked together on the screenplay of Morgan's best-selling novel, *The Great Man,* would do the script for the show, and Ferrer would direct.

Previous to his collaboration on The Great Man, *Morgan had been a foe of team-writing. Creation, for him, was "a solitary, personal, lonely job." The feeling persisted during the early days of the* Man *film; "Joe and I were a little like a bride and groom getting off the train at Niagara Falls—we weren't quite sure who was going to do what, with which, and to whom," Morgan later said. But that job went so smoothly he was able to approach the Broadway collaboration with enthusiasm.*

In the film *The Captain's Paradise,* Alec Guinness played a proper English sea Captain with a tendency to behave most improperly. He had a small boat that ran between Gibraltar (where he kept a mousy English wife) and a mythical African port called Calique (where he was married to a French sexpot). To complicate matters, the mousy English wife longed for adventure and glamor, while the sexpot honed for hearthstone and hominess. The Captain was found out and somehow wound up facing a firing squad. He first took the precaution of bribing the men, who shot their leader. The Captain then did a Fairbanks over a wall and escaped.

Ferrer and Morgan went to work on this basic story, changing the locales to London and Paris. Elaborating on the plot, they decided to reveal that the Captain's first mate had been the husband of the sexpot (she left him because he had been too stodgy for her). They also decreed that the two girls would meet in Paris and become sympathetic toward each other, and that both would give the arrant Captain the air. Then the First Mate and the sexpot—her name was Bobo—would rediscover each other and go off, and the English wife would take the Captain back. In the finale, the four of them would turn the Captain's ship, the S.S. Paradise, into a nightclub. Not much of a plot in these days of the Serious Problem Musical, but it was enough to have some fun with—and the producers began casting about for people to help. They got the famous Jo Mielziner (who has done the sets for 225 shows) and they signed Miles White, whose credits as a costumer included *Oklahoma!, Carousel,* and several circuses (he once designed ballet dresses for elephants). On the advice of Johnny Mercer, Jay Livingston and Ray Evans were signed to do the songs for the show. Livingston and Evans had written about 70 movie scores and had won three Academy Awards, but they had never done a Broadway show. Abbe Lane was signed for the part of the French girl, and immediately everybody began to wonder if it had been a good idea: from Spain, where she was making a movie, Miss Lane proclaimed that her cooch days were over. Henceforth, said she, she would concentrate on Dramatic parts. The producers shuddered and hoped she didn't mean it. With Miss Lane came, as though drawn by a ring in his nose, Xavier Cugat, her band-leader husband, to essay the role of the First Mate. About this time I began following the show like a hungry airedale and keeping a dairy of what I observed and heard. And here it is:

OCT. 17, 1957. NEW YORK. Producers Don Coleman and Howard Merrill, both in their late thirties, have been trying for so long to get this show on, they both already feel like veterans. *They met five years ago in the elevator of the apartment house they live in. Oddly each looks like what the other is. Merrill who was a child star (sixty films), has never been out of showbiz and until recently was a TV writer-producer, but his high-domed face and steel-rimmed spectacles give him the tough-minded, practical look of an attorney; whereas Coleman, who was a lawyer, has a softer face and liquid brown eyes behind shell-rimmed glasses, and the air of a man just visiting this planet before returning home to his muse. Each is a worrier (anxiety is the producer's occupational disease), and each conceals it. Coleman has the harder time doing it; he inclines toward heaviness when things are going well and loses weight when they aren't. His solo producing effort was* Eugenia *with Tallulah Bankhead. It cost him thirty-five pounds.*

The two men are in Sardi's waiting to meet a kid who called them a few days ago. "He says he's raised $25,000 to put in a show," Merrill explains, "and he'll put it in ours if we let him be a production assistant. He's just out of Cornell."

"We've just about raised all our money," Coleman says. "About four years ago I began looking for a property. Thought of *The Captain's Paradise,* but just then the Theatre Guild announced that they were doing it with Danny Kaye. About a year later it was free again. Then began the goddamnedest negotiations—with the company that made the original, with the writer, with stars, directors, and so on."

"They didn't think we meant business because we'd never done a show before," Merrill says. "Once we sent them a $10,000 check to show good faith. It came back—the show still wasn't free. We heard that Don Ameche wanted to do it, and we talked to his agent. He helped us get the rights, but then Ameche couldn't do it. *As soon as we had the rights, Feuer and Martin—they did* Guys and Dolls—*wanted to buy us out. So did Leland Hayward*—South Pacific, *you know. But we hung on."*

"We had the property," Coleman puts in, "but we had no people. Sid Caesar wanted to do it, then decided to go back to TV. We considered George Sanders, Alfred Drake, and tried to get Guinness himself. *No thanks. He said he'd taken two weeks to learn a two minute dance for the film, and No Thanks.* Then we tried like hell to get Joe Ferrer to play it, but no dice. Finally we signed Tony Randall—he played the Mencken part in *Inherit the Wind,* Mr. Weskit on the *Mr. Peepers* TV show, did a few films—*Will Success Spoil Rock Hunter?, No Down Payment,* and so on—and although he's never done a Broadway musical he's one of the best young talents around."

"The English wife was even tougher," Merrill says. "We tried for Maureen O'Hara and Joan Collins but no soap. We thought of Abbe Lane early in the game, but we still don't have an English girl. We're auditioning every day. Actually, we're in good shape. When Livingston and Evans finished the songs, Ferrer and Rosie Clooney—she's his wife, you know—made a recording of them and we played that for potential backers. We raised about $300,000 in three, four week. We figure this to cost around $350,000, about par for a musical now. And the word-of-mouth publicity has been fantastic. We've already an advance sale of about $320,000." Merrill looks up. "Uh—hello."

A thin tense young man of about 21, all spectacles and smile, is standing at the table, looking as though he is suspended from the ceiling by an invisible wire. He is every bookstruck, artstruck, moviestruck, stagestruck kid who ever lived; grave dedication to culture is the sum of his years.

"My name is David Newburge," he says, his voice cracking a little. "I had an appointment . . . ?"

"Welcome to the Captain's ship, David," says Coleman.

NOV. 4. Joe Mielziner begins work on sketches for the sets, *which will be built by Imperial Scenic Studios.* As he has seen it, the script moves from scene to scene like a motion picture. There has to be some way of getting scenery on and off without closing the traveler-curtain and forcing the characters in the preceding scene to step forward and finish on the forepart of the stage. Mielziner, scrawling absently on the paper pinned to his drawing board, remembers an earlier show wherein he used two parallel treadmills running in opposite directions. The stagehands set the furniture on the belts of the treadmills and it floated in neatly.

"But those things never work, do they?" Coleman asks. "They jerk when they start and stop, the actors lose their balance getting on and off, they—"

"They'll work," says Mielziner, quietly.

NOV. 5. Coleman and Merrill believe the name of the show should be changed—so people won't believe they've already seen it, and so the new version can be sold to the movies if it is a hit. Name changed to *Paradise for the Captain.*

NOV. 7. Name today is *Anyone for Paradise?*

NOV. 8. Now it is *Paradise, Anyone?*

NOV. 10. Ferrer suggests *Tail of Two Cities.*

NOV. 11. "Listen, for God's sake," says Coleman to Merrill, "we've got to get a title so we can get out the ads."

"What about Hey, Madam! ?" Joe asks, "Jay and Ray've got a song by that name in it."

"Madahm," says Al Morgan.

NOV. 13. Title changes, once and for all, to *Oh Captain!*

NOV. 14. Jay Blackton, a musical director with many Broadway shows behind him (*Oklahoma!, Call Me Madam, Happy Hunting*), picks the vocal chorus today—eight boys and seven girls. *Ferrer is in transports, "God, how they sing!" he cries. "They gas me, they really do!"*

NOV. 19. Ray Evans and Jay Livingston have been working as a team since 1934, when they met at the University of Pennsylvania, where Ray played saxophone in Jay's band, the Penn Continentals. Livingston, tall and professional, plays piano and writes music; both write lyrics. Today they are working in a room furnished only with a piano and a couple of folding chairs in a 57th Street rehearsal hall.

There are crumpled up pieces of music paper all over the floor, crowding the cigarette butts. Ray Evans, slight and wiry and prematurely gray, says, "We've got 21 songs—counting the three numbers we reprise. This score's gone fairly well. We did it mostly in a couple of months . . . *and we had to interrupt it to write a couple of numbers for Betty Hutton, Jay's sister-in-law. She's taking out a new club act.* Right now we're polishing, trying to make the lyrics better. Columbia is going to record the original cast LP, and *we've given them the rights to release some of the other songs on singles for the jukes and the disc jockeys.* Clooney is going to record *Surprise* —that's the tune the English wife sings when she hears she's won a *cooking contest and a* free trip to Paris. Of course you can't tell, but we think it'll be a hit. *Then, too, Johnny Mathis is going to rocerd one of the songs. We're very hopeful.*"

NOV. 21. *Show people are not like other people, and Joe* Ferrer *is not like other show people. He* sits in a darkened theatre while nearly three hundred pretty, talented actresses, all of whom can sing, dance, act and do a passable British accent, audition for the part of the British wife. None will do. One, Susan Johnson, he remembers from *The Most Happy Fella*—he tells her she won't do for the wife, but he wants to see her later. Then up comes Jacquelyn McKeever, 22, blonde, an ex-schoolteacher, whose previous experience consists of a small part in *The Carefree Heart* which closed out of town and some summer stock. She has a high, throaty voice; she moves awkwardly; she is attractive but no knockout. Ferrer picks her.

"You're crazy," Coleman says.

"She's an unknown," Merrill protests.

"She's got a quality that affects me like Deanna Durbin used to," Joe says. "She'll be great—wait and see."

So they sign her. They send her for acting lessons, they send her for dancing lessons, they send her to brush up on her singing, they send her to Berlitz to learn a proper British accent. And they pray that Ferrer is right.

NOV. 22. Final auditions for the dancers are held at the Phyllis Anderson Theatre, lower Second Avenue. About sixty girls and boys are on the bare stage, their faces eager and apprehensive in the light from the single enormous bulb hanging from a ratty cord. The twittering boys are in tights or jeans; the girls are in old leotards with wrinkled knees, or blouses and pants—all except one, who wears sheer black stockings and red pants that amount to little more than a G-string to show off her spectacular legs.

"We've already picked that one," Morgan whispers.

"And nicknamed her," Ferrer says. "She's The Crotch That Walks Like a Woman."

The choreographer, Zachary Solov, on leave from the Metropolitan Opera (this is his first Broadway show) points to an exotic dark-haired girl who resembles Sophia Loren. "There'll be spots where she'll be effective," he says to Ferrer.

"If you want her, pick her," Ferrer said. "I'm nuts about those four little girls over there." He gestures toward a petite quartet standing to one side.

Assistant stage manager George Quick calls, "Will everybody who's been eliminated please leave?"

About half the kids stand up disconsolately and begin gathering up their coats and bags.

"As an actor, I sweat through this part of it," Ferrer says. "The disappointment in those faces—God! *We try to be fair—we spent from eleven A.M. to three forty-five yesterday picking those four little kids. They complain about the time it takes, but we try to be fair.*"

"How do we decide on the remaining ones?" Morgan asks.

"We'll strip them to the waist," Ferrer says winking. "Look at the one on the left, the blonde." She is wearing a white blouse, flesh-colored stockings, and black pants. She is not exceptionally pretty, but it's hard not to notice her figure. "Got class," he says.

"Character," Morgan says, sardonically.

"Whatever it is," Ferrer says, "she's got a quality I like." He turns to Solov. "Let's have her, Zach." To Morgan and me he adds, with a perfectly straight face, "She reminds me of my mother."

Later, as the girl is leaving, I say, "Did you know you were picked because you remind Joe Ferrer of his mother?"

"Listen," she says indignantly, "I've been studying five years to get a part." She strides to the curb and joins three girls who are waiting there—three who were not picked. She does not want to crow, but she cannot contain her exuberance; her eyes are shining. The other three, as though resentful, stand a little apart from her. "Well," says

one, "Portofino *goes into rehearsal in a couple of weeks . . . and* Say, Darling."

"Sure," says another. "Lots of luck. Well, here goes my last buck for a cab." They got in, leaving the one who was picked standing in triumph turned bitter. . . .

NOV. 25. The front room of Ferrer's apartment, on 57th Street just south of Carnegie Hall, is more cluttered than usual, *with an easel and paints, piano stacked high with music, boxes of English cigarettes, swatches of material from fautz, magazines in various foreign languages, pictures of Rosie and his three children, a pair of typewriters, several chess sets, records, a well stocked bar and hundreds of books.* On either side of the fireplace, all the way to the ceiling, yellow sheets of paper are stuck to the wall with tape, each containing a word identifying a scene.

"First act's on the right, second on the left," Al Morgan says. "We've juggled them every which way, trying to get the proper sequence."

"Break the story down this way," Ferrer says, "and the faults leap out at you."

"The way it goes now is roughly like this," Morgan says. "Open with the villagers singing *This is a Very Proper Town.* The Captain comes on and joins in the last chorus. Then a door floats in on a treadmill, he steps through it as it passes, and he's in his house, which is let down from the flies. Scene with his English wife to show how *stuffy he is and how* she longs for some glamor. He sings *Life Does A Man a Favor—When It Gives Him Simple Joys.* Then it's ten o'clock—beddibys. They undress and go to bed and float out. Villages reprise first song, and it's morning and Captain leaves. Next scene he's on the S. S. Paradise with his First Mate and his crew, singing *Life Does A Man A Favor—When It Leads Him Down to the Sea.* They sing a song about him and do a dance on the dock. Then the Captain, back in the cabin with the First Mate sings a song about his three paradises—England, the ship, Paris. Scene switches back to the cottage. A man comes and tells the English wife she's won a cooking contest and gets a free trip to Paris. She sings *Surprise* and then there's a dream-ballet in which some hobgoblins dress her for the trip. We got Johnny Brascia as the courtier—he's terrific."

"You should see Miles' costumes for this one," Ferrer says, "Crazy."

"The Captain arrives in Paris," continues Morgan, "and he does the *Favor* song again—this time *When it Puts Him In Paree.* He meets a flower girl—played by Danilova."

"You should see her dance," Ferrer says. "You know, she was trained in Russia. She must be over fifty, but she's absolutely sensational. A gasser!"

"They dance," Morgan says. "Then the Captain goes to see his mistress, Bobo—Abbe Lane. She's a stripper. She sings *Femininity*—it ought to stop the show . . . 'Why do I always end up on the tiger skin?' she asks. The scene switches back to the boat. To the great dismay of the First Mate, the English wife arrives. Her name in the show is Maude, by the way. She says she's been looking all over Paris for her husband, *and can't find him.* He offers to go looking for the Captain with her, and they get on a sight-seeing bus. A Spaniard gives Maude champagne and takes a chop at her. The Spaniard is Paul Valentine . . . pretty good. They go to a nightclub, run by Susan Johnson—we wrote in a part for her because she's got such a wonderful brassy voice. This is the same club where the Captain's stripper works, and the first act ends with the Captain and Maude confronting each other as the chorus girls are dancing and Susan's trying to sing."

"The second act's been giving us some trouble," Ferrer says, "but it's just about worked out—the First Mate and Bobo get together, the English wife takes the Captain back, and they turn the Paradise into a bistro. Great. We think." He crosses to a coffee table and knocks on it solemnly.

"We open in Philadelphia January 11," Morgan says, portentously.

NOV. 25. *I run into Mike Sloane, a young producer, whose musical, Rumple, is now in the Alvin, the theatre for which* Oh, Captain! *is scheduled. Rumple is about to close; it was bombed by the critics. "I hear Ferrer's got a million in advance sales," Mike says. "Some guys have all the luck."*

NOV. 26. The show has its first casualty—Zachary Solov, the choreographer. He and Ferrer have been arguing since the end of auditions. "I know I don't know anything about staging dances," Ferrer says, "but I know what I want and what you're giving isn't it." Furious, Solov resigns.

NOV. 27. Coleman and Merrill are going crazy trying to find a replacement for Solov. *Bob Fosse and Gower Champion are unavailable.*

Ferrer has an inspiration. "What was the name of that kid who did the dances on the old TV *Show of Shows?*"

"Jimmy Starbuck," Merrill says.

Ferrer begins to pace, muttering to himself. "*He was good—damned good.*"

"*His last Broadway show was a flop,*" *somebody says.*

"*So was The Great Man,*" *Joe says.* "A guy who works in TV is used to getting numbers on and off fast. That's what we need. *We're stuck. If what he does needs fixing, we'll bring in somebody to help him.*"

DEC. 5. Singers and dancers go into rehearsal today, singers under Jay Blackton, dancers under Jimmy Starbuck.

DEC. 12. *Since the ravenous TV industry began gobbling up most available rehearsal space in midtown Manhattan, the legitimate theatre has been forced to go farther and farther afield to find room. Oh, Captain!* is rehearsing in the Central Plaza, a meeting-hall on lower Second Avenue ordinarily given over to Masons, Shriners, neighborhood weddings and, on week ends, jam sessions attended by college kids. Ferrer and his principals are in the main ballroom, a flowered wallpaper horror, cluttered with artificial blooms, rickety lecterns and funeral chairs. The Hose is sitting on a chair tilted back against a wall, his cap pulled down over his eyes, feet up on a table; around him, in a semicircle, are Abbe, Jackie McKeever, Paul Valentine, Danilova and Susan Johnson. They are mumbling their parts aloud and Joe is interrupting from time to time with suggestions or comments. Co-producer, Howard Merrill, impeccably dressed and emotionally disheveled, is surveying the scene happily. "The advance is up to $1,200,000," he says. "It's a combination of the property and Joe's name—he's one of the biggest draws on Broadway."

Out in the hall, Tony Randall and Cugat are sitting side by side on a bench, earnestly reading lines to each other, holding the book between them.

Ferrer calls a break, *and ambles over.* "The big surprise is Cugie," he whispers to Morgan over coffee. "This morning he handled himself like he's been on the stage all his life. Abbe is a little stiff, but she'll be all right. Come on, let's go watch the dancers."

We go to a room on the floor below, where Starbuck, *a slight, agile man with curly, steel-grey hair that comes to a widow's peak and gives him the look of a satyr's son* is critically inspecting a line of girls as they go through a wild, abandoned dance. "The first act finale," Ferrer says. *Scattered around the room, the chorus boys are limbering up or sitting on the floor talking. One pair is holding hands. "Sweet," Joe says. "And inevitable.* How's it going, Jimmy?"

Starbuck shrugs. "I really can't do much more until I get the costume list from Miles White tomorrow. So far, though, fine."

"Crazy," Ferrer says. "I'll have the staging blocked out by tomorrow evening."

"Tomorrow? So soon?"

"I want to get some idea of how it's going to look."

DEC. 16. By calling a run-through today, Ferrer breaks all theatrical precedent. Musicals usually do not hold run-throughs—with book, singing and dancing—until the third week of rehearsals. This one is a shambles—people don't know lines or dances or songs; they bump into each other, they are confused and bewildered. But it satisfies Ferrer.

DEC. 22. At the stage door of the Alvin Theatre on West 52nd Street, a brown tweed blur shoots by us in a headlong rush for the knob, flings it open with a gasped "Excuse," and shoots inside like an Osborn drawing of motion. This is David Newburge, the kid who brought the $25,000 into the show, now a production assistant and known as Gopher—"Go for this, David," someone will say every minute or two; "Go for that, David." He accepts it with graceful resignation; he is determined to be a producer some day. Or an actor. Or a writer. Or something. *I follow him in and have my usual time-consuming argument with the doorman, who refuses to admit me until Al Morgan comes to my rescue. (All Broadway theatre managers, doormen and box office treasurers are picked solely for their rudeness and stupidity; they cannot get jobs until they pass Blindness, Short-Temper and Stubbornness tests.)*

It is hard to believe that a musical comedy, composed of light and gaiety, can be born in such gloomy surroundings. *The Alvin has the cold, empty air of a place where a dream expired—as indeed, one did recently* (*Rumple closed*). The seats of the Alvin are covered with huge spreads of muslin except for a few rows down front where the production staff sits during rehearsals. The place smells musty and damp, and the deep shadows seem deeper because the only illumination is from the "work light"—the single bulb *that hangs* in the center of the stage. The costumes of the participants give no hint that they are engaged in anything resembling fun. Actresses, to whom acting is not work but second nature, love to have the world believe that they work like sandhogs; they therefore rehearse in clothes the average suburban housewife wouldn't wear to a supermarket. Abbe, in an old blue fuzzy sweater and a disreputable black skirt, looks like an underpaid scullery maid. The chorus girls seem to be the molls of a gang of Brooklyn juveniles. Only Jackie McKeever, new to the theatre and therefore ignorant of the rules, has had the bad taste to come dressed neatly. In her next show—assuming she gets through this one—she will turn up at rehearsals looking as hideous as everyone else, hair in curlers, legs in jeans recently worn for painting a Greenwich Village flat.

Today's run-through goes well enough, but Ferrer is dissatisfied. He sits in the third row, his cupped hand pushing his face into lugubrious lines. He says quietly to Howard Merrill, "We're replacing Cugie."

"We're *what?*"

"He won't do."

"Who'll we get?"

"I'm bringing Eddie Platt from the coast."

"Who the hell is Eddie Platt?"

"You know who he is, for Christ's sake," Ferrer says. "He was with me in *The Shrike* and about six other plays. I just used him in the movie I did at M.G.M."

"How much will he cost us?"

"Not any more than Cugie—well, maybe a little more."

"He's not a name," Coleman says.

"You and your goddamn names," Joe says.

"Why don't you give Cugie another chance?" Merrill asks.

"He won't do," Ferrer says, stubbornly. "He doesn't react properly

—his reactions aren't an actor's. I thought they were at first, but they aren't. Abbe and Jackie aren't experienced, either, but they have instinctive reflexes—they react like a prize-fighter or a bullfighter . . . Cugie reacts like an orchestra leader. He's got to go."

"Who's going to tell him?" Coleman asks.

"I'm the director," sighs Ferrer, "I'll tell him."

JAN. 2, 1958. *I drop into the Alvin for another look.* In the Alvin Ferrer is rehearsing Tony Randall and Jackie in the scene where Maude St. James confronts the Captain in Paris with her discovery of his infidelity. Randall is muttering his lines listlessly; *in the manner of a bored horse who knows he must run a certain number of miles each day before making his race. He is more an actor of the old, or grand, tradition, rather than one of the new dirty-fingernailed school, but like those fumbling mumblers,* he does not believe in turning on the full charge until he is before the footlights. Ferrer seems a bit displeased with him. McKeever is giving it the old Catasauqua, Pa., (her home town) try. She seems semi-hysterical. Her principal dramatic gesture consists of clutching at the bottom of her girdle, through her skirt, which is provocative enough but not especially meaningful.

Ferrer is frowning. He is leaning on a ramp that leads from the stage down to the seats, bending his head so that he appears to be attempting to get an upside-down view of his navel—as though his thoughts, conceived in his guts, are luminous enough to shine through. He starts to give the pair a direction and is interrupted by stage manager Jimmy Russo.

"They're ready to cut the belt," *Russo says.*

"*What belt, for Christ's sake?*"

"*The belt* for the treadmill."

"Will it make noise?"

"Quite a bit."

"Come on, kids, we'll go downstairs," Ferrer says, wearily. They go to the basement of the theatre. In the Ladies' Room Livingston and Evans are polishing lyrics. In the Men's, Starbuck is drilling girls in a routine. Morgan, exhausted by constant rewrites, is asleep on the sofa. "The poor bastard's been getting no sleep at all," Ferrer says.

He turns back to Jackie and Tony. In this scene, Jackie is *supposed to* seize her austere Captain and bend him back in an old-time silent-movie kiss, to communicate the fact that a few days in Paris have let down her British tresses. *She is bending him too far back to suit Joe. "Jackie," he says, "when you bend that way, you look like an ingrown pubic hair," he adds, "on the behind of time." Then he hugs her. This gesture, or his remark, stimulates her to greater efforts.*

Randall is to express astonishment at his wife's transformation, but he is not doing it properly. "Look, Tony," says Ferrer, "it's like the old English joke where the guy comes home and finds his wife in bed with his best friend. He says, 'Geoffery, I *have* to—but *you! ?*' "

After a few more minutes, Joe calls a break. "We're coming along fine," he says. "I couldn't be more thrilled. *Come around* tonight *and see* a run-through—we've invited some friends and we're going to run the whole friggin' thing."

I go back at 7:30 P.M. Ferrer is onstage, *blinking in the naked light bulb,* addressing the invited audience. He says that it is his and the producer's notion that every play has two casts—"Us and you, the audience." He says that we would see quite a complete first act and about two thirds of a second. He *begged* our indulgence for the lack of costumes, lights, scenery, *music*—and for the incomplete book, lyrics and music. "We're constantly changing and polishing," he says.

It is exciting as the piano begins and the singers roll in, jerkily and unsteadily, on the precarious treadmills. The opening is pleasantly Gilbert and Sullivany. Then Randall and Jackie come on in their first scene, which is long and over-expository. The beddibyes scene, in which they take off their clothes and go to bed, drags and drags. So do all the musical numbers and the dances. *It is obvious that Starbuck, realizing he may have to sacrifice some material later, has crammed in as much as possible so that some ultimately will be left.*

Randall has lost some of his afternoon's boredom and takes on a certain authority as he struts about in built-up heels. Jackie, alas, is as smalltown-*Green Room Club as ever;* her high, throaty voice is too stiff, *like that of a road company Shirley Jones.* Abbe Lane is not much better; *cannot hear her.* The Danilova dance seems to take hours.

I leave, frankly disappointed. It does not seem possible that anything can come from this morass of mediocrity, those talented people have managed to sing into.

An hour and a half later, *I go back to the darkened Alvin,* the production staff is meeting in the basement lounge. *They have drawn* up all chairs and sofas into a semi-circle around Joe. Two bottles of Scotch stand on the refreshment bar. Instead of a grim conclave, with intimations of doom, *to my astonishment they are all* manic with joy. Such is the enchantment of the theatre, I gather; to get something on, however bad, is to be transported.

Ferrer is saying, "*It's no panic*—we're so far ahead it's amazing. *What say, Jay.*"

Blackton nods cautiously, "Yes, we're far out in front, Joe—but I need a deadline pretty soon for my arrangements."

Don Coleman says, "*A guy I spoke to—he built our sets—said, 'You guys are practically ready to open from what I saw tonight.'* Also 'Herman Bernstein loves it.' Herman is the Alvin's manager. *He doesn't like the weather, even when it's a nice day.*"

There is a general chorus of congratulatory agreement, after which Ferrer, still feeling high, begins discussing technical points. Someone says, "Any way of getting Susan Johnson back in the second act?"

"That would be nice but not necessary," Ferrer says. "Look at Carmen Miranda in *Streets of Paris.* Six minutes in the first act only and it made her a star."

"Maybe Susan could sing in the finale," Livingston and Evans say, in chorus.

The idea is vetoed, but Jay and Ray are ordered to begin thinking of the second act.

"Everybody thought Jackie was great," Merrill says.

"Well, Joe stuck his neck out on that one," Morgan says.

"Something in her voice got me," Joe says.

Don Coleman came over to me. "We're coming along great," he says, "Don't you think?"

"I think it's too long," I say cautiously.

"Fifteen, twenty minutes too long," he says. "But great—GREAT."

Joe stands up and stretches his arms before him, gropingly, like a blind man. "Well," he says, "so far we're in the room—we're looking for it—we've almost got it."

Everybody begins talking at once. The consensus is that the opening dialogue between Jackie and Tony is too long.

"Oh, crap," says Al Morgan. "A remarkable number of people have joined the Writer's Union during the past four days. People tell me everything is too long. O.K., they even say the strip tease is endless. Look—we have to establish characters. Joe and I just didn't blunder into this thing. We thought it out carefully beforehand, talked for days, thought it over . . ."

"We had a hit show tonight at the end of the first act, I don't care what anybody says," Ferrer says.

"But what about the slow beginning?" Merrill asks.

"Let me tell you a story," Joe says. "In Charlie's Aunt *the first fifteen minutes were supposed to be the dullest thing ever. Everybody said so. But Josh Logan is a little bit like me, or I'm like him, you tell him something often enough he gets stubborn. He kept it in. It played marvelously. It wasn't slow. It'll be all right, the opening. If it isn't, we'll straighten it out in Philadelphia. We have two weeks there to work."*

The meeting breaks up. Starbuck, Blackton, Livingston and Evans go to the Ladies' to discuss some problems. Ferrer follows them. "We've been working until three, four o'clock every damned morning," he says.

JAN. 5. PHILADELPHIA. The show moved here today for several days of rehearsals, one invited-audience preview, the opening, and a two-week run. Herb Gahagan, an assistant propman, says "You know the birds the girls carry in the first-act finale? A guy made us those special. Imported feathers. Everything the best. We're using only *imported* fake birds."

JAN. 6. There is a gossip in every company. This one chatters away: "One of the production staff is sleeping with one of the leads, we think. Another one's got eyes for a singer. So-and-so is shacked up with so-and-so—and her husband's home taking care of their three kids! *We're all sore in the chorus . . . all three girls who were in* Happy Hunting *got understudy jobs. Jay Blackton was conductor of that show, so he gave the jobs to them." (Coleman later denies this indignantly: "We picked the understudies ourselves," he says, "and Jay had nothing to do with it").*

JAN. 8. "My God," says The Gopher, rushing up with his arms full of costumes, "I don't know how we're ever going to get this thing on. We got a dress rehearsal with piano tonight, and these still have to be pressed." He rushes away; he is always in motion.

Nearly everything is in readiness. O'Connell has all his props, the treadmills and scenery are working smoothly, Mielziner is lighting the stage, Miles White has delivered all his costumes. Down in the pit the quiet, conscientious Blackton is working on scores by the light of a gooseneck lamp on the piano. Some of the cast are rehearsing at the Lu Lu Temple, a Shriners' hall across the street, but most of them are here. Ferrer is all over the place, leaping up the stairs to the stage, jumping down, shouting orders and hissing asides to his secretary. *No painter of miniatures ever possessed a finer eye for detail.* I copy down some of his memos and notes:

Make upstairs curtains same as downstairs in Capt. house.

Cut second kiss when Capt. enters.

Bottle on table by his chair should be English beer.

Lights out entirely at end of first scene.

Pipe on table is wrong shape; get curved pipe.

Tony looks hung-up when he goes to mantel to get cribbage set.

Get him something to do.

Those are merely his notes on the first scene; by the time rehearsal is over, there are 57 more. The secretary, a girl with dark, closecut hair, a child's face and the body of a Greek victory goddess, is exhausted. "I worked with Mr. Ferrer on one picture," she says. "*That* was fun. This—I've been working 18, 20 hours a day. I'm going back to Hollywood and rest."

JAN. 11. Opening night in Philly. At rehearsal in the afternoon it is difficult to believe that this show will ever go on. The treadmills are not working. Ferrer is trying to hear lines in the midst of indescribable confusion—stagehands, following Mielziner's directions, raising and lowering bits and pieces of scenery; chorus girls running to stand in costume before Miles White, who pokes and prods them as though examining oxen; Starbuck putting boys through last-minute routines; Vinnie Donahue, Joe's assistant, rushing about on a multitude of errands, his yellow scarf flying behind him; Rafael Ferrer, Joe's kid half-brother, chasing after coffee; The Gopher ready to drop from nervous excitement. Finally, it's back to the hotels for some rest before the show.

A friend of mine has a car and chauffeur; we take Ferrer back to his hotel, the Barclay, after the rehearsal. For once he is silent. He drums his fingers to some secret inner rhythm, staring straight ahead, and leaves the car with scarcely a word.

I spend an hour trying to think of a telegram to send. I do not want to say that I'm sure everything will be wonderful; I'm sure it won't. The show is still slow, much too slow. My friend then suggests a Yiddish phrase, Vesach vus, *meaning "Who knows what?" or, "It's in the laps of the gods." I send that.*

The opening is a sell-out. In New York, an opening demands black tie; in Philadelphia it is optional. Ferrer, Morgan and everyone else on the production staff turn up in dinner jackets, as though to express their respect for each other.

The villagers begin their stately procession across the stage. Tony comes on and gets a hand, but not a big one. He delivers the line designed to get the first laugh:

"I love to see the pippets a-mating on the moor . . ."

No one laughs.

Livingston and Evans look at each other glumly.

"It's because it's Philadelphia," Don Coleman says. "They never heard of pippets here."

"It's because he didn't belt the line," Ferrer says.

A man sitting in the rear row turns around and utters a stern, "Shhhh!"

This audience is singularly unresponsive, sitting on its hands except during the times when the scenery is going in and out on the belts.

"In Philadelphia, they applaud the sets," says Vinnie Donahue.

The dialogue between Tony and Jackie still seems interminable, but then the pace picks up. We realize, with surprise, that the beddibyes scene, where they take off their clothes, has been cut.

"Joe cut it this afternoon," Don Coleman says. "He cut twenty minutes out of the show."

The *Surprise* ballet also has been cut. John Brascia, the star of that number, is standing in street clothes watching the proceedings on stage. His face is a dead white in the shadows; every sound from the orchestra in the pit seems to wrack and stiffen him. He has a run-of-the-play contract; he will draw his salary, which will enable him to study, practice or travel. But to contemplate that now is cold comfort; he has been cut in the hour before his great opportunity, and he is desolate.

The long, long dance by Tony and Danilova is still in, and still much too long; it stops the progress of the book. The audience does not seem to mind. This turn gets the first big round of applause. But mostly the audience sits on its hands.

"That's the way it is in Philadelphia," my friend says. "They don't come to see the show on first night, they come to look at each other."

The statement is borne out during intermission. The richly-furred women stare at each other appraisingly, the men stand around smoking and looking uncomfortable (going to the theatre in the United States is a penance, for the most part, what with the heat and the hard, uncomfortable seats).

"I don't think that Abbe Lane's so sexy," one woman says to her husband at intermission. He gives her a patient look.

"It's her clothes," another woman says. "In that *Femininity* song, she ought to wear something sexier."

Ferrer overhears this. "I've been arguing with Abbe for weeks," he says angrily. "She ought to wear the costume Miles originally designed. Much sexier. But she thinks she's an *actress,* for Christ's sake."

The audience is more enthusiastic during the second act.

"I'll be damned," says Ferrer. "This is supposed to be the weak part of the show."

"It *moves* better, that's for sure," Morgan says. "*We'll have to step up the pace in the first.*"

It does move faster—so much so that the duet between Eddie Platt and Abbe, You're So Right For Me, *in which the French mistress and the mate rediscover each other, all but stops the show.*

Now the audience is hooked, and by the time the finale comes on, and Mielziner's ingenious moving sets transform the captain's ship into a nightclub before the audience's eyes, everybody is ready to stand up and cheer. Howard Merrill dashes in from the lobby, where he has been listening to a Philadelphia radio reporter's commentary on the first three-quarters of the show. "It's a rave!" he cries. "This guy says it's a smash!"

The noise in the theatre, with the people calling for curtain call after curtain call, is deafening. Someone sets up a cry for Ferrer, and others begin yelling for him. He goes onstage, tears streaming down his cheeks (in addition to his other accomplishments, The Hose can cry hose-style almost at will).

Making my way backstage, I collide with Vinnie Donahue. "Joe's done it again!" he cries. "I've seen him do it seven times!"

The Gopher is about to take off for outer space. "A hit! A hit!" he shrieks.

Backstage is a Roman Holiday of mass osculation. An old lady (obviously her grandmother from the home town) is kissing Jackie McKeever, Susan Johnson is kissing Tony Randall, chorus girls are kissing carpenters and stagehands, Rosie Clooney (who came in from the coast *for twelve hours* just for the opening) is kissing Eddie Platt, Danilova is kissing stage manager Jimmy Russo. Peter Witt, the agent, is kissing somebody absent-mindedly, and murmuring to somebody else, "Yes, I put the whole thing together." (All agents take credit like fight managers, except when they are connected with a flop.)

Tears still are flowing from Ferrer's eyes.

"What next?" Morgan asks him.

"Nothing much for a few days," he says. "I'm just going to study it and see what it needs. It still needs plenty."

JAN. 12. *Everybody celebrated last night; everybody has hangovers today. We cure them at a private club, where I overhear a stagehand talking to another. "What a show that was last night," he says. "It made* The Body Beautiful *look sick."* (The Body Beautiful *also is trying out in town prior to going to New York, and it too is a musical.) "Yes, it did," says the second. "I'd give you the whole of the* Body *for one per cent of the* Captain."

Up in Joe's room they are not so enthusiastic. "There's still a hell of a lot to be done," says Ferrer. "On the dances, especially. Starbuck needs help. It's been a tremendous job for him, putting this on singlehanded."

"Who'll we got?" Merrill asks.

"I'm bullish on Ona White," Don Coleman says. "She did *The Music Man*—biggest hit in New York this season."

"Who'll tell Starbuck we're bringing her in?" Merrill asks.

"I'll tell him," says Ferrer. "Look, the only god around here is a hit show. Everybody's expendable, including me."

JAN. 13. Morgan and Ferrer are trying to speed up the first scene between Jackie and Tony. They are working in the living room of Ferrer's hotel suite, *which is furnished in the manner of all carriage trade hotels and differs from them in that it is littered with crushed and torn paper.* The ash trays are full of Morgan's cigarette butts; Ferrer has given up smoking during the show *because, he says, it saps his energy and poisons his system. The walls are covered with memoranda Joe has taped up during the past few days. Rafael Ferrer sits in a corner, ready to run errands.*

"I think we need some jokes," Morgan is saying.

"Jokes or exposition?"

"We got enough exposition! That's why the damned thing drags!"

Ferrer, barefoot, begins to pace. He tries a line or two. Morgan looks sour, shakes his head. Ferrer tries another. Again, the head-shake. "I give up," Ferrer says. "Trying to tell *you* a joke, you bastard, is like one Siamese twin saying to the other, 'Guess who I slept with last night?' "

By the end of the afternoon they get it fixed—they add another page of dialogue. "I know it sounds nuts," Morgan says, "but actually, adding an extra page makes it go *faster.*"

JAN. 14. The Philadelphia newspaper notices were sensational, but they were nothing compared to *Variety.* It says "smash." It says, "Despite trade misgivings about the wisdom of trying to make a legit musical from a click picture, the transformation has been made not only with success but also with distinction."

"I wish I thought it's as good as they do," Ferrer murmurs.

JAN. 15. Morgan and Ferrer go to the Martinez-Turner fight. Ferrer says, "I feel guilty about leaving the show." He is preoccupied all through the fight—and no wonder, since it is a waltz. From time to time he takes out a pad and makes notes. Going back downtown in a cab, he suddenly says to Morgan, "What would you think of cutting Danilova's dance? I think that's one way to speed things up."

"Where would we put her?"

"We wouldn't—we'll just cut her out."

JAN. 16. Rehearsals are still going on every day, and the cast is enraged—for Joe has made no major changes since the afternoon of opening night. All he has done is order Miles White to design new costumes for the second-act finale.

The two collaborators are still trying to improve the book. A laugh is needed in the next-to-last scene. The English wife has deserted the Captain, and Bobo and the First Mate have decided they will get married. The loss of two of his paradises makes the Captain decide to give up his third, his ship. He says he will give it to his First Mate.

Randall, rehearsing in T-shirt and jeans, calls down to Ferrer, "I've got an idea for a laugh. All through the play I've been saying, 'It's a good-sized ship . . . I run a tight ship.' It just came to me—how about if right here I say, 'Take it . . . it's a *little* ship,' and then pause, and then say, 'A *loose* little ship'?"

"Try it tonight," Ferrer shrugs, without enthusiasm.

Randall tries it; it gets the biggest laugh in the show.

"That's the second line he's contributed," Morgan says. "He also thought up the spot in the first act where he says, 'Show me a man who's punctual and I'll show you a man who's on time.'"

Backstage, Jimmy Russo, the stage manager, is missing. Someone explains that he and Ferrer had several disagreements and Russo handed in his notice. George Quick has replaced him.

JAN. 17. Danilova's dance is cut at tonight's performance. Livingston and Evans have finished a new number, *Jubilee,* for Susan Johnson to sing in the first-act finale. It does not work quite as well as her old number, *Give It All You've Got,* but everyone is optimistic. The dances are being altered gradually; Ona White has come in to assist Starbuck. Miles White has delivered the new costumes for the finale; the girls were wearing little black corselettes—now they are wearing red-white-and-blue bikinis.

JAN. 17. "They didn't like it last night," Ferrer says at the production meeting.

"Let's put Danilova back in," Merrill suggests. "The show seems to get small without her—that dance actually *establishes* Paris."

"OK—we'll cut it in half," says Ferrer.

Starbuck looks pained but says nothing.

"That's it," Joe says. "Tony's walking down the street, digging Paris, digging the people—he meets her and they go into the dance. Only now it's a satirical dance. Before it was too damned serious."

JAN. 18. In the second act there is a song sung by the First Mate and the Captain, *I've Been There And I'm Back.* Danilova, wearing an incredibly ancient pair of light blue warmup tights, is doing exercises in the wings. "I been dere," she says, "and I come back." Her number, restaged, has been put back in the show; so has a new version of the dance for *You're So Right*.

JAN. 19. "Even with the restaging, *You're So Right* is wrong," Ferrer says. "I wonder if we don't need a new—"

Livingston and Evans look stricken. "Not a new—?"

"I'm afraid so," says Ferrer. "Get busy."

This is Sunday, but there are rehearsals all morning, afternoon and evening.

JAN. 20. Coleman and Merrill are aglow—and with good reason. Several movie producers have expressed interest in acquiring the film rights, and today a New York syndicate has made an offer to buy out their producers' half.

At tonight's performance, Ona White's restaging of the sailors' dance is in, and Susan sings *Jubilee* in the finale of the first act. *I can't see that either number is much improvement.*

JAN. 21. Ferrer is thinking of cutting *Jubilee* and putting the first number back in. Coleman says he's *got* to make his mind up soon and freeze the show. Ferrer says he'll freeze it when he's ready. Coleman leaves the Lu Lu Temple with his face set. "Joe's style of working gives you ulcers," he says, "because he never makes up his mind until the last minute. That *Surprise* ballet, which he yanked the afternoon of opening night, cost us $8,000. Of course, it was wise to yank it, but why did he have to wait until after we'd spent the money?"

JAN. 22. Bruce McKay, a baritone and one of the Captain's crew, is staring dispiritedly at the backstage bulletin board. "My God, another day of rehearsals—from 11:45 A.M. to 7:45 P.M., tomorrow. I've never been in a show where they worked us so hard." A chorus girl, going by, gooses him and giggles. He catches her by the wrist and embraces her, and she rubs her body against him. It is clear now why the cast seldom complains about the rigorous schedule.

The weather has been miserable; nearly everybody has a cold. Abbe is out with laryngitis tonight. Her understudy, B. J. McGuire, goes on without a reheasal and does a capable job. She looks sexier than Abbe because she is wearing the negligee that Miles originally designed for the star.

"That settles it," Ferrer snarls. "Abbe's going to wear that goddam kimono or *else!*"

In the wings, Jackie McKeever stands fidgeting and wringing her hands. "I'm getting the same thing Abbe has, I know I am," she says, on the brink of tears.

"I'm calling a doctor to get your throat sprayed," the new stage manager, George Quick, says reassuringly.

Jackie's voice holds up until the middle of the second act—but then, in the *Double Standard* number, it cracks and she has to talk the lines.

"The kid's a trouper," Ferrer whispers.

JAN. 23. A new number, written in two days, goes in for *You're So Right*. It's called *It's Not Too Late*. "It's not too good, either," says Morgan, tonelessly.

JAN. 24. George Quick surveys his cue-script, now so changed, altered and scribbled upon as to be unintelligible to anyone but him. "This is an easy show to run tonight," he says. "We've done the whole thing this way once before—first time that's happened for days." Abbe is still out; so is Jackie, who has been replaced by a singer named Sheila Matthews.

Up front, Morgan sees Cugat, who has been at virtually every performance, picking his wife up afterward and taking her home to the hotel. "You must know every damned line in the show by now," Morgan says, kindly.

"I know every part," says Cugie, with rue, "except the First Mate's."

JAN. 25. Closing day in Philly. Ferrer is in good spirits. "I feel like a jockey riding some great horse," he says. "He's twenty lengths behind, then he starts to gain, knocking off horse after horse—pretty soon there are four horses left, then two, then one, then he's home. That's what we've done, we've knocked out the rough spots one by one."

Morgan is not so sanguine. "The book is finished," he says, "but I keep waking up at night, writing it over and over."

"Pray for a bad audience in New York at the preview the night before opening," Ferrer says. "You do a good show the night before, you're down on opening night. If necessary the night before I'm going out on the street and get a lot of squares and drag them in and tell them not to make a sound. Pray." He turns to grab for a chorus girl; she squeals and runs back into the dressing room.

Rafael Ferrer tacks a notice to the bulletin board. It says, ALL PEOPLE WEARING NOSES PLEASE CARRY THEM IN YOUR MAKEUP KIT AS PERSONAL PROPS.

*Joe smiles. He takes off his cap and scratches his head. "This whole tryout has been relatively uneventful," he says, "because we never moved until the last minute. So many directors panic—they listen to what others say, they seek opinions. I'm the opposite. I never talk to anybody. Anybody makes a suggestion, I say, 'No.' I can think better than they can. If you start taking advice, you're dead. You have to operate on how you feel. We still have two major problems," he goes on, closing his eyes, "getting the right song for Mae in the night club—*Jubilee *is wrong—and getting something at the end for Eddie and Abbe. The new song isn't right. Ray and Jay are working on a third. Aside from that, everything's going better than ever." It's true, the show does seem better, somehow.*

Eddie Knill, company manager, comes back to report that receipts up front have been phenomenal. "We broke the house record the first week," he says.

The news seems to inspire the cast to greater efforts, and tonight's performance is the best so far. The company is in high spirits as we get on the chartered railroad car—not even the grimy, sticky seats, patented by this railroad, can depress or even evoke complaints. Bottles are broken out, suitcases are balanced on knees for poker games. The train is late—Pennsy trains are more often late than on time—but nobody minds. The company has become a unit; dey been dere and dey're going back.

"We're going to kill 'em in New York," says The Gopher, his thin face shining.

JAN. 26–30. Rehearsals, rehearsals, rehearsals, rehearsals.

Ferrer methodically puts back everything he cut in Philadelphia —everything, that is, but the *Surprise* ballet. *You're So Right* is back; so is *Give It All You've Got*. New costumes have been ordered for the *You're So Right* dance. Nearly all of Ona White's changes on Starbuck's numbers have been taken out and Starbuck's original movements put back in.

Coleman says, rather disgustedly, "We've spent $15,000 on new costumes, $7,500 on overtime rehearsals, and $10,000 on arrangements and copying for the musicians—and the show is just about the same as it was opening night in Philadelphia."

"No," *says Ferrer,* "*it isn't—and I'll tell you why. When I was a kid I worked for Jed Harris. One time I said to Charlie MacArthur, 'This Harris is the greatest." Charlie said, 'Crap.' Then he changed his mind. He told me a story—he said that when he and Ben Hecht wrote* The Front Page, *Harris fired George Kaufman, the director, the first week, and spent a week screwing around with changes and changes. Charlie and Hecht were up-all-night-style the whole week, rewriting. Then Jed called back Kaufman and they threw out all the changes. And Charlie said to me, 'You know, Joe, the show was exactly the same—but something had been added.' And that's the way it is with this one, Don.*"

"*I hope to God you're right,*" *Coleman says.*

JAN. 31. First paid New York preview—and first disaster. "My God," says The Gopher before the performance, "what problems backstage—there's no room in this theatre to put props or scenery. They have to fly the boat up—they can't just push it forward the way they did in Philadelphia. And it weighs two tons! Something's going to happen."

Something does. As the curtains are about to open for the last scene, frantic shouts are heard backstage. The boat's counterweights are too heavy to lower it from the flies—it will not come down. Ferrer streaks for the door to backstage. The actors face the audience in bewilderment. Finally Tony steps forward. He says to the audience, "We *were* supposed to have the boat here, but something happened." This gets a laugh, and they do the finale without the boat.

FEB. 1. The boat is fixed, and drops nicely.

FEB. 2. *I am standing in the wings beside Doris Einstein, the assistant stage manager, watching her follow the show from George Quick's master-script. Doris' job is to see that George's commands are carried out the instant he gives them. The girls are coming up from their dressing room in their furry fox costumes for the first-act finale. They stand near me, near-naked and shivering, kicking their long, black-stockinged legs high to warm up, shaking their little behinds. Over to one side, one sidles up to one of the male singers and puts her arms around him, as though to draw him into a kiss. It is hard to tell if she is doing it for warmth or for affection; these kids show and use their bodies almost absent-mindedly, and what in other social strata would be acts of love-making can be as automatic and casual as eating.*

One of the little foxes comes up and stands before me. "Are you the man from Playboy?*" I admit it. Her eyes are large and blue and ingenuous. "Can you tell me how I can get to be a Playmate of the Month?" she asks.*

A few hours later, walking home through the gentle snow to my hotel, the proper answer occurs to me—and I favor myself with a bitter laugh.

FEB. 3. The girls are livid—rehearsals have been called for tomorrow, the day of opening night. "How'll we ever get our hair done?" they shriek.

The girl who is deputy for Actors' Equity goes off in search of someone to whom she can complain. Fifteen minutes later she is back, crestfallen and defensive. "No use. They can *call us for rehearsal. We'll have to get our hair done as best we can."*

"Jesus Christ," says Ferrer, who is beginning to get irritable, "the day before opening, and they come to me with hair *problems."*

FEB. 4. Curtain-time is 7:30 P.M. on opening night, in order to give the morning newspaper critics plenty of time to get back to their offices and write their reviews. At 7:00 P.M. there already are crowds of rubbernecks and autograph hunters flanking the entrance to the Alvin Theatre. A mounted policeman stands by to keep order.

In the lobby is The Gopher, arms loaded with small identical cardboard boxes. "Presents from Coleman and Merrill to everybody," he says. "I *been ordered to pass them out. Some job."*

Backstage, Merrill and Coleman are talking to Miles White; all are in evening dress, white carnations in their buttonholes. White's face appears calm, but he is rocking up and down on his toes. Coleman says, "I only lost eleven pounds during this show," and proceeds to attempt to regain some weight by biting his nails. Merrill is taking it worse: "I'm panicky," he says. "I had a drink to relax me, but already I'm panicky."

Ferrer arrives, flushed, staring straight ahead, rushing about shaking hands and muttering. He is not the same confident man he was on closing night in Philadelphia; *it is as though the fact of opening has dawned upon him gradually, and he is only beginning to realize the full import.*

Out front, the audience is streaming in. Harvey Sabinson, the show's press agent, is bobbing about frantically. "What an opening!" he cries. "Everybody in town wanted to come! Know who I turned down this afternoon? Bob Hope! Also Lollobrigida and Paulette Goddard! Couldn't find seats for them. I turned down Milton Berle, too, but somehow he got two seats up in the mezzanine. I let in Walter Slezak because he's got a big laugh—we'll need it."

The celebrities began to arrive: tiny Billy Rose, with the gorgeous Joyce Matthews towering over him; Cugie, with Jayne Meadows (Steve Allen, her husband, is in Cuba); Jim Backus, distinguished in a ruffled shirt and bowler hat; the director Otto Preminger, erect as a Prussian general. Rosie Clooney arrives, wearing a white gown and an apprehensive expression. Here and there come the critics: the mousy, pipe-sucking Atkinson of the *Times*; the genial Watts of the *Post*; the debonair McClain of the *Journal-American*; Gibbs of *The New Yorker*, aloof and reserved. They and their colleagues are the only members of the audience who are not excited; this is just another job, their attitude seems to say.

The overture commences. Ferrer rushes up the side aisle from the door to backstage. A radiator-cover runs along the rear wall of the theatre—he boosts himself up to sit on it.

"Now," he whispers to Morgan, "the agony begins." Morgan nods.

With a start, I realize that I am as nervous as he; I have come to be fond of this show and the people connected with it. I want it to be a hit. All my original objections have long since disappeared.

They are wrong. There is no agony. This is the best audience they have ever had. They begin laughing—which no audience has done before—when the English villagers sing, "We ship our oldest movies overseas to Channel 9." They roar at Tony's "I love to see the pippets a-mating on the moor." Danilova's dance nearly stops the show. The entire first act goes sensationally well, and the finale gets a great burst of applause.

In the lobby, Martin Gabel says, "Very good, I'm enjoying it." His wife, Arlene Francis, nods agreement.

Coleman and Merrill have lost their nervousness. "They *love* it!" Merrill whispers. That appears to be the case throughout the second act, as well. The cast takes eleven curtain calls, and there are cries of "Authors! Authors!"

Backstage is crowded, as Philadelphia was, with hundreds of friends, well-wishers, relatives and hangers-on bumping into scenery, knocking over props, generally driving the doorman and the house manager out of their minds. *For once, there is nothing they can do; for once they must pretend to be gracious.*

It is obligatory for the show's brass to put in an appearance at Sardi's after the opening. The rest of the company and staff show up at a pseudo-Polynesian restaurant on East 57th called Luau 400. One by one the cast members drift in, some in twos and threes, some with wives or husbands or dates, and settle in the fake huts that line the walls and serve as booths. Now that the opening is past and the backstage celebrations are behind them, they are ready to relax—but they are expectant. *The Herald Tribune,* with Walter Kerr's review, will be on the streets within an hour. Kerr is tough, and this season he has been tougher than usual for some reason. Atkinson will follow an hour later; Atkinson is getting crochety. These two have been known to kill a play with their reviews.

The management of Luau 400 apparently has instructed its waiters to take their time serving the liquor. Tension mounts as we wait for drinks. A Hawaiian-oriented trio is methodically working its way through the score of the show, but nobody is dancing; for that matter, nobody is listening. *Bruce McKay, the singer, stops by my table. I congratulate him on the almost-perfect performance the company gave. "Yeah, we went for broke tonight," he says. "Everybody was* up*—but you know, Dick, I'm worried. I can* smell *something."*

The Gopher runs up, harried and stricken. "Bad news!" he cries. "Somebody heard Byron Bentley, the radio critic. Not good—not good at all. Oh, God. I know Kerr is going to give us a bomb—I saw his face as he left the theatre, and he looked sore." The Gopher put his fists to his forehead. "What will I tell all those people I raised the money from?"

Fifteen minutes later the suspicions are confirmed. Word comes from Sardi's that Kerr's review is a blast. Ray Evans, who preferred to be with the company rather than go with the brass, comes in slowly from the telephone, his long, lined face even sadder than usual.

"He hated it," he says, simply.

The word runs through the room, and even the fact that the booze at last has begun to arrive cannot stir a hum out of the silence that has fallen.

The *Tribune* arrives. Kerr's closing lines are, "Mr. Randall . . . keeps bucking everybody up with cheery 'Good show.' It would be nice to be able to echo him this morning."

"Well, there's still Atkinson," singer Stanley Carlson says. "He liked *Jamaica*—if he liked that, he'll surely like us!"

When the *Times* finally comes, we see that Atkinson has written not only a rap but a personal attack on Ferrer. He says, ". . . Mr. Ferrer has substituted leers for wit and generally debased the style to the level of the old-fashioned varsity show. Mr. Ferrer has been away from Broadway too long. New York is a big town now."

"And Atkinson is a small man," somebody says. But the irony is not enough to drive away the disappointment.

Coleman and Merrill arrive, looking haggard. Morgan follows them. "What *happened?*" he says, unbelievingly. "What the hell happened—how is it possible? Is this Hate Ferrer Week for those guys? The audience loved it—what got into the critics?"

Nobody can answer; nobody knows. Ferrer arrives and waves, smiling sheepishly, like a fighter who knows he's been in with a Greb. But the party is over.

FEB. 5. Some notices are such out-and-out raves that it is hard to believe these reviewers are not writing about a show completely different from the one Kerr and Atkinson saw. Chapman of the *News,* Coleman of the *Mirror,* Alston of the *World-Telegram and Sun*—they all love it. Watts in the *Post* is not quite as enthusiastic but is still very admiring. McClain in the *Journal-American* likes the principals, but says he thinks "the Captain's ship lists slightly to starboard." His review is about half-and-half.

Ferrer stands on the steps of the Captain's cottage with the cast gathered around him onstage. This is his farewell address.

"The story is sad on two, pretty good on five," he says. "I have only one thing to say—eight happy audiences a week will make *real* jerks out of those two jerks. You now have a harder job—you have to work harder all the time. Let me point out that we broke the house record twice in Philadelphia, and those people down there aren't idiots. We've got a million and a half advance in the till. We sold a lot of tickets this morning and they're still selling. We've got thirty standees out there today, so we just can't accept the opinions of Atkinson and Kerr as typical. By working hard in every performance, you can crucify the bastards. As it stands, we'll run for a year, anyhow. So, it's up to you. I'll be in every few weeks, to spank you or give you a feel. So—work. God bless."

Everybody cheers as *Ferrer steps down. He puts on his heavy brown tweed overcoat. "What next?" I ask. He scratches his head. "I'm off to the coast—see my kids, get some fun, play some chess, dig some music, lie around and let the money roll in. And sleep. Maybe I'll make another picture. I got five plays optioned for next season. I'll show 'em."*

And he puts on his cap and walks off.

Post Script: In a letter written about a week after he made the assignment, Spectorsky had informed me that I would be limited to 5,000 words—"*Perhaps,*" he added, "a few hundred more." The assignment was appealing and challenging, and I immediately began to plan my approach. John Bartlow Martin once had done a similar piece on *South Pacific* for Herbert Mayes when the latter was editing *Cosmopolitan* as well as *Good Housekeeping.* My principal recollection of Martin's job was that it was a good idea that, perhaps because of the material itself, did not quite live up to its promise. The limited space and the necessity for crediting the many different personalities involved in the musical had forced him into a rather colorless chronology. He had done as well as he could, under the circumstances, but the conventional form of the article had kept him from bringing his people and scenes to life. I knew that in the course of following the show I would witness many brief, lively scenes and overhear many snatches of related yet apparently disconnected dialogue, and in order to keep out of the trap that had snagged Martin I would have to find some method of presenting those diverse elements without resorting to a wearying succession of "and then's" and "next day's." Also, I had to devise some way of indicating that the idea for doing a musical had been in Ferrer's mind nearly six months before *The Captain's Paradise* project was offered him. A daily diary seemed the only solution, and as I began working on the research I found myself writing scenes and bits of conversation. The dates of the diary thus served as the connectives: I had my scenes and I had continuity as well.

In January, when the show went to Philadelphia to try out, I sent what I had finished to Spectorsky to show how I was coming along. The instant I posted the wad of manuscript, I was sorry; reading the carbon, I found that it was lifeless. I could not understand why. Many of the scenes were fairly dramatic and much of the dialogue was bright and witty. The trouble was, there was no immediacy and very little opportunity for the reader to identify with anyone. I solved the latter problem while Spectorsky was looking over the manuscript by putting myself into the piece, permitting the reader to follow the progress of the show through my eyes. And then, one morning when I set out to write a scene I had observed the night before, I suddenly realized I was writing it in the present tense. What caused me to do that particular sequence in the present, I cannot tell—but I knew, as I read it over, that it was the liveliest part I had done to date. I knew then that I would have to do the entire piece in the present.

Spectorsky's letter and my manuscript came back a few days later. He wrote,

As you say, it's a rough. And there are gaps. The diary technique *seems*, at this point, to work okay, but the gaps are fairly startling. What you have sent me, so far, is mostly like a play in which all of the action is offstage, and you only hear about it in dialogue. We "see" no rehearsals, no working session, no descriptions of numbers, no quotes from lyrics, no back-stage action—in fact, Dick, hardly anything except snatches of conversation which refer to events either undescribed or only indirectly described. It may well be that my anxiety on this score is unfounded, and that you plan to fill in these gaps. I sincerely hope so.

There's also the fact that we emphatically cannot assume that our readers will be familiar with the movie which was a smash success as a British movie, but which cannot be presumed to have been seen by our readers, or to have had airing in any but major urban centers. We've got to tell the plot, if only briefly, and the principal characters have to be described, and certainly the departures of *Oh, Captain!* from the original *Captain's Paradise*—with casting comparisons and contrasts—belong in this piece. How you are going to accomplish all this essential conveying of information with the space allottment and the diary format, is (at this writing) hard to envisage. I am assuming it can be done.

Now for some random thoughts, Dick.

Somewhere, very early on, you're going to have to clarify the Morgan-Ferrer partnership with reference to the success of *The Great Man.*

In the event that all here don't cotton to your proposed opening, an easy place to get in a call from the editors of PLAYBOY to you, asking you to do this piece, would be right after your January 27 entry on the second page of the manuscript as it now stands.

The packed terseness that the diary form permits seems excellent on second reading.

Dick, on my own hook, I am not holding a meeting on this material in its present form. Believe me, it is not a good idea. There is also the fact that I must hold people here in reserve for a fresh first reading of this job when it's much further along than it is now.

Before I sign off and rush this off to you, let me reiterate my feeling—a very strong one—that the major problem presented by this rough draft is the absence of event and prevalence of reactions to event.

Incidentally, don't phone in your last entry after opening night—air mail-special will do the trick.

I hope this very candid response won't daunt you: I have said nothing about the things I like, which are numerous, nor about my conviction that you can pull this off splendidly.

Even if Spectorsky had not liked the diary form, I would have gone ahead with it—for I was now absolutely certain that the present tense made it work. His suggestions were sound; some of them I already had anticipated, others I was glad to incorporate.

After the show opened in New York, I set to work collating the diary entries I had made. I found that I had nearly eighty pages of material, most of which was usable. I first went through those eighty pages and slashed everything that, in my opinion, was too esoteric—the Broadway word is "insidey"—for the general reader. Then I began taking myself out of the piece wherever it seemed to me that I intruded upon the narrative. These two cuts got rid of about twenty pages. Next I began cutting unnecessary lines of dialogue —much of the talk was too accurately reproduced, with all the redundancies and unnecessary explanations of conventional spoken speech. Finally I began cutting every bit of description that seemed unnecessary. I now had fifty-two pages; the piece was still more than twice as long as Spectorsky had indicated it should be.

I began to retype the manuscript, and in the process I eliminated five more pages. But a dreadful thing happened. As I got to page ten or thereabouts, I began to have a suspicion that the piece moved too slowly up to that point. Indeed, it seemed dull, particularly in the lead and first three pages. I went back and read them over. Here is what they contained:

JAN. 23, 1957. LONDON. The ebullient, demoniacally energetic José Ferrer is in town, making a movie on the Dreyfus case. When we meet for a drink at the Savoy, he tells me he's itching to get back to Broadway. "I haven't done a legit show for four years," Joe says. "I'd like to try a musical—never did one, it'd be a challenge, a gas—but the trouble is there's so few damned properties. If we can find one, Al and I—you know Al, Al Morgan—we'll do it together. You see our *Great Man?* We did another one, *Jalopy*, but they never shot it. Listen, if you hear of a musical property, let me know, will you?"

APRIL 15. Joe gets a transoceanic call from Kurt Frings, his agent. "Joe, a couple of guys have the rights to *The Captain's Paradise*. They want to make a musical, and they want you to direct and you and Al to do the book."

"What the hell is *The Captain's Paradise?*"

"Alec Guinness movie. Big hit in the art theatres. *You* know it, Joe—there's this English captain, see, he's got this little boat, it goes from Gibraltar to Calique, that's a port in Africa, and he's got a wife in each place, you get the picture? The bigamy hit. Call up British Lion, they'll screen it for you."

APRIL 18. Joe to Frings: "No. I don't like the picture—the idea isn't worked out. The whole thing cheats the audience because the ending's disappointing. Sorry."

APRIL 21. NEW YORK. Joe to Frings: "I can't get that goddamned movie out of my head. Wouldn't that kill you? Do they still want us? I talked to Al—tell 'em we're available."

JUNE 10. Joe and Al sign contracts and begin a series of talks about the projected play's structure. They have seen the original movie a dozen times and agree that it must be changed. Instead of Gibraltar, they will use London; instead of the mythical Calique, Paris. The Parisian girl will be a mistress rather than a wife; the audience may think actual bigamy in bad taste. What bothers them most is moving the action back and forth between the two cities. "Maybe we can do it with a narrator who comes out at the beginning and between scenes," Al says. Joe shakes his head: "Won't work."

JUNE 16. Joe flies to Hollywood to make a picture called *The High Cost of Loving* for M.G.M. Al goes to Hyannisport, on Cape Cod, to block out the first draft.

JUNE 23. HYANNISPORT. Al to Joe on the telephone: "I'm doing all right except for the ending."

"I knew it," Joe says. "That's what's wrong with the goddamned picture. Come on out here and we'll kick it around."

JUNE 28. BEVERLY HILLS. Jan Livingston and Ray Evans, who have written songs for more than seventy movies and have three Academy Awards to their credit, have been signed to do the songs. Johnny Mercer recommended them to the producers. Jay, Ray, Joe and Al gather for their first conference, and Al outlines the plot as it now stands.

"The end's got us bugged," Joe explains. "In the movie, after the Captain's found out, the English wife goes off with some bum—totally out of character. She just wouldn't do that. The French wife gets in a mess with a cab driver and shoots him. The captain takes the blame. He faces a firing squad, but he bribes the men to shoot their leader, goes over the wall Doug Fairbanks-style and gets away."

"It's phony," Al says. "We need something else. One idea is for him to say at the end that a man ought to have his whole family under one roof—then the curtains part and he walks into a harem."

"We've had seven endings, all that bad," Joe says. "Until we figure it out, you guys go on ahead and write songs for what we've got already."

JULY 15. BEVERLY HILLS. Four songs are finished; Jay plays them through for Joe and Al while Ray stands by, chain smoking. Joe is struck by one that begins,

> "Life does a man a favor
> When it brings him
> Simple joys"

The song goes on to describe the small pleasures of home and family life. "There are two variations," Ray explains. "It's also, 'Life does a man a favor, when it takes him down to the sea,' and then the third goes, 'When it takes him to Paree.' Covers all three of the Captain's Paradises—London, the ship, Paris."

"I dig," Joe says. "I like it." He stares fixedly into space and does not say much for the rest of the evening. On the way home he suddenly turns to Al.

"You know, those songs have a lot of heart. Maybe we've been on the wrong track—maybe the concentration ought to be more on the characters, then an ending would suggest itself."

JULY 24. HYANNISPORT. Al telephones Joe, who is still working on his picture in Hollywood. "I think I got it! The English wife is looking for a little glamour—the French girl wants home life, she's tired of night spots, tired of stripping in front of a bunch of strangers."

"How do we end?"

"I'm working on that . . ."

There was no question about it: those pages contained the necessary facts, some color, some dialogue . . . but they simply did not get up and walk. I thought of pulling an exciting part out from the middle somewhere and using it as the lead—but then, how would I get back into sequence? I could not answer that question. I went on retyping, telling myself that I was probably too close to the material to judge it properly. It was undoubtedly all right, I said to myself reassuringly . . . and knew in my heart it was not.

At the end of the retyping job the conviction that the beginning was all wrong was stronger than ever. But I did not know what to do. I sat down and had a martini, ate dinner, and took a nap. I awoke in despair, feeling certain that the lead would affect the *Playboy* editors as it did me. A bad lead can give an editor a sour outlook on an entire piece, and I now had become so certain in my feelings about that lead that I spoke of it as "bad" without giving the word a second thought.

Then I had an idea. Perhaps it would be smoother if I began the story straight and led up to the diary. The more I thought about that, the more excited I became. That week end I was by myself in the country. I washed the dinner dishes, and as I did I kept thinking of lines to put in the narrative-lead. Presently I left the dishes in the sink and went to the typewriter. The lead simply flowed: it was a straightforward narrative of how *Playboy* asked me to follow the show, of my previous meeting with Joe in London, and of the steps he and Morgan took toward putting their book together. It *worked.* And it saved me several more pages. Now I had the manuscript down to about forty-three pages. It was still twice as long, but I believe it was right at that length—and I fondly hoped that *Playboy* would think so too. I went over it another time, then another, but instead of cutting I wrote marginal notes beside paragraphs I thought might still be cut. Then I sent it off. That was a Sunday night. I awoke Monday morning with another intuitive feeling. The ending was wrong, I thought. It needed something more—possibly a quote from The Gopher—to wrap it up. All day Monday I wracked my brain, trying to think of some sort of punch to put in after Joe's speech. Monday evening I was still working at it in my head with no results.

On Tuesday morning, *Playboy* associate editor Ray Russell called. He said the piece was fine, and had two questions about matters that were not clear; they were so trivial, I don't recall what they were.

I drew a final breath and said, "Ray, I'm not satisfied with the ending."

"What do you mean?" he asked, indignantly. "We think it's perfect . . . Joe walking off into the sunset, etc. It works very well, we think."

That settled that.

15 · Post Script

In the foregoing pages I attempted to set down everything I know about writing and selling magazine articles, but upon looking over the chapters I find that there are several other matters, not necessarily related, that probably should be discussed briefly:

When to start free-lancing. For most people, writing at first is an avocation or a part-time job. After a few sales and promises of others to come, the beginning writer quite naturally begins to think about making writing a full-time job. I once had a student at N.Y.U. who, despite a striking lack of talent, was absolutely determined to devote all his time to writing for a living. He was a cost accountant. He had as much chance of becoming a professional writer as I have of becoming a cost accountant. The stories he handed in to the class were feeble imitations of short-shorts he read in *Collier's* and other magazines. Presently he wrote one which I permitted him to read aloud in class (everyone was granted that dubious privilege at least once in each semester). After the class commented on the story, I added my remarks. The young man dutifully incorporated our suggested changes; if we had told him to name the hero Jesus, he would have done that. He sent the story out, and it was turned down. Out it went again, and back it came. On the third sally it was bought. At seven-thirty P.M. that night the young man was pounding on my door (one reason I stopped teaching was that students were always pounding on my door). "I've sold a story!" he shouted. "I've quit my job!"

I wish I could report that that was the first and last story he ever sold. It was not the latter. He sold another about six months later, and one more about six months after that. Presently he went back to being a cost accountant, and he now bends over his ledgers and dreams of the day when he will sell another story and quit his job again.

To rush into free-lancing can be disastrous. I sometimes think that my best writing was, and is, that which I do as a hobby. I try to do a page of my current book each day. Some of the best short stories I've written were done while I was a soldier and had something to occupy me all day long. Writing as a hobby, to be engaged in at night and on weekends, can be absorbing and great fun; writing full time can get to be a bore. (It's never boring to me, but I am admittedly peculiar.) The writer who works in his spare time at his craft and makes an occasional sale is much better off, in the beginning, than the writer who knows he *must* sell if he is to support himself. Not long ago, shortly after *Collier's* was junked by its parent corporation, Peter Maas, who had been an editor there, asked me what I felt should be the minimum preparations a man planning to free-lance should make. I told him I thought he should have five thousand dollars in the bank—or, according to his standard of living, enough money on which to survive for a year—and at least five commitments from editors. More important, perhaps, are the temperamental requirements. There are some people who simply are not emotionally equipped to free-lance. The man who is easily disappointed is taking a giant risk when he free-lances. The man who is easily discouraged is taking an even bigger one. The successful free-lance writer must have a hide thicker than the armor on a tank and the cheerful, philosophical disposition of a Candide. He must realize that, occasionally, stories which by every rule of the game ought to be bought will not be bought. He must get used to the fact that, once in a great while, a story will "fall out" for some unforeseen reason—the death of a subject, the death of an editor, or the changing times. Above all, he must discipline himself. He must regard his writing as a job, set aside regular hours for it and stay on the schedule he sets. He must not indulge his fancies—that is, if he has an assignment to hand in and suddenly gets a compelling idea for a totally different piece, one that cries out to be written at once, he must complete his assignment before taking on the more appealing idea. In recent years I have been doing more and more things that

I want to do, and occasionally I stop midway in an assigned job to do something that is more fun. I can take the risk; I sell virtually everything I write. The beginner cannot afford to do as I do.

Along with discipline goes the necessity for budgeting one's time. The beginner ought to decide, early in the business, how much time he can devote to research and how much to writing, and he should attempt to estimate how long each story will take him to write and whether or not the pay will be worth it. Although he should write up to the very limit of his ability on each job, he should not spend as much time on a *Coronet* story (*Coronet* pays around $500) as he puts into a *Post* story (the *Post* pays twice that, at a minimum). A writer who works on several different stories at a time, according to my W.P.A. system, is not as pressed by this problem as one who does not.

The writer who decides to free-lance is well advised to have "something to fall back on"—a part-time job of some sort, perhaps, or a working arrangement with a magazine or newspaper whereby he is assured of at least a small income. Many of the most successful writers in my acquaintance have some steady source of income. Hollis Alpert writes motion picture reviews for *The Saturday Review* and *Woman's Day*. Ken Purdy works as a rewrite man and trouble shooter for *Playboy*. George Scullin has the same relationship with *Redbook*. I keep my contributing editorship at *Cosmopolitan* and do a jazz column for *The Saturday Review*.

Specialization. The writer who has a specialty or who is an authority on some subject or subjects is far better off than the man who will take any kind of assignment. For years Ken Purdy has made an excellent living because he knows more about old automobiles and sports cars than anyone else in the field. Maurice Zolotow, by specializing in show business personalities, has built up a tremendous store of information and a vast list of contacts. The writer who has two, three or four specialties is in an even more advantageous position. As must be evident from the pieces in the book, I like best to write about show business people, food and crime. I like least to write on some subject I don't understand, and I try to avoid such jobs; they are costly and, on the whole, boring. I seldom do a "how-to" piece. Once, in collaboration with Harrington Rose, I did a story for *Today's Woman* called *Help Your Husband Move*

Up, but I know very little about that kind of article writing, which is the reason I have not discussed it in this book.

Collaboration. There are any number of successful writing teams in the article business these days—Jhan and June Robins, Norman and Madeline Carlisle, Charles Boswell and Lewis Thompson, Ruth and Edward Brecker. Many of the teams are made up of husband and wife, with the one doing the research and the other the writing. In the case of the Robins, both do both jobs, and each may begin to work on the same story at the same time. Apparently there are no hard-and-fast methods of collaboration. In instances when I have collaborated, I usually have left the research to the other person and have concentrated on the writing. One pleasant aspect of collaboration is that it eliminates some of the loneliness of writing. One unpleasant aspect is that it sometimes leads to arguments. Research goes much faster if there are two people on the job, of course—but the writing may go more slowly because of the discussions which naturally will arise. Collaboration, incidentally, is an excellent way for the beginning writer to gradually break into free-lancing; his partner can help him with the research while he is occupied at some job with a guaranteed income.

Submission of articles. In general, it is pointless for a writer to submit a finished article to a magazine. The outline suffices—and, in fact, an initial query, to be followed by an outline if there is interest on the part of an editor, is sufficient. I sometimes write Stuart Rose at the *Post*, "Would you like to see an outline for a piece on so-and-so?" If someone else has already submitted the idea, or if the magazine is not interested, the time that would have been spent in making an outline has been saved. Of course, there are some ideas that simply do not come off in outline—ideas that are so dependent upon the writing, for example, that they cannot be described. My submarine sandwich article was one such.

In Hollywood the agents can submit a property to five or six, or even seven or ten, producers at the same time. In the magazine business, this is not considered proper. The idea must go to one market at a time, and the writer must wait until the editor has declined it before sending it elsewhere. This unfair system conceivably never will change. Some writers attempt to circumvent it by telephoning editors and getting an on-the-spot answer.

Finished manuscripts should be submitted on 8½″ x 11″ white bond paper, preferably of first-class quality. (I prefer Eaton's Corrasable Bond, but cannot always afford it; one can erase typewriter-print on it with a pencil eraser). There should be a title-page, with the writer's name in the upper left-hand corner and the title centered in the middle of the sheet. Some writers put the word-count in the upper right-hand corner; that is not necessary. The subsequent pages should be numbered. Some writers put their own names—"E. M. D. Watson—5" on the numbered pages; this irritates editors, for the most part. Margins should be at least ¾″ at the top and 1¼″ at the sides. Corrections should be made neatly, preferably in ink. If the writer is using a pseudonym, it should appear under the centered title. It is not necessary to bind manuscripts in folders or cardboard backs; indeed, most editors prefer that the pages be held together only with a clip, never with a staple.

Manuscripts may be accompanied by a brief personal letter, but that too is not absolutely necessary. A letter never will influence an editor; again, it may only annoy him.

The promptness with which a magazine responds to a query or an outline depends entirely upon the magazine. The *Post* is phenomenal; it disposes of all business, usually, within a week. *Playboy*, on the other hand, is likely to take as long as three weeks or a month—and, sometimes, six weeks. This is infuriating but apparently unavoidable. As a rule, if a writer has not heard from a magazine within a month, he will do well to write in and ask what happened to his idea. It does not necessarily follow that the longer an editor holds an idea, the better chance it has. It may have been lost, misplaced, or buried under a pile of get-around-to-sometime papers. It also does not necessarily follow that a printed rejection slip, rather than a personal note, means that the story has not been considered. A letter does mean, most of the time, that the story has had unusual consideration—but at *Cosmopolitan* the editors frequently spend long hours in debate over an idea and then send out a rejection slip when they decide it is not for them. However, if the idea is a very near miss or if something about the writer's work makes the editors want to see more of it, a letter goes out.

Magazines sometimes hold stories for long periods of time after buying them. I have one story in the inventory of the *Post*, as I write this, that I wrote nearly two years ago. If a magazine holds a story for more than a year, the writer is justified in writing in to ask what's going on. Sometimes the magazine will return the story and free the writer to sell it elsewhere, retaining the rights to half the profit from the new sale. I once had a story that I sold four times. Magazines kept buying it and then deciding that they had made a mistake. It was finally printed, to my sorrow; I earned nearly $4,000 from that story, and it seemed that I could go on selling it indefinitely.

Photography. I have worked with nearly all the top-flight magazine photographers in the business, but with the exception of Hans Knopf, Genevieve Naylor and Richard Saunders, I have never met one who was remotely competent or talented. To get one picture, the average magazine photographer takes fifty. This realization, born on a trip with a photographer who is regarded as one of the best, prompted me last year to buy equipment to make my own pictures. Since then I have augmented my income considerably. With modern gear, such as the Japanese camera Ricoh, taking pictures requires only the ability to see and move a forefinger or thumb. Magazines these days are going in more and more for photographs. The beginning writer ought to be a photographer as well.

What to Read. Every writer ought to have a basic research and reference library which also includes some books on writing. For the latter, I recommend *Writers and Writing,* by Robert van Gelder, *The Writer Observed,* by Harvey Breit, and *The Writer's Craft,* by Frederick A. Birmingham. For the former, I recommend every encyclopaedic volume the writer can lay his hands on; my own ranges from the *Audels' Carpenters' Guide* to *Living Mammals of the World,* by Ivan T. Sanderson. For a basic reference library, the writer ought to have

A good dictionary, either Webster's New International or the Oxford;

A copy of Roget's *Thesaurus;*

An encyclopedia;

A comprehensive almanac;

A copy of *The Writer's Guide* and *Index to English,* by Porter G. Perrin;

A copy of *Modern English Usage,* by H. W. Fowler;

A copy of *A Dictionary of Contemporary American Usage*, by Bergen and Cornelia Evans;

A copy of *Who Knows—And What.*

The last-named book is invaluable to the article writer. It is an index to authorities on every conceivable subject, and the writer looking for specialists has only to consult it in order to find out who has the last word on any subject he may be working on.

I find it profitable to read both my dictionary and the encyclopaedia or some other reference book for a few minutes each day. I try to learn at least two new words every day; I seldom use them—magazine article editors are suspicious of new or obscure words—but there is a chance that some day I might. I also find word games, such as Scrabble, Jotto or Bali, or the Hollywood writer's pastime known simply as "the word game" useful in developing my vocabulary.

Work. To wind up this book I want to emphasize once more that writing is hard work. Men who cultivate gardens or sail yachts or chop wood for their amusement do not work at those hobbies as hard as men who choose to write. Those who write for a living find, early in the game, that they have taken on not a full-time but a double-time job. I can remember only a few days in the past ten years on which I did absolutely nothing in the way of work—and I could not even count those days, for although I may not be sitting at the typewriter or interviewing a subject I still am thinking about my work . . . and as I have mentioned, what appears to be wasted time will almost certainly turn out at some future date to be time well spent. But not too much time should be wasted. At least a half-hour or an hour should be spent in writing every day, whenever or wherever the opportunity arises. The young writer ought to train himself to work at all times and under any circumstances. I work best in my own workroom, on my favorite typewriter, surrounded by my reference books and with plenty of good materials; but I also can write on trains, aircraft, subways and in automobiles (while someone else is driving, of course). I prefer to work at a typewriter, but I can write in longhand if no machine is available or if the circumstances are such that working on a machine is difficult. I must bow to Bob Considine's ability to work anywhere; his friend Toots Shor reports that once, when he went to a cocktail party at

Considine's house, he found the host sitting off in a corner, quietly writing away at a column while masses of people boiled laughingly around him. I would rather have solitude, of course, but if I can't have it I don't fret.

As I write this I have just wound up a week that was, for me, fairly typical. The schedule, as noted in my pocket calendar, went as follows:

Saturday. 8:00 AM (New York Time). Rose, did a page and a half's work on a book I am writing with Judge Irwin M. Davidson on juvenile delinquency in New York City, did two pages of the original writing for this book, had breakfast.

9:30 AM. Packed for trip to Los Angeles.

10:00 AM. Left for airport.

11:00 AM. Boarded aircraft and set to work on captions for story on *Look Homeward, Angel* for *Cosmopolitan.* Finished that, read for a while, slept, worked for an hour on this book, landed at Los Angeles airport seven hours later.

4:00 PM (Los Angeles Time). Drove to house of Robert Presnell, Jr., with whom I was staying.

6:00 PM. Called Oscar Levant, subject. Called Joe Hyams' house in order to see if Twentieth Century Fox press agent had left message regarding story on Hope Lange and Don Murray. Called *Cosmopolitan* photographer, Lou Jacobs, Jr., to find out what he had done about a picture spread for August issue. Called Ernest Lehman, subject, to set up interview for next day.

7:00 PM. Dinner with Presnells and to party.

Sunday. 6:30 AM. Rose and worked for an hour on Davidson book, then had breakfast and began writing piece on Italian writers for *Cosmopolitan.*

10:00 AM. Went to see Jacobs to inspect photographs.

11:00 AM. Back at Presnells', worked on Levant story from details Marsha Hunt (Mrs. Presnell) had given me at dinner the night before.

12:30 PM. Called Levant to attempt to get interview later in the day, ate lunch, sat around talking with the Presnells.

2:00 PM. Went to Ernest Lehman's house for interview about working conditions for writers in Hollywood.

4:00 PM. Stopped by Joe Hyams' house to borrow his clipping files on Levant, Lange-Murray.

5:00 PM. Returned to Presnell house for drinks, dinner, conversation; picked up more Levant details.

9:00 PM. As instructed previously, called Levant for appointment. Agreed to call him next morning at 11:00 AM. Talked late with Presnell on subject of writers in Hollywood.

Monday. 7:00 AM. Rose and got to work on page of Davidson book, then began writing some of the material gathered from Lehman and Presnell on writers in Hollywood.

11:00 AM. Called Levant and was invited to his house. Drove there and had interview.

1:00 PM. Dropped by I. P. Lazar's office to get telephone number of Cole Porter. Discussed Porter's operation, about which I am writing a story, with Lazar. Went to lunch at Romanoff's; discussed Levant with Mike Romanoff. Had drink with George Rosenberg, an agent, to discuss screenplay based on Eddie Condon's life I plan to write with Rosenberg's client, Bill Morrow.

3:00 PM. Returned to Presnell house to make telephone calls—to Lew Pollock at Screen Writers' Guild; to Mrs. Ira Gershwin to make appointment to discuss Levant; to press agent at Twentieth Century Fox to make appointment to see Lange-Murray, to Joe Hyams to get Groucho Marx's telephone number.

4:00 PM. Worked for two hours on clips in Hyams' files.

6:00 PM. Drinks and dinner with Presnells.

7:30 PM. Drove to studio to see Levant television show.

10:00 PM. Returned to Presnells and worked for an hour on Levant story.

Tuesday. 6:00 AM. Rose and worked on Davidson book, then finished piece on Italian writers. Began work on piece about New York writers (these pieces on writers were for a special section in the August *Cosmopolitan*).

10:00 AM. Spoke to Twentieth-Century Fox press agent and got date with Hope Lange for next day; telephoned Mrs. Ira Gershwin to confirm date; made appointment with Arthur Freed at M.G.M. to discuss Levant.

11:00 AM. Worked on piece about Hollywood writers.

1:00 PM. Lunch at Romanoff's with Ken Englund to discuss Hollywood writers.

3:00 PM. Returned to Presnell house to work on Hollywood writers piece.

5:00 PM. Returned Hyams' clips, had a talk with him about Lange-Murray.

6:00 PM. Went to see Eva Marie Saint to discuss Lange-Murray.

7:00 PM. Dinner with Presnells.

8:00 PM. Went to Gershwin house to discuss Levant with Ira and Lee. Discovered Levant there. Went to his house with him for interview.

10:00 PM. Returned to Gershwin house to continue discussion of Levant.

Wednesday. 7:30 AM. Rose and worked on Davidson book, finished piece on Hollywood writers.

10:00 AM. Called Groucho Marx on telephone to get quotes on

Levant. Called Harpo Marx in Palm Springs for same purpose. Spoke to two friends of Cole Porter.

11:00 AM. Date with Arthur Freed at M.G.M. to discuss Levant.

1:00 PM. Had lunch at Romanoff's with Joe Hyams.

6:00 PM. Drinks and dinner with Presnells.

8:30 PM. Watched Levant TV show.

Thursday. 6:30 AM. Rose and worked on Davidson book.

10:00 AM. Made final calls to variety of people concerning Lange-Murray and Levant.

12:30 PM. Visited Lazar office, then lunched at Romanoff's.

3:00 PM. Interview with Hope Lange.

5:00 PM. Returned to Presnells to pack. Dined with Presnells and drove to airport, boarded aircraft. Aloft, worked on Levant piece and wrote letter to Harpo Marx to discuss book he has in mind. Slept.

Friday. 8:00 AM (New York Time). Drove from airport to New York, worked on Davidson book for an hour.

10:30 AM. Went to *Cosmopolitan* office, had conference with John O'Connell.

12:30 PM. Lunched with O'Connell and discussed record column I am to do.

3:30 PM. Began making New York calls in connection with Levant story.

5:30 PM. Drove to country to write for the week end.

The California trip made this an exceptionally active week—but the weeks in New York are not too much different. It's a full schedule, but I love it. I couldn't wish for a better life.

Index

Set in Electra
Format by Seamus Byrne
Manufactured by The Haddon Craftsmen, Inc.
Published by HARPER & BROTHERS, *New York*